DISCOVERY

Champlain's Route〰〰〰〰 1615-16
Nicollet's   "   "   —·—·—·—·—·— 1634
Radisson's   "   "   ——————— 1658-59
Marquette &
Joliet's   "   "   ‑ ‑ ‑ ‑ ‑ ‑ ‑ ‑ ‑ 1673
LaSalle's   "   "   ·············· 1679-82

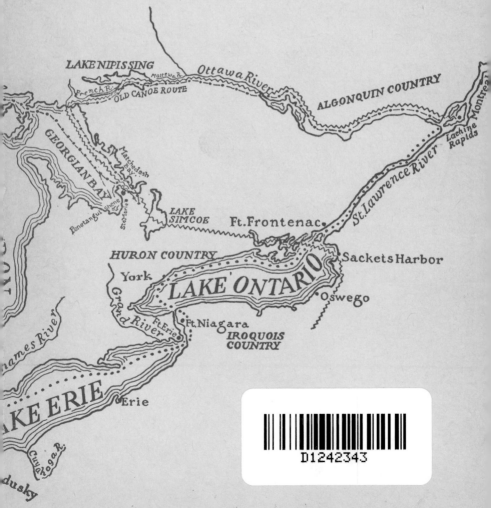

LAKE NIPISSING   Ottawa River
Mattawa R.
French R.   OLD CANOE ROUTE
ALGONQUIN COUNTRY
Montreal
Lachine Rapids
St. Lawrence River
GEORGIAN BAY
Matchedash Bay
Penetanguishene
Sturgeon
LAKE SIMCOE   Ft. Frontenac
HURON COUNTRY   Sackets Harbor
York
LAKE ONTARIO
Oswego
Grand River   R. Erie   Ft. Niagara
IROQUOIS COUNTRY
Thames River
LAKE ERIE   Erie
Cuyahoga R.
dusky

D1242343

THE GREAT LAKES

Lighthouse on South Manitou, established 1839, in which the first steam fog-horn on the Great Lakes was installed. *Photograph by Bob Towers. Courtesy of Black Star.*

THE
Great Lakes

HARLAN HATCHER

OXFORD UNIVERSITY PRESS

London   New York   Toronto

1944

FOR
ANNE GREGORY
AND
ROBERT LESLIE

FOREWORD

THE five interconnecting lakes lying in the heart of the North American continent are descriptively, if not imaginatively, called simply the Great Lakes. The name is apt. No other adjective describes the expanse of the region, or the activity on this greatest body of fresh water in the world. The Lakes are great in size, great in commerce, great in engineering, great in history and romance, great in cities and industry along their shores, great in their interest and their beauty.

They are not so much a region as an area; they are not local but international. It is somewhat hard to hold them in mind as a unit. Lake Ontario, with its busy Canadian cities, seems far removed from the lonely grandeur of the Lake Superior shore line. The great port cities on Lake Erie are nearly a thousand miles by waterway from the thick ore beds and iron ranges of Minnesota, and the wheat fields of the western plains. The green islands of Georgian Bay, the long shipping roads down Lake Huron, seem to be in a different province from Lake Michigan with its big west-shore cities, its steel mills, its orchards and vacation lands.

To the millions of people from all the nations of the earth who live on these shores, the Lakes are a chain of separate and distinct regions. For the people of Prescott and Kingston the region is the Bay of Quinte and the Thousand Islands, and the small, 250-foot vessels that can be locked through the canals on the upper St. Lawrence River. For the people of Niagara it is the Falls, the River and the Gorge, the Welland Canal, and the fruit belt along the foot of the Niagara escarpment. For the people of Buffalo and Cleveland it is the 600-foot freighters coming in with wheat and ore, the breakwaters, and yachts in the basins. For the people of Detroit and along the St. Clair it is a bulk carrier passing every ten or twelve minutes. For the people on Green Bay it is the Pilot Island Light on the island-studded entrance to Lake Michigan, called Porte des Morts because so many schooners went down there—eight in one week in 1872. For the people of the Sault it is the gigantic locks and the coming and going of the ice. For the people of the Lakehead it is a great battery of elevators and the magnificent Thunder Bay.

But to the men who sail the ships, who ride out the storms and fight the ice, the Lakes are a unit and their vast bowl an intimate region.

The ambitions of three nations have circled these Lakes; each has left its stamp and its tradition on their shores. The Lakes form the boundary between the United States and Canada. The border is real enough, of course, but on the Great Lakes it is only an imaginary dotted line cutting across the blue water. It does not so much separate as join together two great peoples. Since the War of 1812 they have lived as neighbors in peace on these shores with the Lakes as a common waterway free of warships and fortifications. Their ships crowd the narrow connecting channels and are lifted around Niagara and the Sault in the same canals. International bridges, ferries, and a tunnel under the Detroit River connect the two nations with a minimum of interference. The tall, 138-foot Rock of Ages Light west of Isle Royal; the 102-foot Stannard Light on the shoal 24 miles out in Lake Superior between Keweenaw and Whitefish Point; Spectacle Reef Light and White Shoal Light at the entrances to the Straits of Mackinac; Fort Gratiot Light and Windmill Point at the north entrances to the St. Clair and Detroit Rivers; the Buffalo Light on the breakwater at the harbor—these and hundreds of lesser lights flash their signals, sound their fog horns, and ring their submarine bells to guide a thousand ships of both nations' registry.

The story of this mighty region—its formation, its discovery, the struggle for its possession, its exploitation, the rise of its cities, the history and romance of its ships—is the subject of this book.

CONTENTS

LIST OF ILLUSTRATIONS

MAPS

xi

Part I   DISCOVERY

Those who shall be so happy as to inhabit that noble country cannot but remember with gratitude those who discovered the way by venturing to sail upon unknown lakes.

FATHER HENNEPIN.

((((I))))

The Great Lakes Bowl

THE Chicago Municipal Airport stretches out across the prairie southwest of the city almost on the imperceptible divide that separates the Great Lakes from the Mississippi basin. When a modern airliner leaves this busy port there is always a last minute catch of expectancy in the air. The uniformed attendants roll away the ladders and the service equipment. The door is closed and the passengers buckle their safety belts. The motors in the huge, bird-like plane are started. The slender gray ship taxies up the field, faces west along the wind, and pauses while the motors roar. Then, unleashed, it rushes down the runway, gains speed, rises, and shoots up like an arrow. The grass races by, becomes a green, parallel swish, then swirls downward and falls away. The plane leans gracefully over on the wind, banks southward into the sun, half circles, and straightens out over the Valparaiso Moraine at Chicago Heights; then with the prairie wind behind it, it heads toward Cleveland, Buffalo, and the East. You have hardly adjusted yourself to your seat and the momentary dizziness of flight, but already the airport is a toyshop and a flag, and you are speeding in a hollow metal tube supported on outstretched wings up among white, lake-borne clouds. They are sailing high above the Chicago roofs and out across the blue over Lake Michigan.

It is afternoon on August 7th. The date is potent in the memory. On this very August day in 1679, La Salle spread the canvas of the *Griffon* to the winds of Lake Erie at the head of the Niagara River, and sailed westward. His green-timbered, 50-ton ship was the first vessel to sail on these waters. That destiny-laden voyage took him across this section of the continent now taking the shape of a gigantic bowl under the wings of our plane. It led him from

3

Buffalo, past Cleveland to Detroit; through the Detroit River and Lake St. Clair; up Huron to the Straits of Mackinac; and around the Upper Peninsula to Green Bay. There he left the ship in charge of the pilot and went down the west coast of Lake Michigan to Chicago; and across the southern lobe of the lake by the sand-dune country to St. Joseph. He spent a man-killing winter in the west lands beyond the portages on the watershed of the lake now falling rapidly away behind us: a winter filled with perils so exacting that it is a marvel even La Salle ever escaped. Then he made his way back across lower Michigan—270 miles of bitter toil over cold, drowned lands; along open grass paths in hostile Indian country; and through jungle-grown timber plots. By some miracle he reached the Detroit River and crossed it on a raft. He was exhausted by the struggle against the bleak and dismal wind, ice, and snow of that March 1680. But he straightway fashioned a canoe of elm bark and paddled on across Lake Erie toward Montreal, to face a crew of creditors and the hucksterer's colonial management of His Most Christian Majesty, the King of France.

There a half mile below us lie the waters and the terrain that were the most tempting and the most trying to the rugged-limbed explorer. With this brisk tail wind pushing at us, we have left far behind the flat plains of Illinois, the Starved Rock, and the rivers of the upper Mississippi, along which in La Salle's time went Indian canoes with pelts for the trading posts at Montreal and Quebec. Chicago's magnificent skyline on the feathery curve of the lake is only a part of the August haze. The lake is a vast, blue-green basin with rim uptilted to meet the sky far away to the north. The lake freighters that look so long when they are tied up at the loading docks at Duluth, and so huge and tall when they receive the first trickle of wheat from the elevators at Port Arthur, are small as driftwood as we look down upon them. They are spaced up and down the lake, each under its plume of smoke, carrying their stupendous tonnage from Lake Superior to the mills of Chicago and Gary, Indiana. The clouds off there in the north drift into formations against the sky that seem in this afternoon light to be a mirage map of that greatest of the Great Lakes.

Now we are over the dunes between Gary and Michigan City. They are remote and desolate looking, tanned acreages holding little pools that flash like silver coins scattered over a wasteland. We are only a few minutes from Chicago, but in that short space we have already flown effortlessly over more of the route than La Salle could cover in a day's hard going. As the curving thread of the St. Joseph River passes beneath us, we can almost see the mighty ghost of La Salle striking a flint to the grass to burn over his trail, or stomping impatiently before the morning fire, munching a few grains of Indian corn for breakfast, waiting for his frozen boots and jacket to thaw out enough for him to plunge again over the series of moraines into the unexplored peninsula—where cherry trees bloom in the spring and the apples are ripening in August.

We fly on, high over the little towns that huddle along the gleaming threads of the highways and the transcontinental rail lines. They curve down in the cup of the moving earth, glide leisurely under the wings of the plane, and disappear to the west, just as another village begins to slide under us out of the east. Farms, gardens, pasture lands, streams, and lakes; barns, silos, dairy cattle, wheat lands, orchards, vineyards, and the smoke of small industries spot the circle of Michigan, Indiana, and Ohio. We look off again to the north. That indistinct carbon cloud on the horizon hovers over the city of Detroit, spread busily along the line of its river. Beyond it we can see in imagination the sandy curve of the southern lobe of Lake Huron, where the St. Clair River begins with a rush, and the endless movement of boats up and down these rivers between Erie and Huron, and along the western shore of Lake Huron to and from the Straits of Mackinac and the locks at the Sault.

While we are yet drawing a map of Huron in the Detroit haze, the western tip of Lake Erie takes shape on the horizon and Toledo on its wide estuary of the Maumee River flows out of its own smoke haze. Its tall buildings whirl dizzily on the moving axis of our flight. There are its high bridges over the estuary; its leagues of docks crowded with Great Lakes shipping; its miles and miles of railroad yards with coal cars close packed and arranged like packages on shelves. There is the great trucking highway in the

bed of what was once the boisterous and overloaded Miami and
Erie canal linking Lake Erie with Dayton and Cincinnati across the
watershed in the Ohio Valley. A few miles to the north where the
yellow Maumee meets the blue-green waters of Lake Erie is the
Presque Isle peninsula, jammed with its forty miles of railroad
tracks, its shipbuilding yards, unloading machinery, and the twenty-
four huge upright gray tubes of the National Milling Company
elevators. The lake freighters are thick in the Maumee, in the
harbors, and in the channels of the lake. When La Salle paddled
wearily back across this lake toward Niagara, and for nearly two
centuries afterwards, the site of these fat farming lands, and of
this busy lake-port workship, was only the edge of the vast, mias-
mic, mosquito-infested Black Swamp. Now it is the greatest trans-
shipping point in the world. Out of that drowned land that once
swallowed up travelers and smote them with the pestilental black
death among the bulrushes and skunk cabbage, the big modern
landing field rises to meet us as the plane circles and sets its wheels
down on the long concrete runway.

In a few minutes it is back in the air over busy, prosperous northern Ohio lake towns, above orchards, wheatfields, and vineyards,
gliding swiftly on toward Cleveland. There is the curving rim of
Lake Erie, with its islands, beaches, and harbors. Perry's monument
on South Bass Island gleams in the sun over Put-in-Bay. There are
the great U. S.-Ohio highways on the terraces that, centuries ago,
were the shores of this lake. There are the quiet little towns and
the big bustling towns on the short rivers with their deep estuaries:
Tremont to the south, Sandusky, Huron, Lorain to the north. Again
the endless flow of freighters moving into these harbors, the spaced
splotches of smoke out on the lake. Then out of the east emerges
the long, wide, and, from high in the air, beautiful spread of Cleveland and its twenty miles of suburbs among the trees along Lake
Erie. The Terminal Tower is a slender point above the formal layout
of the Mall; the Cuyahoga River is dark with fleets of boats, its
smoking mills, its network of bridges in the heart of the city. The
expanse of lake glistens in the sun, and white-sailed yachts flash
among the black ore freighters, some putting in at the Cleveland

harbors, others moving steadily on to the active lake towns farther east. The airport rises to meet the circling, falling ship.

We change planes and soon we are again up among the white, low-flying clouds, winging high above the course of the *Griffon*, of La Salle's returning elm-bark canoe, toward Buffalo at the foot of the lake. We look down upon Fairport Harbor, on Ashtabula and Conneaut. The mammoth freighters are swinging round the break-waters and putting in along the red buoy-marked channels: freighters of such size that any of the giant cranes which load and unload them could grab up the *Griffon* at one bite and toss it into their holds, where it would be lost and unnoticed in the cavernous tonnage. There is Erie by the circling sand arm of its bay and harbor where, in the spring and summer of 1813, Perry built the ships that brought this lake under American control. Then, on that same easy global curve and swing of the moving earth, Buffalo with all **its** wharfs and granaries, its elevators and mills, and its congested shipping rotates into full view. Beyond it is the silver stretch of the Niagara River flowing serenely northward toward the boiling plunge at the Falls and down through the gorge to Lake Ontario. Smaller boats move along this river to be lowered through the Welland Locks 325 feet from the level of one lake to the other. And along the low Mohawk Valley, eastward toward Rochester, Albany, and New York, lies the remnant of the old Erie Canal.

A few miles around the Niagara escarpment, where the acres of orchards and vineyards are ripening in the sun and the temperate lake breezes, the Trans-Canada airliner takes off and rises above Hamilton, key industrial city of Ontario. Smoke from its new war industries, its iron and steel mills, its scores of machine shops and factories thins upward and blows away over the dairy farms. A few minutes' flight brings the plane over Toronto, spread out like Cleveland along the northern shore of its lake front, its harbor lined with elevators and wharfs and breakwaters, with ships and sailing craft moving in and out of the bay to the open waters of Ontario. Small lake towns spot the Ontario shore all the way to Kingston. There the St. Lawrence forms among the Thousand Islands at the entrance to the lake. It is a bright lacework among the green circles of the

islands now growing dark as evening comes on. There is the site of
Fort Frontenac, near which Champlain first crossed Lake Ontario,
from which La Salle sailed his first fleet of small vessels on the
lake, and sent men and tools to build the *Griffon* above Niagara.

And while we relax comfortably in the twilight, glancing down
at the straight wide surface of the St. Lawrence, and reflecting on
the tremendous sweep of this Great Lakes region and the hardi-
hood of the men who first explored it, we lift the lights of Montreal,
and descend among the red beads surrounding the airfield. The
illuminated cross on Mount Royal, high over the city, starts us thinking of Jacques Cartier, the first white man to stand on that prospect
and look with wonder toward the unknown west out of which we
have just flown. He sailed and paddled slowly up this river from
the Atlantic Ocean, but never got beyond Montreal. Within a few
hours we have looked down upon the heart of the basin itself, upon
some of the great cities of the world, some of the busiest ports, some
of the heaviest laden traffic lanes, upon some of the richest and
most thickly populated areas in the hemisphere. For these lakes
with their interconnecting waterways, and with the St. Lawrence
River linking them directly with the sea, join together two thriving
nations and create one of the most diverse and fascinating regions
to be found on the globe.

II

Cartier Sails the St. Lawrence

THE world is now too small. There is even shortage of living space and nations fight about it. Within a few hours a man can fly from wherever he is to wherever he cares to go, be it the ice fields at the North Pole or the lone and level sands of innermost Gobi. This consciousness makes it hard for us to recapture the excitement of younger days when men could still be surprised by the world; when the Pillars of Hercules guarded the entrance to unsailed western seas, and the Great Lakes were neither known nor suspected. We muse in envy on the thrill reserved for Cartier, Champlain, and La Salle, to whom each bend in the rivers of America revealed a new world. We sail in luxury on or above the lakes and the rivers, with full statistics on every aspect of the region at our elbow. But from time to time we must return in imagination to the world as these first explorers saw it when, buoyed up by ambition and an amazing contradiction of knowledge and superstition, they sailed and paddled and marched against the unknown, with fear and faith for what new wonder the next minute or the next mile might disclose.

We blot out of all knowledge the Great Lakes; we shroud the thousand miles of the St. Lawrence in mystery—perhaps, who knows, it is the northwest channel passage to the fabulous wealth of the Orient. We erase time and four hundred years, and it is now the autumn of 1535. Jacques Cartier has been sailing on mile after mile up the complicated shoreline of 'the great river of Canada.' His only pilots were two kidnapped young Indians who were presumed to know something of the intricate channel of the St. Lawrence. Their direction must have been adequate, for Cartier with his ships and men got safely past the bold gorge of the Saguenay, past the green oblong mass of the Isle aux Coudres, past the rock and headlands that begin to squeeze the channel toward the Island of Orleans—promptly called the Isle of Bacchus by Renaissance-minded Cartier, because the island was thick with trees, and the trees were hung with grapes.

It was mid-September. Cartier anchored his three toy ships (the largest was less than 120 tons) in the protected waters of the St. Charles under the rock of Quebec. Perched on this rock was the Indian settlement of Stadacone. Cartier went ashore to pay his respects to the chief, Donnacona. He climbed up through the forest and over the rocks, to find a wretched collection of wigwams and bark huts, swarming with greasy, half-naked, fetid-smelling natives. He learned that Donnacona's high-perched and sorry village was not the center of a rich region, but only a miserable outpost for an interior that was as mysterious as it was limitless. The heart of the land and the Indian capital lay many perilous days' journey farther up this river, through rocky narrows, over rapids, and across wide lakes. It was named Hochelaga, and was set by a mountain at the union of this river of Canada with another mighty stream, the Ottawa. But even Hochelaga by its mountain and its river was not, the Indians said, the end of this new land of fabulous distances. Still farther on to the west where the sun set were thundering waters, and yet beyond that, so the legend ran, were seas of no man knew what immensity.

We study for a moment the Riss painting of Jacques Cartier in the Town Hall at St. Malo, with sword and knife in his belt, an edging of lace at his cuff and neck, a fist rammed in his trimmed beard, and the eager fanaticism of a daring epoch glittering in his eyes. A brief glance, however, would suggest what decision snapped in that brain pan at Chief Donnacona's news. Cartier determined to ascend the river and see for himself this village of Hochelaga and its mountain.

Donnacona may have been only a chief of an evil village, but he was no fool. He had sense enough to see the portentous glint in

the Frenchman's eye at the mention of Hochelaga and the lands
and waters beyond it. He had the foresight to try to scare Cartier
away. He called upon all the wiles of his tribe, short of massacre
or physical violence, to divert and dissuade Cartier from further
intrusion. Three Indians decorated their heads with formidable long
horns. They painted their faces black, and dressed their bodies in
black-and-white dog skins. Then they paddled down the river in
a canoe past the anchored ships. They performed fantastic antics
and shrieked warnings at Cartier and his men in the name of
Coudouagny, the god of these boiling waters. The Frenchmen must
not go any farther. If they violated this region, Coudouagny would
overwhelm them with his storms and snows and drifting ice.

Cartier only laughed at the threats of Coudouagny. He was a
servant of the only true God, and of His Most Christian Majesty,
King Francis I of France; and he was under the protection of the
Blessed Jesus and the Virgin. So he placed his faith on these firm
foundations and, taking the smallest of his ships and two boats,
with fifty of his men he sailed on up the St. Lawrence toward
Montreal. The weather that autumn was memorable. Cartier remarked on the flaming days that succeeded one another as though
they could have no end. Donnacona had not been misled by the
apprehension he had felt in his racial bones when those boats
disappeared around Cap Rouge. For Cartier was impressed by this
peaceful and favored land running gently back from the broad,
straight-flowing river. It was a journey of one hundred sixty miles.
Groups of Indians were quietly fishing along the river bank. The
wild grapes were ripe and hung in clusters from vines running over
the trees along the shore. Cartier tasted them. He found them small
and sour, but observed, like a French husbandman, that they needed
care and pruning. He sailed out onto the broad waters of Lake St.
Peter and noted the three rivers which now give the chief town
on this lake its name. Here he left his ship because of the rapids
above the lake. He went on in the small boats. Indians flocked
down to see him pass. At Montreal he was met and welcomed by
a thousand people. They gave him quantities of food, accepted his

trinkets, and brought their children to him for blessing and a laying on of hands.

Cartier walked back through the cornfields, now the dockyards and east slums of the city, to the village on the terrace by the present public square of Montreal. He read to the assembled multitude a portion of the first chapter of the Gospel according to St. John. Then, on this perfect early October Sunday, he climbed the mountain and named it Mount Royal. From its summit, now the recreation spot of the vigorous city, Cartier looked out upon one of the finest prospects in all Canada. Off to the north, across the flat lands and the network of rivers, the Laurentian Mountains caught the sun on their brown and golden sides. Far away to the south, across the wide valley of the St. Lawrence, were the flame-colored mountains of New York and Vermont. Below him was the village of Hochelaga, the mighty river, the fields of corn, and, five miles away, his boats. And off toward the alluring west the Ottawa River curved into the St. Lawrence at Lake St. Louis and rushed on down the Lachine Rapids that roared and glistened in the sun.

Cartier had seen enough for one time. He descended the mountain, took leave of his hosts, and returned to his camp at Quebec.[1] Cartier wintered on this wind-whipped site in extreme discomfort. The cold was fierce, the rivers froze deeper and deeper, and the snows drifted around them. Scurvy smote and killed twenty-five of his crew, and would have slain more but for the medical advice of a friendly Indian who showed them how to brew a tonic from the green leaves of the ameda tree. It had enough vitamin C to restore the rest of the afflicted. They improved as spring came on; in April the river thawed and released the ships; and white men (some of them) had passed their first winter in this new land.

Cartier spread sail for home with his news. He had seen the great

---

[1] The famous spot, a short distance up the St. Charles and on the east side (directly across from the baseball park), is well marked but desolate and seldom visited. It commands a splendid view of the museum city on its pointed rock. An iron fence surrounds it, and the tiny reed-grown Lairet River runs by it to join the St. Charles. A monument has been erected there, and a huge cross set up, a replica of the one left by Cartier when he sailed away in May 1536. It is decorated with the lilies of France and bears an inscription to her king, Francis I.

river and heard tell of the vast seas beyond it. For nearly two generations talk of these discoveries went the rounds of ship harbors from seaman to sailor on the coast of France and through the drawing rooms of palace and château before another white man saw Mount Royal or heard the roar of Lachine.

III

Pre-historic Shorelines

CARTIER did not know where these mighty waters of the St. Lawrence were coming from. Nobody knew. It would be a full century
and a half before the five Lakes would be uncovered to white men's
eyes, and their boundaries fixed. Even then the explorers would
still be looking for the outlet to Cathay and for the furs they could
pick up along the route. They would not speculate beyond the
immediate surface appearance of the earth or suspect the fascinating transformations through which this region had passed before
it acquired its present shape. Geology was unborn. But these Lakes
had had a birth and a begetting. Their life span had covered a
million years before Frenchmen in their brief hour paddled canoes
across them. In their own language they had written their auto-
biographies. Their parchments were rocks, sand, and boulders, and
their characters were the carvings in the Niagara gorge, the sculp-
ture around the Superior shore, the beaches above Lake Huron, the
waterfalls, the dunes, and the moraines around Lake Michigan.

Men of our day had no more geography to explore. But they
could decipher the record of the immense architecture of the Lakes,
and wander at will backward through time to unfold a cosmic
evolution that taxes as it gratifies the imagination. For it required
a longer epoch to fashion the basins that hold the lake waters in
their saucer-like dip than it took to set man upright and round out
his skull to contain enough brain to explore them. And now, while
the captains on the French coast get ready to penetrate these unknown waterways, we may sweep quickly back over this ageless
process and compress these slow changes into a few swift-paced
acts in a drama that is as engrossing in its way as all that has

happened since Cartier's voyage to grace or trouble these restless
shores.

A million years ago, when the human race was only a Java ape-
man squatting behind the thick bowl of a teakwood tree with a
club in his hand and cunning in his heart, the Great Lakes region
was not a series of lakes but a part of an impressive river system
draining from the Laurentide to the Gulf of Mexico. A half million
years ago, when the bones of the Peiping man were laid down in
the limestone caves of China and prepared for the inspection of
modern ethnologists, the continental ice sheet plowed southward,
melted, and left in the lake region a flat land prolific in vegetation
but with no man yet upon this continent to tend it.

Some two hundred thousand years ago, when the Neanderthal
man was resting his simian thigh bones in a cave in the Dussel Valley after killing a bear with a spear of wood, the glaciers lay thick
and heavy over the Great Lakes and even extended a frigid lobe
across the Ohio River at Cincinnati. When the large-skulled Cro-
Magnon man of 35,000 years ago was domesticating the bearded
wild pony, painting multi-colored pictures on the rock walls of his
cave in southern France, and leaving his skeleton in the grotto of
Cro-Magnon for us to see what manner of man he was, great pools
were forming between the retreating ice front and the moraines in
the vicinity of present-day Chicago and between Toledo and Fort
Wayne. By the time these true men had learned to fashion human
figures in bone and to carve in ivory a woman's head with hair even
then most cunningly dressed, and while the skeleton of the young
'Minnesota Man' woman was being fossilized in the silt of an ancient
lake bed near Pelican Rapids in western Minnesota, to be dug up
20,000 years later by a crew of American road builders, the ice
gave way at the limestone escarpment at Lewistown, and Niagara
began to roar over the falls.

In the long age from 20,000 years to 3,000 years ago, while the
swarthy Azilians were painting their enigmatic pebbles in the cave
of Mas d'Azil; while the first American men of the Yuma and
Folsum types were chasing bisons on our western plains; while the

Browns Valley Man was being ceremoniously buried in the gravel
pit between Lake Traverse and Big Stone Lake 12,000 years B.C.;
while the early Chinese were learning to write; while the little
people of Central America were fleeing from an erupting volcano
through a shower of ashes and plashing their footprints in a layer
of volcanic mud for the Carnegie Institute to exhibit and contemplate; while Father Abraham wandered west to Canaan from Ur
of the Chaldees, and David spied upon Bathsheba, and Solomon
traded horses in Egypt and Phoenicia—in that long period of human
travail, the ice leisurely melted from our region, a small lake formed
in the Erie basin and emptied over Niagara Falls, and the vast
volume of the Upper Lakes poured a torrential overflow down the
Ottawa into the Atlantic, which then reached far up the St. Lawrence Valley. And in those sorrowful and unregenerate days when
Jehu drove his horses and chariot over fallen Queen Jezebel and
left her mangled body for the dogs to eat by the wall of Jezreel,
the water level of the mindless Upper Lakes fell below the divide
at the head of the Ottawa River, and began to flood through the
flat outlets known to us as the St. Clair and Detroit rivers. Only
minor changes were made in this lake system from the time the
Jews were carried into captivity by the river of Chebar in Babylon
to the day when the *Griffon* set sail on Lake Erie.

The recorded evidences of these life stages of the Great Lakes
lie all about the several thousand miles of their shoreline. They are
among the scenic wonders that each year lure tourists by the thousands into the region. Many of them are concentrated on Mackinac
Island that juts up at the straits between Lakes Huron and Michigan. Arch Rock was cut through the limestone by the waves of a
lake whose level was high above the present shore, and drowned
much of the island. Sugar Loaf Rock, standing out white and solitary above the green trees, is another remnant and a reminder of
the abandoned shoreline. The beach ridges of that ancient lake are
clearly exposed on the short target range on the island. Across Lake
Huron on the northeast side of the Blue Mountains of Collingwood, Ontario, this same ancient lake level is marked by the boulder pavement of its beach, which rises nearly two hundred feet

above Georgian Bay. If you wander near Black River, Michigan, you may see the antique contours of this vast lake system traced by the Algonquin Cliff and lake terrace. In fact, all up and down the St. Lawrence and around the Lakes you will come upon these exposures that indicate the areas once covered by earlier stages of these waters. When these contours are projected on the same level around the region, they drown an area of startling dimensions and vividly indicate how radically the outlines of these Lakes have changed.

We can almost see the changes still going on in some places. Within the memory of our grandfathers a large area around Toledo, now fertile with bumper crops, was still the Black Swamp left there by Lake Erie as it slowly lowered its shoreline and withdrew to the north. Much of the margin between Toledo and Sandusky is still a swamp, though a picturesque one with its tall grasses, its quiet bayous harboring motorboats and fishermen's skiffs, and its green rivers that have quietly spread out and gone to sleep.

The signs of the glaciers that formed the Lakes are scattered far and wide on the surface of the land. Time after time they invaded the region. Each time they dumped their glacial baggage in roughly parallel moraines that have undergone much alteration in comparatively recent times. We have already flown over the Valparaiso Moraine. A fast automobile ride across northern Indiana and Illinois gives vivid form to these moraines as the car is lifted and lowered over their pleasing surfaces. The Monooka Ridge is smooth and evenly undulating, but the highway passes over or skirts round kettle-shaped hills, saucer-flat valleys, ponds, lakes, and swamps, that give interest to an otherwise monotonous landscape. Or, if you go across New York a little distance south of Lake Ontario, you will be impressed by the multitude of drumlins, those little hills of unstratified glacial drift that are so thick around Rochester and on east between Lake Ontario and the Finger Lakes. Out in Wisconsin you will see them thrust up against the sky at the end of long corn rows, a few trees usually softening their scarred slopes. All about the countryside are boulders from the Laurentian Mountains scoured into various shapes and sizes, some almost as large as a cabin, some small and round like a basket ball. You see these boulders on the lakeshore, where they have been undermined by the wash of the waters and pulled out onto the beach from among the trees. One of them on Lake Michigan near Glencoe is famous because naturalists and geologists have photographed it so often.

Equally impressive records of the movement of the glaciers have been uncovered on the bedrock of the region. The glacial grooves on Kelley's Island in Lake Erie are celebrated. They were carved into deep, parallel furrows in the solid stone by the heavy hand of the ice armed with rock fragments. They are also exposed at Stony Island, Chicago, and at various other places in the southern lake region. Some of the excavations around Chicago disclose not only grooved, but scratched, striated, and polished surfaces, to bear witness to the slow fury of the glacial alterations in the Great Lakes. In the digging for the Calumet branch of the Drainage Canal at Chicago, huge potholes and deep grooves were exposed where they had been cut and worn in the limestone bedrock. They show how this long disused outlet river at one stage in the history of these Lakes whirled and shoved rocks swiftly down past Blue Island to an outlet south of Mount Forest Island. Even a coral reef, with its concentric circles of growth clearly marked, was uncovered in a quarry at Thornton, Illinois.

Niagara Falls, the escarpment at the western edge of Lake Ontario, Sault St. Marie, the Pictured Rocks, and all the scenic marvels of the Lake Superior shore add their sculptured evidence to that of the old beaches and the glaciers. The basins in which the five Lakes wash about are layers of folded rock. They fit rather tidily over and into each other like a nest of bowls on a shelf—nearly a dozen of them. They warp down under the lake floor and crop out in cliffs above the surface to form the shorelines. The trained expert may be sometimes at a loss to separate and explain all the intricate structures and warpings and age of these layers, but even the intelligent layman who only fishes and boats and tours on vacation in the region must see enough to arouse his interest in these formations.

Lake Erie is shallow. The top Devonian bowl in which it lies has a narrow rim only a few feet above the choppy water. The Niagara limestone sill holds it up there, 326 feet above the Ontario basin. This same sheer cliff sweeps crescentwise around the southwestern shore of Lake Ontario, carrying the railroad over this neck of land and offering unsurpassed views of the fruit farms and the lake below it. It swerves on across the wings of the arrowhead of the Province of Ontario, then reverses its arc and rises between Georgian Bay, North Channel, and Lake Huron to become the chain of islands called Manitoulin, Cockburn, and Drummond. It curves on round to form the north and west shore of Lake Michigan and to create Green Bay.

Lake Superior is contained in the oldest, largest, and most picturesque of these rock bowls. It is a genuine antique, complete with ancient carvings, statues, and hieroglyphs. The panorama of its rim or shoreline is endlessly varied and beautiful. It first crops out at the Sault, twenty feet above the level of Lake Huron. That hard layer of Cambrian sandstone is coarse and resistant. The waters of Lake Superior, channeling down the intimate course of the St. Mary's River, have cascaded over this rim for a long age, but they wear it away slowly. If the edge of that hard sandstone were not up-turned, there would be no falls, Lake Superior would be twenty feet lower than it is, there would be no harbor at Duluth, and the entire contour and economy of the lake would be altered. On the other hand, if it were tilted only a few feet higher, it would reverse the currents of Superior, cut the lake off from the rest of the chain, and send the overflow through the St. Louis River at Duluth into the Mississippi. When it finally wears down, the barrier between the lakes will be removed; but that will be a long, long time. In fact, if the present rate of cutting is continued, this retaining wall will last forever. On the Canadian side are thirsty turbines, mills, and a ship canal lock all using water at the falls. Across the river on the American side is a battery of four locks, the big ones a quarter of a mile long. Day and night they fill and empty and refill their vast bellies from the St. Mary's River every few minutes as they suck in and spew out the unending column of lake freighters. It takes an ocean of water to lift and lower this fleet, and these busy enterprises are now using all the Lake Superior overflow—and then some.

It was not always so. These Cambrian rapids at the Sault were so awesome with their volume and their roar, their foam and rainbow spray, and the rugged but intimate beauty of their green banks, that the Jesuit Fathers who first beheld them named them for the Blessed Virgin herself. But now, much of the time, not a cascade, not even a trickle comes over that stony sill. The once-lovely curtain of water is a dry and glaring yellow slope of barren rocks, sunscorched and desolate, between the furious international activities on its margins. Clumsy ferries below the falls and a black cobweb steel railroad bridge above them link the two countries at this barrier.

On round the Upper Peninsula of Michigan, past the Tahquamenon Swamp, the sand dunes of the Grand Sable Banks whisper under the winds that move them ceaselessly about along the slowly altering Lake Superior shore. Their legend has been preserved by Longfellow.

> . . . the sand was blown and sifted
> Like great snowdrifts o'er the landscape,
> Heaping all the shores with Sand Dunes,
> Sand Hills of the Nagow Wudjoo.

A little farther westward on this varied south shore are the twenty-five miles of Pictured Rocks. It is a rampart of Cambrian sandstone, red and gray and white, facing the lake with a thousand shapes. It has been stratified and hardened through the ages, and it gets its multicolored beauty from the soluble mineral oxides which the waves and the rains have dissolved and used to tint the formations of the escarpment. No wonder the Indians regarded this gallery with awe and hung legends about it. They made it the retreat of Pampeekkeewis when he sped

> Westward by the Big-Sea-Water,
> Came into the rocky headlands,
> To the Pictured Rocks of sandstone.

The ceaseless beating of the storms and the assault of the waves kicked up by the sweep of the wind down the length and breadth

Freighters trapped in the ice on Lake Erie.

The *South Lark* docked in Detroit after a trip from Cleveland. *Courtesy of Acme Photo.*

of Lake Superior have carved out caverns in the wall into which small ships could pass and where the waters roar like the Indian gods who once lived within them. They have created the Colored Caves, Rainbow Cave, Miner's Cave, the Flower Vase, Chapel Rock, Battleship Rock, and other striking configurations. Tourists by the thousands have climbed over them or marveled at them from a boat standing a safe distance off shore.

On westward the rampart goes in graceful contour and profile to the fabulous Copper Country of the Keweenaw Peninsula and Brockway Mountain, along whose precipitous cliffs and high headlands now runs a drive as high as the Skyline at Duluth, and more spectacular. The lonely, unvisited, and harborless shoreline to the west is broken by Porcupine Mountains, sheltering the Lake of the Clouds, and by the green cluster of the Apostle Islands scattered northeastward from the Wisconsin coast.

The Duluth-Superior escarpment along the northwest shore lends an impressive beauty to the cities at the extreme west end of the lake. Without its 800 foot background of deep reddish-brown rock, Duluth would be commonplace indeed. The sharp physical contrasts of its blue lake, multicolored buildings, reddish rock, and green trees make it one of the distinctive cities of America. It accommodates itself to the long shelf on the lakeshore, and has built its houses wherever it could among its rocks. Bare, sun-warmed cliffs, advertising somebody's bread, are as much a part of Duluth as its tall elevators and office buildings. Violence on a cataclysmic scale has erupted here to make possible this spectacle: the Skyline Parkway, complete with parks, towers, and look-out points for sightseers, on the summit and sheer edge of the rampart; the town on the shelf, trying to climb up the cliff; the expanse of the lake hazed over with the scarf of smoke trailed by the fleet of freighters steaming in and out of the compact harbor; and the estuary of the St. Louis River, protected by its long sandbar, lined with countless docks and slips and elevators. You stand wonderingly on one of the high rocky points like Enger Peak and look down on the lake and the river. You imagine the great ice sheet lying thick over the upper lake, damming it off from the east. And you readily understand how a rise of a few feet in the water level at this Duluth lobe (levels clearly indicated by the ancient beaches) would reverse the course of that busy, sluggish river and link Duluth with New Orleans.

The drive along the lake from Duluth on up to Fort William is made a thrilling experience by this continuous bastion, divided at the international border by the ancient valley and the gorge of the Pigeon River. Huge, rugged rock points reach out into the lake and the sun falls upon their scarred sides. The rampart becomes more austere and somber near the Lakehead. Around Thunder Bay it is pre-Cambrian stone, the oldest rocks in the world. They tower above Port Arthur and Fort William and surround the twenty-mile-wide bay with a stern and primitive grandeur. They, too, are legend-haunted. The bay is a magnificent circle that could harbor a fleet of battleships. It is locked off from the open expanse of Lake Superior by two long rock ridges thrust arm-like out in a semicircle from the mainland. They almost meet at the narrow channel entrance through which the boats pass. They have been fashioned into human shapes by the violent hammerings of the centuries. They look like the crude images of petrified gods lying on their backs in the lake, their faces upturned to the sun and the snows. One of them long ago was named the Sleeping Giant and identified with Hiawatha. Seen in a good light from the center of Thunder Bay, it is really a reclining goddess in profile, arms folded, her feet swathed in the restless waters of Superior, and one mammalian breast uplifted to the sky. Across from her is the badly named Pie Island. Actually it is a distinctly masculine figure resting himself at the feet of his recumbent mate, and, when the sun lights up her brown body, glancing at her across the channel. They have calmly watched the birth and brief career of the two cities and the greatest of the lakes that bathes their immobile bodies.

Behind the grain elevators and flying field of Fort William, Mount McKay's sheer cliffs rise up fifteen hundred feet. Lesser but still gigantic cliffs, scarred, scraped, and scrolled, complete the circle of the bay. They produce an indescribable effect of grandeur and mystery as if, like an incredibly magnified Stonehenge, they had been prepared for the ritual of some lost primitive religious revel of giants. The two cities under them are dwarfed by the dimensions of their setting on the bay under the mountains. It takes a steamboat nearly an hour to cross from the entrance by the Sleeping Giant to the dock at Port Arthur. You stand on the foredeck and watch the town take form as you approach; and, though the elevators are so immense that they would dominate Toledo or Sandusky, they are reduced to detailed fresco by the elaborate scale of the bowl at the Lakehead.

All around the wild, uninhabited north shore this rim rises and falls. It goes past Nipigon and on east to Schreiber and Heron Bay. The great transcontinental highway has not yet linked the East with the West over this lonely region which still cuts Canada squarely in two and exaggerates her sectional problem. But its grandeur may be viewed from the lake itself, or from the windows of the trains on the Canadian Pacific, which reaches the coast at Schreiber and bends north around the lake on its way to Port Arthur and the Far West. The faulted, enduring rock, often ornamented with evergreens, rises in places two thousand feet, then folds down almost to the lake level. It pushes bold headlands out into the whitecaps that beat against them as the wind sweeps across the lake and makes its incessant wash in its Cambrian and pre-Cambrian basin.

One other remarkable feature of this landscape is its rivers and waterfalls. They are familiar to casual tourists as well as to fishermen and industrialists. Since the lakes lie in their rock-edged basins, the rivers from the watershed, especially those reaching Lakes Superior and Michigan, must plunge over these rims to reach the level of the Lakes. Most of these rivers are quite short, for the divides that separate the Great Lakes from the Ohio-Mississippi, and from the Hudson Bay are never far from the Lakes.

Some of these streams with their high cascades are famous; around many of them still cling ancient Indian legends; and all have a wayward beauty. Lake Nipigon, really the sixth of the Great Lakes and the upper one in the chain, is 250 feet above Lake Superior. It is drained by the wild Nipigon River that roars over the shelf at Virgin Falls, Cameron and lesser falls, and foams

through Devil's Rapids, White Chute and other picturesque gorges
as it dashes on from one level to another. A few miles west of Fort
William is Kakebeka Falls in the Kaministikwa River. It is a spectacle even in so impressive a region as the Lakehead. The yellow
waters plunge funnel-wise over the ledge. The bottom is so narrow
that it churns the water and causes spray to shoot violently up out
of the gorge like a geyser and rain on the surrounding vegetation.
The Indians named it 'Angry Waters' in the 'River-That-Goes-Far-
About.' It is now called the 'Niagara of the North.' It is higher than
Niagara but only a thin segment of its width. Industry diverts its
volume, and pulp logs lie in confusion above the falls and below
in the gorge. Pigeon River, once the home of immense flocks of
passenger pigeons, cascades down from the high level of the chain
of lakes on the international border, over Partridge Falls, through
The Cascades and other rapids and gorges, over Middle Falls, and
finally takes another sheer drop of a hundred twenty-five feet over
the shelf at High Falls two miles above its mouth at Lake Superior.

The rivers and short streams flowing north into Lake Superior
fall over the Cambrian sandstone ledge and rush through gorges
which they have cut with infinite patience. The falls of the Tahquamenon River, the river of legended Hiawatha, are the loveliest
and best known. Upper Falls, 300 feet wide, beautifully contoured,
flings its waters out of tranquility over a 40-foot cliff of foaming
cataract. Then the re-formed river rushes on through the high forested walls of the gorge, plunges again over the resistant stone of
the Lower Falls, a drop of 43 feet over three terraces, and then,
tranquil once more, it goes leisurely into Whitefish Bay. The other
streams have almost equal grandeur. The Munising River goes over
the Cambrian rim in a 50-foot cataract and through a boiling rapids
that drops another 25 feet. Miner's Falls of 75 feet, Stately Falls
of 200 feet, and the beautiful 100-foot Spray Creek Cascade are
show-places in the Pictured Rocks region. Laughing Whitefish River
falls 100 feet over a series of terraces on land now owned by Henry
Ford.

And a little to the south, other rivers must plunge over the hard
limestone rim of the third bowl of rock, the Ordovician, that is so

clearly exposed along Green Bay. It slopes southward, and the Whitefish, Menominee, and other rivers which have made little progress in wearing it down, must leap over it to reach the bay and Lake Michigan.

These are a few of the physical beauties of the region that capture and hold the interest of all observers of the Great Lakes, and tell in their singular language the slow but dramatic tale of their beginning and their growth. And while Champlain gets the ear of his patrons in France and outfits his little ship to sail back over Cartier's route to the Lakes, we may take a few more minutes to write briefly of their life cycle which got them ready for the visits of the Frenchmen and the cities and farms and ships of the Americans and Canadians.

((((IV))))

Birth of the Lakes

THE first white men who saw the Great Lakes and explored their basin were impressed by the slight elevation that separated them from the Mississippi, the Ohio, the Mohawk, and the Susquehanna Rivers. Joliet himself observed that the divide was almost non-existent between Lake Michigan and the Mississippi and that a canal of 'but half a league' would enable a barque to 'go with facility to Florida.' The barrier is almost on the edge of the Chicago city limits and is only from six to ten feet high. In a rainy season the Chicago River actually joins the Des Plaines on the swampy divide, and canoes have been paddled from Lake Michigan into the Mississippi without a portage. Joliet's canal has long been functioning, and others were cut at strategic points to link the already stupendous navigation lanes of the Lakes with the Ohio River, and down the Mohawk to New York City. For this ridge is little more than a shallow earthen dam piled up on the prairie by the glaciers when they were hollowing out the five basins for the Lakes.

The glaciers spread over the Great Lakes area and retreated many times in their total history. Five of these invasions into the Lake states are plainly in evidence. We need not bother with the records of each, because they do not enrich or advance our story. What really matters is that in the long glacial periods, when it remained freezing cold in Canada and Labrador all the year round, the snow piled up, year in year out, never melting, always pressing down with increasing weight upon the flexible crust of the earth. In the Labrador center it reached a thickness of six miles. It was not anchored like the mountains, but lay loose on the surface. The incalculable pressure pushed out the southern edge of the massive ice field, and started it moving with slow and sluggish but irresistible force, a dozen feet a day, down over the St. Lawrence, down over the lake region, and on into New York, Pennsylvania, Ohio, Indiana, Illinois, Wisconsin, Minnesota. Its moving front edge was fashioned into a powerful cutting tool with rocks and boulders firmly embedded in the solid ice. We have seen how it cut grooves in the rock on Kelley's Island with its century-timed strokes, how it scoured, scraped, and hollowed out the channel at Chicago. In the Upper Lakes and Lake Ontario it crushed and gouged two to three hundred feet below sea level, leaving the bottoms of those lakes to this day in places far below the surface of the Atlantic Ocean. At its maximum depth, Lake Superior is 690 feet below the sea level.

Each southward movement of the ice sheet finally reached a point where the sun still warmed the cold earth and the rate of melting equaled or exceeded the accumulation or the rate of travel. The debris-laden front melted and dropped its cutting edge and its cargo. Pressure from the north for a time kept the southern ice front constant, as the rim of the glacier moved with still more earth, sand, and gravel against the sun. Year after year it came on and melted. The piling up of the debris formed a barrier that mounted higher and higher, until it became the circle of moraines that we now see along the southern border of the lake bowl. And when at last the ice sheet commenced to melt north of these moraines, the Great Lakes began to take form.

The manner in which they were formed is quite simple in principle; though the process was infinitely slow, it has gone on continuously, and it still goes on. Only the rate of change varies. At certain times the Lakes remained so nearly constant for so many thousands of years that they were able to build up those distinct beaches which we have observed on our tour of natural wonders high and dry above the present lake levels. These more static periods have been painstakingly studied and reconstructed by the geologists who have distinguished them with special names and outlined them with detailed maps. Our interest is confined to a few of the more important stages through which the Lakes passed from the time the ice first melted back from the moraines until Champlain's canoe paddled out on Georgian Bay and down the Trent River to Lake Ontario.

It is diverting school play to model to scale the general contours of the Great Lakes basins north of these moraines, fill them with water, and watch where they will overflow if you place soft clay in different places to represent the retreating glacial front at its various stages. It naturally flows out at the lowest available point, and, as we and Joliet have already observed, the differences in elevations around the rim are so slight that an obstruction at one low point will shift the whole drainage pattern. A glance at a topographical map will quickly show where these points are: the present Niagara Falls-St. Lawrence outlet, of course; but also at Rome, New York; at Lake Simcoe and the Trent River Valley in Ontario; at the Nipissing-Ottawa River Valley; at the Maumee River above Toledo; at Saginaw Bay and the Grand River in Michigan; at the Chicago River; at Green Bay and Fox River; and at Duluth. At one time or another in their growth (or shrinkage) the Lakes have used one or more of these outlets with the resulting shift in their shorelines.

In their first stage, with the ice piled high over most of the present system, two small lakes formed between the glacier and the moraine: one in the vicinity of Chicago, the other near Toledo. They drained voluminously down the Chicago and Maumee Rivers into the Mississippi. But when the glacier melted back far enough to uncover the Saginaw Bay on the west coast of Lake Huron, a lower outlet than the Maumee was opened. This outlet was the Grand River valley running crescentwise across Michigan by way of Imlay City and Flint. The forming Lake Erie lay in front of the ice sheet, drowned Detroit, the St. Clair Flats, and spread across this mile-wide valley to join Lake Michigan in the upper dune region of today. Relics of this stage in Great Lakes history are interesting to view in both the Maumee and the Grand Rivers. Green Bay was opened at about the same time and drained off to the southwest into the Mississippi.

Another interesting stage in the building of the Lakes was reached and maintained for a time when the continued warm glow

of the sun drove the ice front back far enough to clear the Finger
Lakes in New York, but not enough to free Lake Ontario. These
lakes, imponding the glacial waters into their basins, but blocked
out of drainage to the north, were then held at a higher level than
now, and emptied down the Susquehanna River into Chesapeake
Bay. At the same period, the entire basin of Erie was cleared of
ice, but since Niagara was still frozen and buried under the glacier,
the level of the lake was determined by the elevation of the Imlay
outlet at Saginaw. Hence the lake in this period of its history
reached almost to Fort Wayne, covered the northern rim of Ohio,
the lower east coast of Michigan, the St. Clair Flats, and the southern littoral of the Province of Ontario. When the ice retreated a few
more miles, the southern lobe of Lake Huron was uncovered. The
interconnecting bodies of water formed one dragon-shaped lake
reaching from the Finger Lakes, round the rim of the ice, and
between it and the morainic dam, all the way to Saginaw. Lake
Michigan was then about half uncovered, but Superior was piled
high with ice.

One more backward push of the ice and the Mohawk Valley was
exposed. It was a few feet lower than both the Imlay-Grand River
outlet to the west, and the Susquehanna headwater to the south,
so another shoreline was formed. The new lake filled the uncovered lobes of Saginaw Bay and southern Lake Huron, all of Lake
Erie and the Finger Lakes. It took this lower eastern exit and
flowed through New York along the route later revived for the
famous Erie Canal and then down the Hudson to the Atlantic.
The Duluth-Lakehead end of Lake Superior was liberated at about
the same time and sent the torrents of its melting ice out through
the St. Croix River into the upper Mississippi.

Another clearly defined stage in the formation of our present
lakes occurred when the ice melted off Lake Superior and opened
up the Nipissing-Ottawa River outlet. At that period all three
upper lakes were joined in one vast body of fresh water. They
were spread out like a great bird flying northeast, with the Michigan lobe for a body and tail, Lake Superior as the outstretched
left wing, and the Huron, Georgian Bay (greatly enlarged), Nipis-

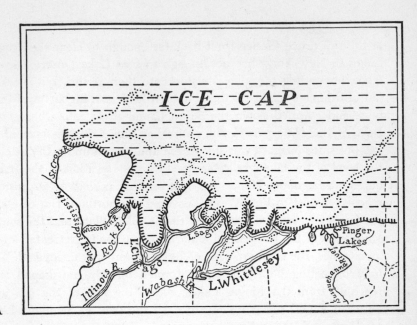

A

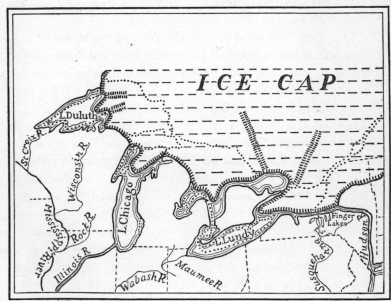

B

FOUR SUCCESSIVE STAGES IN THE

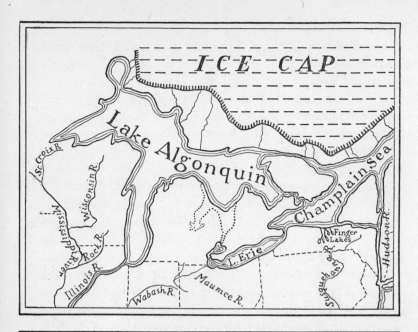

C

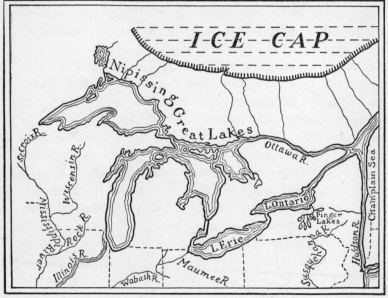

After Leverett and Taylor

D

FORMATION OF THE GREAT LAKES

sing, Simcoe region as an equal right-wing spread—all three members joined by the waters that then covered the Sault territory and drowned all the Upper Peninsula of Michigan.

We have already observed some of the scenic wonders and extraordinary remnants of this tremendous lake that lend interest to the landscape. Its beach line, clearly defined by its boulders, cliffs, and terraces, has been traced throughout most of the region. It reveals both the lake level and the shift of the earth itself that tilted after the ice was removed. At the celebrated Pointe aux Barque at the tip of the thumb of Michigan, the old shoreline is only ten feet above present Lake Huron—and supports a lighthouse and Coast Guard station to warn the big freighters away from the low rocky shore. Down at Port Huron, where the lake rushes through a narrow channel into the St. Clair River, this ancient shore is twenty-seven feet above the lake. Up at Mackinac it rises 221 feet above the present level. Around the south shore of Superior at Munising, called by the Indians 'Place-of-the-Big-Island,' this beach is 147 feet higher than at Mackinac; and it continues to rise another 162 feet in the Keweenaw Peninsula, reaching as high as 1,110 feet above sea level. It also bends up from Port Huron on to the east as far as Kirkfield in the Lake Simcoe region in Ontario, and reaches a crest of 189 feet above Georgian Bay near Collingwood, Ontario. This same beach remains level, however, at the outcropping at Manistee, half way up the east shore of Lake Michigan, at Standish almost due east on Saginaw Bay, at Richmondville on Lake Huron forty miles below Pointe aux Barque, and southeast across the lake at Grand Bend, Ontario; and it stands there to this day to indicate the gentle crescent hinge line on which the earth to the north was uptilted to alter the formation of the Lakes.

At one important stage when all these lakes were still joined as one, they overflowed through three outlets—all to be used a few thousand years later by Champlain and other French explorers. One was out of Lake Michigan at Chicago and down the Illinois River; another went down past Port Huron and Detroit into Lake Erie, which was then almost as it is to this day; and a third flowed

across the low, narrow, arrowhead neck of Ontario through the
Trent River into the enlarged Lake Ontario. At the same time,
since the natural eastern outlet down the St. Lawrence to the
sea was still blocked with ice, the overflow was discharged through
the Mohawk Valley over the present divide at Rome, New York
—a spot made famous a few thousand years later in Erie Canal
days when the destiny of a new nation and its economic development were influenced by this lowland trough through the mountains into the Great Lakes region and the West. The obstruction
of the St. Lawrence Valley kept the Lakes a long age at the
Rome level, many feet above the present shoreline. The Ridge
Road from Rochester to Lewiston runs along the ancient beach
built in this epoch.

Another important and interesting change came over the Lakes
when the ice was melted back on the Laurentian Upland and the
St. Lawrence Valley was cleared. The valley was then below sea
level, and the salt water came in to replace the ice sheet. It
reached all the way west to Toronto and Hamilton, Ontario, and
part-way up the Ottawa Valley. Along the St. Lawrence River
are still visible post-glacial marine terraces now as high as 600
feet above tidal waters.

The most exciting act in the drama of the Great Lakes occurred, according to our best reckoning, about 25,000 years ago.
Niagara Falls was born. The escarpment was already there waiting to produce this eighth wonder of the world, but the thunder-
ous voice of the 'prodigious cadence of water' that was to awe and
deafen Father Hennepin was still buried in silence under the
waters of Lake Ontario, which were then approximately at the
same level, and were linked together by a narrow band of water
that overflowed what we now call the Niagara River. They discharged down the Mohawk Valley. If La Salle had come at that
time he could have built the *Griffon* at Rome, New York, and
sailed calmly through the Niagara strait high above the drowned
cliff of the Falls. But the Labrador glacier was melting back over
the Laurentide rocks, and the earth's flexible crust, eased of its
stupendous load of ice, was, as we have noted, apparently tilting

upward. The invading arm of the Atlantic was slushed out between Montreal and the Thousand Islands, leaving a river to drain Lake Ontario northeastward to the sea. The lake then abandoned the Mohawk Valley for the new outlet down the St. Lawrence. The level of the lake dropped, and the shoreline contracted. Down it went until the hard rib of limestone edged above the water and out into the sun. If that limestone shelf had not been there, or if it had been less resistant, Lake Erie would have been drained and men would now be planting gardens in its basin. But that solid rock, sloping gently up, 35 feet per mile, toward its precipice at Lewiston, held Lake Erie near its present level while Lake Ontario went on down and down toward its final elevation of 246 feet, 326 feet below Erie, now thirty miles away. At that point the waters of the Niagara torrent began first to break, then to cascade, and finally to roar and boil over the escarpment. It had undertaken the long, long task of cutting the six-mile gorge which the white man found when he first came here, and which we now detour through the locks on the Welland Canal.

Interestingly, this hard layer of Niagara limestone which forms the river bed and maintains the falls lies upon soft shales and sandstone. As the water plunges over the sheer cliff of limestone, it assaults these soft underpinnings with stupendous force, cutting back under the edge of the falls and undermining the foundation of the escarpment. When enough of the shale and sandstone has been mined out, chunks of the top layer of limestone weaken, break, and give way. Little by little, it has quarried back toward Lake Erie, leaving the lengthening gorge as an exhibit of its power and patience. The rate of recession has varied, as the uneven width of the gorge plainly shows. In some places it is quite narrow, indicating the resistance of the stone and the decrease in the volume of water going over the edge. In other places it is wide, as at Whirlpool Rapids, where the river had easy material to work on. Here it fell upon a deposit of loose, glacial debris. It carried away the unresisting sand and gravel at a fast rate, carving out a large basin in the gorge, and creating the picturesque rapids of today. Niagara is now working backward at a rate of about five feet per year. Much of Goat Island has already been chipped off. Another huge chunk fell only a few years ago, marring the beauty of the Horseshoe Falls.

At its present rate of change, Niagara will live another five thousand years; but it will slowly decline in grandeur. It will drop in height from its present 160 feet to a final 100 feet, and then, no longer falling sheer over a cliff, it will become a boiling rapids. And some day, when it will not matter at all to you and me, there will not even be a rapids, and the diminishing drainage from these lakes will flow again toward the Mississippi.

The Lakes went right on with their implacable changes, slowly contracting toward the contours familiar to us. For a long time after Lake Erie and Lake Huron assumed approximately their present form, the three upper lakes and Georgian Bay were still joined across the Upper Peninsula from the Straits of Mackinac to Lake Superior, and above the lovely islands of the St. Mary's River from the North Channel to the Sault. They had receded below the outlets over the moraines to the Mississippi, but not yet below the level of the Ottawa. They drained down that wide valley into the salt estuary that still filled the St. Lawrence Valley below Montreal; and they were connected with Lake Erie across the St. Clair Flats above Detroit-Windsor.

The final (for us) stage was, of course, already evident. The salt water was dumped out of the St. Lawrence Valley exposing the rapids that were to interrupt Cartier's voyage, and provoke the controversy over the deep waterway to the Atlantic. The upper lakes fell below the highest point at the head of the Ottawa Valley, and that outlet to the sea was abandoned. It was just barely abandoned, we might note; for when Champlain joined the party of Huron Indians in 1615 to invade the Iroquois Country of Ontario, he went up the ancient Ottawa outlet, took the portage path over the barrier ridge between the Ottawa River and Lake Nipissing, and paddled down the French River into Georgian Bay. The Lakes gradually relaxed into the comfortable confines of their bowls, and no longer struggled for overflow outlets. A small stream cascaded over the Sault out of Lake Superior into the St. Mary's

River, more to make the land and the falls beautiful than to
discharge an important surplus. The sluggish channel across the
St. Clair Flats, now dredged and crowded with commerce, connected Lake Huron with Lake Erie, and Niagara linked them to
Lake Ontario. And so they lay there, green rimmed, teeming with
fish, the haunt of birds and beasts, and, later, the home of red
men, waiting in timeless silence the coming of the commercial and
ecclesiastical Frenchmen, and the alterations of the age of iron
and steel, of ships and machinery.

Ultimately, of course, death with its serene patience awaits the
Lakes as it awaited these exploring Frenchmen and the marble
tombs of conquering Emperors. For it is the fate of all lakes to
drain away and become rivers. Their present monument is carved
in perishable stone—the Niagara escarpment and the Cambrian
rock at the Sault. So long as they hold fast, the Lakes will live.
That will be a long age, quite long enough for our transient
purposes.

((((V))))

Champlain on the Ottawa

THE Frenchmen knew nothing of all these inland seas, lying there quiet as a Provence millpond under an August moon, furious as the Channel off St. Malo under the lashing of a November gale. We see them spread out before our geographic eyes for a thousand miles in all their magnificent detail above Montreal and the rapids which Cartier viewed from the top of Mount Royal. But the Frenchmen will have to discover them slowly, unfolding their mystery league by league, year by year, by struggle on foot, by tireless paddling of canoes, by weariness, disease and death. We shall look on while they gather hints from the talk of Indian traders, while they sketch maps in their minds from these hints, and plan expeditions past all barriers to search out the wonders that were not diminished by the reports of red men. And we shall follow them on a few of these expeditions as with infinite hardship, in constant danger of death, they plunge on through rain and sleet, over ice and into freezing slush, through foaming rapids and around waterfalls; cold, weary, hungry; pestered, stabbed, and almost devoured by mosquitoes; dependent upon Indian guides and subject to their childish caprices, yet always pushing on westward to find the bounds of this region—perhaps discover (who knew?) the passageway to Cathay.

Not all the captains who sailed after Cartier had any wish to risk their necks merely to range over a hostile wilderness. Trade was more lucrative. Greedy merchants from Honfleur and St. Malo soon followed Cartier far enough to drop an anchor in the lower St. Lawrence. But they were well content to dole out knives and beads and axes from the safe harbor at Tadoussac and barter a cargo of muskrat and beaver pelts from the Indians. They listened to tales of great lakes, seas, waterfalls and copper mines lying many leagues and many moons westward, guarded by strange gods and menaced by enemy tribesmen; but they sailed eastward past the white whales in the Bay of Gaspé, past the fishing banks of Newfoundland, back to the rich markets of France, letting the mysterious inland safely alone.

Always, however, there are the unaccountable men with the curious brain, men with restless spirits and adventurous hearts who want knowledge more than furs, and men who want to rescue lost souls more than either. These men also sailed up the St. Lawrence along with the shopkeeper tradesmen. The story of the discovery of the Great Lakes is the drama of a few daring men and holy fathers from Champlain and Brother Sagard to Father Marquette and La Salle.

Samuel de Champlain was still young in years but rich in experience when his king graciously gave him permission to sail to New France with Pontgravé and two tiny ships of only twelve and fifteen tons each. He was already an accomplished explorer, geographer, soldier, sailor, administrator, and colonizer. He was just back from a two-year voyage to the West Indies and Mexico where his quick, empire mind immediately saw the possibility of a ship canal across Panama to reduce the distance to the South Sea 'by more than 1,500 leagues.' No better man in all the kingdom could have been found to plant the first French colony on the St. Lawrence or plan the mapping of the Great Lakes. His love for his homeland only makes more remarkable his willingness to perform his thankless part in a mismanaged venture.

Champlain kept a journal of all that he saw and did. It was dedicated to his king, published in France, and could be had at any time these three hundred years in the book stalls of Paris. We read it now with undiminished interest, and lean heavily upon it for the record of his voyages and discoveries and for its revelation of the man himself, the first of the legended names on the Great Lakes.

We puzzle over the mind and motives of this well-placed young Frenchman from the Biscayan seacoast village of Brouage, who in 1603, at the age of thirty-six, left the sun-drenched vineyards, the pear trees, and the neat gardens of kitchen vegetables that he loved so well, to live out thirty-two years of his life in a barren wilderness across the sea. It was from start to finish a manner of life that might have killed off any man. He first sailed up past Three Rivers to Montreal to retrace Cartier's path. In those sixty-eight years, so transient and hazardous was life among Canadian Indians, every trace of the village where Cartier had been welcomed by a thousand savages had completely disappeared and its exact location became a subject of controversy. Champlain viewed the great river and then attempted to ascend the rapids. He was beaten back by their force, and reluctantly returned to await another and better opportunity. But he learned from the Indians that beyond these rapids were many more, and beyond them were lakes.

Many years passed by before Champlain again got above Montreal. In the meantime he wintered and explored on the tide-beaten wastes of the Bay of Fundy, and, in 1608, he planted the colony and built houses on the rock of Quebec and under the protection of its sheer escarpment. He made friends among the Huron and Algonquin Indians who lived in the vicinity or who came down to trade. To their amazement and delight, he clothed himself in steel and armed himself with fire and arquebus to help them fight their enemy the Iroquois, always making 'the most exact researches and explorations in my power' in the regions through which he passed.

In the spring, like God Almighty, he first planted a garden in his wilderness and encouraged others, including the Indians, to do likewise. In the long and bitter winters, snowed in and limited in food, he watched his men rót with scurvy, saw their lips and gums swell up and burst, their teeth loosen and fall out, their bodies blacken and die; and he had them opened to study their insides and speculate on the cause of this disease that could in a few weeks' time reduce strong men—surgeons and men of rank as well as common workmen—to this pitiful state. We note with satisfaction his conclusion that it came of eating 'salt food and vegetables, which heat the blood and corrupt the internal parts.'

A full decade passed, and still Champlain, who styled himself more highly as Geographer Royal than as Empire Builder, had been no further into the west than the rapids at Montreal. Year by year he learned a little more about the land and waters whence the Indians came in caravans of canoes with their load of furs. They always rejoiced to see Champlain, and every year they invited him to their villages. Each season he promised that he would join them next season. So it was in the year 1608.

He learned from 'our savages' at Tadoussac, who had heard it from other 'migratory savages,' that some fifty days' journey to the north was a salt sea. His interest was stirred, but the shrewd old geographer noted that if the report was true, 'as I certainly think it is, it can be nothing but a gulf entering the interior on the north.' This, of course, was Hudson Bay, into which Henry Hudson sailed just two years later. Champlain had opportunity to look only a little distance up the austere Saguenay River. Regretfully he recorded, 'I have often wished to explore it, but could not do so without the savages, who were unwilling that I or any of our party should accompany them. Nevertheless, they have promised that I shall do so. This exploration would be desirable, in order to remove the doubts of many persons in regard to the existence of this sea on the north, where it is maintained that the English have gone these latter years to find a way to China.'

The year 1609 came and went. This time he did go southward to aid his friendly Indians against their enemies, but more particularly because he was intrigued with their reports of a 'very large lake, filled with handsome islands' and bordered with 'large tracts of fine land.' They directed him to the lake that still bears his name. At the very moment when he was jotting notes about it in his journal, his English rival, Henry Hudson, was beating down the New England coast in the *Half Moon* on his way to the great river that also bears his name and rises near Lake Champlain. The Indians showed Champlain a country so rich in beavers, stags, fallow-deer, fawns, roe-bucks, and bears, and streams so well-stocked with fish that he exclaimed over them. He also noted, however, that because of the eternal tribal warfare, the Indians had all withdrawn from this marvelous hunting ground to escape surprise by their enemies.

The year 1610 came in and again Champlain had to postpone his inland journey. But he was still firmly resolved in his mind to inspect the fabled region to the west; and before sailing back to France in August and September, he sent a young lad of two winters' experience in the new settlement of Quebec to live the ensuing winter among the friendly Algonquin Indians. Presumably this was Étienne Brûlé. Champlain's instructions were that he should learn the language, 'ascertain the nature of their country, see the great lake, observe the rivers and tribes there, and also explore the mines and objects of special interest in the localities occupied by these tribes,' and inform Champlain of the facts. Champlain courteously took with him an Algonquin boy in exchange, and after many promises of friendship and return, separated from them and sailed away to France. But notwithstanding his mounting interest in the region, the following season of 1611 got him no farther inland than the Lachine Rapids, where he again met his friendly savages and received back his boy.

So the seasons passed, each finding Champlain putting off or being prevented from enlarging his knowledge of the Great Lakes. The opportunity came at last on his return to the St. Lawrence at the end of April 1613. As usual he was greeted by his savages 'with great demonstrations of joy,' and he made immediate plans to go up to the Falls of St. Louis (i.e., the Lachine Rapids) to consult with the tribesmen. He found them moody and disgruntled because the merchants had mistreated them the season before; they were too discouraged to come down to the trading mart any more. The greedy merchants were left anchored in the river with quantities of goods but no Indians with furs to exchange. The situation was serious, and the geographer promptly decided to use it as an excuse for extending his long-delayed researches up the Ottawa Valley. He would visit the Indians in friendship, encourage them to come down to traffic, and reassure them of his

wish to aid them in their wars; and, incidentally, he would explore
their country.

It is clear that Champlain had planned his journey before he
left France. In Paris, the year before, he had met Nicholas de
Vignau, a young man who had also wintered among the Algonquins on the Ottawa. He swore before a notary and all that was
holy that he had looked upon the North Sea, that it was only a
seventeen-day round trip from the Falls of St. Louis, that he
found there the wreck of an English ship, that the eighty cast-
away sailors had been scalped when they tried to seize supplies
from the Indians, and that these friendly Indians were holding a
young English boy as a present for Champlain. The explorer entertained fears and misgivings, but at the same time he was greatly
pleased because, as he said, 'I thought I had almost found that for
which I had for a long time been searching.' Combining his two-
fold interest, he obtained provisions and two canoes, took three
of his men, one savage as a guide, and Vignau, whom at the outset of his record Champlain calls 'the most impudent liar that has
been seen for a long time,' and on Monday, May 27, 1613, began
the ascent of the Ottawa River.

It is doubtful whether all the reports of his young men and his
savages had prepared him for the hardships of this journey. The
Ottawa Valley has a peculiar beauty. Flanking it on the north is
the dark mass of the Laurentides, where the shadows play and
make deep blue pockets in their sides. On the south is level and
gently rolling terrain, now a pleasant land of farms and dairies,
then a 'fair and open woods' as Champlain noted, with soil 'very
good for tillage.' A network of modern highways now weaves the
region into a busy and prosperous unit; but Champlain was making his way up the river itself, and the Ottawa is not a free-flowing
and navigable stream. It is a series of island-spotted lakes and
short open stretches of peaceful river with dozens of high and
dangerous falls and rapids. The journey was one of continuous
battle against obstructions that brought him time and again just
short of disaster.

At the beginning of the Long Sault, 'filled with stones and rocks, and where the water runs with great velocity,' they had to get into the water and drag the canoes with a rope. A mile farther up they had to row hard through a little fall, which, the explorer faithfully tells us, made him sweat. Still farther on they fared worse, and Champlain almost lost his life. The current was swift, the river bed was full of big rocks, and the water foamed and roared. The woods on the shore were so dense that they could not portage through them. They dragged the canoes with ropes through the boiling rapids. Champlain had a rope wound tightly around his hand. His canoe caught in a violent eddy and dragged him down into the rapids before he could unwind the tow-rope. By a miracle he landed between two large rocks and escaped with his life, though he says he was badly hurt and his hand nearly cut off. We get another fine glimpse into the mind of our geographer in this crisis. As he was jerked into the rapids, he remembered God and called out to Him for aid, wisely remembering also to help himself by pulling at the canoe. His savage rushed to his aid, but God had already preserved His servant, and the canoe 'was returned to me by the refluent water.' Champlain then praised the Divine Goodness that had spared him, and lay down to rest during the remainder of the day, 'having had enough.'

The going got still worse. He fell in with fifteen canoes of savages from up the river. They were astonished to see him there, still more to learn of his plan to go farther. They told him how bad the way was and that 'we had seen nothing up to this point.' However they courteously gave him a guide for the second canoe, and took in exchange Champlain's 'least indispensable' Frenchman, who returned to the Falls with a leaf from Champlain's notebook.

Thus reinforced he toiled on up the river past the mouth of the Gatineau. Champlain was greatly impressed by the site upon which the city of Ottawa now stands with such pride. He exclaimed over the Rideau River that flows through what is now a select section of the capital, and in his enthusiasm exaggerated the height of its fall over the escarpment into the Ottawa. 'The savages take pleasure in passing under it, not wetting themselves, except from the spray that is thrown off.' They paddled hard against the

current round the point where the bridge now crosses to the many-
towered Hull across in Quebec, past the high gray cliff upon
which the English Gothic Parliament buildings are now enthroned.
They portaged round the Chaudière Falls, below which the fishermen now idle in boats, and where the tankers swing up the channel and ease into the dock beside the battery of giant silver oil-
storage vats. Here the savages placated the gods of the falls by
ceremoniously tossing an offering of tobacco into the cauldron,
now so unceremoniously harnessed into turbines. So they passed
one of the beautiful spots in Canada and paddled on up Chaudière
Lake, that shines in the evening like silver when viewed from the
terrace on Parliament hill at sunset.

The land was now more sandy, the country unpromising. Champlain complained of the hardship, but he did not fail to note such
curious items as the root from which the Indians of this region
made a crimson dye with which to paint their faces and 'also little
gewgaws.' In order to pass the Rapide des Chats, he was forced
to lighten his already spare cargo by storing in sacks his maize
and other provisions, and his least necessary clothes. He kept only
his arms and fishing lines to supply food 'as place and luck might
permit.' Even with this easier load their progress became more and
more difficult. Vignau deliberately tried to lure Champlain into
peril or insurmountable obstacles to end the expedition before his
duplicity could be exposed. He got into heated dispute with the
Indians when he urged Champlain to go through the falls above
the Island of St. Croix. The Indians, with their gift for ironic phrase
which was never lost on Champlain, scornfully told the liar, 'You
must be tired of living.' We can see the old explorer scrutinizing
with mounting suspicion the lying face of the impostor as the
little party huddles in exhaustion at the foot of still another rapids
that leads nowhere but into more wilderness.

Champlain sided with his savages. With their load still further
reduced, they portaged safely around the danger. Champlain says
he himself carried 'three arquebuses, as many oars, my clock, and
some small articles,' including possibly the astrolabe marked 'Paris
1603,' which a farmer in the region turned up in 1870. Champlain

cheered his loaded men on against the vicious mosquitoes that attacked in swarms and with so marvelous persistence that even the articulate geographer gave up in despair the attempt to describe them. Staggering under their loads, for twenty-four hours without any food except a little boiled, unseasoned fish, they finally fell down from exhaustion, cast their lines, and built a fire to drive off the pests. They were passing through sections where blown-over and twisted pine trees blocked their portages, where the pines had been burned over by the Indians to make a little clearing for their grain. These adversities did not affect Champlain's piety. When he first saw a red cypress, he hewed it into a cross, emblazoned it with the arms of France, and erected it conspicuously on an island which he christened Sainte Croix.

Some distance above the island he came upon a settlement of Indians in a clearing of maize. The natives were completely astounded to see Champlain materialize in this remote and unlikely spot. They themselves experienced such trouble in getting through this region of the Ottawa that they could not understand how this Frenchman had managed to come here, unless indeed he had fallen from the skies. Champlain did not disillusion them in regard to his supernal prowess, and he recorded with evident satisfaction the chieftain's belief in 'all that had been told him,' and 'that I accomplished all that I set my mind upon.' So they fed him, gave him tobacco, showed him their fields and gardens, and fitted out two canoes to conduct him on up to the next tribe, who lived on an island in Lake Allumette.

The chieftain of this tribe was no less astounded; he thought he was dreaming when he saw the armed explorer in his village. He, too, banqueted Champlain and took him on a tour of the village, showing him their bark cabins, their cemetery whose shrines struck him with wonder, and their gardens filled with 'squashes, beans, and our peas, which they are beginning to cultivate.' The soil on the island seemed infertile and sandy. Champlain asked why they lived here in this scrubby, desolate spot, and tilled such barren ground, when there was so much fine land to be had elsewhere for the taking. The answer was simple and sad; they had fled here to escape attack from their enemies; better a hard-won little in security than abundance in constant fear of assault and torture.

If the Allumette Indians were amazed to see Champlain, they were positively dumfounded when they learned of his plans to press farther up the river. They assured him that the upper Ottawa was peopled by enemies and sorcerers who could kill with charms and poisons, and that if he went there he would surely die. But Champlain replied that he could be harmed by no witchcraft, and that he was determined to go on to the north sea where lay the English wreck and the eighty scalps which his guide Vignau had seen. That statement threw the Indians into an uproar. They began to hurl invective and abuse on Vignau. They called him a liar and taunted him again and again with deceit. They accused him of plotting Champlain's ruin. If he had ever viewed the north sea, it was while sleeping. In their mounting rage they actually threw themselves upon him 'as if they would eat him up or tear him to pieces.' They demanded that Champlain torture this impostor and put him to death.

All this tumult greatly perturbed Champlain and undermined his waning confidence in Vignau. He went apart to meditate. From his knowledge of the English voyages he believed the report might be true, that the sea could not be more than a hundred leagues away, and that these Indians might not have heard of it. He decided to go on. First he got everything ready for the journey. Then he summoned the impostor. He told him in plainest terms that he was going on up the Ottawa, but if he went further on a fool's errand, he would have Vignau hanged and strangled. Thereupon the liar broke down and confessed. He had fabricated the story out of rumor to get him some honor and place in France, never thinking that anyone would be reckless enough to make the journey that would expose him. Champlain's rage is revealed in the few words of contemptuous dismissal of his wretched liar. 'Overcome with wrath at this, I had him removed, being unable to endure him any longer in my presence . . . I wished to take him to the

Falls to show him to the gentlemen there, to whom he was to bring some salt water.'

Thus ended in treachery and defeat Champlain's first big expedition inland in search of the northwest passage and the Lakes. He had reached the low-lying island now connected by a worn and blackened ferry with the pretty little town of Pembroke on the mainland; a peaceful island with trees and meadows, houses and barns, protected on the south where Champlain landed by a rapids from which, as the natives will still tell you awesomely, no one who has entered has ever emerged alive. Champlain made a cross of white cedar, planted it prominently on the border of the lake 'with the arms of France,' and warned the savages that if they did not preserve the crosses which he had set up, misfortune would overtake them. He promised them to return next year to visit them, fight for them, and to look further into the region. He urged the savages to come to the Falls where he had four vessels of good merchandise to trade with them. Then, honorably escorted in a convoy of forty canoes, he began the return voyage to the St. Lawrence. But the plan that was forming in his head was revealed in one pregnant generality recorded in the journal: 'If I had gone in another direction, according to the report of the savages, I should have made a beginning in a thing which must be postponed to another time.'

Champlain on Huron and Ontario

FOR two long years this 'thing' so near to Champlain's heart had to be postponed while he tarried and awaited the pleasure of others back in France. His impatience at the delay was obviously great. It breaks through the studied restraint of the journal of the voyage and explorations of 1615-16, and even offers a rebuke to his King in the opening paragraph of that vivid record. For fifteen years, he pointed out, he had toiled incessantly to extend his travels over this unknown territory, to cultivate its inhabitants, and to bring them to God under the arms of France. He had a statesman's vision of a vast program for 'a permanent edifice, as well for the glory of God as for the renown of the French.' Yet for all his years of labor he had not been able to advance his designs for exploring the interior of New France. And why? Because His Majesty would not support his efforts with the requisite assistance. Confronted with the royal indifference, he could see no alternative but to abide with such patience as he could command the good pleasure of his king, and in the meantime to use as fully as possible the meagre resources and opportunities that came to hand.

The Prince of Condé finally provided these for the voyage of 1615, and Champlain, already handicapped by the delay, hurried back to the region of the Great Lakes. He sailed from Honfleur on April 24 and arrived off Tadoussac on May 25, 'resolved to go and explore' the Indian country and 'assist them in their wars, in order to oblige them to show me what they had so many times promised to do.'

Champlain met his savages at the Falls. They had complaints to make, and they made them shrewdly. They knew how to use

the wily French for their own purposes. They said they could
hardly be expected to come down to trade with the French when
their enemies the Iroquois 'were always on the road obstructing
their passage.' Champlain had constantly promised them assistance
but he had given little or none. The relation was strained. Champlain's response to this indictment was ready and wholly revealing.
No single passage in the writings of this great explorer throws a
steadier light into the processes of his mind. He concluded, he
wrote, 'that it was very necessary to assist them, not only in order
to put them the more under obligations to love us, but also to
facilitate my undertakings and explorations which, as it seemed,
could only be accomplished by their help, and also as this would
be a preparatory step to their conversion to Christianity.' He then
explained to them his purposes and returned to Quebec to arrange
for an absence of three or four months. He promised to be back
at the Falls in four or five days.

He was gone ten days because of an unexpected delay at Quebec.
When he got back to the Falls, his savages were gone. These
despondent creatures, always expecting the worst, were certain
that he was dead or captured by the Iroquois. They had waited
several days and then broken up the rendezvous in melancholy
surrender, thereby upsetting as usual Champlain's plans for them.
Nonetheless he determined to follow them in his two canoes. He
took with him an interpreter, his man, ten savages, and a heavy
load of food and clothing, and hurried as fast as he could up the
obstructed Ottawa over the same route he had taken in 1613.

Either because he was not guided into hazards by his liar, or
because he now knew his way, Champlain encountered no particular hardship between the Falls and Lake Allumette. He jumped
quickly over these miles in his journal with the brief note that he
had already made 'ample description' of this river. And, indeed,
he had.

Without pause he pressed on up the Ottawa River above the
lake. It was then, as now, a rugged country, thinly populated. The
river winds around the dark foot of the Laurentian Mountains,
plunging over falls and through rapids, and widening into calm

and lovely lakes that reflect the sky. Champlain was not looking
for scenery. What impressed him most was God's goodness in giving for the refreshment of man in 'these forbidding and desert
lands' excellent strawberries and 'a marvellous quantity of blueberries,' which the natives dry for winter 'as we do plums in France
for Lent.' And even to this day the traveler in this region is agree-
ably surprised at the luscious blueberry pie which the most ram-
shackle wayside lunchroom may serve him along this King's Highway.

At the mouth of the Mattawa River Champlain paused. The
Ottawa led to the north around a bend between rock-gray mountains and by a series of portages to Lake St. John and the Saguenay
to Tadoussac—perhaps also to the North Sea. The Mattawa, an
intimate and quiet stream wedged between chains of wooded hills,
came down from the legended lands to the west. Champlain considered the little river and decided to follow it. It is appropriate
that the twin white spires of Saint Anne's should now be the
dominant object in all that lovely valley; that they should look
down upon the confluence of these rivers from the shelf and terrace above them, and lend grace and tranquility of spirit to the
little gateway town of Mattawa, set so daintily among its trees.

The pious explorer would rejoice to see the church presiding
over this historic spot. He would not be so pleased to talk with
the swarthy, sun-scorched fourteen-year-old descendent of his
coureur-de-bois, who leans arrogantly on the guard rail of the
bridge above the reed-grown mouth of the river. He flaunts an
unlighted cigarette in his scarred hands. His growth is stunted;
his black hair, made harsh by sun and weather, is close-cropped;
and his eyes are large and brown. He belongs to the woods, not
to the village.

'Want a light?'

'*Non.* Got plenty.'

He looks at the three crude wooden crosses on the top of the
rugged mountain across the Ottawa, as desolate against the blue
sky as the three crosses with their precious burden at sunset on
Golgotha.

'What are the three crosses up there?' he is asked.

'Boys put 'em up there.'

'What for?'

'Oh, just for hellery.' He smiles, and his teeth are crooked and decayed. He speaks a strange dialect of English and French.

'What are the buildings by the church?'

''Ospitàle. And a school.'

'Do you go there?'

'Non!' he says, contemptuously. 'There's another school over there,' pointing to the village.

'Do you go there?'

'Non!' He spits through his teeth into the Mattawa.

'So you don't go to school?'

'Non! I hunt and trap with my father.'

There is no mistaking the restrained glow of pride in his polyglot voice when he says that. Like his forefathers who were gathered up from the prisons and the streets of Rouen and Honfleur and placed on Champlain's ships, he asks for nothing more. He does not need to explain himself.

The moment of his curiosity is relaxing. He is about to go on across the bridge.

'When did you quit going to school?'

'Never went,' he says, returning to the contemptuous tone and the swaggering manner.

'Why not?'

'Oh,' a shrug of the shoulders, 'I go back in the bush with my father. You learn more tengs.'

So Champlain went up the Mattawa. It did not look like a river that would join the Atlantic by a northwest passage to India and the East. All the explorer found to say about it was: 'We passed several lakes where the savages carry their canoes,' and entered the lake of the Nipissings.' Here he was afloat on one of the most impersonal of the Canadian lakes. It still retains some of its glacial quality, a rather forbidding reminder of the ancient ice age, when it formed a part of the chain of Great Lakes that poured a flood

of melting snow water down the Ottawa Valley to the sea. Its
shoreline is attractive in early morning, and again in late afternoon, at dusk, and by moonlight. Rows of cottages and ugly sign-
boards announcing ale, cigarettes, and tourist cabins disfigure the
shore.

The international publicity turned upon Callander and the little
Dionne girls vulgarized the eastern Nipissing country. Here, in
the region where the Nipissing chief and prominent men courteously banqueted Champlain and took him hunting and fishing,
people from all over the continent came to park in the dust of the
open square, surrounded by souvenir shacks with the most blatant
signs, and to stare at the faded window blinds and the high pal-
ings that shut off the end of the hospital and house from the road,
and at stated intervals to file by and gape at the children.

Champlain was spared all this. Though the lake is too large for
intimacy, and too small and set in too vast a wilderness to have
the color and interest of the Great Lakes, it still has a certain
beauty. Champlain praised especially the north shore, along which
the King's Highway from North Bay to the Sault now runs, calling
it a pleasant land, 'with fine meadows for the grazing of cattle, and
many little streams, discharging into the lake.'

After a two-day rest among the hospitable Nipissings, Champlain
crossed the lake and descended the French River, that drains it
into Georgian Bay. His description of this route which lay north
of the Indian war zone and thus became 'the fur traders' highroad
to the west until the days of steamboat navigation' is still accurate:
'All this region is still more unattractive than the preceding, for I
saw along this river only ten acres of arable land, the rest being
rocky and very hilly.' With that single comment on the French
River, he entered Lake Huron, more accurately Georgian Bay,
called Lake Attigouautan by Champlain.

It was a supreme moment when Champlain with his retinue of
canoes and savages floated for the first time upon the waters of
Huron, the central lake in the Great Lakes chain. It called for
ceremony. Knowing the ritual-loving old explorer, we build up
great expectations of a fitting celebration of this historic discovery.

A lake freighter carrying coal, leaving the Milwaukee docks.

Barges passing Lock 2 at Waterford, N. Y. *Courtesy of Philip Gendreau, N. Y.*

For Champlain had always rejoiced in the chanting of the Mass and in the display in the wilderness of the handsome church ornaments of the Fathers, to the amazement of the natives. He had set up along the Ottawa his crosses of cypress and white cedar emblazoned with the arms of France. For nearly fifteen years he had been anticipating this expedition. Now at last he was looking out upon one of the Great Lakes, the first important white man in history to view its blue-green waters. They spread on and on to the west and northwest as far as the eye could see and then bent over the horizon. It might even be the passage to India. Yet Champlain went into no ecstasies; he recorded no visions of the future; he erected no cross and emblazoned no arms. He only said that the blueberries and strawberries were plentiful, that his savages gathered some squashes, and that they came in handy because these improvident tribesmen, though eating but one meal a day, had as usual gorged all their food and were already facing want in this long journey. It is disappointing. The Royal Geographer, looking for the first time upon one of the mighty lakes of the earth, upon the central waterway of what was to be the richest and busiest region in the world, wrote in his journal that he had found—squashes!

Perhaps that anti-climax prepares us for the events that followed. Champlain paddled close in shore down the island-studded Georgian Bay, which he named Mer Douce, to Matchedash Bay on the extreme south. He visited extensively for more than two weeks among the many Huron villages on the peninsula around Penetanguishene and across to Lake Simcoe. In one of the villages he met brave Father Joseph, whom he had last seen on the St. Lawrence at the outset of his journey. The good Father, who was then preparing to winter among the Hurons, refused to heed Champlain's plea that he remain in Quebec until spring. He had completed his plans, had made the journey into the Huron country, and was already established by the time Champlain arrived. The Father said Mass, they erected a cross outside the village, and enacted a ceremony that impressed Champlain more than his first glimpse of Mer Douce.

Champlain found this region most agreeable, as well he might; for it is now the pleasant center of Ontario, which lies embedded like an arrowhead pointed into the heart of the United States; a region populous and substantial. He praised the corn in the cleared land, but not the bark cabins of the Indians. They were thick with fleas which tormented him so that he could not sleep. He fled outside, only to be followed by 'a girl of little modesty,' as he delicately calls her, 'who came boldly to me and offered to keep me company.' The hardy explorer dutifully records, however, that he sent her away 'with gentle remonstrances, and spent the night with some savages.'

Following his fortnight of visiting among these villages, Champlain met with the Huron warriors near the little village of Hawkestone, on the western shore of Lake Simcoe. They were overjoyed to see him, for they had given him up as lost and had abandoned their projected war for another year. Many of their number had scattered to the villages for the winter. They had to be summoned again, and while they were gathering and their five-hundred promised allies were being notified, Champlain had to dally at a round of banquets and dances tendered him by the natives to express their confidence in the coming victory and their joy in having Champlain suddenly materialize from the grave to help them. They then went northward along Lake Couchiching to await the muster. Champlain records his pleasure in their method of fishing in the narrow strait between the two lakes; they closed off the channel with stakes, and then placed a net at the small opening in the fence to take with ease their winter supply of fish.

Here the war party finally gathered with 'arms, meal, and necessaries.' They decided to wait no longer for the five-hundred promised allies, but to send two canoes with twelve stalwart savages and a French interpreter to give notice to these allies of Champlain's departure for the Iroquois country and to charge them to join his forces at the enemy fort. The procession then set out on its circuitous route to attack the Iroquois stronghold in New York below Lake Oneida. They paddled over Lakes Couchiching and Simcoe, portaged 'about ten leagues by land,' entered Sturgeon

Lake, and, passing five long, impressive falls, reached Lake On-
tario, in terms of present geography, by the Otonabee River, Rice
Lake, Trent River, and the long, beautifully contoured Bay of
Quinte. It was the route of flood-tide glacial waters in ancient
days; of the marauding Iroquois when they harried the land of the
Hurons in the days of Cartier and Champlain.

Somewhere near Amherst Island, where Lake Ontario narrows
around the Thousand Islands to suckle the St. Lawrence, Champlain and his war party paddled out into the second of the Great
Lakes which he was to see on this memorable expedition. Here he
was afloat again in a small light canoe on an open inland sea, gazing at the mouth of the mighty St. Lawrence, upon whose rocky
banks he had planted colonies, and only a couple of hundred miles
from his starting point at the Falls above Montreal. Like the Children of Israel trekking down the grim, scorched route along the
Red Sea, around Mt. Sinai, and through the wilderness of Peran
to reach the Promised Land when they might have crossed quickly
up the coast from Egypt to Joppa, Champlain had made the longest possible detour from Montreal to Kingston to discover Lake
Ontario. Yet this second great moment in the epochal journal
evoked no more enraptured prose from the Royal Geographer
than the first sight of Huron. He remained almost provokingly
cold, matter of fact, and unimpressed. It excited him more to
watch his savages hunt 'stags and other animals' by chasing them
into the water and killing them expertly at leisure with spears.
Of the lake he only said that they traversed it near the entrance
to the River St. Lawrence in sight of 'very large beautiful islands,'
that they proceeded toward the land of the enemy, and hid their
canoes in the woods near the shore. He added on hearsay that the
lake was 'some eighty leagues long and twenty-five wide' (really
quite accurate, for it is 180 miles by 50), and that most of its shores
were peopled by savages. That is all from the Royal Geographer,
on his errand for God and preoccupied with plans for his war on
'our enemies, the Iroquois.'

The plans went awry. The war party arrived before the Iroquois
fort on the tenth of October at three in the afternoon. The Indian

warriors acted like excitable, undisciplined children. They had captured a little party of men, women, and children on a fishing expedition. They then began to work up the martial spirit by hacking off a finger of one of the poor women, an act that revolted Champlain. Then, instead of concealing themselves until the following morning and launching a surprise attack as planned, they rushed hot haste into a skirmish with the enemy. This gave the Iroquois ample warning to barricade themselves in their strong fort and prepare to meet the assault. Champlain castigated his savages 'with rough and angry words' and restored some order among them. He directed them to prepare wooden shields to protect themselves from the arrows and stones shot down upon them by the Iroquois from the gallery of their fort. He ordered them to build a wooden, enclosed platform (a 'cavalier'), which was raised high on a framework and could command the interior of the fort. On top of this he placed arquebusiers who were to rake the galleries with gun fire while the savages, protected by their shields, rushed in to set fire to the ramparts.

It was a good and simple plan, but the Indians could not carry it out. They failed him. They brought up too little wood for the fire. They kindled it on the wrong side, and the wind blew the flames away from the log ramparts, not into them. In their excitement they threw away their shields. They screamed at the enemy and shot arrows promiscuously over the walls of the fort. Champlain shouted orders to set them right, but he records with irony that the only effect was to burst his own head. The confusion was now beyond repair. The Iroquois began to shoot arrows into them and to hurl rocks down upon them from the galleries. They poured water on the fire and easily put it out. The attackers retreated, 'a disorderly rabble.' They had suddenly decided to withdraw and await the 500 allies who had not yet appeared. They were completely out of hand, and all Champlain could do about it was to reflect patiently on the fact that these savages were not warriors, that they would do only what they pleased, and at a whim would break off any plan to form a new one. Champlain himself was sorely wounded with two arrows, one in the leg, one in the knee.

They tarried in the forest, but the allies never came. The battle was lost. In spite of all Champlain's pleas (and he knew how to talk to his savages) they refused to renew the attack. They were determined to give up and go back home. They swaddled their wounded, crowded them 'up in a heap' into a kind of basket, and carried out a skilful retreat, 'the only good point,' reflects Champlain, 'that I have seen in their mode of warfare.' He himself was unable to stand because of the wound in his knee. Suffering more from being bound and pinioned than from the wound itself, he was carried ingloriously from the scene of the battle on the back of one of his savages. 'I lost my patience, and as soon as I could sustain myself, got out of this prison, or rather *gehenna*.'

Champlain's one venture into the region of the Great Lakes had ended in a military defeat. His prestige was so far weakened that he could command no escort back to Quebec, although his savages had promised to conduct him to the settlement after the war. He was unprepared for a winter among the Indians, but, he records, 'not being able to do anything, I was obliged to resign myself in patience.' One puzzles over this entry. Why was he obliged to resign himself? The party had come back to Lake Ontario. The canoes were unmolested where they had been hidden in the thicket. The entrance to the St. Lawrence was in sight. Montreal was but a few days' journey down the same river, as Champlain knew perfectly well. Why did the brave-hearted explorer who knew no fear hesitate to go home that way with or without a guide and an extra canoe? He himself suspected that his savages planned to keep him 'as a security for themselves,' and to counsel with them on the conduct of their future wars.

At any rate, wounded and weary, he went back with them to the grim and drab Huron villages. The journey must have been fully as hard as the one he had just foregone. He struggled along over frozen ponds and lakes and through fallen timber for nineteen days, with a twenty pound load that tired him greatly. Then the ice melted and for four days he toiled through muck and mush that kept him wet to his knees and 'caused us a thousand troubles and embarrassments.' By some miracle he survived all this and spent the winter of 1615-16 observing the life, character, and customs of the Indians. He was treated with great respect and courtesy, and, all in all, it was not a bad winter. He watched them hunt deer, bear, and beaver; he saw them fish; he studied their social organization and methods of government; he observed the ritual of their intimate living; and he wrote shrewdly and vividly of the Indians and their ways in one of the brightest sections of his journal.

Champlain had one disappointment in store for him. When he saw that he must winter among the Indians, he comforted himself with the thought that he could with their help extend his explorations still farther westward. But anger had flamed between the tribes because a chief of the Algonquins had not only failed to torture a prisoner presented to him by the Atignouaatitans, but had actually treated him as a son. Thereupon they sent a man to kill the prisoner; this man was in turn slain in anger by the Algonquins; and civil war was on. It threatened French interests and French security. Instead of going into the west, therefore, Champlain had to use his time and all of his wiles to compose this dangerous feud. 'If ever there was one greatly disheartened it was myself,' he wrote, 'since I had been waiting to see this year what during many preceding ones I had been seeking for with great toil and effort, through so many fatigues and risks of my life. But realizing that I could not help the matter, and that everything depended on the will of God, I comforted myself, resolving to see it in a short time.'

There was no next time. He set down all the things he had learned from the Indians about the peoples to the north and west, about the plains and the buffaloes that were forty days' journey away, and about a great river and a Mer Douce of nearly four hundred leagues' extent. His actual presence in the region would be required to gather exact knowledge, and that would demand assistance and 'men of means, leisure, and energy.' These were to be denied to Champlain; though he labored with indefatigable zeal for New France to the end of his days, he explored no more. With the coming of spring in May, he left the Huron villages and began his long voyage home. His savages conducted him back the way he had come, and after forty days he arrived among the French at the mouth of the Ottawa.

The rest of his life and all that he did is almost irresistibly interesting, but it is not properly a part of the narrative of the Great Lakes. He died in Quebec on Christmas Day 1635. In the park on the escarpment behind the Château Laurier in Ottawa is a splendid statue honoring his memory. The figure of the great explorer is idealized; the pose is cultured and cavalier, the mouth intrepid and firm, the eyes visionary. His back is turned to the Ottawa River, up which he twice toiled; he does not look at the Laurentides to the north or at the white spires of the churches in the valley, immaculate against the dark green forests. He faces the steep gray cliffs softened by trees across the Rideau Canal, upon which are piled the magnificent Gothic spires of the Parliament buildings, transplanted from the Thames, symbol of the capital of this vast Dominion in the Empire of his rivals the British. He seems to contemplate the transformation of his barren wilderness into the lovely city of charm, beauty, and force; he seems to accept with his usual patience and resignation the fate that reduced his beloved homeland to vassalage and elevated his New France into a stalwart center of the British war against the conqueror of his kingdom.

Champlain died unsatisfied. He had lifted the veil from the eastern edge of Lakes Ontario and Huron; he had explored the heart of rich Ontario and pried into northern New York; he had gathered clues and pointed a way for others to follow to the unknown lakes. Perhaps it was enough for one man. La Salle, Marquette, Joliet—the strong men kept coming on. They will carry us into those interesting lands which Champlain saw only in vision from the fragmentary reports of his savages. But before we unfold more of the Great Lakes, we must visit these Indians who held so many keys and barricades to the region; and we must consider the missionaries who went among them for God and opened a way for the empire builders and their wars.

((((VII))))

Indians at the Gateways

BETWEEN the white men and the Great Lakes were the Indians. They were at once the lure and the barrier to the westward movement up the St. Lawrence. Cartier in one century, Champlain in the next had learned through bitter hardship what both meant. Furs brought down the rivers from the interior were the coveted source of wealth for the French merchants. War, with all its barbaric torture and tribal dislocation, always threatened the trade routes and blocked exploration and expansion. So, as we have seen, Cartier braved Indian threats to visit Montreal, and Champlain took the hard detour route around by Lake Nipissing to reach the Huron Villages in western Ontario. The story of the Great Lakes from the first rumors of their existence through the actual sight and survey of them to the final settlement and struggle for possession revolves around the Indians who peopled their shores.

These Indians were an interesting and diversified race of men. Their story already fills libraries and still it is tangled and incomplete. But their part in the tale which we have to tell is fairly clear-cut, and their character as revealed to the successive generations of white explorers and military leaders is not mystifying. Fundamentally they were not very different from their brothers across the sea. Certainly few Europeans of the time (or in our own!) could cast the first stone at these tribesmen.

With the still unexplored chain of Great Lakes and the thousand miles of the St. Lawrence spread out before our mind's eyes over half the continent, we look down upon the tremendous sweep of blue water and green forest to see a few thousand Indians scattered over the region and almost lost in its vastness. With sure instinct, however, they have gathered at strategic points along the lakes and streams that provide for them a pathway through the wilderness. They are grouped in certain large generic families, like the Hurons, Iroquois, and Algonquins; but the ties and the kinship are tenuous at best. The number of separate tribes, each with its own dialect, each with its own modification of Indian customs, and each with difference in tribal character, is enormous. And when we reckon with the Indians' own names for themselves and their neighbors, then with the French names for them, and finally with the English nomenclature and spellings, the result is most confusing. The lay-reader feels that there is no end to the tribes, for just when he thinks he has met them all, a new one appears.

The general pattern of their distribution on the lakes and rivers lying there unrolled before us is reasonably distinct. In the time of our interest, that is, from Cartier on through the crucial years of the seventeenth century, the Iroquois were concentrated and well-placed in the very heart of the region, like Germany in modern Europe. They held the watershed to the south of Lake Ontario and the upper St. Lawrence. They commanded all the southern entrance to this lake and the river from Albany to Buffalo. They held the northern gates to the Hudson, the Delaware, the Susquehanna. They camped on the portages that led from the St. Lawrence to the south—those legendary routes about which Cartier heard from Chief Donnacana. They occupied the region from Lake Champlain to the Genesee River west of the Finger Lakes, that strategic Mohawk Valley of up-state New York that gave them speedy mobility between the seaboard and the Lakes.

It was through this low pass over the mountains, the farms and hunting grounds of the Iroquois, that first the armies and then the pioneers streamed westward. Here the Erie Canal was dug; and now, as one dines leisurely on a New York Central train whirling along the ancient war paths of these fierce tribes, he reads on the wine list: 'Nature Built It. The Indians Used It. New York Central Developed It.' The climate was favorable, the soil was fertile, the hunting and fishing were prolific, and the locale provided a commanding base for military assault against weaker tribes in all directions.

A moment's contemplation of a map will also show how their villages lay on the troubled and contested border between the ambitions of the French and the British. For the French were occupying the St. Lawrence Valley and pushing as rapidly as possible on through the Great Lakes to the Mississippi, to carve for themselves a vast crescent-shaped empire in the very heart of the continent. It encircled the British, who were planting strong and permanent colonies south of the watershed along the Atlantic seaboard. They, too, were slowly expanding westward to the mountains where their interests would clash with the French. Squarely between roamed the Iroquois. They had been alienated from the French by Champlain's attack upon them. But there were shrewd men in the councils of their Long House. They knew how to play off one white tribe against the other. They favored Britain, of course, who, together with the Dutch, supplied them with guns long before the tribes to the west and those allied to the French possessed any. And they used their advantages to the full.

The Iroquois confederation, known to the English as the Five Nations, was a close union of five tribes whose names animate the pages of the history of the Great Lakes. To the east, on the Hudson River and up to Lake Champlain, were the Mohawks. They were aggressive and competent. Legend has it that Hiawatha came to them from the Onondagas with his plan for a league of nations that would bind the tribes into a close offensive and defensive alliance for prevention of the incessant and devastating civil wars. They saw merit in the plan and put it into operation. They were regarded as the Elder Brothers in the confederation that became first the Five Nations, and later, when the Tuscaroras from North Carolina came up and united them, the Six Nations.

Joining the Mohawks on the west were the Oneidas. The beautiful lake around which they gathered their villages still bears their name. Next to them were the Onondagas, the central tribe in the confederacy, also powerful in the councils. Adjoining these keepers of the council fires in the Long House were the Cayugas on the

Finger Lake of that name. And holding the western gate in the Genesee Valley were the Senecas. Closely unified in their league, bold and audacious in planning war, fierce in their striking power, and lightning swift in their movements, this confederacy terrorized the St. Lawrence and the Lake region and raided the tribes allied to the French from Chaleur Bay to the Sault; from the Isle d'Orleans under the nose of the French at Quebec to the Mississippi; from the Ottawa to the Tennessee River; from the hunting grounds of the Montagnais above Tadoussac to the land of the Ojibways on the upper Great Lakes.

Champlain inherited the Iroquois as implacable enemies sight unseen. They were his enemies because the Huron and Algonquin tribes were his friends. These tribes had been driven north of the St. Lawrence and Lake Ontario by the deadly attacks of the Iroquois. They controlled portions of the great waterway and the trade routes to the north and west. At one time they had important towns at Quebec and Montreal. They brought down the furs which the French sailed the ocean to acquire. The French were completely dependent upon them and could maintain their weak settlements in the region only through Huron and Algonquin cooperation. When they pronounced the Iroquois their enemy and asked aid from Champlain, he gave it as a matter of inevitable policy, and we cannot justly blame him for seeing only a little farther than his superiors.

Just when the Hurons, closely related to the Iroquois as they were, incurred the wrath of the Five Nations, and why this sworn war to the death had broken out between them is lost in legend like the origin of feuds among primitive families. Under fierce Iroquois assault the Hurons had made friends with the Algonquin tribes and had withdrawn farther into the wilderness to find safety in distance. They chose the rich region of Ontario between Lake Huron and Lake Simcoe, now as then one of the favored spots in Canada. For a long time it was out of range of the marauding Iroquois. Here in comparative peace for a time they lived in a concentrated area. Like the Iroquois, they built permanent houses grouped in villages—long, crude, communal houses with roofs open to the sky to let out the smoke. In comparison with the Algonquins, they were a settled, agricultural people. They raised corn, squashes, and some vegetables on the good land around Simcoe. They hunted and fished throughout the region with skills and techniques that astonished the white visitors. By Indian standards they lived well. Their frontier towns were fortified after the Iroquois manner with upright logs in double V shape, and a protected gallery on top. They held the northern entrance to the Great Lakes. Through their friendship the French first viewed these waters. The route taken by Champlain, by the Jesuits, and the coureurs-de-bois was protected on the southern flank by their towns. They were the natural field for the Jesuit missionaries when that earnest little band of black-robes went forth to win the savages to the Kingdom of God and the bosom of the church.

Between the stark and lonely trading station of the northeast at Tadoussac on the Saguenay and the western Huron villages around Lake Simcoe wandered the restless Montagnais and Algon-quins. The Algonquins seem once to have been a single family, but at the time when the Great Lakes became interesting to the French they were disorganized, divided into numerous tribes, and scattered about this cold and desolate northern wilderness generally out of reach of the aggressive Iroquois. They must have degen-erated under the combined pressure of their enemy and the in-hospitable northland. Their standard of living was low. Many of the tribes merely roamed from place to place, faring well or ill according to the caprice of nature and the seasons. If the eels ran in abundant schools in the St. Lawrence between September 15 and October 15, they had a food supply. They camped in cabins at Quebec, and lived on eels. Many of them also died on eels, because they cooked them poorly and infected themselves with dysentery. They dried eels and blueberries to tide them over to February while they hunted beaver. But that was precarious, too, because if the water was up and the rivers were out of bank, the hunting was ruined. Then they depended for subsistence upon elk and any other wild beasts they could find and kill, often being reduced to extreme desperation. For they never learned to keep adequate stores; they gorged day and night when the hunting and fishing were good and while the harvest lasted; but when the feast was finished, they starved, for they laid nothing aside.

A group of these improvident pauper Indians were so driven by hunger in the cold February of 1609 that they attempted to cross the St. Lawrence to Quebec through a treacherous, ice-filled channel opened by the wind. The group of Frenchmen huddling through the winter under Cap Diamond watched the emaciated skeletons of men, women, and children embark in canoes, saw the ice floe shatter these canoes to pieces, saw them leap like Eliza to a sheet of floating ice, then to a larger piece which, by some miracle, was driven by the wind to the Quebec shore. They bolted the bread and beans given them by the French without waiting to cook them, they seized and devoured the rotten carcasses of a sow and a dog, which had been thrown out two months earlier to attract black and red foxes and which stank so that the French could not go near them. They even cut down the pole upon which had been placed carrion to attract martens, and they gnawed at the stinking skin and bones.

Occasionally one might come upon a grim little village where a tribe of Algonquins had temporarily settled and built huts. Champlain found a few of these settlements up the Ottawa, on Allumette Island, and around Lake Nipissing where the wretched womenfolk planted maize and garden vegetables in the sandy, burned-over soil. They were always able to give a feast to their great white friend, Champlain, to the despair of his courtesy and the punishment of his body. He was unable to stomach the *tabagie* in his honor on Allumette Island. The guests sprawled unceremoniously on the bare ground in the cabin of the chief, each holding his own bowl and spoon. The chief served them a mess of crushed corn boiled with meat, fish, and other odd gobbets thrown into the common pot without salt. The explorer said, 'as I did not wish any of their chowder, which they prepare in a very dirty manner, I asked them for some fish and meat, that I might prepare it in my own way, which they gave me.' Like the Hurons, the Algonquins welcomed the French to the St. Lawrence and the Great

Lakes because the markets and trading ships were exciting, and because the armed and armored Frenchmen gave them hope of military retaliation against the Iroquois, who had forced them into this cold and barren region.

Cheveux Relevés, known to the English as Ottawas, were among the most picturesque and important of these Algonquin people. They fascinated Champlain when he visited them on the shores of Georgian Bay. They wore ear rings but no breeches. They pierced their ears, polychromed their faces, and pricked their skin into patterns of various shapes. They crowned their muscular and ornamental physiques with long hair anointed with sunflower-seed oil and arranged high on their heads in a coiffure more handsome by far than any fashion the courtiers at His Majesty's palace could achieve with all their 'irons and refinements.' They carried clubs, and were armed with bows and arrows. When Champlain came upon them in that memorable late summer of 1615, they were drying blueberries 'to serve for manna in the winter.' They knew this west country well. Champlain won them immediately to friendship by giving a cheap hatchet to their chief and by exerting that subtle personal spell which the Indians almost uniformly found irresistible. And when he asked about the extent of their country, the chief took a coal in his hand and drew a picture on the bark of a tree.

But the missionaries who came a few years later to live among the Ottawas and try to convert them to the Jesuit God encountered no such friendship. The unfortunate Father René Ménard, who wintered with them on Lake Superior in 1660, found them a set of ruffians beyond all possibility of redemption under the sign of the cross and the solemnity of the Mass. He was deserted and left to die somewhere around Keweenaw Bay. Years later his cassock and breviary were discovered among the Sioux Indians, who worshiped them as sacred relics.

Among the other important tribes between the French and the still unexplored lakes were the Tobacco Nation and the Neutral Nation. The Tobacco Nation took their name impromptu fashion from the fact that they grew a very good tobacco on their lands in rich Ontario, just south of Lake Simcoe and the Huron villages. Like their friendly neighbors, they lived in fairly stable villages scattered over what are now Grey and Dufferin Counties. They were visited by Champlain in the winter of 1615-16. They tried unsuccessfully to avoid the Huron-Iroquois wars.

The Neutral Nation derived their name from their futile foreign policy of seeking security by keeping to themselves and taking no side in the wars. They were a strong and determined tribe, dwelling in villages in what is now the richest and busiest section of Old Ontario. They occupied the neck of land between Lake Erie and Lake Huron. They held the fertile flat strip between the foot of the Niagara escarpment and the Ontario shore from the Niagara River to Hamilton, where Canada's fruit is now grown. Their northern border was the crescent now defined by the teeming port and main factory center of Toronto, the agricultural center of Guelph, the German town of Kitchener that used to be named Berlin, its busy industrial neighbor Waterloo, and the oddly Shakespearian town of Stratford, where the river is called Avon and the houses front on Hamlet, Falstaff, Romeo, and Juliet Streets. But all the hardship of discovery, and all the bitter blood of the wars lie between the smoking huts of the Neutral Nation of 1615 and the peaceful towns of today, engulfed in another war beyond the Lakes, the river, and the sea.

The Neutral Nation bordered the Senecas on the east. And after the Iroquois had destroyed the Hurons and the Tobacco tribes, they turned leisurely to obliterate the Neutral Nation with the ease and the same general technical principles of the Nazi army picking off neutral Holland.

These were the more important tribes between the incoming white men and the region of the Great Lakes. They were encamped at all the watercourses, those highways of the forest in the days when no wheel turned where now the peak of the white man's mercantile civilization is supported on wheels. Waterways, portage paths, and birch-bark canoes were the arduous transportation system into these Indian villages. Over them now came in growing numbers the traders and the missionaries.

Étienne Brûlé: Scout and Bush-Ranger

CHAMPLAIN never again saw the Great Lakes. He wore himself out administering the starved colony at Quebec and in fruitlessly trying to convince his king that a hundred armored soldiers sent over in time could subdue and dominate the Indian menace that flanked the natural approach to the Lakes by way of the St. Lawrence. He never got the soldiers, the Iroquois ravaged the southern route, and the Frenchmen for another generation had to use the rough Ottawa-Mattawa-Nipissing canoe-and-carry detour trail through fifty rock-strewn rapids and across thirty-five portages to reach the Huron villages in western Ontario. But Champlain knew how to train young operatives and send them into regions where he himself could not go. The surprising accuracy of his maps was most certainly due to the generally reliable information brought to him by these rangers. Their bravery and adventure are as significant a part of the story of the Great Lakes as the more formal and spectacular journeys of the great who had style, rank, and language. The name of one has survived, where so many are nameless and forgotten, because he served the purposes and entered the records of Champlain himself. He was Étienne Brûlé.

This unsung wanderer, woodsman, and explorer saw more of the Great Lakes than any man before him—far more than Champlain. If he had had position, or if he had kept a journal like his master or like the Jesuit brethren, he would be a gigantic figure in history with monuments erected to his memory, instead of a shadowy bush-ranger whose story must be pieced together from legend and fragmentary mention by those whose paths he crossed.

Brûlé was one of the most capable of the young men who joined the expedition that planted the settlement at Quebec in the harsh winter of 1608-9. He helped cut down the nut-trees under the rock to clear the spot for Champlain's 'habitation.' He observed the masterly way in which Champlain uncovered the plot hatched against his life by Duval, the locksmith, and the swift reprisal which stuck the rebel's head on the end of a pike and set it up conspicuously on the fort as a grim warning to the disaffected. As the snows accumulated and the winds howled down from the frozen Laurentides, Brûlé often must have looked up at the wizzened head posted as a sign of the violence to be let loose in the New World. He was one of eight survivors of that winter. He helped bury the twenty who putrified with scurvy or died of dysentery.

Any man who could live in reasonable health, as Brûlé did, through two successive winters in that lonely, idle, frozen, pestilence-riddled settlement need fear no evil from the Indian villages. He eagerly volunteered to go up with the Algonquins the following winter, and Champlain made the necessary negotiations with the chieftains, who had come down to trade their furs and do some fighting with the Iroquois. Brûlé was to live as one of them and learn their language. His instructions from his master were to 'ascertain the nature of their country, see the great lake, observe the rivers and tribes there, and also explore the mines and objects of special interests in the localities occupied by those tribes, in order that he might inform us, upon his return, of the facts of the case.' So Brûlé bade goodbye to his countrymen, joined the fleet of canoes on their homeward journey up the Ottawa, and became a forerunner of that strange tribe of Frenchmen for whom the ways of civilization and culture had no gifts to offset the wild freedom of shooting a canoe through a rapids, picking a trail through enemy forests with a scouting party, or taking an Indian woman after a feast and war-dance.

Brûlé got on handsomely with the Indians. He dressed in their clothes, ate their vile mess, and thrived on it. All winter long he sat at their councils, listened to their tales, slept in their vermin-infested cabins and tents. He mastered their language, learned their customs, and grew familiar with the paths through their lands. He became expert in all the ways of the wilderness. He returned as

one of them the following June, in the impressive convoy of two
hundred Indians who paddled their canoes in orderly formation
down the great river to meet Champlain at the rapids at Montreal.
And Brûlé gave him his first accurate information about 'their
rivers, falls, lakes, and lands, as also about the tribes living there,
and what is to be found in the region.' Through Brûlé the Indians
also told of a route to Florida, of a great sea some distance from
their country, and they made charcoal drawings of the places where
they had been.

Brûlé was now fully acclimatized to savage life. When the meeting and the trading were over, he returned to the bush with his new
friends to resume his own informal researches. He may have gone
far enough west at this time to look upon Lake Huron, but the
records are cloudy. He came down again in 1615 to Montreal with
the canoe fleet for the trading, and was at Champlain's side when
he planned the expedition of 1615 which we have already followed.
His presence must have cheered Champlain at that moment when
so many things went wrong with his plans, and Brûlé's knowledge
of the region must have eased somewhat the hardships of that long
journey round by Lake Nipissing and Georgian Bay to the muster
at Lake Simcoe. And it was this expert young woodsman and interpreter who went with the 'twelve of the most stalwart savages'
to mobilize the five-hundred allies and bring them to meet Champlain in the Iroquois country of New York. He was to be gone
three days. He did not see Champlain again for three years.

We have the record of that remarkable expedition into territory
unvisited as yet by white men. It has some importance to our story.

These potential allies were the Andastes, variously known also
as Conestogas and Susquehannocks. They had three villages on
the upper waters of the Susquehanna River, on the other side of
the Iroquois stronghold right in the center of New York. Their
situation was vulnerable. They were separated from their Huron-
Algonquin friends by the most powerful of all Indian tribes, and
they were exposed to attack by the tribes along the Hudson who
had already fallen under the influence of the new Dutch trading
post at Manhattan. Despite their geographical handicap, they held

loyally to their Huron alliance. Brûlé had to pass through this dangerous Iroquois country to reach the Andastes.

The route he chose led him into new discoveries. He might have taken the longer, safer journey through the Neutral territory and across the Niagara River, flanking the Senecas, and so into western New York. But there is no evidence that any of that race of Frenchmen gone native in the bush were ever daunted by danger. He took the more perilous but speedier canoe route by way of the Humber River, reaching Lake Ontario at the site of Toronto. He was dressed like a Huron, he was weatherbeaten by severe Canadian winters, and, seated in a canoe in company with twelve Indians (thus making an ominous party of thirteen), he was hardly distinguishable from the savages. But he was still a white man; and, since he preceded Champlain by a few days, he was the first of his race to stand on the ground now occupied by one of Canada's richest and proudest cities, the first to look upon and to paddle across Lake Ontario. We have no way of knowing how the spectacle impressed him.

The two canoes darted across the upper end of the lake over calm September waters and touched the southern shore a little way east of the mouth of Niagara River. Though Brûlé was within a few miles of the river and Niagara Falls, there is no indication in the records or in the full report he later gave to Champlain that he either knew it or even heard any rumor of their existence.

The rest of that journey takes us beyond the bowl of the Great Lakes, but it throws so much light on the nature of their discovery and on the Indians' habits, and the final result gave such a critical turn to Champlain's career that it deserves just a moment's notice in passing.

Brûlé's party landed safely, hid their canoes in the underbrush, and picked their way around the main traveled trails of the Iroquois, across the southwest corner of the Seneca country in the region of the Finger Lakes. They plunged on foot, as Brûlé told Champlain, 'through thick and impenetrable forests, wood and brush, marsh bogs, frightful and unfrequented places and wastes, all to avoid danger and a meeting with their enemies.' They met only one small group of homeward-bound Senecas. Brûlé's party waylaid them, killed four, and took two captives on to the village of the Andastes.

The eight-hundred Andastes warriors immediately entered upon a frenzied round of feast and dancing to welcome the mission. Nothing Brûlé could do would halt the orgy. After several days of this, they thought it fitting to listen to his message. Then they went into council to consider it. They decided they would send the five hundred warriors to join Champlain. But first, of course, the warriors must be got ready. No warning from Brûlé could hurry them. They could have no notion of their part in Champlain's pincers movement on the Iroquois fort, no understanding of the fact that their few days of dancing were altering the potential course of Great Lakes history and their own destiny.

They arrived several days too late. The Hurons were already defeated, and Champlain was being carried away wounded, agonizing on the back of his stretcher-bearer. The Andastes promptly turned around and went back as quietly as they had come to their fortified village, taking Brûlé with them. They refused him an escort back to Simcoe (there is no mention of what became of his twelve stalwart companions). He was forced to spend the autumn and winter among them while Champlain was wintering among the Hurons and wondering what had become of Brûlé and the allies.

Brûlé was certainly untroubled at the prospect. The climate south of the lake was mild and the country was new. He went exploring while Champlain restlessly composed the civil strife among his Indians. He visited neighboring tribes; he went down the Susquehanna through Pennsylvania, all the way to Chesapeake Bay; and he examined the islands of Maryland. It was a profitable and enjoyable winter.

When spring came, a half-dozen Andastes, who had been thinking about it all winter, decided to escort Brûlé back across the lake to the Huron villages at Simcoe. Somewhere along the forest trail they were set upon by the Senecas, and Brûlé never saw his guides again. He got lost in the woods, nearly starved, and finally, in desperation, walked deliberately into an Iroquois village.

'Do you not belong to that French nation that makes war upon us?' the Iroquois asked.

'No,' Brûlé answered. 'I belong to a better nation that wishes only to be friends with you.'

He made friends with the chief, but the people called him a liar, bound him, trussed him up to a pole, and tortured him. They tore off his finger nails, plucked out his beard hair by hair, and burned holes in him with hot sticks. One of them grabbed at the Lamb of God medal which Brûlé wore round his neck. Brûlé threatened him and his house with death if he touched the sacred Agnus Dei. And just as the Indian grabbed at the medallion, the serene and fair day suddenly turned black, lightning rent open the sky, and deafening and long-continued thunder claps struck the savages dumb with terror. They fled and looked with awe on Brûlé from afar. He was of a better nation than the French. He was a God.

The storm, Brûlé told Champlain, passed as suddenly as it came. He was unbound, feasted, honored, and even escorted by the Iroquois four days on his homeward journey. He parted from them in friendship with a pledge 'to restore them to harmony with the French and their enemies,' and made his way without further mishap back to Huronia.

By this time he was the most traveled and geographically the best informed man in New France. But before he went down to see Champlain he made a ten-day trip up Georgian Bay, paddled across the northern end of Lake Huron, and, according to persistent tradition, actually reached the Sault Ste. Marie, which he called the Sault de Gaston. Then he took the now familiar route down the Mattawa and Ottawa to Three Rivers in 1618, and gave his report to Champlain of all that he had seen and done. Champlain was well content with it, promised him recognition and reward, and sent him back with the Indians to continue his explorations.

The record of his later years are less precise, but they center around the discovery of the Great Lakes. He vanishes and reap-

pears among the Indian villages. He served as traders' agent to
keep the fur fleets coming down to the trading marts. He roamed
over the region south and southwest of Lake Simcoe where Champlain himself did not go on the advice of his Huron friends. He
may have seen Lake Erie. He certainly went west and north, where
Champlain urged him to explore. He passed on beyond the Sault
and looked on Lake Superior from the rocks of the Upper Peninsula
of Michigan, again the first white man to see this lake. Legend also
holds that he went as far west as Duluth-Superior, and on up the
coast to the Royal Island. It is not at all impossible. He was as
restless as he was brave and capable, and he spent twenty years
in the vicinity of the Great Lakes. He even reported accurately
that it was a nine-day journey to the head of Lake Superior, and
he brought back an ingot of copper which he showed to Brother
Sagard.

Brûlé, alas, as we have already regretted, kept no journal and
wrote no book for his king. The details of his amazing exploits in
the west are lost, except as they appear on Champlain's maps.
Other men must go there and report more scientifically before the
region is really known and understood. But Brûlé's legend incited
and directed other men toward the western lakes, and he has a
place of honor in their company. Before we let him go, we must
take a quick glimpse at him in two final, revealing episodes.

One was his betrayal of Champlain, the other was his death. We
know nothing of the motive that led him to go over to the British
in 1629. Perhaps the 'recognition and reward' promised him by
Champlain were never conferred. Perhaps he felt himself defrauded
by the pinching French merchants who profited by his work among
the Indians. For whatever reason, he placed his expert knowledge
of the place and the people at the disposal of Admiral David Kirke
and the British fleet that sailed on Quebec from Tadoussac in late
July of that year. The alarmed and starving Frenchmen on the
ill-fortified rock saw the fleet come round the tree-girt point of
Isle d'Orleans and gave themselves up without battle. Kirke took
the surrender of Champlain and raised the British flag for the first
time over that important rampart.

Brûlé died in the Huron country in a manner befitting his career. Legend had already clung to him and invested his habits of life among the savages with wild tales of licentiousness and the crafty code of the forest. In one of their childish and unpredictable mass moods of hatred and suspicion, Brûlé's Huron friends, among whom he had lived a score of years, murdered him. By a curious coincidence, it was in 1632, the year the English gave Quebec back to the French, the year Paul de Jeune and two other Jesuits came over to convert these same savages. Frenzied by what they had done, the Hurons prepared a feast in their village of Toanche near Penetanguishine. They butchered and boiled the body that was scarred with wounds and torture burns, and made a banquet of Étienne Brûlé. But the God who had saved him from the Iroquois fires had one more miracle to perform. He smote these Hurons with a pestilence and slew half the population with smallpox. The Hurons were thrown into a panic of fear. In penitence, they burned and abandoned the accursed village. A ghostly shape formed above the embers and floated over the Huron country scattering the pestilence before it. Some of their sorcerers said it was Brûlé's sister, others were sure it was his uncle. When the black-robed Father Jean de Brébeuf arrived two years later to establish his mission and further the exploration of the Lakes, the region was stricken and desolate, the village in ashes.

((((IX))))

Brother Sagard: the Gentle Recollect

WE look down again upon the thousands of leagues of the Great Lakes shoreline where the heavy-bodied herons flap their wings low over the waters, where muskellunges break the surface of the lakes, where deer slip delicately out of a birch clump to drink in the evening, their ears erect and alert in motion. We see the Indians loading pelts into frail and precisely balanced canoes, paddling over these waterways to the trading marts at Montreal and Tadoussac, spreading from tribe to tribe the news of the strange white man's lust for furs and his gifts of tools and trinkets. But official knowledge of the Lakes is still limited to the edge of Lake Huron and Lake Ontario.

The news also spreads back to France. It travels from the port cities of Dieppe, St. Malo, Honfleur, to the monasteries as well as to palace and chancellory. Explorers go to map the land and hunt the northwest passage to the East. Traders and wood-rangers go to stimulate the flow of furs to warm and decorate the officers and the courtesans. But the men of God ask nothing more than to live among these poor savages and save their immortal souls. Their faith was unbounded. It had to be, or they could never have endured their tribulations. So good Father Joseph le Caron wrote during the miseries of his winter near Lake Simcoe, 'I must needs tell you what abundant consolation I found under all my troubles; for when one sees so many infidels needing nothing but a drop of water to make them children of God, one feels an inexpressible ardor to labor for their conversion, and sacrifice to it one's repose and life.' Men's inexpressible ardor may be aroused by many motives, and explorer, trader, and missionary sacrificed alike for their own purposes. Yet the three conjoined to open the roads to the Great Lakes.

76

In the annals of that epic the chapter written by the Recollect and Jesuit missionaries is the most ennobling. They followed close behind Brûlé and that growing company of reckless, often debauched, wood-rangers which numbered nearly a thousand at the end of this seventeenth century. The huge wooden crosses which these godly brothers planted throughout the region were foretokens of the myriad now lifted like white symbols on the towering church spires through the length and breadth of the land they tried to save. They bear silent testimony to the selflessness and the martyrdom of these men.

We find it difficult to recapture the temper of that age when well-placed men chose savage poverty to civilized ease, and renounced the world to embrace a barbaric existence in the Canadian wilds to try to annex a few uncomprehending savages to the kingdom of heaven. Yet they did just that, and their name is legion. Their journals and reports fill a whole library. The yearly Jesuit *Relations* alone cover the crowded pages of seventy volumes. They tell of discoveries in the Great Lakes region; they recount miracles and victories over evil; they record torture, defeat, martyrdom, and death. We single out the story of one humble lay brother whose experience typifies the modest but glowing heroism of the men of God in this epic of discovery.

He is the Recollect missionary and linguist, F. Gabriel Sagard, styled Theodat (God-given), author of the *Long Journey to the Huron Country* and maker of the *Dictionary of the Huron Language*.

In mid-March 1623, this gentle and observing follower of St. Francis journeyed along the road from Paris to Dieppe to join the mission to convert the savage people of New France. In apostolic manner he traveled on foot and begged his bread. There was no careful advance preparation; no well-planned luggage train for a winter in the Canadian wilderness. He had no baggage except the few portable necessities of 'the poor Recollect Fathers Minor of our glorious Father St. Francis,' and a childlike faith in God. Thus equipped, he suddenly appears out of an obscure background on the road to Dieppe, and stands full-sized before us like Elijah the Tishbite ready for his mission.

Sagard boarded ship immediately at Dieppe and sailed at midnight. He was not a good sailor. Like his companions he had to 'pay tribute to the sea.' 'I had never imagined sea-sickness to be so troublesome and disagreeable as I experienced it,' he wrote, 'for it seemed to me that I had never had such bodily suffering in my whole life as during the voyage of three months and six days, which it took us, because of contrary winds, to cross that great and terrible ocean and reach Quebec, the residence of our Fathers.' At the end of one furious storm that hammered the ship for eight interminable days and nights, Sagard was still serene among the sick and battered sailors and passengers. One of them was bitter against him.

'You and your annoying pose of calmness!' he lashed out in anger. 'You are no Christian, or you would stand in fear before God at a time like this!'

'We are all in the hands of God,' the unruffled friar answered. 'Nothing will happen to us except by His holy will. I am on my way to the country of the savages to win souls for our Lord. I may endure martyrdom there if such be His sacred pleasure. If His divine mercy decrees that I should die on the way, I ought no less to be content. It is a bad sign to be in such great terror as you are.' And as the small ship continued to toss recklessly about, he added, 'Everyone should first try to put his soul right with God; then he should do everything possible to escape from danger and shipwreck, and leave the rest to Him.'

God and the captain brought the little ship through storms and calms and all the hazards of a voyage in the north Atlantic in the seventeenth century. Sagard amused himself by watching great whales spouting and little whales at play. 'I saw an immense number of them, particularly at Gaspé where they disturbed our rest by their blowing and the chasing hither and thither of the gibars and whales.' Though he was sometimes ill, he preferred to suffer rather than consult with the ship's surgeon, because he was a

Huguenot, with 'little liking for monks' and 'scant courtesy for anybody.'

They sailed at last up the Gulf of St. Lawrence and anchored a few days in the roadstead at Gaspé. Sagard climbed the mountain above the harbor to get a view of the mouth of the great river. There with the magnificent midsummer prospect spread out beneath him, and the unknown interior waiting before him, he took out his knife and scratched crosses and the name of Jesus on the largest trees, 'to signify to Satan and his imps that we were taking possession of that land for the Kingdom of Jesus Christ and that henceforth he should have no more power and that the only true God should be known and worshipped.' This he did because, he said, he always wished to be occupied with some little act of piety, and because it renewed his earnestness of purpose.

Sagard had need of both. Hardships of unimagined nature, bitter tests of his piety and his purpose to the limit of human endurance and beyond awaited him and his brothers up that broad river whose union with the ocean he had climbed the hill to view. But that was in the undisclosed future. He still had before him the pleasant delights of the voyage up to Quebec. He noted the snows still lingering on the Laurentians, he observed the little gardens of sorrel and other small herbs cultivated by the French sailors, the pretty meadows along the river's edge where the French settlers gathered up hay for the cattle at Quebec just as they do to this day. Filled with his pleasure in these pastoral glimpses, he rounded the Isle d'Orleans and surrendered as all have surrendered through the centuries to the stab of awe before the rock and rim of Quebec bursting full upon him. But as he neared the harbor he noted first the wooden fort up on the escarpment where the Château and the Terrace stand, also Herbert's house, farm, and cattle near by; and then, to his enchantment, a young apple tree brought over from Normandy and now laden with apples in the warm June sun. It was a happy entrance into New France with these little familiar tokens of civilization to link him to the homeland.

He went on up the St. Charles River to the Recollect convent, from which he could see the sweep of the valley and the full majesty of the terraced rock. He rested there in the orchard and the garden, and walked in the bordering meadow among the scarlet lobelia, the eight-foot-tall tiger lilies, and the raspberry bushes where the turtledoves played in large flocks. And while he refreshed himself among his brothers, he heard the now familiar plaint against the merchants who had done nothing to improve Quebec. 'If they will do nothing more than in the past Antarctic France will always be a name of fancy, and ourselves an imaginary possession in others' hands.'

Three days he rested in the little convent of the Recollect Brothers in the St. Charles meadows in that summer of 1623, before setting out for the Huron country. The Recollects had been in Canada for eight years. Eager and energetic though they were, they had made slight progress in their mission. The odds were overwhelmingly against them: they were four lone brothers among all the savages, merchants, and the Canadian wilderness, all hostile to the purposes of the gray-robed fathers. These first four had come to Canada with Champlain in the memorable year 1615. They and Champlain were the only ones who were happy over the expedition. Devout Champlain had always placed first, or at least a close second, his responsibility for bringing the Indian tribes, 'living without religion like brute beasts,' into a proper 'knowledge of God.' Winning a single soul for the Kingdom of Heaven was of more value to him than claiming the whole tribe for an empire. He had committed his company to contractual obligations to carry over and support six missionaries to serve the Frenchmen and convert the natives. It was easier to article it in the license than to put it into effective practice. The merchants were not keen on making Christians of their savages. The missionaries wanted the Indians to live in or near the settlements where they could have both 'the teaching and example of good monks.' The merchants wanted them back in the bush, hunting furs. Their own *coureurs-de-bois*, who had learned the language of the natives, were rude to missionaries and even refused to aid them in any way to overcome the barriers of speech and customs.

Seven long years had gone by since the colony was planted under

the rock of Quebec and still there were no priests. The Huguenots
considered this no hardship. But Champlain persevered. When he
went back to France in 1613 for the long stay that lasted through
1614 and into the spring of 1615, he took specific measures to secure priests for his mission. He found them among the Recollects,
a noble and pious order with a convent in his own native Brouage.
He approached the King's secretary, who controlled the important
salt works there, and this pious official, and friend of the friars,
recommended the Recollects as the most likely order to undertake
the grievous mission. The Recollects were willing, but they were
a beggarly order, without accumulated wealth, dependent upon
alms. In fact they were a new and stricter reform branch of the
order of St. Francis. They were pledged to a return to the strict
code of the gentle saint himself, from which the now popular and
well-placed order had somewhat relaxed. In contrast to the retire-
ment and plenty of the monks, they accepted anew the indigence
of friars, to walk among men in the streets and marketplaces, to
minister to the sick, the poor, and the outcast, to eat the dry crust
of God's bread given them at doorways, and to nourish their souls
with meditation, or, as the name of their order suggests, by recol-
lection. The movement had begun in Spain a century earlier, but
had only reached France about the time Champlain was embarking
on his voyage to the Spanish West Indies and Mexico. The Recollects in France, therefore, were only about twenty years old in 1615
when, with the sanction of the Pope, Fathers Joseph Le Caron,
Denis Jamet, Jean d'Olbeau, and Lay Brother Pacificus Du Plessis
came to Quebec with Champlain, arriving at the end of May after
a reasonably fast voyage.

They built at once a small house in the lower town near the
present wharfs, where the boats rise and fall in their slips with
the tides, and erected the first chapel in Canada, where they said
Mass for the first time in June 1615. Then, eager to win souls to
God, they divided labors and separated for the uncharted wilderness. Father Joseph Le Caron hurried on to the Huron villages
where, as we have seen, Champlain found him later in that same
season. Father d'Olbeau undertook the equally harrowing mission

to the wandering and shabby Montagnais. Father Jamet and
Brother Du Plessis nourished the station at Quebec. The stupendous
task of making Christians of Canadian savages and keeping the
French settlers in the faith was begun. The first results were meager,
however, and the effort in the wilderness languished for seven
years while new recruits were gathered. Fragments of news about
the savage peoples and their need of Christian light circulated in
France. Curiosity to explore the mysteries of this new world was
in the very air of the times. The church was eager to spread the
good news. And thus it came about that in 1623 another little band
of Recollects, including Gabriel Sagard, were again in canoes on
the broad St. Lawrence bound west on the 'Long Journey to the
Country of the Hurons,' as Sagard entitled his travel journal.

That journal, which we are now following, glows with a naïve
realism, and throbs with life as Sagard tells in detail just what it
was like to travel with and live among the native peoples of the
Great Lakes. For Sagard was alert, his restless eye missed nothing,
and his vivid pen preserved what he saw. In company with the
veteran Father Joseph Le Caron and Father Nicholas Viel (who
was tossed into the rapids of the Rivière des Prairie by the Hurons
and drowned at Sault-au-Recollect in June 1625) Sagard sailed up
the St. Lawrence from Quebec in a pinnace. He was exuberant
over the charm of the countryside along the banks of the river,
where the tree-shaded villages now flourish and the long meadows
stretch in narrow ribbons back toward the hills. He joined the
Indians at their camp a few miles below Lachine Rapids at Montreal. They were feasting on a bear which they had driven into the
river and killed with arrows and clubs. They hugged the stewing
kettle of flesh and sang a song that amazed Sagard and carried him
away with its sweetness. But he went without supper because he
could not swallow their mess, and because the improvident savages
had eaten his bag of sea-biscuits. He had brought along enough
of them, he thought, to last him to the Huron country; but the
Indians liked their taste and, having no notion of rationing, devoured them all at a single meal. He lay hungry, cold, and hard

on the ground under two sloping pieces of birch bark with a stone
for his pillow.

That first wretched night was only a mild portent of what was
to come. 'In order to practise patience in good earnest,' the gentle
Sagard wrote, 'and to endure hardships beyond the limit of human
strength it is only necessary to make journeys with the savages,
and long ones especially.' He was wedged in a small canoe with
five savages. They were not clean-limbed nobles of the forest; they
were 'dirty disagreeable fellows,' and the fastidious Frenchman
confesses that he was almost overcome by the stench which they
emitted 'almost constantly.' When they were 'under the necessity
of making water in their canoe,' they used a birch-bark bowl which
each man carried for himself. In the evening when they pitched
camp and boiled a kettle of sagamité, always mixed with 'dirt and
refuse,' they fed from these same bowls, unwashed, and the unpleasant smell took away Sagard's appetite. He marveled at the
skill with which the savages located their caches of grain which
they had buried in little bags of birch bark along the route, and
at their endurance between feedings; for they ate only twice a day,
smoking often in the meantime to deaden their hunger. Sometimes,
if they were in a hurry to set out, they would omit the morning
sagamité. Sagard almost perished from lack of food. But after he
had reached the Huron country and could boil a pot in his own
style, the savages refused to eat his sagamité because it 'smelt bad.'
Instead of seasoning his corn stew with rotten fish, carrion, dog,
or any handy gobbet of flesh, Sagard had spoiled it for them with
pot herbs like wild marjoram, purslane, balsam, and small onions.

If sitting in a crowded canoe, trying to keep out of the way
and be as little troublesome as possible, was hard, the long portages
were worse for Sagard. He wore the robe of the Franciscans, a long,
undyed wool habit with a pointed hood whose natural sheep color
gave them the name of Greyfriars. On his feet were sandals with
wooden soles. In this costume, so becoming to friars in the open
lanes of Provence, so grotesquely unsuited to the Canadian wilderness, Sagard toiled westward. He waded through marshes; he
climbed over sharp stones; he pushed through dense woods, part-

ing the limbs with his head and hands, and crawling over fallen and matted trees and rotten logs; and all the way he fought off clouds of vicious mosquitoes that poisoned his face, hands, and legs with their stinging and biting. 'If it had not been for my care in protecting my eyes by means of a piece of thin stuff which I had covering my face, these fierce creatures would have blinded me many times.' He walked so slowly because of his costume and his weakness that the Indians always put him in the lead at a portage to prevent him from getting lost.

But in this band was one remarkable Indian, humane and thoughtful. He took pity on the kindly, weakening friar. He relieved Sagard from rowing or paddling; he carried Sagard's bundles in addition to his own heavy load of goods over 'the vexatious and powerful trails'; he shared his own bearskin covering with Sagard when it rained; and at night he made him a bed of cedar branches and spread for the dependent friar his own little reed mat which he carried for his own use on long journeys. In this manner Sagard after many days finally reached the Freshwater Sea, which he hastened over in his narrative, like Champlain, with the observation that they 'passed from island to island, and landed in the country so greatly longed for on Sunday, the festival of St. Bernard, about midday, with the sun beating down perpendicularly upon us.'

Friar Gabriel Sagard Theodat makes an incongruous picture as he enters Huronia on his mission. Clothed in his sheep-gray robes and wooden-soled sandals, now torn and muddy, he staggered along under his load of clothes and bundles which now he had to carry for himself. For the journey was nearly over, the canoe was hidden away in the woods, and the Indians were on the long, overland trail to their villages. Sagard bent under his load, the sweat dripping from his nose, fighting mosquitoes, and almost fainting from hunger and exhaustion. The savages as usual placed him at the head of the file because he could not keep up with their pace. He was too worn out to notice his route. He took the wrong track and got lost. We see him stand dully at a crossing of trails not knowing which one to take. Two Huron women came by, stopped and stared at this strange creature.

The Ford Motor Company's River Rouge Plant, at Detroit. *Courtesy of Philip Gendreau, N. Y.*

The Hill Annex Iron Mine, Calumet, Michigan. *Photograph by Erling Larsen. Courtesy of Frederic Lewis.*

'Which road do I take?' Sagard asked in his halting Algonquin.
'How do I get to the town?'

The women tried to understand but could not.

'But I do not even know the name of the village,' he said and
gave up. Again God looked after him and guided him. He chose
a path, followed it, and after a while he came upon his savages.
They had sat down to wait for him 'in the shade under a tree in a
fine large meadow . . . much troubled as to what had become of
me. They made me sit down beside them and gave me stalks of
Indian corn to suck which they had gathered in the field near by.'

Revived and restored, he entered the village in triumph. The
three-hundred households emptied themselves out of the thirty or
forty lodges into the street in an uproar of enthusiasm. They thought
him a great chief and war leader. He was borne down the street
to the lodge of the parents of his savage. They received him 'with
extraordinary caresses,' and made him welcome as though he were
their own child. The excited savages crowded so thickly into the
lodge on this hot day, emitting such rancid odors, that poor Sagard
was forced to climb up on top of the platform to escape their pressure and keep from fainting. The hospitable Hurons turned one
small household out of the communal dwelling and gave all their
space to their guest.

Sagard was now at the end of his 'long journey,' settled among
his savages on the east coast of Lake Huron, ready to attempt his
mission. He felt desolate and his loneliness was almost more than
his faith or his Christian zeal could bear. He had no idea what had
become of his two brothers, for he had not seen or heard of them
since they were separated at Montreal. He worked out a routine
for himself to keep up his spirits. In the morning he would escape
from the Hurons, take his sundial with him, and go apart to pray
and recite his office in peace. At mid-day he returned to the lodge
and fed on cooked pumpkin. In the afternoon, he records, 'I used
to read some in a little book I had brought, or else write.' In the
evening he sang hymns to improve his morale while the always
curious Indians gathered close around him to watch and listen.
At night his sleep was broken by the screaming and the weeping

of the mother of his savage, who was troubled with nightmares. He would lie awake thinking about these poor creatures who were so 'simple and ignorant' that they asked the Frenchman 'to go and kill the thunder, which they supposed to be a bird, asking us if the French used it for food, and if it had much fat, and why it made such a noise.' And he would try to find a way of explaining these things and the religion of Jesus to these savage children.

In this manner Brother Sagard passed his homesick days and nights. Then one day Father Nicholas, in robe and sandals, came walking into the village. Sagard was overcome with joy to see his brother. He determined at once to go back with the Father to his village and to find Father Joseph. He made the most delicate diplomatic preparations and excuses to his hosts to avoid offending them, and took his leave. They found Father Joseph in a neighboring village. 'I cannot express to you the joy and satisfaction we felt at seeing ourselves all three together again, nor did we omit to give thanks to God.'

Sagard took strength from companionship with the Brothers and began in earnest his year's work. Together they built a bark hut of their own to live in. Sagard was happy to find among the Hurons the pioneering custom of house-raising; when a man had no lodge, these good savages with one accord all lent a hand and did not leave him until it was done. They were equally courteous to the Recollects. They built a hut twenty feet long and ten feet wide. They roofed it with bark, leaving a vent Indian-fashion to carry out the smoke. They partitioned off one end for a chapel, with an altar and safe storage place for their vestments and small articles which the Indians liked to finger and carry away. The only trouble with their dwelling was that the bark was unseasoned, and it split, buckled, and cracked open. Rain poured in, and, when winter came, the cold wind lashed them and snow piled up in their living room. Sagard says that they would huddle together in a corner in the cold and watch the rain put out their fire. Sometimes they spent whole nights without sleep in this miserable posture. Their only light was from candles made of 'little twists of birch-bark which did not last long.'

But in true French fashion they had immediately fenced in a garden and planted peas and herbs, which 'did quite well.' They made sacramental wine from the wild grapes. They drank beech-tree sap as a tonic. And they survived. They patiently welcomed and entertained the constant flow of savages who crowded into their cabin. From them they learned of the Lake Huron region and of the peoples who lived farther west among the Great Lakes, though the lakes were the ocean in the minds of the listening Fathers. They hoped to visit these people, who, they thought, 'might be some civilized race and nation living in the direction of the China Sea, which bounds this country on the west.'

With his two Brothers for companions, and their cabin as a refuge, Sagard put in a busy and fruitful year. He visited the Hurons in their lodges, and they liked him because he was never arrogant and scornful like the traders, but always kind, affable, and friendly. He was fascinated by the ceremonies they performed when they fished, by their marriage ritual and their burials, and he noted down a hundred odd things that relieved the tedium of his days and nights. He discovered that they took sweat baths in season exactly as the Finns do to this day. Some of their habits were almost more than he could stomach. He disliked having to smoke a pipe with a stem fresh and wet from the mouth of a stinking tribesman. He was nauseated at the sight of 'the women savages eating the lice from their own bodies and from those of their children,' as if they were 'something very good and tasty.' He was outraged by the ceremonial of mass fornication around a sick woman's couch while at each end of the house the chiefs sang and rattled tortoise shells all night long. He called upon God to end 'such damnable and wicked' ceremonies, and threatened the Frenchmen 'who foster them by their evil example.'

Except for their occasional excesses, Sagard found the people around Lake Huron an industrious and kindly tribe, in some respects even better than the French back home. For these savages gave hospitality to the needy, and they could not understand why there were so many indigent beggars in Sagard's country. They thought 'that this was for lack of charity in us, and blamed us for it severely.' In truth, Sagard observed, 'if they were Christians these would be families among whom God would take pleasure to dwell.'

Sagard could never find how to make Christians of them. Fine linguist that he was, he was saddened to discover that they had no words for his holy religion. He could not explain to them the Pater Noster. He could not put into their language the meaning of Sanctification, or the most Holy Sacrament, or even the Kingdom of Heaven. When one of the chiefs begged Sagard for his cross and rosary, he called them 'Jesus—the very name they give to the sun.' And the Christian phrase, 'Leading into temptation,' simply could not be translated into their vocabulary. They could understand the fact of a miracle, but not the God of Sagard who performed it. In April and May the rains were so heavy that their corn was rotting and they feared starvation. Their own sorcerers could not stop it. They turned to Sagard.

'Call upon your god. You tell us he is good and all-powerful. Ask him to stop the rain or we shall face famine.'

'Give up your superstitions, vices, and bad habits,' Sagard said, 'and He will treat you like His own children.'

'Oh, my nephew,' the chieftain cried, 'I want to be a child of God like you!'

Sagard and his Brothers took some corn into their hut and prayed. Then they walked in solemn procession around their dwelling, 're-citing the litany and other prayers and devotions.' And while they marched, the rain stopped, and not another drop fell for three weeks. But the Indians did not become children of God like their gray-robed spiritual Fathers. They looked upon them as magicians who could make God do what they asked. And in later years, some of the priests who followed Sagard met death because the Indians believed they had asked for the disasters of war, disease, and famine that befell their villages.

If Sagard failed to make of them a dwelling place for God, or to visit the nations on the China Sea, he could prepare a dictionary of the Huron language to help others to carry on both missions and communicate more freely. We have a graphic picture of gentle scholarly Sagard at work on his lexicon. He would seat himself in a smoky, fetid lodge in a snow-bound village off the east coast of Huron, fingering his beads and talking to his Indian friends. They would pack themselves close around him, gaping and chattering.

'Aviel,' they would say, for they could not pronounce 'Gabriel.' 'Aviel, take your pen and write.'

Then Sagard would take his pen and paper from his gray robe and add new items to his dictionary. No lexicographer ever had more willing or interested informers. They would make dramatic and ingenious signs, gestures, and noises to explain the meaning of their words, and their names for objects. The nouns were easy, but their idea words were hard to understand. They would draw pictures on the ground with a stick, or act out the meaning with their bodies; and, Sagard says, 'they were not ashamed to make very unseemly movements' to instruct him.

Sagard's dictionary and his journal were the most tangible results of his labors. He had lived on the western limits of discovery, and he probably knew as much as any living man about the people and the hardships still to be faced before the district could be uncovered and the Indians made into New Frenchmen and Christians. In the summer of 1624, he started the long journey back to France with his reports. He met up with the ubiquitous Brûlé, who feasted him and a select group of savages on boiled dog and led the flotilla of canoes across Lake Nipissing and down the Ottawa to the St. Lawrence. And we can understand the regretful conclusion with which Sagard summed up his researches in Huronia: 'To make a beginning there is no necessity for very learned men, but there is indeed for persons who fear God and are patient and full of love; and it is in this that one must chiefly excel in order to convert this poor people and draw them out of their sinfulness and blindness.'

((((X))))

Nicollet's Dash to the Sea

WE have lingered over Sagard's mission at Lake Huron because it is typical of what all these men, the nameless and the great, priests and laymen, endured to open up the Great Lakes for American ships and farms and cities. A mere list of their names and a terse summary of their accomplishments would fill a volume. But when Father Brébeuf and Father Lalemant, Fathers Raymbault and Jogues go on among the Lakes, when Father Allouez and Father Marquette make their perilous way to the south Superior shore to live among the nations there and explore the watershed and the Indian paths, we shall remember Gabriel Sagard's journal and let it fill in the details of their solitary hours.

So we hasten on to the era of rapid discovery and the men who used Sagard's Huron villages as a base of operations. And we meet first the notable figure of Jean Nicollet, going about among these villages and preparing his epic-making expedition beyond the Huron sea.

Again we cast our eyes over the vast sweep of the Great Lakes, and then remind ourselves that the St. Lawrence between Montreal and the Thousand Islands is unexplored, and Niagara and Lake Erie are unknown because the Iroquois have closed them tight to their French and Huron enemies. And all that lies west of Georgian Bay and the Sault is still unknown except for the sketches on Champlain's map of 1632, based upon Indian signs and Brûlé tentative reports. Only the familiar portage route up the Ottawa, round by Lake Nipissing and down the Georgian Bay, and a part of Lake Ontario are mapped and certain. Jean Nicollet now goes into the unknown west.

He was another of those gifted young men who entered Champlain's service. He was born in Normandy. He came across to Quebec in 1618, still in his 'teens. He went up with the Algonquin canoe fleet and lived native among the Indians on Allumette Island, to learn their language and the technique of managing them. He became expert in both. Then he went on to dwell in the same manner with the Nipissings, and was among them for almost a decade. When the British gave Canada back to the French, Champlain, now nearing the end of his frustrated career, sent Nicollet to find out officially the truth about this great sea to the west about which he had heard for more than a quarter of a century. The year was 1634.

The experienced Nicollet made careful preparations. He packed a wardrobe suitable for calling upon the Emperor of Cathay. He revisited his friends along the Ottawa and at Lake Nipissing. Then he went on down into the Huron country. There he engaged an escort of seven picked Huron warriors and navigators and set forth in canoes. He sent advance emissaries to announce his coming and assemble the tribes to receive him. He first paddled up to look at the Sault, already described by Brûlé and named Sault de Gaston on the map. He did not go on to Lake Superior, but explored the channels among the mass of green islands between the St. Mary's River and Lake Huron. Then he crossed Potaganissing Bay at Drummond Island and steered through the Detour channel into the Straits of Michilimackinac. Nicollet was not a journalist. We can only speculate about what went on in his mind when he first saw that important waterway opening up new reaches to the West. Did he see it at dawn when the Straits lie dark and brooding between the low shores of the two jutting peninsulas? Did he come upon it at mid-day with the sun falling sharp on the tree-girt islands and glistening on the water? Or was it late afternoon, with the sun making a path of gold to suggest the future channel for ships laden with wealth that would sail from lake to lake? Of one thing we can be certain: he thought that just beyond this narrow and picturesque Straits lay the China Sea, and he would be the first to enter it from the Northwest. For he had packed away in the cramped space of his bark canoe impressive damask robes decorated with Chinese birds and colored flowers for his ceremonial greeting to the people beyond the sea.

Nicollet paddled on west through the Straits and entered the new sea. Like the one he had just left, however, it was without salt. As the shorelines of Lake Michigan spread out to the west on his right hand and to the south on his left, with St. Ignace Point dominating the connecting band of water behind him, he must also have noted the future strategic importance of the strait through which he and his Huron savages had paddled. The trade which he hoped to send from the west—to him the golden East—would flow through this waterway. But first, of course, he must find the people of the East, the mysterious men-of-the-sea—Winnebagoes they were called—and make peace with them. He searched for them across the northern end of Lake Michigan. He swung down around Point Detour, passed through the curtain of islands, and entered Green Bay. He saw the Menominee River falling over the escarpment bowl of rock into the bay, and met some Menominee Indians there. Then he continued southward in the narrowing cul-de-sac of the bay that ends at the mouth of Fox River. And there he found the Winnebagoes.

They were not Chinese, and there was still no salt water from the eastern seas. But his emissaries had told them that the white god was approaching, and several thousand tribesmen were gathered at the head of the bay to receive him. Nicollet, with a Frenchman's proper attention to ceremony in the wilderness, unfolded his damask robes which he had so carefully guarded, arrayed himself splendidly, seized a pistol in each hand, and progressed toward them, firing into the air as he advanced. As soon as the poor Indians recovered from their panic and when the feasts were finished, Nicollet made peace with them. Then he reconnoitered in the Winnebago country. He paddled the length of Lake Winnebago and entered the upper reaches of the Fox River. He paused only when he had stood on the narrow portage strip of land on the low watershed between the Fox and the Wisconsin Rivers—the mile-wide dividing point between the Mississippi Valley and the Great Lakes-St. Lawrence basin.

There Nicollet gave up and turned back in spite of Indian reports of the 'great water' to the west. It is surprising. He confidently declared that another three days of traveling would have brought him to the Eastern Sea. Then why not make the insignificant journey, we ask? What are three days more in the life and explorations of Jean Nicollet? He did not go on. He folded his damask robes and turned east, back to the Huron country, back over Lake Michigan and through the Straits, back down the Ottawa to the French settlements with his news.

Men of God and Martyrdoms

THE Jesuits went along with Nicollet as far as the Huron country, and then followed his trail to fill in and extend discovery
from the reference line which he had drawn. Their story is as
important to the uncovering of the Great Lakes as it is astounding
in its disinterested valor and fortitude. A portion of it belongs here.

On the little sailing boat that bore Brother Sagard back to
France in 1624 was another Recollect, Friar Irenaeus Piet. He was
on a private mission to the Jesuits to ask their aid in making Christians of the natives around the Great Lakes. The Jesuits had wealth
and prestige, the Recollects had neither. They were also resourceful, tireless, and experienced in extending the Kingdom to the
danger zones in the uttermost parts of the earth. The gentle Recollects had seen enough of New France to realize that their strength
alone was not enough to plant the faith among its vast wilderness
of savages. They invited the Jesuits to come over and help them,
and the Jesuits came.

Three Fathers of that order, Charles Lalemant, Ennemond
Masse, and the incomparable Jean de Brébeuf, sailed for Quebec
in 1625. Their reception was a portent of the trials and final
disasters that were to reward their sacrifices. They were not welcome at Quebec. They were not even allowed to get off the ship
when it anchored upon the rock. The company's officials refused
to take them into the fort. The company resented the article in
their charter which compelled them to support six missionaries,
and they attempted to evade their contract. They did not want
the priests to spoil their fur-bearing savages. Moreover, the Frenchmen in Quebec were dominantly Huguenot; if they must have
priests among them, they said, let them at least not be Jesuits.

The three Fathers were quarantined on their ship and threatened with deportation.

The generous Recollects finally rescued them and set apart half of their own small convent for the Jesuits' use. They left the ship and took shelter there for two years until they could erect a house of their own. The Jesuits, therefore, had made little progress with their mission when Kirke sailed in with his English fleet in 1629 and took Quebec from the French. Because of their hatred for the order, the British wrecked the Jesuit convent and carried the priests, who had been called in from their posts, as prisoners across the Atlantic to England. This left the missions untended; they fell into ruins and discovery languished. But the British, in sportsman-like manner, handed Canada back to the French because the attack had been made after an armistice had been signed between England and France. The Frenchmen returned in 1632; with them came the Jesuits, but no Recollects. The Jesuits began systematically to re-establish their work and prepare for the spiritual conquest of the country.

And so it came about that when Nicollet started west in 1634, Father Jean de Brébeuf, with two companions, was in his party, returning to the Huron villages. His experience was almost a duplicate of Sagard's. His companions got lost from him along the Ottawa. At the foot of Georgian Bay, Brébeuf's savages dumped him and his baggage on the desolate shore of Thunder Bay, and hurried off, leaving the tired priest unattended, far from any village. The undaunted Brébeuf knelt and thanked God for His mercy. Then he concealed his precious churchly equipment in the bush, and followed a path through the woods in search of a settlement. It soon proved to be familiar ground. He came upon the ashes of the chapel where he had said Mass years before in the village of Toanche. The town also had been burned. He traveled on. At dusk he emerged into the clearing where a new village had been built. The astonished Indians rushed out to meet him, welcoming with shouting and with joy their long-lost man of God. They went with him back to Thunder Bay that same evening to get his baggage, and at one o'clock in the morning, Brébeuf with his friends and his goods re-entered the village and began the new phase of the Jesuit mission to the Hurons.

Here Brébeuf's two lost companions finally joined him. They were exhausted, toilworn, and famished, for they had been ill-used and then deserted by their guides. All together again, they settled in this friendly village, where the natives helped them build a house. It had the usual three compartments: the main hall, the kitchen-dining room, and the chapel. It was a place of endless entertainment to the childish natives, for it was full of marvels. It had wooden doors that separated the rooms. Inside was a hand mill, which they loved to grind. There was a magnet that made steel jump and stick fast; a prism that shattered light into rainbow colors; a glass that made a flea look like a giant mosquito; a lens that transformed a single spider into a colony of eleven; and, wonder of wonders, a clock that struck the hours. When it spoke, the savages were completely mystified. The solemn Jesuits were not above hoaxing their guests harmlessly with this marvel and using it in self-protection. The Hurons called it 'the captain of the day.' They would sit by the hour to hear it speak. 'What does it eat?' they asked. When it spoke, they eyed the black-robes to make sure they were not manipulating it. 'What does it say when it talks?' they wanted to know. The wise Jesuits answered, 'When he strikes twelve times, he says, "Hang on the kettle"; and when he strikes four times, he says, "Get up, and go home."'

So at twelve they boiled the pot of sagamité, and at four they left the Fathers in peace to meditate and do their work. These trinkets, like the candles, the images, and the service for the Mass itself, made a profound impression on the Indians. They came from miles around to gape at them. 'All this seems to gain their affection,' Brébeuf wrote, 'and make them more docile in respect to the admirable and incomprehensible mysteries of our Faith; for the opinion they have of our genius and capacity makes them believe whatever we tell them.'

If the priests received homage for good, they had also to take blame for evil, and evils were plentiful among the Hurons. When a drought threatened to destroy the crops in that sandy soil, or when plague ravaged the villages, the fault was the Jesuits'. The squaws kept them out of their lodges, and some of the braves threatened to kill them. Brébeuf himself wrote what he thought would be his farewell letter in October 1637. 'We are perhaps on the point of shedding our blood and sacrificing our lives in the service of our Lord and Saviour, Jesus Christ . . . If you should hear that God has crowned our labours, or rather our desires, with martyrdom, return thanks to Him, for it is for Him we wish to live and die.'

But it was His wish that they should not yet die. Brébeuf was an evangelist who loved to baptize new souls, but Lalemant, his immediate superior, was a practical functioner. As the Iroquois war clouds began to gather over Lake Ontario, and the hostility and suspicion of the languid, diseased, and unprepared Hurons continued and increased, he saw the approaching danger to these scattered missions. He determined to centralize them in one stronghold where they could have some measure of safety. From it the Fathers could go out two by two into the field; to it they could foregather in time of peril or for refreshing their spirits when their hearts were heavy.

The spot chosen by the Fathers for their outpost fortress of God in 1648 was on the Wye River, about three miles east of the present town of Midland, which spreads along the Gloucester bight of Matchedash Bay at the south end of Georgian Bay. They deliberately selected a site up in the more isolated and protected wilderness far from the center of Indian life or Iroquois invasion. They built a fort of stone to surround and protect their living quarters, which had a hospital, a chapel, and accommodations for sixty men. They named it Ste. Marie, and its isolation and its strength gave new prestige to the Jesuits. Soon there were eighteen priests here, together with four lay brothers, and from forty to fifty French engagés. Indians in great numbers came to the mission, usually to be fed, because the French planted gardens and had quantities of grain; and the Jesuits went out from it to preach and baptize and explore.

This Jesuit center is now an object of pilgrimage. A modern

stone church with square towers broods comfortably there on the
gentle slope above the east bank of the Wye, between Mud Lake
and the Bay. Near by is a cabin enclosed in a stockade, and a
rude pile of stones topped by a statue of a Jesuit missionary. It is
called the Martyrs' Shrine. It pays tribute to the unfaltering
bravery of Father Brébeuf and his fellow martyrs, who astonished
their murderers even more in their death than in their life. The
Iroquois war parties moved northward across the St. Lawrence,
and on into Ontario. They practically cut off communications between Montreal and Lake Huron. At their leisure they crushed
and scattered the Neutral and Tobacco Nations. They swooped
into Huron territory, laid waste the villages, pillaged and burned
them, slew, scalped and tortured their victims. The Jesuits could
not rouse the Hurons to their danger, or shake them from the
paralysis of fear. In these frightful ravages the Jesuits also perished. Fathers Jogues and Lalande had both been tortured, and
then murdered with a hatchet as they bent their heads to enter
an Iroquois tent on a mission of peace.

When in 1649 the Iroquois assaulted the mission village of
St. Louis a few miles east of Ste. Marie, they captured Brébeuf
and Lalemant. The two Jesuits had refused to flee. They were
tortured and taunted. Brébeuf was bound fast. To silence his
words of encouragement to the other captives, the crazed warriors singed his body, cut away his lower lip, and shoved a red-hot
iron into his throat. They poured boiling water over him, shouting,
'We baptize you that you may be happy in Heaven; for nobody
can be saved without a good baptism.' They cut out pieces of his
flesh and ate them, jeering, 'You told us that the more one suffers
on earth the happier he is in Heaven. We wish to make you
happy.' The brave man never once flinched or weakened. Finally
they scalped him, drank his blood to get some of his courage, and
a chief seized and ate his heart. Lalemant was wrapped in bark
strips coated with tar and burned.

The Brothers from Ste. Marie found the relics and remains of
the two martyrs and bore them back to the fortress and buried
them. Then they loaded their grain, vestments, and belongings

on a raft and joined the sorrowful band of Huron survivors and refugees who sought safety on the Isle St. Joseph or Christian Island in Georgian Bay. They burned their chapel and fort at Ste. Marie, and closed in apparent failure their mission to the Hurons. It is, indeed, the Martyrs' Shrine.

((((XII))))

Stations in the West

NEITHER martyrdoms nor the Iroquois could stop the now rapidly moving advance of white men into the Great Lakes. While Ste. Marie was flourishing the Fathers had traveled widely and gathered reports about the West. Fathers Raymbault and Jogues went on a seventeen-day journey from the fort to the Sault to meet a concourse of two thousand Indians of Algonquin kinship—the Sauteurs and the Ojibways. The Ojibways of the Sault told them in turn of still more tribes another eighteen-day journey across Lake Superior—a nation known as the Nadouisseux, or Sioux, as we know them. They also told of a big river cutting through the forests of their hunting lands.

Those who went south to the Neutral Nation brought back reports of exciting interest about the region in the Iroquois war zone. Their accuracy is striking. Father Vimont's Relation of 1641 mentioned the 'famous river of the Neutral Nation' as the outlet for 'our great Lake of the Hurons.' He recorded that 'it flows first into Lake Erie, or the Lake of the Cat nation, and at that point it enters the territory of the Neutral Nation and takes the name of Onguiaaha up to where it is discharged into Ontario, or the Lake of St. Louis, from whence rises the St. Lawrence River, which flows past Quebec.' As for the rumored eastern sea that Nicollet thought he had almost reached, Vimont recorded the still prevalent conviction that it was part of the sea 'on the north of New Mexico and by it a passage to Japan and China.' This conviction would soon be put to final test, at least in its relation to the Great Lakes, by the few Jesuits and laymen explorers whom we have yet to mention.

The Iroquois had murdered the priests and annihilated the

100

Huron missions between Lake Ontario and Georgian Bay. But they had not destroyed the faith or the zeal of the Jesuits. Ste. Marie was burned and abandoned, but the mission moved on west over Nicollet's route and beyond. Four more outposts at strategic points were founded by the intrepid Fathers: one at the Sault Ste. Marie; one honoring St. Esprit at La Pointe on Chequamegon Bay, three hundred miles west of the Sault on the lonely south shore of Lake Superior near Ashland, Wisconsin; one on the point at St. Ignace on the Straits of Mackinac; and one named for St. Francis Xavier at the mouth of the Fox River at the head of Green Bay, where Nicollet had donned his robes and fired his pistols. The paths and waterways linking these posts formed the first network of western inter-lake communications. Around these settlements gathered Indians and traders. To them came the commercial explorers and unlicensed wood-rangers. They were the immediate forerunners of La Salle's epic-making voyage of the *Griffon*.

From the day Brûlé first saw the St. Mary's River tumbling over the Sault, there was never any doubt about the importance of that picturesque spot as the gateway and crossroads of the upper lakes. Father Dablon, Superior of the western missions, after he had made a tour of the region chose it for his headquarters. The civil authorities were equally impressed. They took formal possession of it with their usual spectacular pageantry. Duamont de St. Lusson went out as the representative of France. On a morning in mid-June 1671 he dressed himself in his most splendid uniform and stood before his troops drawn up on the bank of the graceful river near the falls, with the cascade of the waters sounding in their ears. Around him in full regalia were the chieftains of fourteen tribes summoned by St. Lusson from far and wide. Representatives of the church in their robes, vestments, and black habits were there, with crosses and prayer-books. They lifted a huge cross and set it up as the symbol of God's rule. They sang, 'The Royal Banners forward go, The Cross shines forth with mystic glow.' Then they placed beside it a cedar post emblazoned with the arms of 'the Most High, Most Mighty, and Most Redoubted Monarch,

Louis, Fourteenth of that name, most Christian King of France
and of Navarre.'

St. Lusson lifted his sword with his right hand, held it above a
lump of the earth clutched in his left, and declared that the Sault
and Lakes Huron and Superior now belonged to his monarch. And
while he was thus laying claim to the Great Lakes, he also acquired, with the ease of shouting a few liturgical phrases at the
Indians who did not understand his French, 'all countries, rivers,
lakes, and streams contiguous and adjacent thereunto; both those
which have been discovered and those which may be discovered
hereafter, in all their length and breadth, bounded on the one
side by the seas of the North and of the West, and on the other
by the South Sea.'

Just how much territory the Most Christian King back in comfortable France had thus acquired neither he nor St. Lusson had
the faintest idea. The chant of the *Te Deum,* the volley from the
soldiers' guns and the cry *Vive le Roi* died away, the sound of
the falls of St. Mary's was heard again, and the explorers went
on with their super-human labors of mapping Louis's new boundaries.

The saintly Father Allouez founded the mission far to the west
on Lake Superior at La Pointe on Chequamegon Bay in 1669. It
was an endurance rather than an exploration. For this region had
already been seen, lived in, and wandered over a decade earlier
by those remarkable brothers-in-law, Pierre Esprit Radisson and
Médard Chouart, Sieur des Grosseilliers (the English merely called
it Gooseberry). There is a poetic ring in the syllables of their
names appropriate to discoverers of so beautiful a land. They slip
off the tongue like the paddles of a seven-man canoe dipping and
rising at sunset in the waters of Green Bay. This Radisson had
survived the wildest adventures since he arrived in Canada in
1651. He had no finger nails; they were pulled off by the Mohawk
Indians when they captured him and bound him to a stake for
slow killing. Chouart (des Grosseilliers) had gained his experience as an *engagé* of the Jesuits among the Huron missions. He
knew the country and the waterways to the west. He became a

fur trader in his own right a few years before the Radisson family arrived at Three Rivers. He married one of the Radisson girls, and formed the partnership with Pierre Esprit. They wanted to see the tribes of the far west; perhaps they might glimpse the China Sea; certainly they would find new sources of fur.

Their caravan set forth in mid-June 1658. Above Montreal some of the canoes were ambushed by the Iroquois. The more experienced leaders escaped and took the old route up the Ottawa, across by Nipissing, and down into Georgian Bay. They followed the shoreline around Lake Huron; they camped for a time on the Manitoulin Islands; they made friends with some Pottawatomies who were visiting the Ottawas near the Straits. There they joined with the returning Pottawatomies, crossed Lake Michigan, and went up Green Bay, over the route followed by Nicollet. Here they spent the winter and spring of 1658-9. They wandered about Wisconsin, up the Fox River and over the watershed at Portage. They proved that Nicollet's extra three days would have brought him out upon the Mississippi River instead of the China Sea. Just fifteen years before the memorable journey of Marquette and Joliet, Radisson and Chouart dipped paddles in that great river of the West.

Then they roamed about over Lake Michigan. Radisson, who had a flair for phrases as well as for hardships, called it 'the delightfullest lake of the world,' and, like other far-seeing explorers, lamented that the suffering serfs of his native country could not be transplanted to this good land. They went back through the Straits of Mackinac and up to the Sault. Then, still urged on by lust for the unknown, they paddled on up the St. Mary's River into Lake Superior itself. Here they turned westward again, the first known white men to traverse this first of the Great Lakes. They followed that storied shoreline past the Pictured Rocks, round Keweenaw, and into Chequamegon Bay. They spent the winter of 1659-60 there among the diverse nations who had formed colonies in this fine hunting ground and fishing bank, far from the depredations of the Iroquois. They found in the colony refugees from the Tobacco Nation and the tribes around the Sault. Radisson during the winter crossed the corner of Wisconsin over the narrow watershed between Lake Superior and the Gulf, and came again upon the Mississippi River. When the brothers-in-law got back to Montreal in August 1660 they had almost completed the uncovering of the lake region.

Father Allouez was, therefore, going over a route already mapped when, though deserted by his Indian guides, he pressed bravely on, reached the Sault, and made his desolate way to La Pointe to erect his chapel and bring his God to the peaceful tribes near the end of Lake Superior. Then he went on down to Green Bay and founded the mission of St. François Xavier at the mouth of the Fox.

These three mission posts were fairly well established when Marquette, among the most famed of the Jesuits, came into the western lakes. From his peaceful home at Laon, that city in the fertile fields of northern France on the invasion road to Paris, where the cathedral with its legendary oxen on the hill dreams over the slain on the battlefields below and summons the pious peasants to prayer, Father Marquette came to Canada, passed on through the Sault and carried on Father Allouez's work on the shores of Lake Superior. From La Pointe he went to St. Ignace on the Straits, in the summer of 1671, to instruct in the ways of God the 'untutored minds' of the Ottawas and the Hurons, 'who know only the devil' and, as the good Father regretfully stated, 'often relapse into the sins in which they were nurtured.' He had been two years on the Lakes when Louis Joliet came to St. Ignace.

Joliet was sent expressly to settle the question of the Mississippi River and the eastern sea. Father Marquette joined him. They laid careful plans and prepared supplies. Then they departed in birch bark canoes over Nicollet's route to the Fox River. They crossed the watershed, as Radisson had done before them. Then they went down the big river as far as the mouth of the Arkansas. Historic though the voyage was, it added nothing to the known geography of the Great Lakes except greater certainty that they lay in their own immense bowl and were entirely separate from the legendary sea and river of the West.

Only one other major journey yet remained to be taken before the complete contour of the Lakes was made distinct. For Lake Erie still lies there under the cloud of threat thrown up by the flanking Iroquois, and Niagara still roars, rumored but unseen, between Lake Erie and Lake Ontario. La Salle and his aides, Tonty of 'the silver hand,' and Father Hennepin, were to brave these perils and open the southern waterway.

((((XIII))))

La Salle and the *Griffon*

LACHINE is by now a place name to stir memories. It suggests the master passion of a generation of explorers who kept pressing on into the mystery that shrouded the Great Lakes. It links our minds to those of the men of three centuries ago who could see the alluring wealth of China at the end of a few days of sailing west-north-west over the wilderness sea. It records the derision on the tongues of lackeys when the robes and spices of the Orient dreamed of by their masters faded into mere buffalo hides and wild onions on the endless earth that locked in the freshwater seas. It is a sprawling monument to the greatness and the misfortunes of La Salle.

From the stillness of the top of Mount Royal jutting up high and solitary out of the busy heart of Montreal you may see the village lying low and indistinct in the thin haze that always hangs over the suburbs of the Montreal island. The tram line runs through acres of colorless town and through open fields to the village, where the Ottawa's yellowish waters make a band beside the blue of the St. Lawrence in Lake St. Louis. Busses travel the highway along the river and down by the Lachine Rapids. The river breaks at the bridge and ripples, swirls and foams down over the rocks. A skilled captain can take a boat over them, but when the water is low, he runs a risk and may ruin the record of a lifetime, as one captain did in 1941, by wrecking a fine boat on the shoals. (Joliet was wrecked here, and lost his notes on the trip with Marquette.) The Rapids gleam white and silvery in the sun. Fishermen stand in the shallow waters casting lines, much as they did in La Salle's day. The Lachine canal is a narrow passageway for commerce around the falls. Boats, piled high with wood and lumber, work up the Lachine canal and ease their way through

106

the skimpy stone locks. There is only a hand's breadth to spare on each side. The stones show the marks of frequent scratchings. The highway bridge is open a long time as the boat, hauled along by its thick rope cables, inches through the locks. Traffic collects in long lines on both sides of the canal. Armed soldiers stand guard. The boat eases out into the free water above the falls, the bridge goes down, the cars, trucks, and buses go on their way—it is the spectacle of life in Lachine.

The ghost of La Salle hovers over the region where the remnant of his house may still be seen, for this was once his seigneury. It was given him in 1667 by the Seminary of St. Sulpice when this favored son of France and the Seminary arrived in Canada at the age of twenty-three. The land was thick with forest, and there was no road but an Indian trail along the interrupted highway of the river. He cleared a space for his house, and induced a few settlers into his holdings; but his eye and his heart were on the waterway from Lake St. Louis to the west and the tales the Senecas told of that land and the rivers that crossed it in the long winter evenings around La Salle's fire in 1668-9. For the Huron wars were over and a troubled peace with the Iroquois made the upper St. Lawrence and the lower Great Lakes for the first time reasonably safe for travel. He determined to see the region, to explore it, and to conquer it for trade and empire. The rest of his life was spent in tracking down that dream. It became an epochal adventure in the story of the Great Lakes.

Like Champlain before him, La Salle had to use up more time and energy in breaking through the petty court jealousies and the unimaginative restrictions of the bureaucrats and politicians in France than in launching his broad enterprizes in the Great Lakes wilderness. He had to go back and forth across the Atlantic time after time and cool his heels in Paris anterooms while fussy men who had scarcely set foot outside the capital considered the advisability of his bold plans for expanding the Empire and enlarging trade. He toiled ten long years to get the rights and the financial backing he needed to build a ship to sail the Lakes. And when at last he got the authority, he had to drag after him a heavy load of obstructions and debt.

In 1674 he was granted the Seigneury at Fort Frontenac at the foot of Lake Ontario. He paid dearly for it. He agreed to improve and complete the strategic fort in stone and to maintain at his own expense a garrison equal to the one at Montreal. He also undertook to form a colony under protection of the fort, to maintain a church, and to support at least one Recollect friar. He did not get all these things done, but the obligations indicate how La Salle became more and more involved in a net of mortgages that finally strangled him. It wasn't easy, however, to defeat such a man. He moved on from Lachine to Lake Ontario, and with Fort Frontenac as a new western base, planned his venture.

The fruit of another visit to France in 1677 was a charter from Colbert that authorized La Salle to go into the Far West with full authority to arrest unlicensed traders (there were many of them), to set up trading posts, to treat with the Indians, and, most importantly, to build boats and navigate the Great Lakes and the Mississippi River. Equally important, as events turned out, was the discovery of one of the few capable men who also remained faithful to him. This was an Italian refugee who called himself Henri de Tonty, after the French style. His father, Lorenzo Tonti, was a political exile from Naples and a notable insurance man in France. Henri was at loose ends, in the service of the Prince de Conté, when La Salle was lining up patrons. Tonty was recommended by the Prince as aide to La Salle. He had acquired important military training in the provincial wars. One of his hands was lost in a battle in Sicily. The steel claw which he wore in its place gave him unexpected prestige among the Great Lakes Indians. His prowess in bashing in skulls or knocking out the teeth of disobedient or disorderly men, and the dispatch with which he could rip open a fish or hook a ship's timber, inspired their awe. They called him the 'silver hand.' This unusual man bore the heavy brunt of La Salle's enterprise and of the formidable side-excursions in the bitter winters during which they formed, and fell into disaster. La Salle also added to his staff La Motte, and the Franciscan friar, Louis Hennepin, who left a racy account of many of its episodes.

So after a decade of preliminary scouting and planning and pleading. La Salle with his three aides now hurried forward with his labors. He engaged a retinue of skilled shipwrights, carpenters, blacksmiths, and helpers. He assembled materials and supplies; saws, adzes, iron, hammers, anvils, cauldrons, ropes, sails, guns, a commissary, and an altar and a cross. He sent these over Lake Ontario in one of the three small ten-ton ships which he operated on this lake. La Motte and Father Hennepin were in charge. It was a cold and blustery week in mid-November 1678. The little craft hugged the north shoreline; it was temporarily frozen in near Toronto, but it was cut free, and it passed on round to the mouth of the Niagara River, which it reached on December 6th. There Hennepin found a small Seneca fishing encampment. The Indians were as impressed with the sailing vessel as with the *Te Deum* the grateful Father sang when his boat nosed into the protected river. Then Hennepin went up the river through the narrowing gorge as far as the canoes could go. He climbed up the steep escarpment and walked through the forest to the Falls. He was the first European to see and describe it.

In this modern age of water power and honeymooning at Niagara, when the Falls are listed among the natural wonders of the world, it seems strange that no white man had seen or reported the stupendous phenomenon before La Salle's advance party went there on their way to build the ship. The formidable Iroquois, apparently, had scared everybody away. Champlain had heard vaguely of Niagara. He got the idea that it was a rapids, somewhat higher and more dangerous than those at Lachine. He marked it on his map of 1632 from hearsay. He never saw the Falls. Even the ubiquitous Brûlé, who wandered widely in the region, made no mention of Niagara. Father Galinée on a mission to the west in 1669 passed through the vicinity, but was more interested in arriving speedily at an Iroquois village farther on than in taking time to view this reported wonder. So he too passed it by. Nor did that hardy and experienced explorer, Louis

Joliet, go over to look at it. He was quite near it, too, for he had come down the short route through 'détroit' (the first white man to paddle through that river) and had crossed Lake Erie as far as Grand River. But there he detoured north through Ontario to avoid the Iroquois and passed Niagara by.

So it was left for Father Hennepin at the late date of 1678 to look first upon this spectacle. It was a tremendous sight, roaring and foaming in the cold December solitude. Hennepin drew a detailed picture of the gorge. He can be forgiven for estimating its height at 500 feet, and even for raising that figure another hundred feet when he wrote of the Falls fourteen years later in retrospect. Uninstructed summer visitors make equally false estimates.

In the light of the known rapidity of change in the contour of Niagara (it has been retreating on the average five feet each year), it is interesting to study Hennepin's sketch of the Falls as he saw it almost three centuries ago. Both the drawing and the verbal description are reasonably accurate except for the height of the cataract itself. Table Rock, now lying among the debris at the foot of the canyon, was still holding on in Hennepin's day. Horseshoe Falls was more extended then, and there was another trickling cataract just west of it. He climbed down this west side and felt the icy spray in his face. The east side was too precipitous to be scaled. He peered under the American Falls just as visitors still do. And he estimated, probably again with inaccurate eye, that four carriages could pass abreast between the sheet of water and the wall of rock.

The Falls was impressive, but gazing at God's natural wonders saved no souls and built no sailing ships to step up shipments of fur. Hennepin looked and wondered and sketched, and then went on with La Motte to select a site above the barrier for a shipyard. They found it at Cayuga creek. Here on the east side of the river —the spot is now appropriately named La Salle—they built a shipyard in the edge of the forest and set up wigwam living quarters and a workshop. Hennepin's sketch of the colony shows a forge under an open shed—a roof supported by eight posts, a huge three-

legged cauldron, and men working on the deck railings of the ship.
The Seneca Indians looked on with apprehension while the ship
took form. As its naked ribs rose from the keel and rounded out
to look something like a Dutch galliot, a massive giant many times
larger than the biggest Indian canoe, they grew more hostile. They
cut off the supply of corn, threatened the ship, and tried to intimi-
date the men. They did not need empire minds to see what loads
of fur this monster could carry, or sense its formidable power
afloat under full sail, with cannon bristling from its portholes, and
La Salle shouting orders from the quarter-deck. For it was 60
feet long, of from 45 to 60 tons (Hennepin), mounting five cannon,
roomy enough below for the builders and crew to sleep in ham-
mocks, and moored by an anchor that required four men 'well
stimulated with brandy' to carry it around the Falls. In spite of all
obstacles it was finally rigged and afloat, the first commercial vessel above Niagara, ready for its momentous maiden voyage westward over little-known Lake Erie.

It was christened the *Griffon* with the customary pomp that
relieved the savage tedium of the wilderness. The blessing of God
was pronounced over her bow, the men sang the *Te Deum,* they
fired a salute from her guns, the Indians watched with awe from
the shore, and then got drunk on French brandy while the ship's
timbers swelled in the water. She was then towed up to Lake
Erie. Her two great square sails were spread, the *fleur de lys*
flapped in the fresh breeze, her prow, ornamented with the ar-
morial griffin of Frontenac's house, was pointed toward the west,
and on the morning of August 7, 1679, she set sail. It was a proud
moment for La Salle. We can see him standing on the quarter-
deck, above the carved spread eagle that looked over the rudder
and the wake, shouting commands to the crew of thirty-two. His
bold and courtly manner is becoming to him in this setting, now
that the intimate tree-lined shore of Lake Erie begins to move,
and he feels the live ship under his legs and hears at last after
more than a decade of effort the thrust of the wind in his own
sails. A glance at his surviving portrait, the sharp eyes deep set,
the long, straight, high-bridged nose, the firm mouth and arrogant

thread of mustache, suggests what vast plans and ambitions must have been taking new form and conviction in his busy brain as the *Griffon*, bearing trinkets for barter, sailed on up Lake Erie. He may not have anticipated disaster during those three days of almost perfect sailing as the *Griffon* crossed the route now plowed daily by hundreds of long lake freighters carrying iron and coal, wheat and machinery, between busy ports. But La Salle was too much a man of the world versed in the quick alteration of fortune, and had seen too much of the treacherous life in both Old and New France to be unprepared for sudden reversals.

Some premonition must have disturbed La Salle soon after the *Griffon* had closed behind her the smooth expanse of Lake Erie and nosed northward into the *détroit*, the narrow strait now called the Detroit River. It was a day of sun-lit August calm. From the railing on the new quarter-deck La Salle looked down upon that scene of never-ending delight. Where now one sees the impressive spread of the booming automobile city, its skyscrapers and its massive smokestacks gleaming in the sun by day and lighted up like ghostly altars by night, La Salle in 1679 surveyed flat grass lands, and virgin timber with purple grapes hanging from wild vines on their limbs. Bears and nervous-eyed deer lifted startled heads to look at the strange winged boat on these lonely waters. Flocks of wild turkeys ran away into the brush and tall grass, and the swans swam and flew off as the great bird sailed toward them.

Marveling at the beauty of 'this fertile and pleasant strait,' La Salle took the *Griffon* into the wide bulge in the river. It was Ste. Claire's day, the 12th of August, and he named the lake in honor of the blessed abbess of Assisi. The shallow swamp bottom is now dredged deep into channels to float the giant freighters. They ease along at reduced speed in order not to churn up the mud. La Salle's men felt their way through by taking frequent soundings from the *Griffon's* railings. They came out safely into the St. Clair River. It is narrow. Its shores are now lined with houses, its waters alive with small craft of every description. The big lake boats seem to fill up all the space and glide right up against the cottage yards. The ships' captains and the mates wave to their families and friends and call to them through megaphones as they go by. The sonorous whistles of the passing ships speak to each other day and night. But in that August of 1679, the *Griffon* was the only ship afloat on these western rivers and seas. When a head wind rose, La Salle's men walked on the shore and pulled the boat slowly against wind and current and brought her out into Lake Huron above the rush of the water under the present bridge at Sarnia.

Then the lake storm struck, one of those sudden squalls now so familiar to all Great Lakes sailors. It blew with quick fury out of the northwest, it swept down over the point at Alpena, and lashed the waters off Saginaw Bay. It caught the *Griffon* head on and tossed her around like the osier-wattled raft of Ulysses. The master and the crew exhausted their seamanship and were still helpless before the wind and leaping waves. With the touching inconsistency of that age, they turned to God and His saints and prayed. They shouted promises into the wind. They offered to make St. Anthony of Padua the patron saint of this first voyage on the Lakes and to build him a chapel if he would still the waves and save them from death in shipwreck. The incompetent, complaining saltwater pilot Lucas, angry and disgruntled, preferred to curse La Salle for the humiliating death that was now come upon him not in the wine-dark sea but in 'a dirty lake' in a lost wilderness. The curses or the prayers, perhaps the solicitude of the saint, or the waywardness of the winds, possibly all combined, who knows (for these wary adventurers besought all likely aid in moments of danger), cut off the gale and smoothed out Lake Huron. La Salle and his men got off their knees and the shaken *Griffon* sailed calmly on up the serene lake into the Strait of Mackinac. No chapel was built to St. Anthony of Padua.

The *Griffon* put into the sheltered bay before St. Ignace. A few astonished and disquieted French traders, and a swarm of incredulous Hurons and Ottawas gathered on the beach. They watched in amazement as the ship furled her sails and dropped anchor. They saw La Salle, arrayed in his ceremonial cloak, all scarlet and gold lace, climb down the ladder from the 'floating fort' and row ashore. His rich robe shone splendidly among the half-naked Indians and the drab wilderness garb of the traders. La Salle greeted them with his usual imperious dignity, and then went past the row of crude huts huddled near the shore to the little chapel of St. Ignace to celebrate Mass. The chapel of rough logs and bark had been built only eight years before, when Jacques Marquette founded the village by establishing a mission here on this strategic site. Under the floor where La Salle knelt lay the bones of the good Father. They had been found just two years ago on the desolate eastern shore of Lake Michigan by a band of friendly Indians, who had cleaned them after their custom, carried them back to the mission, and planted them in a coffin of birch bark in the consecrated spot. Perhaps La Salle's mind wandered during his devotions to thoughts of this remarkable priest who had given up his life to explore these waterways and to beseech God to touch the hearts of these savages with His grace 'while we stammer in their ears.' He could not have been unmindful of the fact that the same fate might be awaiting him beyond the strait through which he now proposed to sail on westward.

La Salle talked with these suspicious traders—about his commission, about his King's policies, about the fur trade. Among them he found four of his own men, four of the fifteen he had sent out last year to trade for him and prepare his way. They had, as usual, betrayed him. He arrested them on the spot. No doubt he examined the store of furs collected at the trading post, lifting the pelts of mink, muskrat, and beaver, smelling them and feeling their texture with his fingers. Doubtless also during the week he spent at St. Ignace he formed in his mind the scheme to send the *Griffon* back to the marts laden with such furs. Then he weighed anchor and departed through the wide Straits, where now in the late afternoon the steady procession of ships to and from Lake Michigan form black silhouettes against the gold pathway reflecting the sun. The Ottawas and Hurons paddled out to see the big 'wooden canoe' glide effortlessly away, the repercussion of its saluting cannon still pounding in their ears.

La Salle sailed the *Griffon* out through the Straits and across the northern end of the lake. Without further adventure he lifted the arm of islands that screen the entrance to Green Bay. Here he found friendly Indians with a store of furs to trade for his knives and trinkets and axes and blankets. Here too he found some of his advance party who had been faithful to their trust. They had bartered well and had a goodly pile of pelts for their master. La Salle decided to take quick advantage of the market and his apparent good fortune. He promptly ordered the furs stored in the *Griffon* and dispatched the ship back to the East under the command of the godless pilot Lucas, who had taken no part in the prayers on Lake Huron. The vessel sailed away laden with a good part of La Salle's fortune. Neither the *Griffon* nor the pilot, or any member of the crew or any fragment of the cargo, was ever again seen or heard of. There has been much speculation on their fate. My own guess is that the malicious storm which had spared the pilot on Lake Huron a few days before now turned temperamentally upon him for St. Anthony's sake and tossed him headlong into the fresh-water grave he had feared.

La Salle had gambled and lost. The *Griffon* went down, but the voyage had shown how easy it would someday be, despite all hazards, to place fast sailing fleets in commerce on these lake waters. After that voyage across Lake Erie, up the rivers to Huron, through the Straits of Mackinac, and over Michigan to the innermost heart of the fur country, even though disaster did overtake it, the hard route of paddle and portage around by Nipissing and down the Ottawa could be only a detour makeshift. La Salle's ship sank, but in her disappearing wake rose the vision of other men and other ships that would build some of the world's greatest cities around these shores and set mansions among the trees on these islands at Green Bay where La Salle stood to watch the *Griffon's* sails drop behind the eastern curve of the lake.

When the ship was gone, La Salle turned resolutely to confront the wilderness and to explore as widely as possible before the approaching winter fell upon him. Under vicissitudes that make a book in themselves, he re-explored much of the region previously visited by Marquette, Joliet, and their predecessors, and at last toiled homeward overland, back among his enemies and a staggering debt, as we saw him in our mind's eye in the opening chapter. Many details of shoreline and topography would be filled in as the years came and went, but the Lakes with all their rich future were now unveiled and ready for the hordes of ingenious men who would effect their transformation. La Salle himself was to have no further part in the discovery or development of the Lakes. He built no more sailing vessels, and his nine remaining restless years of explorations carried him out of the region into the Mississippi Valley and on to the southwest. Fate pursued him there and finally overtook him. He was only forty-three when he was ambushed by some of his own surly men in the tall grass near the banks of the Trinity River in Texas. They shot him in the head, stripped his body, threw it into the underbrush and left it there. It was a piteous end for the great explorer whom the faithful Tonty rightly called 'one of the greatest men of this age.'

Part II   CONFLICT

The Duke of Wellington to Viscount Castlereagh on being pressed to accept command of His Majesty's forces in Canada in 1814:

'Neither I nor any one else can achieve success, in the way of conquests, unless you have naval superiority on the Lakes.'

XIV

The Crescent Empire

It is a navigator's straight line west along the forty-sixth parallel from Quebec and Montreal, over Lake Nipissing to the Sault and on to Duluth. This was the paddle-and-portage route of French canoes in the age of discovery and through the period of the wars for possession of the Lake region. Canada's Highway 17 still follows that route; it runs past lonely railroad towns and distributing centers for the settlements in the northland, past army camps, and through Indian reservations where the remnants of shattered tribes offer rugs and baskets for sale on the roadside as indifferent motorists speed by.

Another navigator's straight line runs due southwest from Quebec and Montreal up the St. Lawrence River, across Lake Ontario to Buffalo, and over Lake Erie to Cleveland, Toledo, and Detroit. This is the heavy-laden modern route of ships. The northern route is isolated and desolate. The southern shipping lane is the mightiest artery of commerce in the world. Champlain died without knowledge of its existence. La Salle saw its potentialities. But it fell to the British and Americans to open it to ships.

In the geographical vagary of these two routes to the West lies the origin of the drama of a hundred years of war between the French and British for control of the Great Lakes. Those wars themselves are an old story embedded in a thousand textbooks and histories that recount the evil deeds of acquisitive mankind. They began in age-old conflicts in Europe's palaces and battlefields; they spread over the ocean to these shores; they reached bloody swords and bayonets into American forests; and they started cannon firing from warships on the Great Lakes. They were world struggles, and one of the prizes was America itself with its pro-

119

digious network of lakes and waterways. Those wars, fortunately, are not our story. We shall take our station on the Lakes, on the outer rim of the intrigues and the battles, and briefly tell why and how their destiny was altered by the conflicts though neither Englishmen nor Frenchmen in the time of their fighting foresaw the full glory of their possession.

The French were not in America to create a new home for French families from the Old World. They came to get furs for the big trading companies of France. These trade-combines fought each other at court for their exclusive privileges. Their operatives moved westward to the Lakes primarily to increase the yield of peltry and not to plant flourishing colonies for men to live in. From the outset they crossed the wilderness by the northern canoe path to escape the danger of the formidable Iroquois Indians along Lake Ontario. They let this southern route severely alone; instead of reaching Lake Erie, they headed northwest to the falls on the St. Mary's River. Other Frenchmen opened up Louisiana and the Mississippi River far to the south, and gradually joined the two enormous waterways at the low, narrow portages in Illinois and Wisconsin. Theoretically, therefore, the French held as empire that vast crescent of the New World from the Gaspé down the St. Lawrence to Quebec and Montreal, and, sweeping around Lake Ontario and Lake Huron, and the wall of the Appalachian Mountains, to New Orleans and the Gulf of Mexico. We say 'theoretically' because the French claim was established only by the fact that explorers like Marquette and La Salle had toiled over the terrain, looked at the land, and impressed the local Indian tribes with their fire-arms and their sense of décor. Their claim was supported by a few scattered log forts poorly manned and supplied, and by crosses ceremoniously set up at the important corners and crossings, emblazoned with the *fleur de lys* of France. They commanded the Indians to obey their new white fathers, and warned all intruders to stay off these premises. Until 1702, in all that fabulous expanse of territory west of Montreal, there was no white woman at any of the trading posts, no wives or families or colonies—only a few thousand soldiers, traders, trappers, and missionaries.

In the bulge of that crescent, between the Atlantic Seaboard and the chain of mountains whose northern rampart is visible from Mount Royal and the Plains of Abraham, were the Dutch and the British, and soon only the British. They had arrived on the New England coast with wives, household goods, and farming tools about the same time that Champlain's men were dying of scurvy in the masculine colony at Quebec. The British had come to stay. The French paid little attention to them. Neither were the English greatly interested in the Frenchmen's frozen northland on the Great Lakes which they had discovered. The Atlantic Ocean and the streams flowing into it gave them all the water and wilderness they wanted or could use. It looked for a time as though the two peoples would not get in each other's way.

The barriers between them were extensive and stubborn. The English considered Fort Royal in Acadia a French invasion of their boundaries and repeatedly sent ships to attack it. But in general, men from Massachusetts had no wish to get across the mountains of New Hampshire and Vermont into the St. Lawrence Valley. The colonists of New York and Connecticut faced to the east; they felt no desire to cross the Iroquois country and set houses on Lake Ontario. The people of Pennsylvania and Virginia had all the land they needed between the mountains and the sea; they did not lust for Lake Erie or the Mississippi Valley. That happy separation of the two rival peoples lasted without serious interruption for more than a hundred and twenty-five years.

That was quite long enough for the French and the British to establish firmly their divergent colonial policies and habits of living. The differences persist to this day—as a witness to the civilized tolerance and racial pride of both nations. Britain has owned and governed Canada since 1763. There were only about 65,000 Frenchmen there at that time. In 1942 there were some six million of them, and most of those six million still differed more radically from the British than do the citizens of modern France. They rear big families of twelve to sixteen children. They are loyal to their church, which gives them spiritual comfort and assurance in return for a tight control over their lives by their priests, a rigorous church organization which exacts a 4 per cent tithe on all their grain harvests, and forbids birth control. These French Canadians and their villages and farms seem like archaic museum pieces preserved in our time to show what life among the French was like in the days of La Salle and Frontenac. They have never known, or cared to adopt, the proud independence, local enterprise, and experimental liberalism of their English neighbors, who had already disowned the Pope and would soon disavow their King. When the contest between them did come in the years immediately preceding the American Revolution, the paternalistic system and remote control from Paris proved unable to withstand the determined thrust of the freedom-schooled English colonies.

How was the issue joined on the Great Lakes? There was one natural breach in the bastion that shut out the British from the crescent empire of New France. That breach was the ancient glacial overflow outlet of the Lakes down the Mohawk Valley and the Hudson River. It was as fatal to the New France on the Lakes as the gap at the end of the Maginot Line was disastrous to the Old France of 1940. The Dutch had already discovered it and used it during their brief half-century (1609-64) of trading with the Indians. When the British took over, they drove a wedge through this natural salient to the shore of Lake Ontario. Their maritime eye quickly saw the strategic importance of the two lower lakes. And it was through the Mohawk gap and on Lake Ontario and Lake Erie that the British finally took control of the region. It is an exciting and instructive chapter in the story of the Lakes.

Englishmen on principle had always looked upon Frenchmen in America as intruders. The shrewd ones, like Governor Dongan, abhorred the idea of a French empire circling the colonies at their back door. In fact Dongan had no modesty about saying as early as 1683 that the French were on 'our lakes,' and that their claims and holdings might be 'very inconvenient to the British.' One of his successors, Governor Bellomont, wanted to build forts at the northern crossings to block off the Indians, because, as he said, 'to pursue the Indians again and again to the forests was as useless as chasing birds.' He had no faith in the French system of posting the boundaries with cedar crosses. By 1721, Governor Keith of Pennsylvania was urging forts on the Lakes themselves 'to interrupt the French.' And in 1727, Oswego on Lake Ontario was actually fortified. That was a provocative act on dangerous ground, and the English and French were now to meet in conflict on the Great Lakes. They were soon racing to control these all-important southern lakes which France had so long neglected.

The French were not particularly brilliant or imaginative in their strategy. They had used the Ottawa route so long as the link between the East and West that their minds could conceive no alternative. They did not therefore move boldly across the two lower lakes, securing bases as they went; in fact they made no further attempt to sail ships on Lake Erie after the loss of the *Griffon.* They did plant a fort at what is now Kingston, at the foot of Lake Ontario. Then they jumped all the way to Mackinac at the head of Lake Huron, which they reached by way of the Ottawa and Lake Nipissing. From these two widely separated points they projected a primitive and cumbersome pincers movement on the British wedge at Oswego—though even this operation in its first stages was made with a sharp eye on the fur trade.

The first step in closing the pincers was the building of Detroit. Here again it was primarily trade rather than empire strategy that moved the French. Cadillac, the last of the mighty names in New France, picked the spot. He was one of old Count Frontenac's capable young men, as Brûlé was Champlain's. Frontenac sent him out to Michilimackinac to control that fort and trading post on the Straits. But this imperious and imaginative young soldier was wise enough to see that the road to the future was south and not north, and that the Detroit River, not the Straits of Mackinac, was the key to the Great Lakes. He proposed to move down there. The saintly but wily Jesuits saw in the proposal only more brandy-drinking, sin, and licentiousness, and tried to stop him from founding a new and independent trading center. But Cadillac was also too wise to waste himself in controversy with the Jesuits at that mission. He out-maneuvered the priests, whom he strongly disliked, by sailing round them and over the head of local authority straight to Colonial Minister Ponchartrain in Paris. The minister caught Cadillac's vision of Detroit as the key and central link between the Lakes and the Mississippi River, and a barricade against British ambitions in the Northwest. He also acquired some of the young man's fiery zeal, and gave Cadillac what he wanted. Cadillac came in by the northern route. From early June until late July 1701 the Indians along the 700-mile Ottawa-Nipissing waterway from Lachine to Detroit saw the procession of twenty-five heavily loaded canoes, commanded by Cadillac and manned by fifty soldiers and fifty settlers, paddling, unpacking, carrying around the interminable rapids and waterfalls, reloading and paddling again to the frontier post that was to become the first American city on the Lakes.

That city perpetuates in many ways the name of the forty-year-old Antoine de la Mothe-Cadillac, who picked this site and rhapsodized over it in his letters more extravagantly than any of its admirers before or since. Cadillac Square is the heart of downtown Detroit. The automobile center of the world has added its luster to his memory by naming one of its finest motor cars in his honor. And it is quite fitting that the Detroit-Windsor tunnel under the river, linking the two nations in commerce and friendship, should have its busy tubes erupt into Cadillac's American city near the very spot where he drove the oak-log bastions of his little fort of about an acre in size along Jefferson Avenue. Here on the bank where the river narrows after it passes around Belle Isle, Cadillac built dwellings, a storehouse, a chapel for Ste. Anne, and laid out garden plots for his men. In his happiness, or as Detroit's first publicity agent, he wrote that 'the climate is temperate, and the air purified through the day and night by a gentle breeze. The skies are always serene and spread sweet and fresh influence which makes one enjoy a tranquil sleep.' Nostalgic words for a colony and a city that had before it the two and a half centuries of war and commerce that have raged in its streets and along its busy waterfront.

Cadillac's sleep must have been anything but tranquil. In fact it is an effort to imagine that restless, dominating, and scheming gentleman sleeping at all. He was a busy man during his decade at Detroit, trading, intriguing, drilling his soldiers, struggling to improve the new post. He cultivated the Indians and lured them into settlements near by for the profit of their fur trade. He sent for the brave Madame Cadillac and the wife of his captain. They came by the southern route, up the St. Lawrence to Fort Frontenac, over Lake Ontario, around Niagara, and across Lake Erie, in the spring of 1702, indicating that the French were beginning to see the importance of that easier waterway. They were the first white women to take up residence in a western French port. Other women followed their example, and before many seasons had passed Detroit was a fully organized colony with feminine-managed households, abundant crops, a public windmill, a blacksmith shop, priests, nuns, nurses, and schools. All that Cadillac did in his firm and often irritating manner was, as he put it, for 'its utility for the glory of God, the progress of religion, and the good of the colony.' Life in the colony, however, was not exactly tranquil. It was troubled by fire and Indians and unauthorized French traders. Cadillac himself exploited where he could, and tried to enforce a tight monopoly over the fur trade. But settlers continued to come in, and by the time the virile founder was sent in 1710 to govern the post at the southern end of the crescent in Louisiana, the little colony was firmly rooted on the Detroit River as the Gibraltar of the western lakes. It survived mismanagement, neglect, and Indian hostilities, and was strong and relatively prosperous when, a few decades after Cadillac's departure, it became the chief western anchor of French defense against growing pressure of the British.

XV

Warships on Blue Ontario

THE expanse of Lake Ontario and Lake Erie and the length of
the Niagara River lay between Detroit and Fort Frontenac. English Oswego pointed a bayonet at its heart, and English merchants
yearly diverted more of the fur trade from these lake shores down
the Mohawk and Hudson Rivers. The French saw the imperative
need of a strong fort at the Niagara bottleneck to wall out the
British and block their further advance. But that would require
the permission of the Iroquois, who still dominated the Niagara
region.

The French went to them with proposals. They solicited,
wheedled, flattered, threatened, and bribed the Five Nations, and
finally got from them the right to erect a building near the foot
of the path that led down from the escarpment to Lake Ontario.
The Iroquois had seen enough of the white man's wiles to be
suspicious. They specified that the house must be made of bark;
they did not want any French strongholds of stone on their lake
front. But to give an inch was to yield a mile. Before the Indians
quite knew what was going on, the French had not only built
the bark house, but they had summoned from France the celebrated military engineer Chevalier Chaussegros de Léry to build
a thick-walled stone bastion on the east bank of the Niagara River
about 130 sailing miles west of Oswego. He built it so solidly that
it still stands and may be seen to this day. The French diplomat,
suave Chevalier de·Longueuil, explained away the broken promise to the Indians: the furs did not keep well in a bark house; a
stone house was much better for the purpose.

The French also extended their military labors along Lake Erie
and down the Ohio, where the British traders were, in their opin-

ion, usurping French territory and trading rights. They seized old
Fort Sandoski on Sandusky Bay from the British traders—'usurped
by the French in 1751' as the British noted on their map of the
region. In the season of 1754 the French built Fort Junundat on
the east shore of Sandusky Bay to control the portage routes to the
south. Over at Presque Isle, Pennsylvania, where Perry was later
to build his victorious Lake Erie fleet, the French also erected a
fort of squared chestnut logs to dominate the portage down to
the headwaters of the Ohio.

This belated military activity gave the French a line of forts
on the Lakes, anchored at the ends to Detroit and Fort Frontenac.
But the communication lines between them were still tenuous.
The forts were isolated islands of defense in a vast wilderness,
connected only by canoe caravans. When de Léry made his inspection trip to Detroit and Mackinac in 1754, he traveled in a
caravan of twenty-seven canoes, each burdened with ten men and
'packages of provisions.'

The strategy of British attack was, therefore, perfectly simple.
If they could subdue the main base at Fort Frontenac and cut
behind the lines of the dependent western forts, the whole frail
structure would collapse. And that is precisely what happened.
It was the Great Lakes aspect of the Seven Years' War, 1756-63.

The British anticipated the war on the Lakes. They worked
hard and furiously at this beachhead on Lake Ontario. All through
the summer of 1755 this shipyard at Oswego rang with hammers
and whined with saws.

In mid-August, a 43-foot sloop, christened the *Oswego* and
gaily brightened with British flags, slid down the ways and
splashed in the water of Oswego harbor. She was cheered by the
soldiers, the builders, and the onlookers—including many wide-
eyed Indians—standing around the new shipyard. And well might
they cheer the launching, for it was the first English ship to float
on the Great Lakes. Her timbers touched water just seventy-six
years almost to the day after the *Griffon* first set sail across Lake
Erie.

The *Oswego* was a warship, armed with twelve cannon, five

guns, and a swivel on each side. She was a trim figure against the
late summer blue of Lake Ontario's surface and sky. She wore a
wide, orange-yellow girdle around her middle and a black band
above and below it to the water edge, where it met the line of
the white tallowed bottom. Her spiring single mast, filled with
billowing canvas sails, was fifty-three feet tall, and her graceful
main boom was fifty-five feet long. She was fifteen feet in the
beam amidships. Her draft was only seven feet when loaded, because Oswego's harbor was but eight feet deep. She was swift
and quick on the turn. Under her quarter-deck were the staterooms for the officers, and in her forecastle were a cooking stove
and cramped bunks for her crew—'the beef on the rope'—twenty-
six men in all. The magazine stores were amidships.

The *Oswego* was both a symbol of England's might and purpose, and a triumph of organization and skill amid all the hazards
of a frontier shipyard. The man of force behind the achievement
of her launching was Governor Shirley of Massachusetts. He had
gone to Alexandria to talk with Dinwiddie of Virginia about the
menace of the French at their back doors. He wrote that Dinwiddie 'purpos'd to build some vessells at Presque Isle for securing the navigation of the Lake Erie,' and that these boats, in con-
junction with those he himself designed to build on Lake Ontario,
would 'Make us masters of the Great Lakes . . . untill the French
can get a superior force upon these Lakes, wch it seems very difficult if not impracticable for 'em to do, when our vessels shall be
cruizing upon them.'

Just how difficult indeed it was even for the British is indicated
by the hardships which Shirley encountered in getting ships afloat
on Lake Ontario. He had to hire artisans and workers of all kinds
in the seaboard villages and persuade them to go through a danger zone of wilderness to a menaced port in enemy territory.
Indians with anger inflamed by the French lurked in the bushes
along the Mohawk. They ambushed one party of twelve carpenters; they scalped eight of them and saved the other four for
the more leisurely pleasure of torturing them. But the brave men
kept coming on to Oswego.

The problem of procuring and transporting material was formidable. Shirley bought the thousand and one items needed—hammers, saws, adzes, smithies, bolts, clamps, screws, ropes, tar, sails, guns, powder, tents, medicine, and provisions of all kinds—and assembled them at Schenectady. He sent soldiers and axmen in advance to Oswego to clear the way of trees, and of the hostile Indians who were paid by the French to bring in English scalps. Then he got whaleboats and bateaux and canoes to haul the supplies up the Mohawk River. That was a twenty-day journey and a tough one. It led up the Mohawk, over the toilsome interruption of the 'Great Carrying Place near Wood Creek,' down to Lake Oneida, across that lake to the Onondaga River, and on to Oswego-on-the-Lake. Some of the rapids on this route were as treacherous as those on the Ottawa or Upper St. Lawrence. Shirley's own whaleboat was dashed in one of them, and he himself barely escaped drowning.

Men and material nonetheless arrived at Oswego. But that was only half of it. The work itself was arduous. Sawyers, one on top, one in the pit, reduced green oak logs to thin planks and ships' timbers. The planks then had to be steamed or soaked in boiling water, bent to shape around the hull, and fastened in place with clamps to fit the curves of the ship. The seams had to be calked and tarred, and the mast hewn, hoisted, rigged, and made fast. Frontier shipbuilding was a laborious undertaking, but Shirley's crew at three pounds ten per month fell to with energy, and lusted to get 'a crack at the Monsheers' before the autumnal freeze-up beached their ships.

A few days after the *Oswego* was launched, a sister ship *Ontario* slid from the stocks, and shortly thereafter two small schooners, christened the *George* and the *Vigilant*, were sent down to complete the first British fleet on the Lakes.

The fleet built at such cost deserved a more rewarding history and noble ending than it got. Like the great English battleship *Repulse* that went down with the *Prince of Wales* 150 miles northeast of Singapore on December 10, 1941, under an attack of Japanese torpedo planes, having cruised 53,000 miles without ever fighting a single battle, neither the *Oswego* nor the *Ontario,* or the

London, the *Halifax,* and the *Mohawk* that were built the following year, ever got their 'crack at the Monsheers.' For the French
were also furiously building even more heavily armed ships at Fort
Frontenac, and the defeat and death of Braddock down in Pennsylvania allowed his papers and the English plan of attack on all
the French strongholds to fall most untimely into enemy hands.
The French had warning and time to prepare to meet the English.
Shirley could not get enough men together to risk an attack on
either Fort Niagara or Fort Frontenac. His little fleet was reduced
to patrol duty. It would sail out on the lake for a day or two at a
time to see what the French were up to, and then return to its
base at Oswego.

The fleet was privileged to have only one short and disappointing brush with the French. That was on the morning of June 27,
1756. The *Oswego* and the *Ontario* and one schooner had put out
from Oswego harbor to patrol as usual and chart the waters of
the lake. As dawn began to break, the lookout sighted two enemy
ships bearing down on them before a strong westerly wind. The
English vessels tacked sharply into the wind and made for them,
to close distance and have a look. That took only a half-hour—from
4:00 to 4:30 a.m.—with the wind behind the French. When they
were about 1,200 yards apart the two advance French ships hauled
up into the wind, tacked into position, and opened fire. That was
the first salvo between warships on the Great Lakes. Captain
Broadley, in command of the English ships, saw at once that his
small light guns were out-ranged. After a hurried consultation with
his officers, he decided to run rather than risk destruction of this
nucleus of a British lake fleet. While the poorly placed French
shots rained into the water short of his ships, Broadley ordered all
sail close hauled, and ran away to the southeast before the wind.
Eight hours later he had dropped the French under the curve of
the lake, and on the following morning he sailed back into Oswego
harbor. The slow twenty-ton British schooner, however, fell behind
and was easily taken by the enemy. That was the prudent but
unsatisfying end of the first naval battle on the Lakes. Just to note
how morale-building propaganda was handled long ago, we record

Hocquart's broadcast of the engagement: 'Our little fleet on Lake Ontario, in number about five vessels, having met the English fleet amounting to ten gave them battle. We have taken the English Admiral. Afterwards we put the others to flight, and obliged two to run ashore with all sails set.'

Perhaps Broadley should have slugged it out with the enemy after all, for poor management and scanty supply brought disaster to the British shortly thereafter, and all their ships were captured or destroyed. It was almost a duplication of the Hong Kong and Singapore debacles, where guns were sent on one ship, ammunition on another, and when one was sunk the cargo of the other was useless. Montcalm of Quebec fame took personal command of the French. With a fleet of small paddle boats he slipped from Fort Frontenac along the east and south shore of Lake Ontario under protection of the desolate wilderness that lined it, and fell upon Oswego. The British ships that could be got out of the harbor to shell the French, who had landed along the shore, were easily out-ranged and out-fired by the French shore batteries. No reinforcements came to relieve the British. Broadley had to surrender. It was August 14, 1756, just a year after the launching of their first ship. The Indians gorged and got drunk on the supplies, Broadley and his officers were sent captive to France, the fort and shipyard were razed and returned to the wilderness from which they had barely emerged, and the British had lost the first round of their war.

((((XVI))))

The Gateways at Niagara and Quebec

THE calamity at Oswego did not change the nature of the problem or the strategy of the English. Even the armchair strategists of the day could see that the English must get control of the Lakes, that Forts Frontenac and Niagara would have to be taken, and that when those hinges and supply bases fell, the whole French structure on the Lakes from the St. Lawrence to Lake Superior would collapse.

A contemporary columnist summed it all up neatly in a tract of 1757 called 'The Contest In America, &c.' He reviewed the French 'encroachments . . . to annoy and attack us.' He observed that Oswego was only '370 miles in all' from New York, with waterway connection 'except about twenty miles of easy land-carriage.' Oswego, he said, 'not only commands this passage to the great lakes, and all the inland navigation of North America . . . but it is the only place we have that gives us any access to that continent beyond the precincts of the sea-coast that we have settled upon.' He then pointed out that Niagara was 'the principal and most important place, perhaps, of any, in all the inland parts of North America.' He made an eloquent and accurate description of Niagara as the bottleneck pass between the mountains and the Great Lakes, 'with the whole continent open to it on the west and our colonies on the east . . . Here the waters of those great lakes, that spread over the continent far and nigh, are so narrow and shallow, that they are even fordable for passengers on foot; whilst, on all other hands, they form seas near 100 miles broad, and 1,200 miles long. By this means Niagara is the chief, and almost only pass into the interior parts of North America, both from north to south and from east to west, either from the French settlements or ours . . . It is by this pass, and this alone, that the French go to the river Ohio, Fort Du Quesne, Detroit, the Mississippi, and all their other encroachments on us except Crown-Point . . . If we were possessed of this one place, we might be free from them, and all their incroachments, incursions, devastations, etc.'

Concerning all these references to French 'encroachments,' by the way, the British claimed full title to the region by deed from the Five Nations made at Albany in 1701. Our tractarian writes with characteristic vigor and conviction that 'these lakes, especially the two lower ones, Lake Ontario and Erie, with great part of the two next adjoining to them, Lake Huron and Michigan . . . have been made over to the Crown of Great Britain; by many solemn and formal acts and deeds; and the same was acknowledged by France itself at the Treaty of Utrecht.' And he regrets that the French have overstepped the privileges graciously granted them by Britain to make a few settlements in the country where they could trade and stop to refresh themselves 'in passing backwards and forwards, as they pretended when they made them.'

To take Niagara was precisely what the English intended to do. But first Fort Frontenac had to go, otherwise the flank and rear of an attacking force on Niagara would be exposed to assault from that base. Fort Frontenac fell—as easily and suddenly as the defenses of northern France in June 1940. Oddly enough, after all the shipbuilding on Lake Ontario which went for nought in 1756-7, not a warship was involved in the exploit. The English merely duplicated the feat of the French in taking Oswego. Colonel Bradstreet led a brigade of whaleboats, bateaux, and canoes up the old Mohawk route to the ruins of Oswego. From that port he took them secretly down the lonely south shore of Lake Ontario, and silently disposed his 'Bradstreet's Boatmen' at night around Fort Frontenac within two hundred yards of its stone walls. Incredible as it seems, on that fatal morning in late August 1758, the French commandant had only 110 men at this key fort. When daylight revealed that he was encircled, he surrendered Frontenac almost instantly. Uncontested, the British seized all the stores accumulated at this base for shipment to the western posts. They took all they could use or carry away, and burned the rest of it or gave it to the allied Indians. They seized two French ships and put the torch to seven others, which they surprised in the harbor.

With this central link of the French chain broken, the other links could be shattered with relative ease. Niagara was next to go, but it put up a real battle. Both Oswego and Fort Frontenac had been taken by armies transported on the lake by small boats, but that was no proof that warships were not of the greatest importance in the war on the Lakes. The French set to work with a frenzy to build more ships to scout Lake Ontario, to keep the British out of the St. Lawrence River, and to supply Niagara more quickly. They had a small fort down the St. Lawrence near present Maitland, Ontario. It is on the first rapids in the river, and was, therefore, the foot of ship navigation on the lake. Here they built a shipyard and rushed to completion a brig (the *Outaouaise*) and a corvette (the *Iroquoise*) in April 1759—the last boats, incidentally, built by the French on the Lakes. They also had hurriedly constructed a dockyard at Fort Niagara, where they were building two medium-sized schooners when the British struck their blow.

Again the British used whaleboats, bateaux, and canoes for transport. General Prideaux and Sir William Johnson moved 2,300 men through the now familiar open corridor up the Mohawk, over the Carrying Place, and down the lake and river to Oswego on Lake Ontario. Then, hugging the south shore, they paddled and rowed the 130 miles up to Niagara. They beached their boats a safe distance away and moved up to the fort on foot. They dug trenches close up by the walls and opened siege. The engineering was stupid, and many lives, including brave General Prideaux's, were needlessly lost. But under Sir William, the English persevered. The French garrison of 600 men under Captain Pouchot was actually trapped inside the fort. Their only hope was relief through outside reinforcement. Pouchot sent messengers to the western posts to summon help. He waited days and nights on end for this help to come, watching his stores dwindle and his men die. Relief finally came, several hundred strong, down Lake Erie in small boats, and down the current of the Niagara River to the portage above the head of the Falls. But it never reached the fort. The French beached their boats, and picked their way over the seven mile path down to the old bark trading station, and then more cautiously along the river bank toward the fort.

Sir William's men, aided by the allied Iroquois warriors, were waiting for them behind a trench already prepared a short distance up the river to cut them off. The French attacked, but the English guns mowed them down. The French gave up in disorder, and fled back up the portage to their boats, pursued by the English. The rout was complete. Nearly every French officer in the attack was either killed or taken prisoner. Sir William took the captured and wounded back to his headquarters. After another heavy bombardment of the fort, he ordered a trumpet sounded, and sent a courier to Captain Pouchot to invite surrender. When Pouchot learned of the repulse of his reinforcements and saw the list of the captive officers, no help being in sight from the east, he surrendered Fort Niagara to the British on July 25, 1759.

The terms were chivalrous. Their civilized gallantry is a rebuke to the inhuman barbarity of our own age. The officers kept their arms and baggage. 'Those women who chuse to follow their husbands are at liberty to do so.' The others would be honorably transported to Montreal. No officer or man would be 'subject to any act of reprisals whatsoever.' The sick and wounded who could not move from the fort would be 'allowed a guard for their security' and have 'liberty to depart with everything that belongs to them, and shall be conducted in safety, as soon as they are able to support the fatigues of a voyage, to a place destined for the rest of the garrison.'

The fall of Niagara gave the English firm hold on the key to the 'French encroachments.' They promptly took over the shipping at Niagara, and completed the two vessels which they found on the ways. They restored Oswego and began shipbuilding again at that important point. For they had only to clear the French from the upper St. Lawrence in order to take full and final control of Lake Ontario. That meant driving the remaining French boats into

the cul-de-sac between the Thousand Islands and the rapids at
Maitland (Presentation was the French name for the post).

This venture, undertaken in August of the next year, was made
easier by the fall of Quebec just forty-nine days after Niagara, on
September 13, 1759. That brilliant action still stands as one of the
thrilling military exploits in history. It seems far away from Fort
Niagara, but Niagara and the Lakes do not seem remote at Quebec.
The great river narrows there between the rock wall of Quebec on
the north and the rock wall of the Lévis shore on the south, where
twice daily the twelve- to eighteen-foot tide rises and falls.

From the Dufferin Terrace at the Château Frontenac, under the
shadow of Durenne's fine statue of Champlain that turns its back
on the magnificent scene to look toward the interior of the continent, you sit in the sun and watch the big ships and the black
freighters coming and going on the river. You follow them until
they disappear behind the bend of rock on their way to Montreal,
or watch their fanlike wake as they turn into the South Channel
around Point Lévis and the Isle d'Orleans. You cannot mistake the
feel of being at the entrance gateway to the Lake region, with all
its cattle and grain and ore. The vast waterway and hinterland
press close upon the city. For Quebec, like Montreal, is in reality
another lake port, and its fall to the British was as much an event
of the Lakes as the capitulation of Niagara or the surrender of
Detroit.

General Wolfe's capture of Quebec was one of those bold and
daring, even desperate, exploits that might as easily have ended in
catastrophe as in triumph. A dozen coincidences had to synchronize
and mesh to the moment with carefully prepared plans. On this
one moment, just when he was about to give up the whole venture
in despair, luck rode with him. He had sailed up the St. Lawrence
with Admiral Saunders and arrived in the channels below Quebec
on June 26, 1759. From the fort and the city on the rock, Montcalm with his nondescript soldiers and the astonished citizens and
Indians looked down on the formidable spectacle of the black and
yellow banded British fleet rounding the Isle d'Orleans and drop-
ping anchor in the harbor out of range of their shore batteries:

forty-nine warships and over two hundred auxiliary and supply vessels. As sea power it was overwhelming and superbly managed. But sea power alone could not reduce the city; that required a landing party. Where could they land? All summer long Wolfe had studied that expanse of impregnable rock wall from Sillery Point to the fortified town, and the more open shore from the St. Charles River to Montmorency Falls, for a place to form a bridgehead and strike at the city. He placed guns on the Lévis escarpment to bombard Quebec across the river. He tried a landing near Montmorency, but it was beaten off in disaster. Montcalm seemed to have anticipated all the moves and fortified himself against them.

The British fleet maneuvered up and down the river, wearing out the French forces by keeping them on the run along the walled shore to guard against a landing. The French in their turn loosed expensively prepared fireboats on the British, but they lit them too soon, and while the hopeful Frenchmen watched from their walls, the blasé British seamen caught flaming barges with long poles and towed them over to the south channel shores, saying, 'Damme, Jack! Did you ever take Hell in tow before?' So the summer days and nights wore on. September came in with its cold nights warning that winter was on its way, the ice was soon coming to trap the fleet, and time was running out. General Wolfe was growing desperate.

One day as he was scanning the rock wall for the thousandth time through his glass, he saw some women washing clothes in the river, and their wash spread out to dry on the cliff above the cove at L'Anse au Foulon. How could they get up and down the escarpment if there was no pathway? And if washerwomen could negotiate it with a bundle of clothes, why not British soldiers with mortars and muskets?

Wolfe must now either make a move of chance or give up in defeat and sail away. He resolved to plan minutely and venture boldly. He did not even confide with his officers until a few minutes before he was ready to strike. At 11 p.m. on the twelfth his troops embarked. They moved up the river under cover of darkness and the fleet. At 2 a.m. the perfect signal system of the fleet was touched off by a light on the topmast of the *Southerland*. The task force crossed the river above Point Sillery and dropped down toward the cove. The first boatload was challenged by the French guard.

'Who goes there?' he called down.

'France,' whispered Scotch Captain Fraser in excellent French.

'What regiment?'

'The Queen's.'

'Why don't you speak up?'

'Hush! the British will hear you.'

At 4:01, just a minute off schedule, Wolfe ordered a squad of twenty-four men up the cliff with the words, 'The officers and men will remember what their country expects of them.' The suicide squad then climbed the cliff. The result of the entire venture, and the fate of the Great Lakes, was in the balance of the next few minutes. Neither General Wolfe who ordered the ascent, nor Captain De Laune who led it, knew what awaited them at the top. 'I don't know whether we shall be able to get up there—but we must make the attempt,' Wolfe said as they began the climb. They picked their way up over natural obstacles and over fallen logs and debris laid by the French to obstruct the hazardous path. Even today, over the new carriage road that winds up from the cove, it is a stiff and exhausting climb. But Wolfe's men got to the top. They assaulted the sentry and the small guard in modern commando-raid tactics. Some were captured, some fled.

The British shout announced to the waiting Wolfe and his army below that all was well. By early morning the General had an army of 4,829 men with guns and cannon up the cliff and disposed across the Plains of Abraham, where Abraham Martin's cattle were wont to graze in Champlain's day. Dressed in a resplendent scarlet coat that must have caught the eye of every opposing French marksman, Wolfe led his troops to the battle, and was shot three times. But his incredible performance had caught the dispersed French off guard. Even Montcalm could not retrieve the disaster. Six minutes after the battle opened the French army broke. A few more minutes and it was all over. Wolfe, dying now behind the lines, heard the British cry, 'They run, they run.'

'Who runs?' he asked.

'The French, Sir! Egad! They give way everywhere.'

'Now God be praised. I die content.'

Montcalm, also with three bullets in his body, died at dawn the next day in the little house on St. Louis Street.

For the second time Quebec was delivered over to the British. This time they did not give it back. Its surrender was also chivalrous. The two generals were equally honored. Monuments to each were erected at the spots where they fell, and their unique joint monument stands in the Governor's Garden a few steps west of the Château Frontenac. The resident French changed overlords with little strain and almost no alteration in their manner of living. And when, under a brilliant sun on May 17, 1939, the *Empress of Britain*, bearing King George VI and Queen Elizabeth, glided past the city and docked near Wolfe's cove; and when they drove up the path taken by Wolfe to greet the 60,000 people gathered on the Plains of Abraham to welcome the first reigning British monarchs to visit the Dominion of Canada, both English and French cheered them and the National Anthem was sung in both languages.

With the Quebec entrance to the Lakes in British hands, and Fort Frontenac and Fort Niagara already taken, the remaining forts on the Lakes and the river were rather easily mopped up. The British added three more warships to their Lake Ontario fleet in 1760, one from Oswego and two from Niagara. They also built five gunboats, serviceable craft, forty-five feet long, ten feet in the beam, with very shallow draft, and mounting six pound howitzers. They carried lug-sails, and were specially cut away amidships to accommodate six or eight oars on each side. With this fleet, supplemented by Bradstreet's Boatmen, the British moved down Lake Ontario on August 10, and with great difficulty threaded their way among the Thousand Islands to close in on the St. Lawrence forts. They hunted down the only two remaining French warships, sinking one and capturing the other. Presentation fell quickly on August 18, and Fort Lévis, just below it on Isle Royale, capitulated on August 26 after several days of sharp bombardment. Then the victorious British repaired their boats and, under General Amherst, ran the rapids down to Montreal. They lost forty-six boats and drowned eighty-four men in the process. Montreal surrendered on September 8, 1760, after a two-day battle. Amherst's terms were honorable in the high tradition of the times. We note one touch of sentiment and pageantry in the articles of surrender. The colors of Shirley's and Pepperell's regiment, taken by the French at Oswego in 1756, were 'marched out of Montreal by a detachment of grenadiers and a band of musick, and carried down the right of our line to the head quarters, where they were lodged.'

Thus the French were cleared from Ontario and the St. Lawrence, and Detroit and Mackinac were the only two important posts left to them on the Lakes. Their surrender is a short story by itself.

Rogers' Rangers at Detroit

THE capitulation of Montreal carried with it also the surrender of all the French frontier posts on the Lakes. In the third article of that gentlemanly worded document dictated by General Amherst and signed by His Excellency, the Marquis de Vaudreuil, Governor, and Lieutenant General for the King in Canada, in the little house that may still be seen on the Côte des Neiges Road which leads off to the west around Mount Royal, was this simple sentence that sounds somewhat like an afterthought: 'The troops who are in our posts, situated on the frontiers, on the side of Acadia, at Detroit, Michilimackinac, and other posts, shall enjoy the same honours, and be treated in the same manner.' Article 39 added that none of the French at those colonies or posts, neither the married nor unmarried soldiers, should be transported to the American colonies or to Old England, and 'they shall not be troubled for having carried arms.' And Article 41 guaranteed that those who wished to remain could do so with no obligation 'to take arms against his most Christian majesty or his allies, directly or indirectly, on any occasion whatsoever.' Only a strict neutrality was required of them.

On the fifth morning after the signing, Major Robert Rogers was on his way west from Montreal to Detroit with two hundred men to receive the surrender of the French posts. He was General Amherst's personal choice for this mission. It was both delicate and hazardous, for it led over still-hostile Indian ground to French commandants isolated in the west who had not yet heard of the calamity that had befallen them at Quebec, Montreal, and on the length and breadth of Lake Ontario. Rogers' fame (resurrected, refurbished, and brilliantly dramatized into a modern best-seller, *Northwest Passage*, by Kenneth Roberts) was already legendary

when he encamped with Amherst before Montreal. This hard-
bitten New Hampshire man had grown up almost within sight and
sound of the Indian road through the Connecticut-St. Francis River
gateway between the St. Lawrence and the Atlantic over which
so many English captives were taken north by the Indians, along
which so many met torture and death. As the leader of the Rangers,
this tall, restless mountaineer with the big nose, vain mouth, and
limited mentality had become the foremost frontier warrior of the
Seven Years' War.

   With a select detachment, Rogers left Montreal on September 13
in a fleet of fifteen whaleboats—those long, narrow rowboats that
had become so popular and serviceable on the lakes and rivers.
He took them up the St. Lawrence, laboring through the Lachine,
Cedars, Galops, Long Sault and lesser rapids on that rough stretch
of river that drops 223 feet in the 165 miles between Lake Ontario
and Montreal. They pulled hard against the late September winds
over Lake Ontario, skirted the north shoreline, like Hennepin
before them, and reached Niagara in the chill of the first day of
October. They lugged their heavy whaleboats around the portage,
paddled up the Niagara River, and rowed out on choppy Lake Erie
at Buffalo. They followed the south shore of Lake Erie, close in,
to Presque Isle (Erie, Pa.). Rogers left his men there while he
dashed down to Fort Pitt in a birch-bark canoe to hand some
official papers to the English commandant. Rogers then rejoined
his men, and led them on westward around the Erie shore. His
succinct Ranger's diary of the expedition, supplemented by his
book of 1775, *A Concise Account of North America*, with its individual place names and lordly spelling, contains many illuminating
details of this first expedition of an English detachment on the
Lakes west of Niagara. The weather was dirty, the wind high. The
Rangers were more familiar with the technique of dodging behind
trees than of handling whaleboats in a Lake Erie tempest. With his
usual precise attention to details, Rogers instructed them 'not to
mind the waves of the lake; but when the surf is high, to stick to
their oars, and the men at helm to keep the boat quartering on the
waves and briskly follow, then no mischief will happen by any

storm whatever.' It was good advice, as all Erie boatmen know, but the October weather got too rough for the Rangers' seamanship. They had to put in and make camp in the forest on the Cuyahoga River, or the Chogage as Rogers writes it, near the spot where Moses Cleaveland later founded his city.

While they were scanning the clouds with weather eye and watching the surf break on the low rocky shore, Ottawa Chief Pontiac (in Rogers' spelling 'Attawa' and 'Ponteack') sent his emissaries to intercept them and ask the meaning of this unauthorized intrusion into his domain. A few hours later the great chief, who signed his name with a drawing of an otter, appeared in person before Rogers. He was ornamented with a feathered turban and a nose ring that covered most of his upper lip. Rogers says that 'he puts on an air of majesty and princely grandeur, and is greatly honored and revered by his subjects.' He was by far the most astute chief among all the Indian tribes. He rivaled the Europeans in conceiving, in his untutored way, an empire strategy that held for many years under his personal dictatorship most of the Indians of the Northwest.

The meeting of the tough woodranger with 'the King and Lord of the country' was a momentous drama enacted there in the wilds on the shore of tempestuous Lake Erie. They saluted each other in fitting manner. Then Pontiac demanded, 'What is your business in my country? Why did you dare to enter it without my permit?'

'I have come with no design against you,' Rogers replied. 'I am only here to remove the French out of your country. They have been an obstacle in our way to mutual peace and commerce. I am going to Detroit to take over the French forts in the name of His Majesty, the King of Great Britain.'

Rogers gave him 'several friendly messages' in much wampum. But Pontiac returned solemnly to his tent for the night to think it over, warning Rogers that 'he stood in the path I traveled in till next morning.' Sleep eased Pontiac's objections. Next day he sent Rogers several bags of parched corn and 'some other necessaries.' He came again to meet Rogers, bringing the lit peace pipe, and ready to call the King his 'Uncle.' The wet pipestem passed back and forth from Pontiac's mouth to Rogers', while the chief assured him that he might pass through the territory and receive the protection of the Indians. Pontiac sent his messengers to all the Indian towns around Lake Erie to tell his people that Rogers had been granted friendly passage through the region. It was a great diplomatic victory for Rogers, who was certainly not equipped at the moment to fight his way through Pontiac's land along Lake Erie. The meeting over, the weather cleared at last, and the British, on November 12, again rowed westward in their whaleboats toward Detroit. Rogers says that Pontiac 'sent one hundred warriors to protect and assist us in driving one hundred fat cattle, which we had brought for the use of the detachment from Pittsburg.' He even went on to Detroit with Rogers, and preserved him 'from the fury of the Indians, who had assembled at the mouth of the strait to cut us off.' Rogers sent one of his officers on ahead with a letter to the French Commandant, M. Beleter. That was Beleter's first knowledge of the disaster. Naturally he did not believe the English letter and he fell into raging defiance. He mounted an effigy of Rogers' head on a staff, and placed a crow on the head to symbolize to the Indians how he would scratch out Rogers' brains.

But he didn't. The Rangers moved up the Detroit River with their usual caution and encamped in a field half a mile below and in full view of the fort. Rogers sent over a copy of the terms of the capitulation of Montreal. That document changed the mind of the commandant, and he yielded up his fort. In another of Rogers' impressive acts of showmanship, the blue-coated French were drawn up in military formation before him and his guard. As the drums rolled, the *fleur de lys* of France on its white field was solemnly hauled down and the British flag was smartly run up over the fort. The French garrison then marched out of their quarters and laid down their arms before Rogers on the brown November grass. The Indians were astonished to see the once boastful French surrender without battle to this small company of Englishmen. They were dumfounded when the victorious English did not massacre their victims, but actually left them their houses and their goods. They told Rogers that 'they would always for the future fight for a nation thus favored by Him that made the world.' The curve of British prestige was vertical. With this little frontier drama, the destiny-marked city of Detroit passed over into the hands of the English in its sixtieth year after Cadillac founded his trading post there.

Rogers attempted to hurry on up the Detroit River and up Lake Huron to take over the other four important French posts at Mackinac, at the Sault, at St. Joseph (near present Niles, Michigan) and at Green Bay. But he reckoned without the annual autumnal freeze up. He had barely started when he ran into the December ice and northwest snow storms and was forced back to Detroit. The posts on the Great Lakes remained in French hands until late in the year 1761. Rogers did not linger, or wait to take them over personally. He delegated his command at Detroit, and returned overland through Ohio to Fort Pitt and the East.

((((XVIII))))

Michilimackinac

MICHILIMACKINAC on its still-isolated strait did not capitulate immediately. A harrowing, but not unique, story of treachery and starkest barbarism accompanied and followed its surrender. The central character was a British trader named Alexander Henry.

The minute Montreal fell, certain British traders began to get their packs, canoes, and trinkets ready to go inland to reap the harvest of the fur trade. Among them was Alexander Henry, a young adventurer from New Jersey, who thought he saw a chance to make his fortune in the bush. Like Brother Sagard, he is famous where so many are forgotten because he was literate and left a vivid account of his experiences in his *Travels and Adventures* published in 1809. He accompanied Amherst's expedition from Oswego. He lost three of his boats at the Rapides des Cédres, where so many boats and men met disaster. Leaving Montreal on August 3, 1761, with a passport, he took the route of Champlain and Nicollet up the Ottawa-Nipissing-Georgian Bay entrance to the outpost of white authority and junction center of the upper lakes at Fort Mackinac.[1]

The route had not changed in the century and a half since Champlain's day; it was still as wicked and toilsome as ever. But custom had standardized the canoes at a length of 33 feet and a width of 4½ feet at the middle. The men who paddled and portaged them were, in Henry's day, a loosely organized profession. They hired out to take canoes back and forth from Montreal to Mackinac. In Henry's caravan there were eight men to a canoe on the paddles. The skilled men were placed in the bow and the stern and paid

[1] By the way, whether it is Michilimackinac, Mackinac, or Mackinaw, it still is Chippewa for 'Great Turtle,' and, regardless of French or English spelling, it is pronounced MackiNAW, not MackiNAK.

146

twice as much as the unskilled 'middlemen.' The cargo of each canoe was done up in 60 packages, each weighing about 100 pounds, for convenient loading and portaging. Each man was permitted to take along one personal bag of 40 pounds. A floating canoe, therefore, was carrying a total weight of about four tons, yet it bore the load easily. On the lakes, when the wind was favorable, each canoe might hoist a sail.

Henry set out on his perilous journey in one of these standard caravans. At Ste. Anne's each man received, according to custom, a gallon of rum when they stopped there to go to confession and offer their vows to that patron saint of Canadian canoemen. Henry was sorry to see them guzzle their entire ration on the spot in a supreme orgy before they proceeded further. 'My men,' he said, 'surpassed, if possible, the drunken Indian, in singing, fighting, and the display of savage gesture and conceit.' The carousal over, however, these men continued their hard journey. They unpacked, carried, and repacked each canoe around those multitudinous obstructions on the route—always fighting flies and mosquitoes. Accidents were too frequent. Henry says that so many men were ruptured, strained, or injured for life that a fund had to be established at Montreal for the relief of 'disabled and decayed *voyageurs.*' They reached Georgian Bay at last, and Henry exclaimed his relief when he first saw 'the billows of Lake Huron which lay stretched across our horizon like an ocean,' and found that the heavy-burdened canoes rode the high running waves of the lake 'with the ease of a sea-bird.'

Henry himself admitted that his trip was 'a premature attempt to share in the fur-trade of Canada.' He was soon to learn just how premature it was. As he neared Mackinac, he found out that Englishmen were murderously hated by the Indians, and that some of these Indians were already demanding a share of the pillage of his goods as soon as he was scalped—as he most certainly would be. The scared young man decided to camouflage himself as a Frenchman for self-protection. Indians, as he observed, loved the Canadians. 'I laid aside my English clothes, and covered myself only with a cloth, passed about the middle; a shirt, hanging loose; a molton, or blanket coat; and a large, red, milled worsted cap.' He also smeared his face and hands with dirt and grease. When Indians approached his canoe, he seized a paddle and thus had the satisfaction of passing several hostile groups unnoticed. There was still an Englishman under the disguise, however, and the Indians were soon to smell him out.

With this retinue, and in this disguise, trader Alexander Henry, aged twenty-two, reached Mackinac Island early in September, and then hurried on across the Straits to the fort. He arrived several days before the English detachment came up to take Mackinac away from the French.

The fort was no longer at St. Ignace; it had been moved to the south point of the Straits at present Mackinaw City, where you may see the reconstruction of it in the state park while you wait for the steamer to ferry your car across the six or seven miles of choppy water to Mackinac Island or the Upper Peninsula. It was so near the shore that the high waves, so continually kicked up by wind, washed against the cedar posts of the stockade.

Naturally this English trader with his load of goods was received with no enthusiasm at Fort Mackinac. The fort was included in the Montreal capitulation, but it was strictly French. Frenchmen had explored the region, they had built the post, they had established the mission, they had made friends with the Indians, and the fur trade was a French monopoly. They tried to scare the young trader away with horror tales and hints of danger. He had better escape at once to Detroit, they said, before the Indians learned that an Englishman was in their midst. But Henry stayed by his goods and went on with his plans.

Then the Indians came to see him. He tells how he was waited upon one afternoon by a formidable band of Chippewas who paddled over from Mackinac Island. Sixty of these warriors crowded into his small house. Their naked torsos were daubed with patterns in white clay. They exuded a foul odor of grease, mixed with charcoal, which they had smeared on their faces. Many of them had feathers thrust through their noses. Each had a tomahawk in one hand, and a scalping knife in the other. An 'uncouth, if not frightful assemblage,' as Henry described these 'visitors' whom he now faced.

They sat in complete silence while they gravely smoked their pipes. They smoked a long time while Henry studied their impassive faces and wondered what was coming. Then the chief took a few strings of wampum in his hand and made a speech to the Englishmen. He said that their father, the king of France, was tired out from warring with Britons. He had fallen asleep, and while he slept the English had grabbed Canada from him. Now he was stirring again, asking about 'his children, the Indians,' and, as soon as he got fully awake, which would not be long, he would utterly destroy these intruders. He suggested that the spirits of those killed in the wars could be appeased by covering their bodies with presents. Since Henry had come to them bravely, unarmed and in peace, to trade with them and supply them with things they needed, they would call him brother. 'You may sleep tranquilly, without fear of the Chippewas,' he concluded. 'As a token of our friendship, we present you with this pipe, to smoke.' Henry smoked, shook hands with each Chippewa, and served them 'English milk (meaning rum).' Then, to Henry's unspeakable relief, they rose and paddled back across the rough strait.

Henry now set quickly to work to get his canoes manned and provisioned for the winter trade journeys before the ice closed in. As he was completing all the details of buying corn and engaging men, he was again visited by Indians. This time they were the corn-growing Ottawas, who were living on Lake Michigan only twenty miles west of Mackinac. Two hundred of these warriors came to the fort and billeted themselves for the night among the friendly Canadians there. The next morning they sent for Henry and a couple of other merchants who had followed him up from Montreal. The Indians said they had received news of the merchants' coming with goods which the Indians needed, but they had learned that the Englishmen were loading canoes to send their merchandise on to 'the Mississippi, and other distant regions' where their enemies lived. They ordered the Englishmen to give to each of their warriors fifty beaver-skins' worth of merchandise and ammunition on credit until the following summer. Naturally the merchants refused. They would have been stripped of all their goods and left without security of any kind. Just when this war of nerves was at its height, news came that the long-awaited English detachment from Detroit was approaching to take command of the post. The traders armed thirty of their men with muskets, barricaded themselves in Henry's house, and determined to fight until help came. Two days later Lieutenant Leslie with 300 men beached their canoes, marched in, and quickly took possession of Mackinac. Henry concludes his account of this crisis with these words: 'The Indians, from all quarters, came to pay their respects to the commandant; and the merchants dispatched their canoes, though it was now the middle of September, and therefore somewhat late in the season.'

The crisis seemed to be over, the English were in command, and Henry settled in for the winter. He has left an engaging account of his trip to the Sault, where he spent much of his time; of the fishing there, and of the ups and downs of winter life and travel at a frontier post. He thought he was getting along very well, making friends with the Indians and learning their language and their ways. Then he got caught in one of the most grimly dramatic episodes in all the struggle for the Lakes. It was a minor act in Pontiac's carefully planned counter-attack against the white man's encroachment on the Indians' homeland.

It begins down at Detroit. Pontiac had prepared his attack with a military skill worthy of a trained European general. He organized the Indians throughout the Northwest. He sent detachments to attack simultaneously by ruse and stealth all the forts held by 'these dogs dressed in red.' The plan was sprung in May 1763. It began with a Trojan-horse move against Detroit. Pontiac sent his warriors to the fort to give a dance before the officers, and while they danced, a spying party went around to note the arrangement of the post and the disposition of the troops. A few days later, Pontiac himself arrived with sixty braves in canoes and filed up to the fort. Each brave was draped in a blanket, and under each blanket was a sawed-off gun or scalping knife. Major Gladwin, the commandant, had wind of the strategy. He ordered the guard to let them in.

Pontiac was surprised to see the garrison alert and fully armed. He was even more disconcerted when he entered Gladwin's headquarters to find the major and his officers in military dress with pistols and swords at their sides. Gladwin kept the calm and fearless pose that has through the centuries enabled a few Britons to rule their populous colonies. He carried out his act through the exchange of speeches. He watched Pontiac finger the wampum belt with which he was to give the signal for the Indian attack. Gladwin did not waver. Either his confident manner or the rattling of arms in the garrison outside made Pontiac hesitate. Then Gladwin boldly rebuked Pontiac for attempting deceit. He stepped over to one of the warriors and pulled away his blanket to show that he knew of their treachery. Pontiac did not order the massacre. Instead he rose with chieftain dignity, and said, 'My brother does me wrong; he does not believe. Then we will go.' And they marched from the chamber and out of the fort. A few days later Pontiac's men murdered an English sergeant, and the war, centering around the siege of Detroit, was on.

The simultaneous attack at Mackinac was more ingenuous and the English were less alert. The traders returning to the Straits brought back rumors of unrest among the Indians. More and still more Indians gathered around the fort. A Chippewa friend of Henry's came to warn him. With tears in his eyes, he pleaded with Henry to leave the fort and go back to the safety of the Sault. But his friend spoke in elaborate figures which Henry did not understand. The warning left him unmoved. That was on June 2, 1763. The next day was the King's birthday. The Sacs and the Chippewas planned an international match of lacrosse to be played in the mile-long stretch outside the fort, with the commandant and his men as guests and spectators. Henry urged Leslie not to permit it, but Leslie only laughed at him and went to the field to watch the game.

As played by these Indians, it was confused and violent. Each side had bats four feet long with a racket on the end. They put a ball in play in the middle of the field and attempted to throw it forward until it passed the opponents' goal post. One side worked the ball down toward the fort amidst the heated excitement. Then one of the Indians batted it clear over the protecting wall of cedar pickets into the fort. The yelling Indians all rushed after it. By that ruse they entered the English enclosure.

Henry did not go to the game. A canoe was being got ready to depart the next morning for Montreal. Henry wanted to send letters with it, and at the moment when the Indians were approaching the fortification, he was at his desk writing. A friend came to ask him to go down to the beach and get the news from a canoe that had just come in from Detroit. Henry told him to go on down, and he would follow in a few minutes. This man had hardly left the room when Henry heard the fierce Indian war-cry and the screams of Englishmen. He rushed over to the window and looked out. What he saw made him shudder. Here are his own words: 'I saw a crowd of Indians, within the fort, furiously cutting down and scalping every Englishman they found . . . I saw several of my countrymen fall, and more than one struggling between the knees of an Indian, who, holding him in this manner, scalped him, while yet living . . . I observed many of the Canadian inhabitants of the fort, calmly looking on, neither opposing the Indians, nor suffering injury.'

Henry ran for shelter to the house of M. Langlade, one of these unmolested Canadians. Langlade was standing with his family at a window watching the slaughter. The Indian slave hid Henry in the garret of the house. Henry looked out through a chink. He saw the dead lying scalped and mangled, the dying writhing and shrieking; 'from the bodies of some, ripped open, their butchers were drinking the blood, scooped up in the hollow of joined hands, and quaffed amid shouts of rage and victory.' The Indians had caught the English completely unprepared. Only twenty of them escaped murder.

Henry's escape was nothing short of a miracle. Four Indians, dripping with the blood of their slain and brandishing tomahawks, broke into the Frenchman's house to search the attic for more Englishmen. Henry had just crawled into a dark corner and burrowed into a heap of birch-bark vessels used for making maple sugar. One Indian was close enough to touch him, but the window-less garret and Henry's dark clothes concealed him. The Indians went away. Madame Langlade, however, was frightened by the idea of harboring an Englishman right in her own house. With irresistible womanly pressure, she forced her husband to betray him. Langlade slunk off to inform the Indians. Naked and drunken they came to get Henry. Their leader Wenniway was over six feet tall; his whole face and torso were smeared with grease and char-coal except for a white spot around each eye. This formidable savage, Henry tells us, 'seized me, with one hand, by the collar of the coat, while in the other he held a large carving-knife, as if to plunge it into my breast; his eyes, meanwhile, were fixed stead-fastly on mine. At length, after some seconds, of the most anxious suspense, he dropped his arm, saying, "I won't kill you!"' The warrior with knife poised above his victim like Abraham's arm over young Isaac was reminded of his lost brother Musinigon. Henry became Wenniway's man and was called after his dead brother.

The way the Indians toyed with him in the next few days was fantastic. He and the other prisoners were placed in canoes and made to paddle west toward the Isles du Castor in Lake Michigan, where they were to be killed, cooked, and served. Henry was almost naked and the weather was rigorous. He begged old Lang-lade for a blanket, but was refused because Henry could now offer no security. Good Samaritan M. Cuchoise gave him one. Fog drove the flotilla close in shore, bringing it up to the Ottawa village twenty miles west of the fort. These Ottawas were furious because the Chippewas had attacked and robbed the fort without consult-ing or inviting them. They lured the flotilla up to the shallow water on their beach, and then a hundred shouting warriors jumped out of the bushes, splashed out to the canoes and seized the prisoners from the Chippewas.

The dazed and battered Englishmen were now loaded into Ottawa canoes and taken right back to Michilimackinac. The Ottawas wrangled with the Chippewas while the English languished in prison, some of them trussed up to the roof pole with ropes, all famished because the only food offered them was bread smeared

with English blood and Indian spit. The canoes coming in from
Detroit and Montreal were seized as they landed and the Englishmen made prisoners. One chief, returning to the fort too late for
all the fighting, took his knife, went into the prison, and carved
up the seven Englishmen who were bound to the pole. Henry was
not bound. By another miracle, his old friend who had tried to
warn him before the lacrosse game arrived at the fort. He went
into council with the Indians and bought Henry away from them.
He hid the young trader in a cave while the Indians caroused on
rum and ate the flesh and drank the blood of Englishmen. Then
he shaved off Henry's hair, daubed his face with black and red
paint, garbed him in Indian clothes, placed feathers on his head,
and transformed him into a savage. Henry thus again escaped
death, but in this sorry state he saw his business collapse and his
canoes come back empty. A little later his Indian friend took him
to live through the winter as his brother in safety in the north,
where he heard only rumors of the progress of the war and the
siege of Detroit.

While Henry was witnessing or enduring these barbarities up at
Michilimackinac, Detroit lay under the siege of Pontiac himself.
There is a physical limit to the atrocities which may be committed
even in savage warfare on the Great Lakes. Those perpetrated at
Detroit were in pattern a duplicate of those we have just recounted.
We need not harrow ourselves with repetition. Detroit held out for
five months against all the wiles of Pontiac.

It was ironic that the chief who planned the total operations
should fail while all his warriors were successful in attacking the
other English forts. One important reason, besides Gladwin's determined leadership, was British boats. They saved Detroit. The British had learned the value of ships on the Great Lakes in their
campaigns against Quebec, Montreal, and around Lake Ontario. If
they were useful on Lake Ontario and the St. Lawrence, they were
doubly important on Lake Erie. There were no land routes between
Niagara and Detroit, but the lake was an open road. Shortly after
the surrender of Fort Niagara, the British moved in above the Falls
and built a shipyard at Navy Island in the Niagara River. They

promptly laid the keels of two eighty-ton schooners for communication and supply between Niagara and Detroit. One of them was
christened the *Michigan* (sometimes listed as the *Gladwin*) and the
other the *Huron*. They were almost identical in structure and armor
with the Lake Ontario schooners. They were the first ships to sail
on Lake Erie since the *Griffon*. And they were ready just in time to
help the British in the struggle against Pontiac.

These schooners were lying in the harbor in the Detroit River
when Pontiac began his war on the fort. The *Michigan* weighed
anchor and, with a good breeze behind her, sailed through the
Indian gauntlet down the river and out onto Lake Erie. She carried
the news of Detroit's plight to General Amherst at Niagara. Pontiac
attempted to close the river to these ships, but in spite of his bold
attacks, the schooners managed to get in and out. They had to fight
their way. On one of her trips up, the *Huron* was attacked by a
whole fleet of Indian canoes. The captain anchored his ship in
mid-stream and allowed the Indians to drift in close. Then he
suddenly opened fire with ball and grape. The canoes in the vanguard were sunk outright, and the attack was beaten off with heavy
casualties to the Indians. Then with a favorable wind, the vessel
sailed smartly up to the fort with men, food, and ammunition,
pouring gunfire into the Indian encampment on the Ontario shore
as she glided by. The *Michigan* had a narrower escape. She was
actually boarded by Indians while she lay becalmed one night
near the shore of Fighting Island, just below Detroit. The captain
and five of the crew were killed, but the quick-thinking mate
ordered the magazine fired. The frightened Indians abandoned
the ship in panic, and at dawn the survivors of the crew were able
to sail her in under the protection of the Detroit guns.

The bateaux that tried to cross the lake were more vulnerable.
Lieutenant Cuyler was sent up with ten of these boats to relieve
the hard-pressed garrison in the early weeks of the siege. While
he was camping for the night on Point Pelee in Lake Erie, Pontiac's
warriors surprised his company, killed several, captured the rest,
and forced them to paddle the bateaux on to Detroit. The watchers
at the fort shouted for joy when they sighted the supply train com-

ing up the river. When it drew nearer they saw to their horror that it was commanded by Indians. Some of the captive soldiers tried to leap overboard and swim to the fort. They were slain in the attempt. Two soldiers in one of the boats clubbed their captors and drove the bateau ashore. Its cargo of barreled pork and other provisions was retrieved by the garrisons. The rest of the boats were taken on to the Ottawa camp. Some time later the guards at the bastions of Detroit saw the mangled bodies of the captured English soldiers tied to logs float slowly past the fort.

This sort of thing went on for 153 days before Pontiac gave up the effort and sued for peace. Indian temperament was unsuited to siege warfare. Their supplies ran out. News came that their father, the king of France, had never quite wakened from his long sleep, but had abandoned his children to a new father, His Britannic Majesty. The French who, like the men of Vichy, had merely looked on or secretly aided the Indians, accepted status under the English. Word also ran among the Indian villages that General Bradstreet had massed 3,000 men at Niagara and would soon be at Detroit in force. Resistance dissolved. Pontiac withdrew. Bradstreet's army rowed up Lake Erie in specially built barges in July 1764. The neighboring Indians came in to give the English their allegiance. The fifteen months of war was over. Two years later the capable but defeated Indian statesman, Pontiac, went down to Oswego to meet Sir William Johnson. He concluded the peace with great personal dignity, leaving the English free at last to exploit the Great Lakes.

In Bradstreet's expedition were Israel Putnam, the Connecticut farmer who gained in the long French and Indian War the military skill which served his country during the American Revolution; and our friend Alexander Henry. Henry had gone from the Sault to Niagara with sixteen Indian delegates to the council with Sir William Johnson. Amherst placed Henry in command of ninety-six Indians to go back to Detroit, to retake Mackinac, and incidentally to recover Henry's property at the Straits and at the Sault. All but ten of these warriors deserted and fled back over Lake Ontario. Four Missisakies joined him, and Henry with his fourteen Indians rowed one of the Bradstreet barges up Lake Erie. For some odd reason they portaged the barges over the neck of land at Presque Isle, straining the timbers and wasting time, as Henry reports. They camped at Sandusky, then paddled on up to Detroit. They reached the fort on August 8, after a twenty-five day voyage. After the peace of August 26, Henry joined Captain Howard's detachment of 300 Canadian volunteers and embarked up the St. Clair and up Lake Huron to the scene of his terror at Michilimackinac. 'We met not a single Indian on our voyage,' he says. The Ottawas and Chippewas were summoned. They came and made peace. Indians at the other lost forts followed suit. The British were back in permanent control of the Great Lakes. Henry went on to the Sault to spend the winter and recoup his fortunes. In this, he adds, 'I was in part successful.'

((((XIX))))

Strife Between Brothers and Neighbors

THE Revolutionary War almost passed by the Great Lakes. They were a minor and an indirect cause of trouble with the mother country. No sooner had England taken over the vast American possessions from the French than she issued a proclamation (1763) particularly annoying to the colonists. It ordered them to stay out of the Great Lakes region, including the rich valleys west of the Alleghenies and the St. Lawrence River. The order meant that this luscious land of savannahs, forests, and fur, and the broad highway rivers and lakes of the French Empire in America were fenced off and forbidden to the very men who had given their blood and worldly goods in a seven years' struggle to wrest them from the French. The old crescent empire was, in effect, still there on their back doorstep and still swarming with hostile Indians. In their view, the colonists had got rid of menacing Frenchmen only to be confronted with equally menacing Englishmen.

In view of the worsening relations with Britain, the new menace seemed to the colonists more dangerous than the old. For Great Britain also had formidable sea power on their Atlantic front door as well, an advantage which the French never enjoyed. The resentment of the Americans, and their natural desire to enter and exploit this western region, was one cause of the Revolutionary War.

No important battle in that war occurred on the Great Lakes or in the lake bowl. The battle for the Lakes, in fact, was fought in Paris by the diplomats at the Peace Conference in 1782. Where should the boundary line be drawn between the United States and Canadian Great Britain? At the end of the war, let us remember, Britain still held and still garrisoned her forts on the south shore of the Lakes. They were not assaulted or taken by the Americans.

But the Americans demanded a boundary line that would follow the old canoe route of the French up the Ottawa and across Lake Nipissing to Lake Superior. That would have given to the United States all the wealthy and vital industrial heart of modern Canada. Naturally Great Britain resisted that proposal. She did agree, however, to compromise on the present border, which splits four of the Great Lakes.

Britain also agreed to evacuate Oswego, Niagara, Presque Isle, Detroit, and Mackinac, which were all south of the border. But a subtle phrase was slipped into the agreement: four words that said, 'with all convenient speed.' Speed seemed to be most inconvenient. The British had a good excuse for not evacuating. The Americans had agreed, among other things, to be kind to returning Loyalists and to pay indemnities. They did neither, and Britain continued to hold the gateway forts as security and incidentally to keep in her own hands the lucrative Great Lakes fur trade.

In the meantime the Northwest Territory, including the Lake states of Ohio, Michigan, Indiana, Illinois, Wisconsin, and a part of Minnesota, was created, with its enlightened Constitutional Ordinance of 1787, and it was beginning to fill up with settlers along the Ohio River and on the eastern shore of Lake Erie. The presence of British-held forts within this territory galled the Americans. Fortunately all the outstanding differences between the two nations were settled by the negotiations of John Jay in 1794, and two years later the British withdrew to their side of the border. They had moved their Mackinaw fort over to Mackinac Island in 1780-81; they now withdrew from the island and planted their garrison on St. Joseph Island in the North Channel at the mouth of the St. Mary's River. They abandoned Detroit and crossed over to Malden a few miles below present Windsor. They also vacated the American side of the Niagara, and took up defensive positions at Fort Erie and Fort George.

Memories of this friction at key points on the Great Lakes lingered as the two countries once more drifted into war—happily for the last time. That war involved the Lakes in their most critical conflict.

We take no particular pride in the conduct of our ancestors in the War of 1812. Its justification was doubtful, and its conduct was, on the whole, stupid, although there were many brilliant exploits. From the point of view of Britons and Canadians, it was a treacherous stab in the back. For Britain was fighting a desperate battle for her life against Napoleon. In that uncertain hour the Americans struck at the vulnerable, weakly-held, two-thousand-mile-long border of Canada. They did not wait for a formal declaration of war. That came on June 18, but in May our own Lieutenant Woolsey, in command of our only large naval vessel on Lake Ontario, the *Oneida,* halted the British *Lord Nelson* right out in the open lake. He trained his guns on the ship, forced the captain to surrender, put a prize crew aboard, and sailed her into Sackets Harbor, the new American shipyard and base at the east end of Lake Ontario. The *Lord Nelson* with her cargo of flour was condemned and sold. (The United States in 1928 paid Canada $23,644 damages for this unlawful seizure.)

Lieutenant Woolsey was out of line, but he did not act without precedent. As he stood on the quarter-deck of the *Oneida,* studying the *Lord Nelson* through his glass before ordering his cannon stripped for action, he may have been thinking of that bitter June day back in 1807 when the British warship *Leopard* fired upon the U. S. *Chesapeake* in American territorial waters off the Virginia coast, killing three and wounding eighteen sailors before our ship yielded to search and impressment of American seamen. He may also have remembered that the British farther west had been arming Tecumseh and his Indians and encouraging them to make war on the Americans in the Northwest Territory. For William Henry Harrison of Tippecanoe fame had reported after the defeat of Tecumseh in November 1811, 'The Indians had an ample supply of the best British glazed powder, and some of their guns had been sent so short a time before the action that they were not yet divested of the lint coverings in which they are imported.' Woolsey could claim that he was merely taking revenge when he anticipated by a few weeks the actual declaration of war that came on June 18, 1812.

It is true but meaningless to say that the war should never have been fought. It was fought on or around the Lakes. Both sides did too much preliminary boasting. The British said they would not let American ships even so much as cross from New York to Staten Island. They were confident because they had a good thousand ships of war, while the poor little American navy had only fifteen. Henry Clay phrased the American boast when he said that the Kentucky militia could take over Canada single handed. With proper military leadership and planning, the Kentucky militia could have fulfilled his boast. There were only about a half million people in all Canada, most of them French. A majority of the English-speaking citizens were Loyalists who had fled the Colonies during the Revolution. Very few had been able to return, in spite of the treaty, because they were still tarred and feathered by the Americans when they crossed the border, and their property was not returned to them. There were only about 5,000 soldiers in all Canada, and they were scattered in a thin line along the thousand miles of the St. Lawrence and in isolated garrisons around the Lakes. While she was at death grips with Napoleon, England certainly could not greatly strengthen her Canadian defenses. If a trained army had struck at that moment with concentrated force across the Lake Champlain gap against the anchor fort and base of supplies at Montreal, Ontario and the Lakes would have fallen like autumn leaves, just as they did in 1761 when the British took the city, and there would have been no war on the Lakes themselves. But instead of driving at the center, the Americans dissipated their strength in weak assaults around the edges. These ill-advised tactics brought a series of miserable disasters to the American forces that was unmitigated until Perry won the crucial naval battle of Lake Erie off Sandusky Bay on September 10, 1813.

About the only extenuating reason for the lack of elementary planning in the war was the firm belief of the Secretary of War and General Hull that the men of Canada hated the British as poisonously as the Americans did, and would rise up in revolution when the Americans appeared. In this conviction General Hull marched his army up through Ohio to Detroit, chopping a road through the forests as he went. He had no naval support on Lake Erie, and the British seized the supply ships that attempted to sail from Maumee Bay to Detroit. He crossed over the Detroit River into Ontario, invested the British force, and confidently appealed to the citizens of Ontario in these words: 'The arrival of an army of Friends must be hailed by you with a cordial welcome. You will be emancipated from Tyranny and Oppression and restored to the dignified station of Freemen.'

After all the bad blood and unfriendly dealings between the two shores of the Lakes since the outbreak of the Revolution, the Canadians may be forgiven for their failure to join Hull's banner of liberation. There was nothing in the background relations on the Ontario border to dispel the Canadian suspicion that this was another American attempt to annex the valuable territory between Lake Nipissing and the lower Lakes. The refusal of the people of Ontario to be 'emancipated from tyranny and oppression' seemed to leave poor old General Hull completely befuddled. There is hardly a doubt that he could have occupied the Canadian bank of the Detroit River if he had struck decisively with his full force. But he did not strike. Instead he hesitated in uncertainty and then moved right back across the river to Detroit. That inexplicable action was a cue to the British, and the war was joined on the Great Lakes.

The British moved promptly back across the border to retake the forts which they had evacuated only a few years before. And they retook them almost without challenge from the American garrisons. The Americans had only fifty-seven men under Lieutenant Sinclair up on Mackinac Island when war was declared. The British under Captain Charles Roberts mustered an assortment of regulars, trappers, and Indians at St. Joseph, about a thousand men in all, and made a landing by night on the west shore of Mackinac. They lugged cannon up to the heights commanding the fort, and when daylight came, Sinclair found himself looking up at their muzzles. Resistance was useless. The British had achieved overwhelming conquest of the island. The Americans were unable to counter attack until 1814, and then they were decisively repulsed. The two American warships covering the movement were seized by the British in a daring move, and they were still in firm control of this gateway to Lake Superior and Lake Michigan when the war ended.

The situation at Fort Dearborn was equally critical. The Americans had discovered the strategic value of the site of present Chicago. Captain John Whistler (grandfather of the artist and wit) with a company of soldiers had built Fort Dearborn there in 1803, near the little trading settlement on the Chicago River. Only a small garrison of soldiers and a few white settlers, with their wives and children, about a hundred in all, were there in menaced isolation among hostile Indians when the war began. Hull feared for their safety. He ordered them to leave. They dumped their supply of rum and whiskey into the river, threw their surplus powder and shot after it, and broke up the guns they could not use, all to prevent these dangerous items from falling into the hands of the numerous Indians gathering about the fort. This act inflamed the anger of the Indians. They restrained their wrath and abided their hour. The caravan of ninety-three whites, with the twelve women and twenty children, escorted by the Indians, left the fort on August 15, and began their trek around the foot of Lake Michigan. Among the sand dunes on the Lake shore, just two miles from the fort (now Eighteenth Street, with a monument), the escorting Indians suddenly spread out, surrounded and attacked the train. In the furious battle that immediately followed, forty-three of the soldiers were killed, six women and fourteen children were slaughtered, and the rest taken captive.

On the following morning, August 16, General Hull surrendered Detroit to the British. They had scared him into paralysis. They had seized the supplies which he had sent on in advance to Detroit at the outbreak of the war. Their guns across the Detroit River were within range of the poorly provisioned American fort. And since the British fleet dominated shipping on Lake Erie, they were able to cut Detroit's communication line. Hull thought defense was useless. To the supreme disgust of his subordinate officers, he gave Detroit to the British without firing a shot. He surrendered all his stores and two vessels of our meager Lake Erie marine, a brig and a sloop. For this cowardice Hull was court-martialed. Thus in less than a month, the British were back in all the key western posts, and in firm control of four of the Great Lakes.

The Americans were but little better off at Niagara and on Lake Ontario. Our command in the Niagara sector was rife with bickering. It actually reached the disgraceful pass of generals' accusing each other of cowardice and fighting duels instead of fighting the enemy and getting on with the war. The British met little resistance when they struck across the Niagara River at the village of Buffalo. The citizens fled for their lives up Buffalo Creek, their path lighted by the flames of their burning homes. In their turn, the Americans made a commando raid across Lake Ontario to strike 'Muddy' York (present Toronto). The poorly disciplined soldiers gutted the sorry little village, burned the government buildings, and looted the church, stores, warehouses, and private dwellings. (It is reassuring to record that General Dearborn had forbidden such conduct, and that Commodore Chauncey collected all the books and stolen plate he could find and returned them to Toronto after the war.) In general the raid was unfortunate, though the loss of their stores did not hamper the British when they finally engaged Perry in battle on Lake Erie. But the British, on the other hand, burned the White House in Washington in retaliation for the burning of York. We need not be surprised at the episode reported by A. L. Burt, that only forty years ago in Toronto 'some Canadian boys had a lively altercation with American visitors of their own age, each group crying, "We licked you in 1812!"—so different were the versions they had been taught.'

In spite of Henry Clay's boast and Britain's preoccupation with Napoleon, America was in grave danger of losing back to the mother country at least the entire Great Lakes region and all the Mississippi Valley. The one obstacle was the profile of the Great Lakes and the St. Lawrence River where Niagara Falls and the many rapids and waterfalls walled out the overwhelming British

Atlantic fleet. Naval power on the Great Lakes had to be an independent operation, with shipyards and bases above the rapids and
the Falls; and here in the long run the British were at a disadvantage. The sagacious Iron Duke of Wellington understood this. When
his country asked him to undertake the reconquest of North America, he pointed out that nothing could be done there without control of the Great Lakes; and that would be an undertaking in
which the odds would always lie on the side of America.

Wellington was right. The only important victories of the war
were won on the Lakes: MacDonough's repulse of the British on
Lake Champlain, and Perry's victory on Lake Erie. We are concerned only with Perry. His victory was impossible until September 10, 1813. The British had continued to add to their lake
fleet after the fall of New France in 1763. Between that date and
the end of the War of 1812 they had built twenty-eight ships of
various sizes on Lake Ontario, ranging up to the big 510-ton *Royal
George* (later *Niagara*), built at Kingston in 1809, and manned
by a crew of 200 men. Above the Falls, on Lake Erie, in the shipyards at Navy Island, Detroit, and Amherstburg, they had constructed during the same fifty years twenty schooners, sloops, brigs,
and ships. These included the 400-ton *Queen Charlotte* (which
helped defeat Hull at Detroit) and the 230-ton *Lady Provost*, both
of Amherstburg, 1809 and 1810. Both were in the battle with
Perry on Lake Erie. Several of these twenty ships had been
wrecked or had become obsolete by 1812, but compared with the
insignificant American marine, particularly on Lake Erie, the British
navy on the Lakes was strong. Our efforts at shipbuilding at
Sackets Harbor on Lake Ontario and our skilful seamanship offset
some of our disadvantage below the Falls, but the situation on
Lake Erie was critical.

When Oliver H. Perry took command on Lake Erie, he had to
build enough ships to meet the British lake navy above the Falls
under Commodore Barclay, based chiefly at Malden. In the general darkness of a year of disasters, the building of those ships
was a brilliant accomplishment worthy of the great monument at
Put-in-Bay.

Perry was only twenty-seven years old when he arrived at Erie, Pennsylvania, on March 27, 1813, to supervise the construction of his ships. He was a Rhode Island man of a naval family; his father had been a naval officer in the Revolution; and his twelve-year-old brother was a midshipman on Perry's own flagship in 1813. Oliver had come up through the grades of the service, and had seen action with the fleet in our first war in Tripoli. He knew that the British navy on Lake Erie had to be eliminated before the losses in the west could be regained.

Speed was essential, and speed was attained. Allowing for the circumstances, which included the transport of skilled workmen and supplies over the snow-covered roads from the east, in some cases a five weeks' journey, part way by sled, and the raising and training of seamen and gunners to man the vessels. Perry's men chopped down trees, hewed out boards and timbers, and built ships under the shelter of the long sand arm of Presque Isle. So feverishly did they labor that by July 25 two brigs, the *Lawrence* and the *Niagara,* a schooner and a gunboat, were launched, rigged and equipped ready for service. These ships were reinforced by units built or refitted by Sailing Master Dobbins at Black Rock, and hauled up the Niagara River into Lake Erie by men and oxen; and by the *Caledonia,* which the Americans had captured from the British in a daring night action at Fort Erie. This fleet was assembled at Erie without molestation by the English, though we hesitate to think what Barclay might have done to it as it was being worked across the Presque Isle sandbar if he had chosen to attack. He did not choose to attack, but retired to Amherstburg and Malden. He remained there during the month while Perry sailed up and down Lake Erie, training and preparing for his attack.

The dwindling food supply of the British army in the west at last forced Barclay to venture a voyage down to Fort Erie. He sailed his entire fleet except the *Nancy,* which was up on Lake Huron, from Malden before dawn on September 10. With a fair breeze behind him, he was out in the open waters of Lake Erie by sun up. Perry was waiting at Put-in-Bay, where he kept a con-

STRIFE BETWEEN BROTHERS AND NEIGHBORS

stant lookout for Barclay's fleet. As he saw the white sails in the morning sun, he knew that at last his great moment had come— his chance to engage the entire British fleet in a decisive struggle. He sailed out to meet it. He was forced to beat against the breeze to get out into battle position. Then the breeze died, making it difficult to maneuver into favorable contact. The two fleets, with the destiny of the Lakes awaiting the outcome of their clash in the next few hours, came slowly into battle line under a September sky that was blue and cloudless. Perry had nine ships: 3 brigs, 5 schooners, and a sloop with a total of 54 guns and about 400 effective men. Barclay had six vessels, described in Perry's 'we have met the enemy' victory dispatch as 'two ships, two brigs, one schooner, and one sloop.' They mounted nine more guns than Perry's fleet and had about fifty more effective sailors, though many of them were without training.

Perry placed the 112-ton schooner *Ariel* in the lead, with a second schooner, the *Scorpion*, behind her. His own black-and-yellow banded, 480-ton flagship, the *Lawrence* (a model of it may be seen in the museum at Erie, Pa.), came next, followed by the big *Caledonia* and *Niagara*, the other three schooners, and the little 60-ton sloop, the *Trippe*. Barclay led with his 70-ton *Chippewa*, followed by his big flagship, the *Detroit*, the brig *General Hunter*, the frigate *Queen Charlotte*, and the brig *Lady Provost*. The small sloop *Little Belt* closed the British line. At fifteen minutes before noon the two lines had drawn near enough to fight. The band on the British flagship struck up 'Rule Britannia,' and Barclay opened fire on Perry's *Lawrence* with long-range guns from the *Detroit* and the *Queen Charlotte*. Perry's ship took this fire for ten minutes before the *Lawrence* could get in close enough to reply. But the ship did close in to 250 yards despite the desperate shelling it was receiving, and began to rake the *Detroit* with all its fire power. Three other vessels from time to time got in close enough to support Perry in this central attack. Fighting these small wooden sailing vessels at close range was a fearsome and bloody ordeal. Timbers splintered and shattered, masts and shrouds fell, fires raged, ropes and sails tore and split, and the wounded and dying men screamed on the blood-drenched decks. The three hours and fifteen minutes of action in this battle of Lake Erie were furious and deadly. It lasted until 2:30. By that time both flagships were shambles. The rigging in Perry's ship was shot away, the ship itself could not be maneuvered, its guns were ruined and useless, and most of the crew were killed or wounded. The *Detroit* was equally stricken. Barclay had been hit eight times, sorely wounded, and forced out of action; and his first officer was dying. The smaller boats were almost equally punished. A gun on the advance *Ariel* burst under the strain of firing and killed several men. One of the *Scorpion's* cannon exploded, broke loose, and crashed down a hatchway, killing and wounding gunners and some of the crew below. Perry escaped injury by what miracle we know not.

At this critical moment in the progress of the battle, Perry performed his amazing exploit of crossing in a small boat under British guns from the stricken *Lawrence* to the *Niagara*. He left the ensign flying, but he carried with him his symbolic blue battle flag with the white letters DON'T GIVE UP THE SHIP. He ran this flag up on the mainmast of the *Niagara*, and immediately took that ship in for another half hour of close and furious action. She was supported by the schooners which had fallen behind and had to be worked into firing range with long oars. The crippled British ships could not absorb this final assault. At three o'clock Barclay lowered the *Detroit's* flag and surrendered the entire Lake Erie fleet to Perry. Perry received Barclay's sword in the great chivalric tradition. The wounded were immediately cared for, and the remnants of the two fleets limped slowly back to Put-in-Bay to recuperate.

Perry's victory was complete and overwhelming. In one afternoon his ships and men had ended British sea power on Lake Erie, and had ended, except for a few sporadic clashes, the long era of strife on the Great Lakes. General Harrison followed up Perry's victory by taking Malden, Detroit, and all that region of Old Ontario, from General Proctor. The engagements at Niagara and on Lake Ontario were concluded in the following year, and peace formally returned, with statesmanlike compromises on both sides, on Christmas Eve, 1814.

The two neighbor nations, whose boundaries became fixed at the Great Lakes which each was to share, were convinced that naval warfare on those waters was suicidal. As a wise British officer wrote to his superior in 1815, 'The preservation of Canada by means of a naval force on the lakes will, in my opinion, be an endless, if not futile undertaking.' In 1818 the Great Lakes were forever neutralized by the Rush-Bagot gentleman's agreement. It has been faithfully observed in letter and spirit by Canada and the United States. The only armed vessels on those waters are some old training ships and those built in World War II for service on the Atlantic convoy lanes and in the Pacific for the mutual protection of both countries. The old forts, relics of an era of distrust nearly a century and a half outlived, have decayed or been turned into museum pieces. And where once the fleets sailed to prevent the entrance of one people into the domain of the other there are now eight magnificent international bridges and a tunnel linking them in amity at the key points on the Lakes: The Thousand Islands, the Roosevelt at Cornwall, the Lewiston-Queenston, the Lower Arch at Niagara, the Peace Bridge at Buffalo-Fort Erie, the Ambassador at Detroit, the Blue Water at Sarnia, and the Detroit-Windsor Tunnel.

Part III   POSSESSION

By blue Ontario's shore,
As I mused of these warlike days and of peace
    return'd, and the dead that return no more,
A Phantom gigantic superb, with stern visage ac-
    costed me,
Chant me the poem, it said, *that comes from the
    soul of America, chant me the carol of victory . . .*
*And sing me before you go the song of the throes
    of Democracy.*

                              WALT WHITMAN.

((((XX))))

Lake Towns and Steamships

THE warlike days were ended at last. Peace and permanent neutrality had returned to the Great Lakes. It was like the quick escape of spring bursting full blown from the arms of winter at Montreal, where over night the blanket of snow evaporates, the children put away their sleds and climb Mount Royal in warm sun to pick flowers. We look down once more upon this vast waterway at the end of its long winter of strife, at the beginning of its season of seed time and harvest in 1818. The scene has altered somewhat since we last surveyed it. Three wars, with brief interludes of armistice, had made the colonies and the states lake-conscious. The wars had been world wars; the booming of guns in the conflicts in Europe and on her bordering seas was echoed and relayed over these waters deep in the heart of America. The eyes of the world were on the fabulous region of the Lakes. News of their wonders was already spreading from feudal farm to peasant village, from Norway and Sweden and Finland, to farthest Calabria and Sicily. Soon these peoples would be streaming across the communication lines of Perry's Lake Erie fleet. Dreams of these lakes as a Northwest Passage faded away. Who cared about a mere passage when squarely on the legendary route lay more wealth for the taking than was ever dreamed of in Cathay? Wise men laid plans to exploit it.

British and American sailing ships dotted the blue waters of Lake Ontario and Lake Erie with their masts of white canvas in 1818. A few canoes still labored up and down the Ottawa and over Lake Nipissing, but that ancient route had become obsolete with the passing of the French regime, the conquest of the Indians south of the Lakes, and the era of ships that came in with the wars.

173

The British had abandoned it to the voyageurs, the Indians, and the wilderness after one last desperate attempt and failure to use it to reinforce their garrisons at Mackinaw and Malden after Perry's victory in the closing year of the war. Ontario's future lay on its great lakes, not on its obstructed northern rivers. Her towns sprang up on Lake Ontario and down the St. Lawrence as far as the first rapids. We see, with one sweep of the eye, the little Canadian villages planting firm roots at Prescott on the north shore of the waterway; around the unused fort at Kingston; at Toronto, now rapidly rising out of the burned and gutted ruins of Muddy York; at Niagara and Fort Erie at each end of the river. We see on the American side the cluster of houses and wharves at Ogdensburg, opposite Prescott, the thriving bay and shipyard at Sackets Harbor; and the busy, growing village around the docks at Oswego. A few miles back on the ancient beach ridge, Colonel Nathaniel Rochester and friends from Maryland have taken up a hundred-acre tract at the falls of the Genesee River, where the rapids will turn their millwheels. Now, in 1818, the Colonel himself is moving in to live on his land, where the big city that bears his name will rise and spread down the river to the Lake Ontario shore.

People and goods were on the move around this lake. Its waters were their roads, and they needed ships. Sailing ships were beautiful and relatively cheap; they were also slow, hazardous, and dependent upon the vagaries of lake winds. Merchants gathered around their wharves and warehouses to talk about the miracle of steam. Steamboats were already solving the problem of cheap mass transportation in the Hudson and the Mississippi, and they were now puffing up and down the American rivers. Was not this new invention the key also to transportation on these expansive lake waterways? Both the Canadians and the Americans rushed into the race to find the answer and profit by it.

Over at Kingston the seven gentlemen of the firm of Forsyth, Kirby, Marsh, Markland, Mitchell, Herchmer, and Yeoman met in the company office with their neighbor Henry Murney to view with alarm the fact 'that Lake Ontario becomes a nursery for American seamen, and that the marine interest of the country cannot increase while such carrying trade is principally carried in foreign vessels.' These Canadian shippers raised £12,000 to build a steamship that would capture their share of the Lake Ontario trade. The ship was launched on September 7, 1816, and appropriately christened the *Frontenac*. This first steamship on the Lakes was a trim and graceful vessel of 700 tons. She was 170 feet long, 32 feet wide at the beam, and carried 3 tall masts and a funnel. Her engines of fifty horsepower were brought over the Atlantic from Birmingham, and hauled at great expense in time and money around the various rapids in the St. Lawrence. (Canals would soon have to be built around those obstructions!) She did a good business between Prescott and Niagara, with the intermediate villages as ports of call and an occasional stop at Oswego on the American side.

The Americans were not to be outdone. Over at Sackets Harbor, Smyth, Lusher, and Company hurried the construction of the *Ontario*, a fine 220-ton steamer. It was launched just six months after the *Frontenac*. Through the season of 1817 the thin bluish wood-smoke plumes of these two rivals drifted over the white caps on Lake Ontario and cast a shadow under the morning sunshine. People gathered at the wharves to wonder at these strange ships with a smokestack in their rigging and a paddle box on each side.

We shift our view farther west above the barrier of the Niagara escarpment to Lake Erie. Shipwrights are hammering and sawing on the ways at Black Rock in the fast upper Niagara River current. More than a score of Lake Erie sailing vessels put in here and worked out again, usually with some difficulty against the prevailing wind. Near-by Buffalo was an ambitious suburb of Black Rock, a few houses on low, flat, ox-bowing Buffalo Creek. It was rebuilding after the war. Its plan called for broad streets running off from a central hub after the design just approved by Jefferson for the National Capital. As a port and maritime center it was still insignificant in 1818. But on the preceding Fourth of July Governor De Witt Clinton had ceremoniously dug up a shovelful of earth to start the digging of the Erie Canal, which would link the Lakes with the Hudson and the Atlantic. The scoffers called it, derisively,

'Clinton's Ditch'; but the men of Buffalo were already laying big plans to profit by this 352 mile bridge to the ocean.

The sailing ships needed from five days to a week to cross Lake Erie from Buffalo to Detroit. The farms and villages of Old Ontario had been ravaged by the war, and the north shore was still rather barren. The ships called at the healthy little villages springing into life on the southern shore before beating up the Detroit River to the group of houses reaching out from the forts at Detroit and Malden. The ships were very busy on this lake in 1818. People were making their way in great numbers to the westlands on the lake shore. Ever since Mad Anthony Wayne had defeated the Indians on the Maumee near Toledo at the battle of Fallen Timbers in 1794, the seaboard states had been sending a stream of settlers into the Ohio Valley. The Ohio River was their main wilderness road. But Ohio had enough people in it to become a state in 1802, and nearly three-fourths of Ohio's northern border was the shoreline of Lake Erie. Moreover, that shoreline all the way to Sandusky, and the rich adjoining land in the Erie drainage bowl as far south as Akron and Youngstown, belonged to Connecticut. This part of Ohio was reserved by that state when it gave over its western lands to the new Federal Government in 1786. This famous region, still known as the Western Reserve, fronted on Lake Erie and looked to that lake for transport.

Tacked on to this lake tract was still more Connecticut property, a half-million acres in Erie and Huron Counties known to this day as 'The Firelands.' The land was granted to Connecticut people, 1,870 of them, whose houses had been fired and their property damaged or destroyed by Tory raids in the Revolution. Lake Erie was, therefore, a natural lure for enterprising citizens from Connecticut. They began energetically to clear away the forests to make room for those pretty little New England villages which distinguish the region along Lake Erie and its short tributary streams, and so strikingly duplicate the towns on the Connecticut coast. Ashtabula, with its superb harbor, was first settled in 1796; Lorain, almost equally well-favored, was founded in 1807, and was building lake boats in its shipyards in 1819; Vermilion on its river was settled in 1808; Huron on its beautiful little stream was founded in 1805; and Nowalk and Milan farther upstream in the Firelands were laid out in New England fashion in 1816.

Toledo was not yet born; it had to await the digging of the Miami-Erie Canal and the beginning of Lake traffic. But half way across the Western Reserve on Lake Erie at the mouth of the Cuyahoga River, where Major Roberts had met Chief Pontiac, the settlement planted by General Moses Cleaveland in 1796 was struggling along toward prosperity and dominance. It was being steadily augmented by new families from the East. They erected log houses on the river bank, eighty feet above the surface of the lake, within sound of the hammering and sawing in the busy shipyards. Since 1804, bateaux and sailing boats had been built here and launched for the growing Lake Erie trade. The village now awaited only the new interconnecting waterways—the Erie Canal and the Ohio-Erie—to link it with the East and South. Then it would become the metropolis of Lake Erie.

Out west Detroit, despite its favored setting on its river, was marking time. Fire had completely destroyed it back in 1805, but that was a blessing instead of a calamity. The old stockade and village had become a mangy ensemble that only flames could improve. It was rebuilt over a farsighted plan. But it did not immediately become a settling place for men looking for new permanent homes for their families. For some strange reason, jaundiced-eyed Surveyor-General Tiffin and his operatives had stigmatized and blackened the character of that village and its hinterland. He reported officially in 1815 that the land was swampy and sandy, with scarcely one acre in a thousand fit for cultivation. His slander helped detour hordes of immigrants away from Detroit and send them thronging down the Ohio River. Nonetheless, the village that was to become the industrial wonder-city of the world held its own as an important fort, and a shipbuilding and trading center for the Upper Lakes. And it was, of course, the western port of the rapidly increasing Lake Erie traffic.

The villages of Old Ontario helped to swell the volume. Maitland, Selkirk and Dover were the outlets for the region east of

Long Point. Port Stanley served St. Thomas and the mid-lake area, and Chatham sent its small vessels down the Thames to Lake St. Clair and Detroit. Farms already lined the Detroit and St. Clair Rivers and reached back in thin strips from the water front. West and north from Detroit, Lake Huron, Lake Michigan, and Lake Superior washed desolate shores whose loneliness was broken only by a few forts and trading posts—Mackinac, St. Joseph, Dearborn, and the Sault.

This was the general picture of the Lakes in 1818, when the Lake Erie Steamboat Company of Buffalo built and launched at Black Rock the third steamboat on the Lakes and the first on Lake Erie waters. She was the big 135-foot-long, 32-foot-beamed *Walk-in-the-Water*. A 30-foot smoke stack jutted up beside her two proud masts that carried enough sail to speed her along when the wind was favorable. Her two 15-foot paddlewheels could skim her passengers across the lake from Buffalo to Detroit in a day and a half for $18.00 cabin or $7.00 steerage.

As the first of her kind, and the forerunner of the era of steam and steel that was to make the Erie shore one of the wealthiest and busiest water fronts in the world, the *Walk-in-the-Water* captivates the imagination and holds our interest on her structure and her brief but adventurous life on the lake. Her design was experimental. The first steamboats were built for river traffic on the calm Hudson and the smooth-flowing Ohio. No storms or high seas had to be reckoned with. The timbers could be light. But the lakes were broad and often wind-swept, and the gales could kick up waves as furious and battering as the ocean itself. The builders did not always understand this; Noah Brown, builder of *Walk-in-the-Water*, had no table of stresses on stormy Lake Erie. He constructed his ship lightly for fair weather, not reckoning with the gales that would beat her to pieces three years later. She looked fit enough on that August morning when, with her one vertical engine puffing and her paddles clawing at the Niagara current, she was towed upstream by twenty yoke of oxen (a 'horned breeze' in sailor jargon) into Lake Erie. Her huge paddlewheels were encased in a half circle of wood box, ornamented with the ship's name, that rose about nine feet above the deck. The smokestack was forward between the masts.

Stripped of her anomalous paddlewheels and smokestack, however, she would have been taken for a graceful early model of the new, fast clippers that the New Englanders were developing for express service on the seven seas. Her prow was thin and pointed, her stern high, sweeping gently upward and overhanging the rudder. Her hull was eight and a half feet deep. She could not enter the shallow Buffalo harbor, or the Cuyahoga River; she stood elegantly off shore and was tended by small boats. Her cabins, forward for gentlemen, aft for ladies, carried twenty-nine passengers on this first run, though she was equipped to accommodate a list of one hundred. Her four-pound cannon on the forward deck served for a whistle. A megaphone at the mouth of her captain, who bore the name of Job Fish, was the forerunner of the modern bell signals to the engine room.

This majestic steamship left Buffalo at 1:00 p.m. on August 23. She made her maiden voyage across the lake in forty-four hours and ten minutes, according to the log and Captain Fish's turnip watch. She had taken plenty of time out to load on firewood and to be admired at Dunkirk, Erie, Cleveland, and Sandusky as she lay at anchor off shore. She was the unbelievable wonder of the lake to the wilderness folk who gathered at the villages to see her chug by. She reached the Detroit River just as darkness fell on the evening of August 25. She anchored there for the night in order to make her triumphal run past the gaping populace of Detroit in daylight. Prominent citizens boarded her at Fighting Island, like one of Grover Whalen's parties meeting celebrities coming into New York in the gala 1920's. In the bright morning light of August 24, the handsome steamer sailed up to the new wharf that had just been built out from the river bank across the shallow water to the edge of the channel, where the necessary ten-foot draft could be had to receive her. The wharf and its runway were crowded with spectators. They watched the marvel ship as she was maneuvered by the orders of Captain Job Fish, who stood on the paddlebox and shouted through his megaphone. They felt the wharf shake and the piles give as the *Walk-in-the-Water* banged roughly along-side and was finally made fast by her lines.

This first run of a steamboat on Lake Erie was a great financial and navigational success. For three years the *Walk-in-the-Water* sailed back and forth across Lake Erie from Black Rock to Detroit, with an occasional voyage up the St. Clair and Lake Huron to Michilimackinac. In the late afternoon of October 30, 1821, she sailed from Buffalo with a distinguished list of passengers. The weather was dirty. The waves grew higher and fiercer as she steamed slowly westward against the wind. She made little head-way. The storm increased in ferocity. It lashed the lake and beat against the ship. Her comparatively frail construction began to weaken under the battering of the waves. Her timbers trembled and the seams loosened. She could not go on. Captain Jedediah Rogers finally put her about and headed back toward Buffalo. In the rain and the darkness he lost his bearings. He did not know where he was; water was pouring into the hull and he was afraid to go on. So he dropped three anchors to hold his position, and started the pumps, hoping to last out until morning. But the waves tossed the ship about like a corked bottle, breaking up dishes, bat-tering the passengers, and hammering more seams open. Water poured in faster than the pumps could handle it. Captain Rogers was now certain that if she stayed where she was, the ship would sink in deep water before morning. He cut her loose from the anchors and let her run toward the shore. She grounded well off shore on a sandbar, twelve miles from Buffalo. She settled on her side and the waves washed over her. Sailors fought their way ashore with a hawser and secured it to a tree as a life line for the passengers. They were worked ashore in a small boat, and all were saved. Haggard and storm-shocked, they were taken back to Buf-falo in carriages. Fortunately Mr. J. D. Mattheis visited the scene of the disaster and made a sketch of the grounded ship before she broke up. It preserves for us the 1821 equivalent of a photograph or news reel of this first steamship on Lake Erie.

The ship, of course, was a total wreck, except for the engine, which was a precious piece of machinery in 1821. A salvage crew

Grain elevators overlooking Buffalo Harbor. *Photograph by Tom Peck.*

An inboard motor boat used in commercial fishing, Lake Superior. *Photograph by Erling Larsen. Courtesy of Frederic Lewis.*

removed it from the broken ship. It was placed in the new *Superior*, which in the following season took the place of the *Walk-in-the-Water*. It drove that ship over choppy Lake Erie between Detroit and Buffalo, and occasionally on the Upper Lakes, for more than a decade. In 1824 the *Henry Clay* was launched and went into service on Lake Erie. These two steamers provided four-day passenger service between Buffalo and Detroit, and were the forerunners of the fleet of ships that would soon be scurrying back and forth over this busy shipping lane.

XXI

Waterways to the Great Lakes

GREELEY's 'Go West, young man,' meant New York's Mohawk Valley, not the corn fields of Illinois or the grazing ranges of Wyoming. With all its stirring action, its sailing ships and new steamboats, the region of the Lakes, as we have seen, was still sparsely settled when the *Walk-in-the-Water* foundered in the waves and the *Superior* docked at Detroit. The great mass of restless, roving Americans, hunting fortune and the good life, were still streaming westward over other routes. The first migration had gone around the Cumberland Mountains, keeping to the valleys south of their forested wall, down the Clinch River and up into Kentucky from the south. The second wave at the turn of the new century crossed the mountains of Pennsylvania to Pittsburgh and drifted down the Ohio River in every possible contrivance that would float—from a few logs lashed together to hold a cow, a chicken coop, and a family, to the noisy new steamboats skirting the undredged sandbars opposite Wheeling. The Ohio River, not Lake Erie and Lake Michigan, was then the center of population. When Illinois was admitted to the Union in 1818, her people looked to the river as their life line. Chicago was a desolate and dangerous military outpost in what was publicized as a flat, sterile, and unhealthy region.

But the population was moving steadily northward. Wise, lake-minded men saw the day coming when the Lakes would supersede the Ohio River as the center of shipping and industry, and they laid plans to hasten it and to profit by it. They saw the graceful yellow-masted schooners like the *Nancy*, with their square topsails and their fore-and-aft rigged fore- and mainsails, making good way into Buffalo before a Lake Erie west-northwest wind. They watched the *Walk-in-the-Water*, then the *Superior*, and the *Henry*

Clay get up steam and put out against the wind for a two-day run up to Detroit. They knew that with only a little time and much hard work these Lakes would become the main life artery of America and Canada.

Lack of navigable outlets and inlets to and from the Atlantic were all that now stood between the Great Lakes and their destiny. Until they could be connected with the sea, they must remain isolated inland waters. For they still lay with all their potential shipping lanes high behind Niagara, ridged off from the Ohio-Mississippi by the upturned rim of their basins, and cut off from the North Atlantic by the many rapids on the upper St. Lawrence. Clearly these barriers must be overcome. Canals, the empire-building Frenchmen had said two centuries ago. Canals, the big businessman said again after the War of 1812. Let us dig canals.

The era of canal digging began.

The New Yorkers led the way, backed by their Governor De Witt Clinton. The unimaginative, the faint-hearted scoffed. How could you build a 363-mile canal through all that Mohawk wilderness, over all those 586 feet of barriers, across all those streams, and through those rock canyons, from the Hudson River to Lake Erie? How could the unheard-of sum of eleven million dollars be raised to pay for it? Or how could the debt be paid once it was incurred? 'Clinton's Big Ditch' was another folly.

Vision, toil, and perseverance made the folly a triumph. Back of it all, of course, was a realistic Yankee trading sense. New York entrepreneurs saw the opportunity of draining off the profitable commerce from Lake Erie into the Mohawk and Hudson Valleys and out through the port of New York. Why let it go down the St. Lawrence? Moreover, this new route was ice-free for a longer period each year than the northeastward flowing river. The canal was smart business.

In 1816-25, the digging, or building, of that canal was a near miracle. The engineers did not know how to control and use nature's own rivers and creeks. They had to dig a completely new channel. There were no steam shovels to gouge out a car load of rock and dirt at a scoop; that era would come out of the Lakes

themselves when the canals were dug to them. Now it must be
done by Irish muscle with picks and shovels and wheelbarrows.
Thousands of men sweated in that ditch—a few Yankees from the
rocky farms of Vermont, a number of Negroes who dropped with
malaria, but mostly the 'bog-trotting' Irish, who left their famine-
ravaged island in droves and sailed to this valley to battle rock,
sand, mud, and mosquitoes in the path of the ditch. These hard-
working, hard-drinking Irishman could move the ditch forward
about 16 feet per man each week. Scores of them died in the
swamps from the fever. Scores died from accident and exposure.
Many were maimed or injured in blasts, in landslides, and in the
wild berserk brawls on Saturday nights when they took their
relaxation from kegs of frontier whiskey. But the ditch lengthened
on, 40 feet wide and 4 feet deep, between the five long stakes
driven by the surveyors through the wilderness toward the shim-
mering lake. Simultaneously in three sections it crawled forward
between Albany and Rome, from Syracuse to Montezuma, and on
to Buffalo. It went through the gorge at Little Falls on a shelf
exploded from the rocks and protected by a wall lifted up 30 feet
from the bed of the Mohawk River. It hurried across the 69-mile
'Long level' from Utica to Syracuse, where no locks were needed.
It climbed up above the boggy Cayuga marshes on a huge fill,
and awed spectators were soon to see water flowing and boats
passing at a height of 72 feet above them. It crossed over the
Genesee River on an aqueduct. It burst through hills at Lockport
in a 20-foot cut and by ten locks in two flights of five each that
lifted and lowered the boats across the remaining 60-foot barrier.

There was sharp controversy over the terminal point at Lake
Erie. Black Rock, center of shipbuilding, and with a good port,
wanted it, but Black Rock (now a portion of Buffalo and the
terminus for the Barge Canal) was about three miles down the
Niagara and ships usually had to be towed against the wind up
to the free waters of the lake. Buffalo, on the other hand, had no
usable harbor, because of the big sandbar that lay across the lake
entrance at the mouth of Buffalo Creek. The ambitious Buffalo
citizens, however, were undaunted. They organized, raised money,

cleared away the barrier, and became the entrance port. By October 26, 1825, the ditch was dug, water flowed through it, the boats were ready, and the ceremony of opening it to traffic began.

De Witt Clinton started the pageant. It was all in the exuberant manner of the young nation feeling itself grow. The Governor and his distinguished entourage marched from the Buffalo courthouse and went aboard the brand-new cedar-timbered *Seneca Chief*, tied up at the head of the canal. From this rostrum he spoke the proper words in an address to the happy multitude. They took aboard two kegs of ceremonial Lake Erie water, they fired off a cannon, a double span of gray horses bent their necks to the towrope, and the *Seneca Chief* began the historic voyage by water from Lake Erie to the Atlantic port of New York. All along the route were men and cannon to relay the news that the boats were coming, and within just one hour and thirty minutes New York knew that De Witt Clinton had left Buffalo on the Erie Canal.

Followed by five other boats, the *Seneca Chief* was towed through 83 locks and over 18 aqueducts. The procession reached Albany on the sixth day. All along the route there had been pageantry, band playing, receptions, and speech making at the important villages where the excited crowds had gathered at the basins to see the boats come in. The *Seneca Chief* was in the lead bearing Governor Clinton, and the *Noah's Ark* in the rear displaying a bear, two eagles, two fawns, two Indian lads, and varieties of lake fish. A few towns came to mourn because the canal had passed them by and given their trade to rivals. But the prevailing spirit was one of awe and rejoicing. It was enough to make the frontier populace gasp to see these boats, towed by horses and mules, float right across the Genesee River itself in a man-made river on a bridge high above the natural river channel. It was an equal marvel to see them lifted and lowered from one level to another at the various locks. From Albany, Clinton's boat was towed down the Hudson to New York by steamboat. And there, amid wild celebrations, the Governor poured out the Erie water from his kegs to marry the Lake to the Ocean. Phials from storied rivers of the world—the Thames, the Seine, the Elbe, the Rhine, the Nile,

the Ganges, the Orinoco—were added, and the first through waterway across the new nation into the vast heart of the continent
was officially opened. Returning boats brought Atlantic salt water
to be poured into Lake Erie to complete the double ring ceremony.

The pageantry over, commerce began to flow, and the country
boomed. Captain Samuel Ward promptly pointed the way toward
the future of the Lakes by sending his tiny, schooner-rigged *St.
Clair* from Detroit down to Buffalo. He sailed her into the new
harbor, where the sandbar had been cleared away; and then, instead of transhipping his cargo to a canal boat, he lowered the
St. Clair's masts so they would clear the bridges, and proceeded
under tow right on across New York to Albany, and sailed again
down the Hudson. It was the first through voyage from the Lakes
to the sea. The cost of moving freight from Lake Erie to New
York harbor dropped from $120 a ton to $4.

Almost every little town along the route began to build canal
boats. The boats multiplied until every basin swarmed with them.
Soon 4,000 of them were hurrying back and forth across the route
once traveled only by moccasin-footed Iroquois. Twenty thousand boats a season would pass above the Cayuga marshes, dragged
along by mules under the whips of underprivileged little boys
(5,000 of them) who got $10 a month for their job. Night and day,
on the average of one every seventeen minutes, the boats dropped
through the locks at Schenectady, steersmen and deckhands jostling and fighting for priority at the gates. Fast packets hurried
by, each year carrying more and more emigrants, men, women
and children, jammed on their decks and joining in the great mass
migration of Europe and the Atlantic seaboard to exploit the fabulous region laid open by the canal. The packets would glide them
comfortably through the wilderness, bed them, and board them, for
four cents a mile. Freight boats would slacken and drop their tow
lines to let the passenger boats hurry by. If they didn't give way,
a sharp scythe-like blade at the bow of the passenger boat might
snip their towropes for them.

The original canal, of course, was immediately outgrown. Its
dimensions as opened were far too small for this rush of boats and

goods that glutted and swamped it. It could take only 30-ton boats with drafts under 4 feet. Ten years after the opening the canal had completely liquidated its debts and work was immediately begun to enlarge and deepen it to 7 feet. The improvements went on through the years. By the time of the Civil War it could accommodate 240-ton canallers and carry them over the creeks and rivers on limestone aqueducts so wonderful to behold that people came to view them as they did Niagara Falls. The one over Schoharie Creek a few miles west of Schenectady was 624 feet long, with 13 piers to hold up the water trough, and 14 arches to bear the tow path and strengthen the piers. It still stands as archaic as a Roman aqueduct—and as impressive. But the canal itself is still very much alive. It was rebuilt and reopened in 1916, a hundred years after its first beginnings, with 36 locks, each 328 feet long, 45 feet wide, and 12 feet deep, and a 339-mile-long channel, 123 feet wide on the waterline and also 12 feet in depth.

The Canadians did not sit idly by in their Ontario, St. Lawrence ports while New York drained away the commerce from the Upper Lakes. They had plans and visions of their own. The Niagara portage was a traditional route, well worn by Indians and voyageurs carrying canoes and fur down its long incline and sharp sides. The time had obviously come to supplant it with a canal that could compete with the Erie. The Canadians surveyed the route from Port Dalhousie on Lake Ontario, along Twelve Mile Creek back to the escarpment, up to the summit, down the Chippewa or Welland River and up the Niagara River. Clearly all the advantages did not lie with the New Yorkers. Lake Erie was only 25 miles from Lake Ontario, while Buffalo was 363 miles from Albany. Once around the Falls, ships could sail with the wind down the lake; barges had to be towed at mule pace down the canal. So the Canadians formed the Welland Company in 1824, and began digging in 1825 as the Erie swung open to traffic. Before the ice closed in on the navigating season of 1829, on November 27 to be exact, a Canadian schooner christened *Annie and Jane* made the first ceremonial passage up the canal. It was less extravagant than the American pageant, as befitted the British on the other side of the lake, but it had its own solemnity. A schooner-rigged ship was a graceful object on the Great Lakes. *Annie and Jane* was especially handsome as she floated into the first of the locks and secured. Her tall spars pointed high above the new wooden gates that closed behind her, and they did not have to be lowered for canal bridges. The water rushing into the lock quickly lifted her deck above the heads of the cheering spectators. The upper gates opened and she moved on into the next level. Again the gates closed and the *Annie and Jane*, now followed by an American ship, the *R. H. Boughton*, rose again to the third level. So, step by step, she climbed the 325 feet through the 40 timbered locks up to Port Robinson. There she was taken in tow by the 'horned breeze' of yoked oxen and pulled down the Welland and up the Niagara until she could spread her canvas free to the Lake Erie winds. She sailed over to Buffalo, traded cargo, and returned the following day, descending the steps of the Welland locks as easily as she had climbed them. The days of laborious portaging were over, and Canada was still in the competition.

The Welland-Niagara route soon proved itself unsatisfactory and in 1831-3 the canal was extended from Port Robinson up to Port Colborne on Lake Erie. In its new location it handled the through traffic for over half a century. It was supplanted in 1887 by a new system that reduced the number of locks to 25, enlarged them to 270 by 45 feet, and deepened them to 14 feet. It has been further improved by the big Welland Ship Canal, which was formally opened on August 6, 1932. Great Lakes men were now canal minded. The fever swept down the St. Lawrence and out through the western Lake Country, and a digging boom was on to tap the wide waterways with more canals at strategic points.

Down at the Lachine Rapids there had long been a need for a canal for the big canoe fleets and the bateaux that came down to Montreal. Much work had already been done to clear the rocks from the north bank of the St. Lawrence so that boats could be towed up the Rapids. But a serviceable canal was now urgent, and in 1818 a company was formed to construct it. While the sweating, bare-backed Irishmen were taking the Erie over the

Cayuga marshes, the Canadians were building nearly nine miles of canal with seven locks around the foaming St. Lawrence barrier. It, too, was opened to traffic in 1825. Like the other canals it was shallow, and could only take boats up to 4½-feet draft. It also had to be deepened to 9 feet in the busy 1840's and enlarged again in 1885 to its present size with five locks, each 270 feet long, 45 feet wide, and 14 feet deep. It is crowded with traffic, and the ships, built to the last inch limit of its width, fit so snugly in the locks that they scrape its sides. Some steamers under skilled captains still shoot the rapids, but it is hazardous business and ships occasionally get out of hand and smash on the rocks.

Canals were also dug in the 1840 boom years around the Long Sault Rapids in the St. Lawrence—the 11-mile-long Cornwall Canal; and at Farran's Point, Rapide Plat, and Galops—the Williamsburg Canals, over 26 miles long including the usable strips of the St. Lawrence River itself. This system overcame the last hazards on the direct route from Lake Erie to the Atlantic via Montreal and Quebec.

Meanwhile other outlets were being hastily constructed to connect the Lakes with the Ohio-Mississippi chain of natural waterways. If a canal could be dug across New York, how much easier it would be to build others across the corner of western Pennsylvania, or carry them through the compact, growing state of Ohio, or over the low Lake Erie watershed to Indiana, or down the Chicago River to the Illinois—or wherever they might be needed. Rich farmlands languished in wilderness isolation along these routes; fat hogs and bumper grain crops needed only a market outlet to bring prosperity and more people into the new states. Indians had passed quickly up and down the water courses across Ohio, Indiana, and Illinois from the great river to the Lakes over these flat valleys. Their canoe-and-portage routes were natural locations for canal systems.

Ohio rushed forward with plans to build a thousand miles of canals to link her thriving Ohio River trade with the Lakes. Governor De Witt Clinton himself came out to the opening ceremonies in the canal wonder-year of 1825. He lifted a spadeful of earth near

Newark to start the construction of the Ohio-Erie Canal. It ran
from Cleveland over the ridge at Akron and down the fertile Scioto
River Valley to join the Ohio at Portsmouth. Then he went on over
to Middletown on the Great Miami River and performed the same
ritual for the Miami-Erie. It linked first Dayton, and later Toledo
on the Maumee, with thriving Cincinnati, the Queen City of the
West, as that big supply center was already known. By 1832 both
canals were swarming with traffic and far-seeing eyes were already
turning from the river towns to the new and growing lakeport
cities, where boats laden with grain and timber, flour and whiskey
crowded the wharves and basins. New York and New Orleans—
both were now the seaport towns for the Lakes and the Middle
West.

Down across Indiana from Toledo also went the Wabash and
Erie Canal, and by 1843 canal boats filled with produce from
Indiana began to arrive from Lafayette at the Toledo port—the
joint terminus for the Miami and the Wabash-Erie canals.

Out at Chicago the Illinois and Michigan Canal was pushed
forward to connect Lake Michigan with New Orleans. In times
of high water, as we have already seen, canoes could pass over
this low watershed between the Chicago and the Des Plaines
Rivers without portage. Joliet had been of the opinion that a mile-
long canal would link the two streams. But La Salle toiled across
that route in a drier season. He saw that a canal must of necessity run the whole distance of the portage. He was right. The canal
was opened to traffic in 1848 and it was nearly a hundred miles
long.

Seven major outlets now were available to the Great Lakes:
six of them tapped Lake Erie—around the Falls by the Welland
Canal, down through New York from Buffalo by the Erie, or down
to the Ohio River from Erie, Pa., Cleveland, or from Toledo across
Ohio or Indiana. Only one barrier remained in the vast lake and
canal waterway system, and that was the 19-foot falls in the St.
Mary's River between Lake Superior and Lake Huron. An active
trading post had grown up at Sault Ste. Marie by the portage
where the fur caravans were carried round the falls. As the fur

trade was driven farther back into the west and the Lake Superior hinterland, the volume of traffic and the increasing size of the bateaux justified a canal that would save all the time and trouble of unloading and reloading for so short an obstruction. So in 1797 the Northwest Fur Company, rival to the smart Hudson's Bay Company outfit, dug a short canal with timbered flume 300 feet long and a single lock only 39 feet long with a lift of 9 feet on the Canadian side of the river. The other 10-foot drop could be negotiated by the boats without too much danger.

This small utility was blown up by our American troops who raided the region in 1814 during the unfortunate war with England. It was replaced forty years later, long after the fur trade was gone, when the iron ore and copper mines of the Lake Superior shore made new locks inevitable. We shall consider that new and fabulous era a little later on. In the meantime we see the rushing St. Mary's River, unharnessed, abiding its destiny as the busiest by far of all the canals and locks in the whole wide world. Pending that day, the American Fur Company built a tramroad on the Michigan side of the river with horse-drawn cars to haul the goods down to the Lake Huron level. A few ships, both schooners and steamers, were actually pulled up out of the water and dragged across the Sault to sail on Lake Superior. And the growing commerce on the Lakes made all this construction and effort profitable.

XXII

Fur

THE sound of steamboats chugging across Lake Erie and the shouts of busy men on the canals and wharves and in the ship-yards did not disturb the primeval stillness of the Upper Lakes. During the decade of the 1820's, when the modern industrial pattern of the Lakes was first designed, the ancient fur trade of the great Northwest was just reaching its spectacular zenith. In retrospect, at least, the era of fur was one of the most adventuresome cycles of activity so far seen in the Great Lakes region. It is time to examine that drama of the fur trade before the steamboats and sailing ships carry enough immigrants into the hunting grounds to cut off the timber, drain the swamps, and scatter the pelt-bearing animals into the Far North.

To men of our day, the Great Lakes are synonymous with steel and wheat, with giant ore and grain freighters floating down the dredged channels of the St. Mary's River one behind the other only about fifteen minutes apart. But for over two hundred long and battle-scarred years, fur and not ore or grain was the treasure of the New World for which men toiled and froze and starved and died. The quest for fur caused shrewd Frenchmen at Paris and St. Malo to organize companies, recruit explorers and colonists, outfit ships, and send them to the American wilderness. The fur trade kept these men huddled under the rock at Quebec through bitter winters of ice and snow and the freezing gales that howled down upon them. Fur kept the wavering French capitalists interested in the Lake country. Desire for fur in ever larger quantities drove Frenchmen farther and farther into the bush around the Lakes. Fur was the cargo of the *Griffon* with which La Salle hoped to pay off his debts and reap a handsome profit. And the lure of fur led the English from the south into conflict with the French on the north.

In Champlain's day, as we have seen, the Indians brought their season's catch of fur down the canoe-and-portage route to Montreal, Three Rivers, and Quebec to trade with the French merchants whose ships lay at anchor in the little settlement harbors. That scheme worked well for many years for both French and Indians. Fur was the only cash crop of the natives of the Great Lakes. It was the one product they could exchange for the marvels brought over from France in the trading ships. They were wide-eyed and covetous as children before the goods piled up on the deck, on the wharf, or in the trading shacks. They had little idea of the relative value of furs when they began to trade them for kettles, knives, guns, and tin cups; for chiefs' coats, calico, scarlet cloth, and vermilion; for ornamented brass rings, silver armbands, wristbands, breast broaches, and earwheels; for buttons, handkerchiefs, and moccasin awls; and for the scores of other desirable wonders, including, above all, the potent mystery of gin, rum, and whiskey.

For these compensations the Indians hunted and trapped through the long severe winters to acquire a bartering stock of peltry. They went up the Fox, the St. Croix, and the Pigeon; they crossed over to the Illinois and the Wisconsin; they hunted at the waterfalls of the Upper Peninsula; in the quiet streams, around the lakes and ponds, through the forests and across the prairie, where beaver, otter, muskrats, mink, fox, deer, and other fur-bearing animals lived and flourished before the white settlers came. They set crude traps of their own devising, or the ingenious steel traps which they got on credit from the traders, mortgaging the winter and spring catch in advance to pay for them. They found the neat ponds where the beaver had gnawed down trees, engineered dams, and constructed their dwellings with mound-like roofs sticking up a few feet above the water. They stole up on the colonies, snared the animals in traps, or dug them from their burrows with sticks and hoes. For years beaver pelts were the most valuable of all the furs; they were the gold standard in all trading. They were done up in neat 100-pound packs, 70 to 80 skins to the pack, and exchanged for brass kettles pound for pound.

The otter were large creatures, three to three and a half feet long. They fished at night. The Indians moved silently along the streams or around the solitary ponds wrapped in the stillness of a northern winter night, and speared them while they fed. The muskrats were round and chubby little chunks of fur, eight to ten inches long, with slimy tails as long as their bodies. The Indians searched out their nests, and shot, speared, or clubbed them to death on the creek banks. The mink were slender, brown, and serpentine. Their heads were like the heads of snakes, and their teeth were long and sharp. The Indians speared or clubbed these murderous animals while they stabbed wild geese and gulls with their teeth and sucked their blood from small holes punctured in their necks or breasts. The marten were about two feet long, and dark brown or black in color. They lived on birds, eggs, rodents, and berries. The Indians stalked these cat-like animals in the forests, or pulled them out of their rocky burrows, and clubbed them to death. They set traps far and wide for foxes, and they stalked deer in force. And when the braves brought in the catch, the squaws spread the skins, scraped away the flesh, smeared the hide with the creature's brains, and made the pelts ready for the next season's journey back down to the trading marts.

This system was primitive, but it was good. There were just two things wrong with it. If the interminable tribal wars happened to be raging, the Indians might forego the joy of the trading season, and the heavily laden ships might lie at anchor in the St. Lawrence with goods to trade but no Indians to trade with. The other difficulty was that the appetite for fur in the capitals and courts of Europe was insatiable while the supply was temperamental. Instead of waiting for Indians to fetch their furs to Montreal or Quebec, the French pushed back into the wilderness to set up trading posts on the hunting grounds. They established trading centers at the Sault, at Mackinac, at Detroit, at Green Bay, on the south Superior shore, at Fond du Lac and Grand Portage.

They not only traded with the Indians back in the Lake country; they became trappers themselves.

The artisan, garden-growing, grape-raising Frenchmen adapted themselves with remarkable ease to the woods and the Indian ways. They slipped out of the settlements of New France, contrary to orders, and disappeared by the scores into the forests to hunt and trap and trade. An official report in 1680 listed 800 men, out of a total population of 10,000, who had slunk into the wilderness to take beaver and mink and muskrat along the streams that fed into the Great Lakes. The number increased year after year as trading posts were established, and protective stockades were built farther and farther inland.

These traders and trappers built up their own tradition, their own habits and distinctive costumes. When the fleets of 35 to 60 cargo canoes paddled along the upper Michigan shore or around the islands of Georgian Bay, sun-tanned, dark and weather-bitten Frenchmen were always in the procession. When the early autumn migration back to the woods and trapping regions began, Frenchmen were in the canoes. They were not greatly different from their successors of the present day who guide businessmen hunters and fishermen back through northern Ontario to the quiet lakes and cool trout streams. Short, dark, and with inexhaustible endurance, they roamed the region. Their diet seems incredible to a vitamin-conscious age of processed foods. Alexander Henry tells how the traders at the posts would buy corn from the neighboring Indians in exchange for a few knives and trinkets. They boiled the grain in strong lye to remove the husks. Then they mashed it with pestles and dried it. In this concentrated form it could be stored in crowded canoes without taking up too much precious cargo space. For canoe transport it was a great improvement over the bags of bulky parched grain carried by Rogers' Rangers on their Canadian exploit. The ration was one quart of this dry mash per day to each man, or one bushel per month. On this meager and monotonous diet, these swart, vegetable-loving French Canadians could go week after week and month after month, paddling, portaging, tramping, wading over killing terrain, surviving summer heat

and polar winters, and return to the posts in the late spring with
canoes bulging with the season's take of fur, and looking strong
and eager for the carouse that would celebrate the end of the
trading.

The trading was usually in late June or early July. Into the posts
at Grand Portage on Lake Superior and at Mackinac on the Straits
the trappers crowded. They filled the huts and stores at Green
Bay, at Sault Ste. Marie, at Saginaw, and Detroit. They gathered
at Grand Island off the Pictured Rocks, and at the stations on the
Illinois River. And many, of course, came on down with the caravans to the fur marts at Montreal.

The July trading days were as rousing as a camp meeting in the
frontier days of Ohio and Kentucky. Trappers and traders from
the headwaters and the Lakes gathered at the posts for an orgy of
drinking and the excitement of a crowd after the solitary months
in the bush. They beat the dusty pelts and watched the factors
and clerks sort them and weigh them and place a value upon
them. Indians, vivid in paint, beaded skins, and polychrome blankets, congregated to sell and share in the festivities. They camped
in tents outside the stockade and danced and drank. Sometimes, as
at Grand Portage and at Mackinac, important men from the fur
companies would come out to lend their impressiveness to the festival. The great hall at Grand Portage was 60 feet long, and the
stockade enclosed 16 log buildings. The post had a canoe yard for
150 canoes. Its storerooms had inventories of French goods, and
its resident keeper, in traditional French fashion, cultivated a
kitchen garden and milked his own cows. They gave a big July
trading feast in the hall. Then the tables were cleared, the rum
flowed, the flutes and violins piped and played dance tunes, and
the Frenchmen from the woods sang and regained their Gallic
graces as they danced with the Indian girls. The nights were wild
and Dionysiac. 'You would be amazed,' La Hontan wrote, 'if you
saw how lewd these peddlers are when they return; how they feast
and game, and how prodigal they are, not only in their clothes, but
upon their sweethearts.' The Frenchmen were vain and childlike,
and boastful under the stimulus of the rum. Many of them were

naïvely proud of their costumes; they stuck Cyrano-like plumes in
their red caps and wrapped colored sashes around their blue
capotes.

The feasts were too soon finished, the rum was too quickly drunk,
the lechery ended. Then once again the fur brigades loaded their
canoes with provisions and trinkets, and departed for another season in the wilds, while the companies carried the peltry on to the
markets at London, Paris, New York, and Canton. The traders and
trappers went docilely and willingly, puffing at their pipes and
chanting their songs to the rhythm of their paddles as they broke
the surface of the lake water. It was the docility of these French
Canadians that caused Astor's company to employ them exclusively.
As Astor's agent, the blunt and successful Ramsay Crooks, wrote,
the Americans were 'to independent to submit quietly to proper
controul,' but the Canadians had 'that temper of mind to render
him patient docile and persevering in short they are a people harm-
less in themselves whose habits of submission fit them peculiarly
for our business.'

These men, and of course the Indians, spread themselves over
the far-flung empire of fur. The profits were extravagant. The take
in the decade of the 1780's was a million dollars' worth of peltry
each year. Twenty years later, six million pelts were coming out
of the traps of the Northwest each year, and they were selling at
the fur marts at prices ranging from 15 cents to $500 each. No
wonder, then, that the fight for monopolistic control of so rich a
harvest was so fierce and determined that it involved nations as
well as individual men and companies.

For a time the history of the Lakes revolved about the muskrats
on the upper streams of the Mississippi, the marten, the mink, and
the beaver at the end of the canoe route from Fond du Lac to
Sandy Lake, and the central trading posts at the Sault, at Mackinac,
at Grand Portage, and at Detroit. Governments both national and
local tried every means to keep the trade in the hands of certain
monopolistic companies. Private citizens were forbidden to buy
from the Indians. Only licensed traders could tap the market. Such
restrictions were consistently and adroitly violated from Cham-

plain's day to Astor's. Frenchmen disappeared from the colonial
towns and launched themselves illegally in the trade. Citizens in
frontier towns on the edge of the Iroquois territory simply went
back into the forest and traded. Bushrunners, they were called in
derision, but who cared about the name?

Gradually, however, control did come to center in a few big,
powerful, politically entrenched companies. The Hudson's Bay
Company generally worked the region north of the Great Lakes
watershed, and therefore does not directly enter our story. But the
Canadians formed the Northwest Company to exploit, primarily,
the lakes and streams to the north and west of the Great Lakes.
It was organized in 1783, the first of the big syndicates. It had
twenty-three partners, of whom the famed Scot explorer, Sir Alexander Mackenzie, was the best known. They had a working capital
of over a million dollars and kept some 2,000 men—factors, clerks,
interpreters, traders, trappers, et cetera—at work in their far-
flung hunting grounds. They ran the thriving post at Grand Portage
at the western limits of Lake Superior, where the trading festivities
were always spectacular. They brought their yearly yield of fur
down to the Montreal market. And they were protected not only
by the license laws that kept intruders from the trapping and frontier trading grounds, but also by the laws which required that fur
for export must be routed via London. A New York merchant, for
instance, was at their mercy. He couldn't send his own brigade
into the fur territory because it was reserved for Canadians. And
if he wanted to buy some choice furs at, say, Montreal and bring
them to Broadway, he had to import them from London. It was a
thriving racket.

The other big organization was the Mackinaw Company. It too
was Canadian. It was only a little less powerful and wealthy than
the Northwest Company. It had a capital of $800,000, and it ex-
ploited the region below the Lakes. Its big western supply and
trading post was at Mackinac on the Strait, a spot so long associated
with discovery and strategic dominance of the crossroads to the
west. This company sent its fur brigade over the divide to trap
and trade in the Wisconsin territory and along the upper Missis-

sippi and Missouri. By the time the Americans awoke to the wealth of fur trading, this Canadian company was collecting nearly a half-million dollars' worth of fur every year right in their own back country. Obviously something should be done about that.

And something was done.

The man who led the attack on the Canadian monopoly was John Jacob Astor. He was one of the shrewdest men ever to operate on the Great Lakes. He left his stamp on the region and on the lives of thousands of men who came in with him and after him. His career is the now familiar saga of the poor little immigrant boy rising in fabled America to the eminence of a multi-millionaire. He came from Waldorf, Germany. He was the butcher's son, born on July 17, 1763. At the age of 16 he slung a bundle over his back and left the butcher's shop to seek his fortune. Legend has it that he stopped outside his village to make his pledge 'to be honest, to be industrious, and never to gamble.' Except possibly for a few slumps in his driving energy, he did fulfil the second of the articles of his pledge.

He made his way first to London, where he arose at four in the morning to read his Bible and Lutheran prayer book until breakfast time. The ultimate lure, however, was not staid and class-bound London, but free and hopeful America. He sailed in 1783 on the *North Carolina*. He was on board that ship for four months, and finally reached land before his ship did. The ship got caught in a calm off Chesapeake Bay and froze solidly in the January ice of 1784. Since he was entitled to bunk and board while in passage, he thriftily stayed on with the ship; but the idleness finally got irksome and he walked across the ice to shore. The story goes that there were several Hudson's Bay officers aboard coming back from trading in London, and that their talk excited him over the future of the fur business. Legend also recounts that a communicative young German boy aboard the *North Carolina* spent the tedious hours of the passage by instructing John Jacob in the arts of the fur trade. He told how fur could be picked up in odd lots on the wharves of New York, and how, with a few knives and beads and blankets, you could trade with the Indians below Lake Ontario.

He even explained some of the tricks of the trade, such as how to judge and value the pelts, how to sort and pack and transport them, and how to sell. The boy from Waldorf obviously listened with acute ears and an organizing imagination.

Astor then hurried on up to New York, where he peddled cakes for his brother. In after years, when his success had sharpened the tongue of his sister Catherine against him, she was wont to exclaim, 'Yakob vas noting put a paker boy, und solt preat und kak.' He did not sell cake for long. He soon found a job with a furrier, one of his many tasks being to beat the dirt out of the pelts. In a small way he began to buy and sell furs for himself. In a short time he had become a familiar figure in upper New York. Settlers saw him trudging back and forth across the state trading for fur. Once they saw him emerging from the wilderness where he had been lost for days. Others reported seeing the hard-working German wading out of a swamp, bedraggled with mud, after losing his wagon and his gold in the deep mire. But he was making progress in this fur business. Soon he was shipping furs to England and importing musical instruments to sell in New York—flutes, clarinets, fifes, chamber organs, and scores by the masters. He broke into the trade with the Iroquois on the upper Mohawk. By 1788 he was already visiting the greatest North American fur center at Montreal. By 1790 he was even buying 'futures.' In that year he ordered 15,000 good muskrat skins, of which 12,000 must be 'spring gotten skins.' He knew his business. By 1800 he had even entered the China trade, and was sending pelts out to Canton and bringing back tea and brocade to sell in America.

Astor was hampered, of course, by the Canadian-British monopoly. But he was shrewd enough to see that one prize of the endless wars between England and France, and then between the United States and Great Britain, was the fur trade around the Great Lakes and in the woods and on the streams beyond. And when Jay's long-drawn-out negotiations with Britain finally culminated in the Treaty of 1796, Astor rejoiced. For Britain gave up Mackinac and Detroit to the Americans, and that meant the end of their exclusive rights to the lucrative trade that rolled through those posts. 'Now,'

Astor exclaimed with supreme satisfaction, 'I will make my fortune in the fur trade.'

He made the hard first million rapidly. His agents multiplied and he set up his trading posts hither and yon. He cultivated and influenced the Congress, he won support from the great American Democrat, Thomas Jefferson, and he wove his private Astoria empire steadily westward toward the Pacific. By 1808 he had clutched the trade so firmly in his two hands that he could change his name from John Jacob Astor, Fur Trader, to the American Fur Company, capital one million dollars, subscribed to and furnished by himself. He had become an impressive symbol of the original 'Robber Baron,' the German butcher boy risen to the heights of American business with a Congress to do his bidding. He sat there in lower New York in his small, cluttered, old-fashioned office, scheming the downfall of his rivals, and speaking to his agents in broken, Katzenjammer English. He said 'brining' for 'bringing,' 'easch' for 'each,' 'cam' for 'came,' and 'tham' for 'them.' And he wrote to his agents that 'mush Depends on the coller of the Martin and Mink the Darker the better & providd they are taking in Season.'

Astor still had several rivals to liquidate before he could be supreme in his monopoly. He was soon powerful enough to take care of them. One of them was the Government itself. Some of the private traders had become notorious for their unscrupulous dealings with the Indians. They plied them with rum and whiskey, corrupted them and cheated them. For a gill of whiskey costing the trader three or four cents they got from the Indians three or four dollars' worth of beaver. Conditions were so bad that both the Church and the State stepped in to try to stop the evil—though we may mitigate our sympathy by remembering that the Indians were shrewd, too, and knew how to do a bit of cheating on their own. They got credit in advance from one trader, and then took their furs to his rival the following season. If a trader got back a third of his loans, he was doing very well. The American Government set up its own trading posts, called 'factories,' to deal justly and temperately with the Indians and counteract these evils. In this respect, the Government was actually in the fur trade as a serious rival of private business.

Astor did not like this competition, and he loathed the principle upon which it was based. He believed with all his individualistic heart that the Government should stay out of business and keep its hands off except, of course, to protect and aid private exploitation. He went directly to Washington, and was influential in getting a law passed in 1816 that refused trading licenses to anyone except American citizens; any goods taken by unlicensed foreigners were subject to seizure. That law was one of the fruits of the War of 1812; it was aimed at the British at Fond du Lac and Mackinac.

That helped.

With this victory behind him, Astor induced the Government to build military forts out in the Northwest Territory—Fort Howard at Green Bay, Fort Crawford at Prairie du Chien, for example— to afford protection for his men and his expanding empire. Then in 1821-2 he was successful in persuading the Government to abolish its factories. The withdrawal of the Government from the hunting and trading grounds handed the lucrative fur business over to John Jacob Astor's thriving organization.

At the same time, Astor was also busy crushing out his private rivals. The little fellows were in business everywhere around the Lakes. They were more of an annoyance to Astor than a threat to his income. He ordered his agents to go to their trading posts and outbid them at the fur sales. If they insisted on buying at high prices, Astor went a step further and undersold them on the markets. His million-dollar resources and wide connections enabled him to accept these temporary losses, while his poorer rivals went bankrupt. Many who were capable and expert in their knowledge of the fur trade he absorbed and took over into his own company. Some of these men served him well and helped him spread his empire westward to the Columbia River and the Pacific. Others suffered complete disaster. There was, for example, an old, influential, and well-established firm of French traders at Green Bay— Grignon, Lawe, and Porlier. When they needed capital, Astor sewed them up with a mortgage on their extensive land holdings, and then took over for himself. Lawe wrote a pathetic letter about their ruination at the hands of Astor. 'They made us form a Company at the Bay,' he said, 'but it is a Mere Burlesque for to throw us into misery & trouble & they pretend it is for our own Good.' One by one these little traders were cleared from Astor's path. Only the few big, well-financed companies remained to challenge him.

He bought out the Mackinaw Company and absorbed it into his new American Fur Company. He not only wanted their business, but he particularly desired Mackinac Island for his western headquarters. As soon as the British and American soldiers got through fighting there in the War of 1812, Astor ordered his sagacious agent Ramsay Crooks to buy a parcel of land on the island 'with two stores and other dependencies thereon erected.' He paid only £200 for it. So he established headquarters on the cool green island athwart the blue waterway crossroads of the Great Lakes where canoes, sailing ships, and Mackinaw boats by the hundreds came in, anchored, and put out as the carriers of the million-dollar fur trade of the Lake country. For the year was 1817, and Astor had timed his deal perfectly to capture the fur business just as it began to revive and to boom after the ruinous slump of the war years.

During the next fifteen years, the busiest and most lucrative the fur industry was ever to enjoy, Astor was in full possession of the hunting grounds and trading posts on the American side of the border. His only rival in the Lake country was the Northwest Company. But Astor did not trouble himself about that outfit. He had got what he wanted and his sense of orderly monopoly was not violated by the activities of the Northwest Company. Foreigners were excluded by law from the United States hunting grounds, and he was protected now by his own regional monopoly. Moreover the drawing of the International Boundary line presented Astor with a neat windfall and accomplished his purpose for him without any effort on his part. The line was drawn right down the Pigeon River a few miles above Grand Portage. That placed squarely on American soil the most flourishing trading post of the Northwest Company. To Astor's immense gratification, they had to move out. They transferred their entire organization to Fort William far to the north on Thunder Bay under the towering rocks well out of the way of Astor's empire. It merged with the Hudson's Bay Company in 1821.

The operational base on Mackinac Island was a beaver pond of activity throughout the fur decade of the 1820's. Agents, factors, interpreters, sorters, packers, etc., lived at the post, received the season's take from the returning traders, trappers, and Indians, and shipped it on to the world markets, over which Astor himself kept diligent watch. They outfitted the well-organized brigades and sent them back after the trading into the hunting grounds. Back and forth across the Lakes went the canoe fleets, caravans of 30, of 50, or of 60 canoes in late August, laden with rations, stowed with trading articles doled out by Astor's astute factors on the island. It was reported that in 1817 Astor was able to outfit and dispatch 240 'boats,' each manned by two traders and six hands. His agents were resourceful. They struck off medals bearing the stamp of Astor's head upon them and distributed them to the Indian chiefs to win them from British rivals. When they had difficulty in recruiting French Canadians for the brigade to Astoria, these agents invented a garish Astorian uniform, set off with cock's plume or an ostrich feather in the cap. Such impressive and exclusive finery broke down all their resistance and they went over to Astor's service with enthusiasm.

The Astor fleets seemed to be everywhere. Travelers saw them going down toward Green Bay, paddling west past Green Island, penetrating the St. Croix and the Minnesota lakes, going up to Saginaw. Down in New York, Mrs. Astor herself, with her adroit and delicate eye for quality in fur, sorted out the prize pelts for her husband, who paid her, on her demand, $500 an hour for her professional services. Over in London and Paris, in Hamburg and Moscow and Smyrna, in far-away Canton and Hong Kong, men bought these furs for their wives and mistresses and for impressive-looking hats for themselves.

John Jacob's millions accumulated, though he was always talking about his formidable losses and urging his agents to supply fewer pelts. Yet, in one of the peak years, in September 1827, he wrote glowingly that in less than twenty-four hours he had unloaded 200,000 muskrats at Public Sale, and 350,000 at 'Private Sale; 'so many have never in the world been sold in one day.' The average price was thirty-six cents, and he still had in stock 200,000 skins.

This was opulent business. It lasted into the 1830's. Then Astor sold his Mackinac post, and got out of the business in 1835. The empire did not crumble; it merely metamorphosed and was superseded by even wilder speculative profit in land and lumber. These fur traders had spied out the land, explored the routes of travel, and brought reports back to the East. Land-hungry, adventure-thirsty men picked up their goods and chattels and followed the fur brigades, not to take pelts but to get land, to cut timber, to plant grain, to raise cattle—and all these activities were natural enemies of the fur trade. Advance trading posts like Green Bay, Prairie du Chien, Chicago, and Saginaw became centers of settlement. Green Bay was, even in Astor's heyday, already a settled community with gardens and corn fields, and long narrow 'ribbon farms' characteristic of the habitants of the St. Lawrence, reaching back from the lake or river into the wilderness. When the canal fever raged across New York and around the Lakes, and a thousand barges passed along their noisy channels, it was not primarily to transport beaver, mink, fox, and scraped deerskin, but to carry grain and pork and whiskey from the new agricultural West to the markets on the seacoast. Astor saw the trend of the times and converted himself from supreme American fur broker to the supreme American landlord. His fur empire had had its day and done its work.

Remains of that empire are still scattered about the Great Lakes. They are mildly interesting, but the memories they stir are not nostalgic. The post on lonely Grand Island, off the Pictured Rocks country of Lake Superior, still stands on the shore overlooking Furnace Bay. It huddles under the arm of a great brooding tree. Another stands on the edge of Brady Park in Michigan's Sault Ste. Marie where the ore fleet is raised and lowered in the new MacArthur lock in the Soo Canal. The ancient buildings on Mackinac are joined together, weatherboarded and ornamented with steamboat Gothic porch banisters, and are used as a boarding house.

Cities have grown up around others where the only remains of the post itself is a cross to mark the spot where it stood. Enormous grain elevators have replaced the great hall of the Northwest Company at Fort William.

The fur trade itself is still alive, but its ways are not the ways of singing French voyageurs and the factors on Mackinac Island. Science has invaded the industry. Perhaps it is best typified by the big peltry farms of Ohio and the Middle West. Here carefully selected animals are bred and reared. Then, in late September, they are crated and loaded on trucks and hauled back to the cool Lake Superior country, where the cold autumn and early winter perfects and seasons the rich pelts for milady's jacket and neckpiece. So great is man's control of nature and his improvement of her bungling ways.

XXIII

Sails

THE topsail schooner *Illinois* sailed out of Sackets Harbor at the foot of Lake Ontario on a fine May day in 1834. She was bound for the faraway port of Chicago. She was stowed to capacity with 104 passengers and their essential gear of wagons, plows, hoes, pots, children, and bedding. The hold was full, the cabins were overcrowded, and the decks piled high. The wagon wheels were lashed to the shrouds like the spinning wheels of the Puritans. Enthusiasm and excitement ran through the ship. For these men and women were headed for the fabulous lands of northern Illinois, where the fur trade had flourished and where the Black Hawk War (1832) had just been fought by the frontiersmen. Now the Indians were cleared from the hunting grounds and the country was open for settlement. A gigantic land boom hit the region. Its headquarters was the little fort and row of log houses near Lake Michigan on the Chicago River. Only 150 people lived there when the year 1832 began; 2,000 scurried along its muddy streets before the year had closed. Twenty thousand people sailed in from Buffalo that season; they passed on through Chicago and spread out over the Illinois land. The entire Lake country stirred with youthful activity. The only highway for this enormous shift in the population and for the commerce west and east which naturally followed was the shipping lanes of the Great Lakes. The call for ships and still more ships was loud and insistent.

The *Illinois* was one of those ships, and her name signified her mission. She had been specially built to the dimensions of the locks on the new Welland Canal (80 x 20 x 8) in order that she might sail from Ontario ports to the Upper Lakes and back at will. The voyage to Chicago in the early 1830's was still a great adventure.

It was a full month's cruise: across Lake Ontario, up the Niagara escarpment and around the Falls, up the Niagara River with the 'horned breeze,' against head winds and choppy Lake Erie waters off Long Point, through the Pelee channel, and up the river to Detroit; then by sail or tow over the shallow Lake St. Clair and through the swift current at Port Huron into Lake Huron; up the rolls and swells of Lake Huron to Mackinac Island; westward through the Straits of Mackinac, and southward with quartering winds to the foot of Lake Michigan to drop anchor outside the sandbar barrier which lay across the mouth of the Chicago River. The weary, seasick, but eager passengers went ashore in the ship's boats. Their plows and wagons were ferried in on rafts. With her draft eased, the *Illinois* was then hauled across the barrier by ropes manned by Chicago citizens and the ship's crew, and she was finally secured at the new wharf on the Chicago River water front.

That scene and that experience was repeated over and over again all around the new ports on the south shores of the Lakes. In 1835, 255 sailing ships arrived in Chicago. Nearly a thousand arrivals of sailing ships and 990 steamships were recorded in Cleveland harbor in 1836. Chicago and Toledo were both incorporated in 1837. At that time there were 8,000 people in Chicago. Detroit had 10,000. Thousands of immigrants disembarked at Sandusky and spread over the fat wheat lands of Ohio. On a single day in October 1838, 285 wagons drove into that little lake port, with produce for the eastern cities.

All this activity, still only a bare portent of what was to come, gave rise to the storied era of the sailing ships. Steam was already on the Lakes; and steam would in a few decades drive away the sails in competition for the ever-increasing tonnage of bulk cargo—grain, coal, and ore, those golden, black, and red rivers that traced their channel across the Lakes. But in the meantime, in the half century cut through the heart and center by the Civil War, when much of the shipping was deflected to the Lakes from the inland waterways, the sailing ships had their era. Even the United States Navy clung to sails down to the 1880's, and the ships of the 'White Squadron' built in that late decade used steam as auxiliary to the familiar rigging of sails. Hammers, saws, and adzes pounded and burred and swished in a hundred shipbuilding yards on the Lakes. Every town had one yard or more. Ships slid down the ways at Sackets Harbor, Toronto, and Oswego; at Buffalo, Erie, Cleveland, Lorain, Sandusky, and the little Ontario river and lake towns; at Detroit and Saginaw; at Milwaukee, Manitowac, and Chicago. Ropes, cables, masts, spars, and acres of canvas lay on the wharves. The smell of tar and sawdust and damp lumber hovered over the water fronts. The harbors and wharves were a forest of masts interwoven with halyards and rigging.

In the shipyard offices the designers and builders worked over plans for new and better models. They studied weather, winds, harbors, and cargo on the Lakes. They discussed captains' reports on keels, hulls, and winddrifts. Just how should a sailing ship be built and rigged for best performance on these Lakes? The harbors were generally very shallow. The *Illinois* couldn't get in over the sandbar at Chicago. The *Walk-in-the-Water* had to anchor well out at Cleveland. The first ship to call at Kenosha, Wisconsin, in 1835 with a cargo of lumber had to stand well out of the harbor. Passengers went ashore in boats, and the lumber was tossed overboard and floated in to the village. The first canals were also shallow affairs, only about four and a half to six feet deep, though they were later increased to eight or nine feet. Before you built a ship in those days, therefore, you had to decide whether it was to operate through the canals and whether it was to unload off shore or go into the new wharves that were being built at Cleveland, Detroit, Chicago, and other key ports. Smart business called for ships with the largest possible pay load that could be moved in the shortest time with the fewest operating crew. Strike a balance of all these points and what kind of a ship do you get?

The answers were various. The ships were generally built by or for small individual owners. Captain-owners were then as now singular personalities with their own pet notions and ideas about the design of ships. Every conceivable type of sailing ship appeared on the Lakes at one time or another.

The old 'canallers' were a familiar sight, particularly on Lake

Ontario and Lake Erie. They were purely functional. There was
nothing trim about them—no rakish sweep of cutwater bow with a
carved and ornamented figure under the bowsprit bespeaking the
pride of the captain in his vessel. They were heavy, stubby, and
square Hollander-type ships. Their bottoms were flat and their
bows nearly perpendicular like a box, designed to fit snugly into
the tubby locks of the canals. Those locks still limit the size and
structure of ships that operate from the Lakes to the Atlantic, and
give rise to the controversy over the improvement of the St. Lawrence Waterway that rages in our time.

The old square-riggers had their day on the Lakes. They were
the favorite rigs for warships. Barclay's flagship *Detroit,* which he
surrendered to Perry on Lake Erie, was a square-sailed three-
masted frigate. All three of Perry's larger ships, the *Lawrence,* the
Niagara, and the *Caledonia,* were brigs with square sails. It was a
good rig for fighting ships, because it was made up of twelve
to sixteen independent sheets of canvas, with their edges turned
toward the enemy's broadside, and a shell tearing through a fore-
sail or a hit on a topgallant yard would still leave the lower and
upper topsails intact to keep the ship under way. These rigs were
not so good, however, for commercial ships, because too many
hands were needed to operate them. Navies with all their man
power could handle them, but private commercial ships could not
afford it. The square-riggers, however, did sail well coming loaded
down the Lakes with the wind constant behind them, and largely
for that reason a few were built and kept in service.

The brigantines, or brigs, were more in favor. They were two
masters, of all sizes from around 100 tons on up to as much as 500
tons. Like most of the Lake sailing ships they had square sails on
the foremast. It was the brigantine *Columbia,* with the U. S. flag
flying proudly at the gaff above her huge fore-and-aft mainsail,
that brought the first load of Superior ore through the Soo Canal
in 1855 and unloaded it at the busy port of Cleveland.

Up at the little town of Manitowoc, Wisconsin, William Bates
had a shipyard and also a new idea. He developed the first distinctive type of sailing ship to appear on the Lakes. He was trying

to get a ship that would be fast, carry a good cargo, and be easily handled, and yet at the same time one that would draw a limited draft and not yaw about too much in a wind or drift off the leeward. His answer was the trim clipper type schooner, the *Challenge*, that first sailed out on Lake Michigan in 1852. Her shallow draft was equalized by using a centerboard in the keel. It was a simple and effective device. A stout piece of timber about 12 feet long and 6 to 10 feet wide was boxed in the keel and pivoted on a pin at the bow end. A weight was usually attached to the stern end. When the ship had cleared the shallow harbors, or had passed through a canal or lock, the stern end of the centerboard was dropped with a tackle, and this fin acted as a stabilizer.

The *Challenge* had two masts, the foremast square rigged and the main fore-and-aft rigged. The ship easily attained the phenomenal speed of 13 knots and was noted for her agility and regularity of schedule. Her plan was taken over to France as an example of the Great Lakes type of clipper centerboard schooner. Bates constructed a fleet of these schooners. The *Clipper City* of 1853 had a centerboard and square topsails. The *Manitowoc*, a noted Lake clipper, followed the *Clipper City* down the ways, and these Bates-designed ships soon captured and monopolized much of the Lake trade.

The Lake schooners grew in size as more and more tonnage piled up at the ports for transportation to the East or out across the Lakes to the big outlet city of New Orleans. The larger schooners were usually three masters—fore, main, and mizzen. They generally retained the centerboard, and carried square topsails. While the American clipper ships were making history on the seven seas, the Lake schooners were sailing by the hundreds back and forth over the blue Lakes. The Lakers, as they were often called, were longer and narrower in the beam than the salt-water ships. They were also a little more rakish in silhouette. On an Atlantic 'tern-schooner' all three masts were of approximately equal height—about 91 to 93 feet. But a Lake schooner would have a 98-foot foremast, a graceful main that reached up to 102 feet, and a mizzen that dropped down to about 86 feet. And when a Huron breeze swelled the jib, outerjib, and flying jib well out beyond the bow to complete the sweep of the full sail, these Lakers were about the finest examples of harmony and grace of movement to be seen on any body of water anywhere.

Some minor modifications of rigging were introduced from time to time. The *Moonlight* of Milwaukee, embodying the theories of the early 1870's, was rigged with a billowing triangular topsail or raffe above the square lower sail on her mainmast. This type of sail, which seems to have originated on the Great Lakes, was fairly common in the closing years of the sailing-ship era. But the schooner or barquentine rig proved over the years to be the best for the peculiar natural and economic requirements of the Great Lakes. Unlike the square rigger, their running gear was easy to store, and the booms could be quickly swung round out of the way while loading or unloading.

These two- or three-masted schooners became standard in the great days of the sailing ships. They performed all sorts of feats astonishing to their age. The little schooner *St. Clair,* as we have noted, was taken from Detroit down the Erie to New York, the first ship to sail to the sea from the Upper Lakes. When the stampede of '49 was on, and the typically American mass rush shifted for the moment from the grain fields of the Great Lakes hinterland to the gold fields of California, the *Eureka* took on 59 passengers and sailed out of Cleveland bound for San Francisco. She crossed Lake Erie, locked through the Welland Canal, ran with the wind down Lake Ontario, threaded her way down the St. Lawrence and through the canals, and, just as though she were a salt-water clipper from Gloucester, Mass., she sailed down the Atlantic, rounded the Horn, beat up the Pacific, and safely deposited her fortune seekers at the Golden Gate.

Other Lake schooners crossed the Atlantic. The *Sophia* of Kingston, rigged as a topsail Lake schooner, sailed from her home port to Liverpool in 1850. Several others followed from Great Lakes ports in the ensuing decade. In fact it was a profitable enterprise to build ships on the Great Lakes and sell them to English firms for salt-water traffic about the Empire—a portent of the desperate

Split Rock Light, on the north shore of Lake Superior; a net drying reel in the foreground. *Photograph by Erling Larsen. Courtesy of Frederic Lewis.*

A fishing village near the ferry to Washington Island, on Green Bay, Wisconsin. *Courtesy of Philip Gendreau, N. Y.*

days that were to come nearly a century later when these same
yards from Kingston to Port Arthur would be furiously building
submarines, frigates, and corvettes to protect the North Atlantic
shipping lanes against the Nazis.

The *Sea Gull* out of Toronto opened still another market for the
Great Lakes when she sailed out of Lake Ontario with a cargo of
farm machinery, wagons, buggies, and flour for the new community
of Durban, South Africa, and its farms in the back lands. The *Sea
Gull* made the round trip in record time and was back in Lake
Ontario before the ice closed in on the navigation season. The
schooner *Dean Richmond* loaded a cargo of wheat at Milwaukee
in 1856 and sailed directly to Liverpool—the first through shipment
between those ports. These schooners even reached Lake Superior
in the decade before the Soo Canal (1855) was opened. It was an
accomplishment not incomparable to that of sailing round the Horn.
The schooners had to be hauled out below the Sault, placed on
sleds, skids, or rollers, and dragged up to the Superior level of the
St. Mary's River. There they were re-launched and sailed off to
pick up the trade in the little communities already springing up
on the south and west shores of Lake Superior.

Foreign ships also entered the Lakes. Norwegians were among
the first and most frequent visitors. They were led by a sloop from
Bergen, a rather stubby single master with an enormous, billowing
mainsail stretched between a rakish gaff, topped with the blue-
cross Norwegian merchant flag, and a main boom that swept back
over the deck and out over the stern. Her symmetry was preserved
by two triangular head sails carried on the bowsprit and jibboom.

And there were the inevitable absurdities of a new enterprise
that found amusement in ludicrous horseplay, as when the old and
honorable schooner *Michigan* was bought by some sideshow businessmen in 1827, loaded with live animals, and run under full sail
over the Falls of Niagara while thousands of gawk-eyed people
looked on at the crash and watched the helpless camel, elk, deer,
and dogs drowning in the spray-filled gorge.

Deep-sea sailors might feel a pardonable scorn for the fresh
water of the Great Lakes, but there is no record of any complaint

that the winds and weather over the Lakes were not sufficiently boisterous and capricious to hold their interest or task their seamanship. The Lakes lie in the heart of the North American continent in the center of the cyclonic system of storms. They are surrounded by thousands of miles of flat plains and prairies where the thermometer climbs well above a hundred degrees in summer and drops to frigid sub-zero readings in winter. They stretch a thousand miles across the fighting front of the big air masses. Heavy polar-chilled air from northern Manitoba and Saskatchewan and from Mackenzie Territory in Canada races down over the spring wheatfields and the autumn stubble. Warmer, moister air, pushed up from the sub-tropics of Florida and Texas, crowds in over southern Lake Michigan, over Lake Erie and Lake Ontario. The two conflicting masses often meet and fight over the shipping lanes of the Lakes. Gales, blizzards, squalls, and thunderstorms batter the thousand ships. The weather fronts move from west to east across the Lakes on the average of two a week. Atmospheric pressures run up and down the scale from highs of around 1,045 millibars to lows in the 980's. Temperatures slide up and down with equal abandon, despite the equalizing influence of all the square miles of water. Winter temperatures may be 20° to 30° higher on the east coast of Lake Michigan, where the cherry and peach trees bloom in early spring, than on the chill Wisconsin shore. A ship might leave Buffalo on a clear warm summer day, and yet have to take refuge in Erie harbor from storms or fog a few hours later. Warm air blows in from the fields over the cold lake water, where it is chilled and reduced to a blanket of fog lying so thick and soupy on the surface that no ship could sail through. The most competent seamanship was required in sailing-ship days to cope with the weather and the vagaries of the cyclonic winds. Hundreds of ships were wrecked, but on the whole the captains and crews on the Great Lakes were skilled and resourceful.

They had plenty of opportunity for practice. The crews were relatively small and versatile. In fact both the salt- and fresh-water clippers were celebrated and envied by British competitors for this reason. A thousand-ton Yankee ship with only forty hands would

overtake and leave behind a wallowing thousand-ton East India-
man with a crew of eighty. They sailed with equal facility on the
Lakes. The little sloop *Sophia* had started the long list of record-
breaking runs back in 1795 by sailing against the prevailing winds
from Kingston to Queenston, Ontario, a distance of more than two
hundred miles, in eighteen hours. Speed and economy counted in
Lake competition, and the crews, whether sons, relatives, and
neighbors of the captain-owner, or water rovers signed on for the
season at Buffalo, found stimulation and fun in the neat handling
of their ship on the long easy runs and in the quick crises that
were always blowing up on the Lakes.

The routine was well set in tradition. The holds were filled and
the hatches battened down at the Buffalo wharves. The efficient
bustle of getting under way began. The anchor was hove short by
drawing the ship by her cables until she was directly over the
anchor. The capstan was turned and clicked to the rhythmic chant
of sailors' voices. Then the 'mudhook' broke out and was hove up
and secured. From the quarter-deck by the wheel came the shouted
order, 'All hands make sail.' On the Lake ships that would mean
a couple of mates and a dozen sailors or less. The mates take
charge, hands scurry up to loose the sails aloft, others man the
ropes. The jibs and spankers stretch up to take the first wind and
aid the wheelsmen to steer the ship out into the lake. As she begins
to make way, the staysails go up with a flap. The ship hastens
forward and leans gracefully over on the lee rail. Then the sails
are trimmed to the Lake Erie wind and the ship, spreading out
a half acre or more of canvas, crowds her way toward Detroit,
Mackinac, Milwaukee, Chicago. At the canals, or when passing
through the joining rivers and Lake St. Clair, the sails generally
had to come down while the ships were towed in long columns by
the steam tugs. But that indignity was soon over, the sails were set
again, and the ship sailed on as before.

Generally the hands sang as they worked the ropes and halyards.
Singing while you work was one of the traditions on the Lakes.
The voyageurs had sung mournful ballads and lively chanties for
two centuries as they dipped their paddles into the rivers and lakes.

Songs lightened the toil and shortened the hours, and, under their
magic, men would paddle eighteen to twenty hours at a single
stretch. Good singers got extra pay. Boatmen carried on the custom.
Governor Lewis Cass, that rugged, tireless, and great statesman of
the Northwest, read the classics while his men sang and rowed him
up and down the lakes and rivers to treat with the Indians. On one
occasion it is reported that a Chicago citizen at breakfast heard
singing in an approaching boat and, without even looking, announced the approach of the Governor. He was right. A Mackinaw
boat hove in sight on the Chicago River with twelve oarsmen and
a steersman singing a chanty, and Cass himself sitting in the stern
to make the fourteenth. These singing men had been rowing him
sixty to seventy miles a day. On the sailing ships sailors chanted
the rhythm of the capstan weighing the anchor, and the haul on
the halyards as they mastheaded the yards to the beat of 'A-hay!
A-high! A-ho-yo!' And, like their Nova Scotia and deepwater brethren, they set sails to the solo chant of

> *Haul on the bowlin', the fore and maintop bowlin'*—

while all joined in the chorus

> *Haul on the bowlin', the bowlin' haul!*

Most of these old songs, like the libretti of forgotten musical com-
edies, sound harsh or feeble in the cold print of collectors' albums.
But when the watch was aloft belaying a mainsheet off Milwaukee
harbor, or when one big sail was spread to port and the other to
starboard with a lubber's wind dead aft down Lake Huron and the
watch had a moment to smoke and relax, even the most limping
of the songs sounded good in the ear. The nearest they can be
carried back to their proper setting in our time is when an old
sailor, now retired and sitting on a bench on the water front at
Sarnia watching the 625-footers go down the channel, recalls the
sailing days and rolls out one or two old favorites like 'Blow the
man down. Give us some wind to blow the man down,' as you offer
him a cigar and indicate your interest. Or when, too rarely, you go
aboard a fishing boat on Lake Erie and find a sailor who remembers

the days when song accompanied the slap of the waves against the bow off Bass Island.

There was no time for singing, however, when the cold frontal storms broke over the Lakes or a squall struck at the taut canvas with devastating fury. The master and his men had to be prepared for these crises. They had to know the harbors and how to read the skies and make their own predictions. There were no weather maps, no sequence reports, no forecasts or long-range prediction. Every man was his own aerologist. A few seasons on the Lakes made sailors good weather prophets. The lives of the crew and the safety of the ship depended upon how well the master read the storm warnings of the sky. That first sailing ship on the Upper Lakes, the *Griffon*, most likely went down in one of the sudden Lake Huron storms. The *Ontario* foundered on the lake for which she was christened when she was hit by a storm in 1780, and 172 souls perished at a time when that many people were a large proportion of the white population of the Lakes. Year by year others went down: the schooner *Lexington* with a cargo of whiskey sank between Detroit and Toledo in 1846; the *New Brunswick* in 1859 with a load of walnut and oak timber; the *Fay* plummeting to the bottom of Saginaw Bay with a cargo of steel—and they continue to go down. For the Lakes, though spacious, are still shore lined. Ships cannot run indefinitely with the wind. Moreover, they were navigated near the shore and many were cast up on the rocks.

Disasters like these make men weatherwise. The captains knew nothing of air masses, weather fronts, or millibars, but they did know that cirrus clouds sifting out like spindrift high in the western sky and a halo of cirro-stratus around a golden moon meant storm and trouble over the Lakes on the morrow. They could not chart the vertical and roll currents in a swift-charging cold-front thunderstorm, but when the waves began to kick up and the wind died down for a few minutes, then shifted 180 degrees, these captains knew that the topgallants must come down fast and that even the main lower topsail had better come in. In their own practical way they summed up a chapter of modern scientific meteorology in two handy sayings:

If the clouds seem scratched by a hen,
Better take your topsails in.

When the wind shifts against the sun,
Watch her, boys, for back she'll come.

The hen-scratched clouds, the wind shift, and other natural
weather flags were almost constantly hung out on the Great Lakes
sky. The big freighters may generally ignore them but the smaller
ships must still take care. These storms can roar down over Michigan
and hit the long, exposed strip of Lake Huron with terrific force.
The plumes and tufts of the first warning high cirrus have hardly
reached Georgian Bay before the anvil-headed cumulo-nimbus
sweep over the pine forests and hit the waterways. The waves roll
and the fresh gale wind at 40 miles per hour carries their crests
forward and banners the lake with scud or foam streaks. The
smaller craft race to shelter in protected bays and harbors. On the
rocky promontory of Presque Isle, Michigan, stands one of the first
few lighthouses to be erected on the Upper Lakes. It was built of
stone in 1819. It is now privately owned. The top is floored and
the proprietor has placed deck chairs up there behind the protective banisters of stone. The view is superb. A half mile to the northwest the tall new beacon flashes signals to passing ships; they see
it 16 to 20 miles away and check their course. Below it is the all
but abandoned Presque Isle harbor. Off shore you may count eight,
ten, seventeen ships spaced and passing. And as the wind sweeps
down, you hold on to the stone railing and watch tugs and small
fishing boats scurry in from open Huron to the quiet of the protected bay to drop anchor and wait out the blow.

The sailing captains often employed that technique. For many
decades there were no aids to navigation. The Lakes were not surveyed and charted until 1889, though this work had been started
for certain Canadian waters as early as 1817 by the Royal Navy,
and for the entire Lake system by the United States Army in 1841.
Few lighthouses flashed any warning or direction. There were no
red and black buoys carefully marking the channel through
dredged or hazardous waters, no ship-to-shore radio, no system of

harbor lights and fog horns to warn of coast dangers or pilot the ship to its wharf. There were a few lights on the Canadian shore of Lake Ontario in the pre-1812 days. The Americans added their first lights at Buffalo and at Erie in 1818, and built one at the treacherous Lake Huron entrance to the St. Clair River in 1825. The first light on Lake Michigan appeared at Chicago in 1832; and the first on Lake Superior was set up at Whitefish Point in 1847. You sailed by contact or by dead reckoning, and perhaps put into a harbor at nightfall. But the ships, nearly 2,000 of them in the peak years, sailed with phenomenal regularity and with relatively few losses carrying their endless cargoes of lumber and grain and men up and down the chain of lakes.

It was a colorful era, those sailing decades. It has passed. The last of the schooners was built at Manitowoc in 1875. She served the trade for over half a century, and was wrecked in Lake Michigan in 1929. The yachts and small fishing boats that put out on Sunday morning from Toronto, Cleveland, Detroit, and Chicago, with their tall white sails flashing in the sun and leaning over with a fresh breeze, give only a bare and imperfect suggestion of the picture of the Lakes when 2,000 ships lifted their masts full of canvas from Duluth to Kingston. Only a few aged and retired captains still remember the time when they sailed independently about from port to port, chartering their ships for the voyage, picking up here a load of grain, there a cargo of lumber, and a hold full of coal to take back to Kenosha or the Sault. Volumes could be filled with the names of ships, the personalities of their captains, mates, and crews, the adventures of the voyages through ice, storms, fire, and collisions. They held on toughly against the lengthening bulk-cargo ships of steel and steam, which little by little stole their trade. By the 1890's the sails were dropped to mould on the wharves, the masts were pulled down, and the once-proud sailing ships were reduced to tow barges under the dirty streamer of smoke from their conquerors. Hollywood alone was left to rebuild the ships and give them life on a stage set before the camera. And Longfellow's verses, inspired by the sight of one of the most famous of

all the clippers, the *New World*, live on to sing the spirit of the
time:

> *Build me straight, O worthy Master!*
> *Staunch and strong, a goodly vessel,*
> *That shall laugh at all disaster,*
> *And with wave and whirlwind wrestle.*

XXIV

Bound East for Buffalo

NAVIGATION of these sailing ships in the middle years of last century could be astonishingly casual. Among the more detailed logs of voyages on the Lakes in this period, none is more graphic or revealing than that of the keen-eyed and sharp-penned English visitor, Harriet Martineau. She came over to America in September 1834, and immediately visited the Great Lakes. She toured the country for two years, and then in the summer of 1836 she made a second trip to Niagara Falls, crossed Lake Erie to Detroit, and took the lower carriage road across Michigan to Chicago. At Chicago she gratified one of the whims cherished by all the Romantics by making a day's journey out upon the prairie to get the feel of God and the great open spaces of America. Heavy rains over Michigan closed the upper carriage road over which she expected to return to Detroit. So she indulged another romantic desire, encouraged by her friends at Chicago and at Detroit, and sailed up Lake Michigan, through the Straits of Mackinac, and down Lake Huron to Detroit.

She boarded the new sailing ship *Milwaukee* on June 28, bound for Detroit and Buffalo. There was only one other woman aboard, and no stewardess; the rest of the passenger list was a rowdy, swearing, ill-mannered group of men from Milwaukee who had been to the land sales at Chicago. They were most annoying to the ladies. They crowded into their cabin, lounged on the cushions, puffed clouds of smoke, and spat. They rushed into the dining room at meal time, seized the chairs, and indifferently refused to pass food to Miss Martineau until the captain lectured them sternly on shipboard deportment in the presence of ladies. They gambled, and

entertained themselves betimes by singing mock hymns and paro-
dying a Methodist sermon.

With this crude assortment aboard, the *Milwaukee* put out over
the sandbar at Chicago harbor and set sail up the lake with fair
weather and without mishap. Ships sailing directly for Mackinac,
then as now, set their course for Point Betsie, about thirty miles
south of the Great Manitou Island.

Ships calling at the west-coast ports kept near the shore, passing
the Waukegan light at 36 miles, the Kenosha light at 52 miles, the
Racine light at 62, and the Milwaukee light and harbor at 86 miles.
Harriet's ship set course for Milwaukee. The captain had never
before navigated this lake. He was apprehensive, and his nervous
uncertainty was communicated to the crew.

Milwaukee in 1836 had a population of 400, of whom 7 were
female. The harbor was still unimproved, and the treacherous sandbar still lay across the entrance. In the next two decades, the city
spent over $100,000 to deepen the channel and make the harbor
safe except for strong east winds. But in 1836 the sandbar was still
dangerous. Our inexperienced captain promptly ran his ship
aground. All hands had to fall to and unship the cargo to lighten
the vessel. She swung free on July 1, hove round, and cast anchor
in deep water near 'an elegant little schooner' that pleased the
English lady. The obnoxious men from Milwaukee disembarked
in small boats and were rowed into port. Miss Martineau watched
their departure with sweet satisfaction which was heightened by
the antics of one rude man whose hat blew off into the Lake. The
steamship *New York* came plowing down the bay, three weeks
overdue because of storms. She too promptly ran aground on the
bar.

While the *Milwaukee* lay at anchor, small boats plied back and
forth from the three ships to the wharf. They brought out apple
pies, cheese, ale, and strawberries to relieve the ship's diet of salt
beef, pork, potatoes, sea-biscuits, and tea without milk. The captain
and steward went ashore to buy food, but all the fresh meat was
gone and there was no milk, 'only two cows being visible in all the
place.' The entire feminine population came out to the ship to sit

with the English woman and just look at a member of their own sex. Harriet marveled that four hundred men should have good stores, a printing press, and a newspaper at Milwaukee before they had women. She was touched by the pathetic appeal inserted in the first issue of the paper calling upon the women of the more populous towns to cast a favorable eye upon this promising settlement of bachelors.

The *Milwaukee* took aboard one of the ship's owners and made sail for the Manitou Isles, a little over a hundred miles northeast across the lake, and about a hundred miles from the Straits of Mackinac. The owner demanded quarters in the ladies' cabin. Harriet fastened up a counterpane with four forks to divide his space from hers, and with this modest protection they got on very well. He told her about the fur trade in which he was engaged, and invited her to his farm on Mackinac Island. He also pointed out the wreckage of one of his schooners, which was run aground and lost on the Michigan coast in a November snowstorm in 1835.

As they neared the Michigan shore they ran into heavy fog. Toward evening on Sunday, July 3, it lifted a bit. The captain himself climbed the mast to see where they were. They were off Cape Sable, forty miles from the Manitou Isles. One of the great flocks of pigeons, so common over the lake in those days, flew by like a cloud. The sailors shot six and recovered two. But they were served to the mate, because he was sick. On the Fourth of July, the passengers were up at five o'clock to see the islands. They had hoped to be at Mackinac for the celebration at the fort, but the fog had spoiled their plans. The islands were green and beautiful in contrast to the high and sandy shore off northern Michigan. The prettiest sight of all was the glittering white sails of two schooners on the horizon to the south.

The *Milwaukee* reached the Straits in the late afternoon. An 'ugly light-ship' came into view at six o'clock, sailing west to tow vessels through the Strait at night. The *Milwaukee* was too early to need this aid. She reached Mackinac Island before darkness fell. The barracks on the terrace caught the evening sun and gleamed white across the water against the dark background of the isle. All the little vessels in the pebbled harbor, of which there were scores, were dressed with flags, and the national ensign was fluttering proudly over the garrison. The ship dropped anchor in the crowded harbor. A schooner sailed in behind her in fine style, 'sweeping round our bows so suddenly as nearly to swamp a little fleet of canoes, each with its pair of half-breed boys.'

The distinguished traveler was enchanted by Mackinac, the fleet of vessels at anchor, the canoes and Mackinaw boats scurrying around the two small landing piers, the piles of firewood for the steamers, the Indian lodges on the beach, the old French houses, bark-roofed and shabby looking, near the shore, the fine sweep of the three terraces up the rugged sides of the hill, and the good houses among the trees along the first level of the terraces. She went ashore, and the prospect reduced her enraptured pen to inadequacy. It more than lived up to all the eloquent advance notices given her by the officers' wives at Detroit who had been stationed there. She was entertained by the Commandant, and she faithfully set down the old saw of the northland as he told it to her: 'We have nine months winter and three months cold weather.'

The impatient captain had to wait while Harriet made her tour of the Island. Late in the day, Harriet returned, and he made sail and set a course down Lake Huron. The lake was squally, as usual, but the whitefish was abundant and made a welcome supplement to the dwindling rations aboard. The passengers responded to the brilliant sunset over the lake and to the sensational display of the Northern Lights that followed. On the seventh of July they were only twenty miles from the outlet into the St. Clair River. There they hit a south wind head on. They beat against it all day long. By the afternoon of the eighth day they were just in sight of Fort Gratiot. They veered and tacked endlessly in long runs to the east and west. Other ships were struggling against the adverse winds; they made a small fleet of sails converging toward the foot of the lake, racing each other for the opening at the St. Clair. Another squall hit the *Milwaukee* and broke one of her chains. She fell out of the race, took in sail, and dropped anchor to ride out the thunderstorm that was sweeping up from Detroit. It lasted only twenty minutes. Then the sun came out again, clouds of pigeons flew over, an 'immense herd of wild horses' passed near the shore, and the crew began once more the monotonous routine of tacking. The ship almost ran aground as it swept from one side of the lake to the other without making perceptible headway. The keeper of the Gratiot light and the people on shore stood idly watching the ship fight for headway against the wind. Squaws cleaning fish looked up, and a big Indian, wrapped in a blanket, stood immobile in a poster pose gazing at the ship as it finally reached the swift current at Port Huron-Sarnia.

The navigation of the ship, which had been lax and uncertain throughout the voyage, now reached complete incompetency. The current of the St. Clair, which most ships rode boldly, seized the *Milwaukee* and twisted her round and round in the eddies. She was helpless. One final slap of the current threw her fast aground within a stone's throw of the Indians. She dropped anchor wearily for the night, as mosquitoes swarmed over the ship. She had spent two days in making a bare twenty miles and had ended her efforts on the shoals. The exhausted sailors turned in for rest, all except two who went ashore to try to find some milk.

Next morning the *Milwaukee* got free and went floating down the river, stern foremost, swinging crazily from shore to shore in the eddies. This idle passage gave Harriet leisure to observe the country. Settlers' houses were continuous, set on long, shoestring strips, after French Canadian custom, from the water front back into the wilderness. The sound of cowbells came pastorally over the water, children were playing, horsemen were riding by chatting and swishing at the flies with leafy branches. Poor houses sat forlornly in the swamps; spacious houses with paling fences in thriving fields dotted the more prosperous Canadian side. Indians were fishing in the river. Great piles of cordwood for the steamers and shingles for the Detroit market were piled up on wharves. Altogether it was a pleasant and refreshing scene.

But aboard the *Milwaukee* things went from bad to worse. On July 10, the captain got sick and had to turn in. The sailors went ashore to get him some brandy and butter. The first mate was still

too ill to take over. The second mate was incompetent at everything but swearing. The sun was hot and the wind was still against
them. They made no progress that day. When she awoke on the
eleventh, Harriet heard the groaning of the ship's timbers, and she
knew they were under way again. The wind was now fair, but
Detroit was still forty miles away and the captain was ill in his
cabin. No one in charge knew the channel. They kept the leads
going. Four miles from Detroit the ship again ran aground with a
groan. The water was so shallow you could touch bottom with a
walking stick. There seemed no hope of getting off the reef. Not a
scrap of meat or bread was left on board. The cook chopped wood
to build a fire. The patience of the passengers was exhausted. The
mate hoisted signal to a passing schooner laden with shingles. It
came alongside. Its captain agreed to take Harriet and the rest to
port. Fifteen of them piled themselves on top of the shingles and
'sailed gently up to the city.' And at our last view and knowledge
of the *Milwaukee*, she was still aground, with a sick captain, a sick
mate, and a barren galley, but still bound east for Detroit and
Buffalo.

XXV

Passenger Steamships

SAILS filled the ship channels across the Lakes through the nine-teenth century, but steam had come, and, in spite of boiler explo-sions, burnings, and disaster, it had come to stay. As the United States and Canada settled down in peace as neighbors on a com-mon seaway, steamships slid down the ways in a score of port towns on both sides of the border. They joined the growing Lake fleet that chugged steadily along, with the wind, against the wind, or through calms that immobilized the brigs and schooners. Sacketts Harbor and Oswego, Black Rock and Buffalo, Erie, Cleveland, Lorain, and Detroit launched each year newer and bigger steam-ships. Small steamers were launched at Chatham on the River Thames, 46 miles above Windsor; they ranged from the small, 60-ton *Little Western* of 1834, up to the 456-ton *Ploughboy* of 1851, which ran up to Sarnia and along Lake Huron. Other yards were active at Port Dover, Chippewa, and Collingwood, and at Toronto and Kingston.

The engine in *Walk-in-the-Water* was salvaged, as we have seen, and placed in the bigger, stouter *Superior,* where it continued a long and useful life. When the Black Hawk War flamed up on the prairie west of the muddy village of Chicago, Lieutenant General Winfield Scott was able to charter this ship and three other steam-ers to transport his 950 troops from Black Rock and Buffalo to Chicago harbor. It was not the fault of the new steamers that few of these troops ever reached Chicago or the war. For 1832 was the horrible plague year that scourged and panicked the lake-shore towns, and cholera out-raced General Scott and his ships. It had spread like wildfire across Europe from its culture zone of Hin-dustan, and had leaped the Atlantic to strike at Quebec and rage

227

westward to Buffalo. General Scott's soldiers carried it aboard the *Superior*, the *Henry Clay*, the *Sheldon Thompson*, and the *William Penn*, and sailed it across Lake Erie to Detroit. It was most virulent on the *Henry Clay*, which was jammed with five or six companies of the troops. The men sickened and died, or went mad with fear as the epidemic spread through the ship. The ship's surgeon got drunk and went to bed. Along the Detroit River and at Fort Gratiot the soldiers leaped overboard and fled along the trails through the woods, where they died or straggled into the villages with the plague. The General reached Chicago on the *Sheldon Thompson* with 52 dead in passage and 80 stricken with cholera. And all around the Lakes the dead were hurried into shallow mass graves by the few who survived.

Plague could not long hold back the flood of passengers who sought quick passage across the Lakes to the promised land of the West. They poured in through the Mohawk Valley to Buffalo, where they jammed the big hotels American, Clarendon, Commercial, and Mansion House on Main Street and the Western facing the Terrace. They looked out over the Buffalo harbor, where from three to four hundred craft could anchor at one time without using more than half of the available space. As the steamers came in, the eager travelers crowded aboard. The *United States* carried 700 of them to Detroit on a single voyage. Ninety steamships docked at Detroit in May 1836. The famous liner *Great Western* began her voyages on the Lakes in 1838. She was a smart and impressive side-wheeler with three masts fore and aft of the two tall smokestacks for her canvas when the wind was favorable. She was the first of the upper-cabin steamers. She sailed proudly with the national ensign on her yardarm, and her own name pennant fluttering from the foremast. Margaret Fuller, who sailed aboard her in 1843, was thrilled by her performance and by the sight of the other ships on the Lakes 'panting in from their rapid and marvellous journey.' In 1831 it took 25 days to sail goods from New York to Chicago. The big *Indiana* made it in 17 days and 6 hours in 1836. But in that same year the steamer *Columbus* set a new record between Chicago and Detroit, up Michigan, through Mackinac, and down

Huron; she made the run in just 68 hours, and also made headlines in the Detroit paper.

The speed records did not of course stand long unchallenged as the mid-century luxury liners appeared on the Lakes. Great rivalry sprang up among the ships, each company or captain-owner trying to outdo the others in the faster schedules and superior appointments of the cabins and the common rooms. The *Chesapeake,* running between Buffalo and Detroit in the 1840's, was famous for her cuisine and her band of musicians and for her upper structure. She was the first to have two tiers of cabin decks. The innovation proved unexpectedly, even miraculously, useful when this fine steamer went down in the dark not long after midnight of June 8, 1847. She was racing along toward Cleveland on a course parallel to another ship when a schooner, bound for Buffalo, collided with her off Conneaut. The schooner sank first and her crew were rescued by the *Chesapeake*. The *Chesapeake* then sank as she tried to reach shore. But as she went down with her crowded passenger list, the upper cabin broke loose from the hull and floated on the surface of Lake Erie. The passengers clung to it as a lifeboat until they were picked up. Only seven were drowned.

The *Empire* appeared in 1844 to surpass the *Chesapeake*. She was launched on the Cuyahoga as the pride of the Cleveland yards, and of the Lakes. She was a 1,220-ton ship, 260 feet long. She went into service between Buffalo and Chicago in the year when over 20,000 passengers made that journey by steamship. Her cabin space ran almost the full length of the ship. She boasted separate salons for ladies and gentlemen. She had a luxury dining room and bar, a library of popular literature, and a good band for concerts and dancing. And to appeal to the immigrant trade she had four large dormitories in steerage, one exclusively for females.

Even this fine steamer enjoyed her superiority for only three seasons before she was outclassed by the *Hendrik Hudson*. This splendid ship made her first run out to Chicago in 1847. In their advertising, the owners featured her elegant appointments: large, full-framed looking glasses; silk velvet settees with spring cushions; walls gilded and embossed; thick and luxurious carpeting; cut-glass chandeliers; spacious dining room and salons; and, as a special snob-appeal, they pointed out as an added attraction the 'novel sight of foreign immigrants in the steerage.' By using the combined facilities of the New York railroads and the *Hendrik Hudson,* travelers in 1847 could go from New York City via Buffalo to Chicago in a mere five days.

Two innovations had a stimulating effect on the development of steamships. One was the propeller and the other was the railroads. The small, 138-ton sloop *Vandalia* was launched at Oswego on Lake Ontario in 1841. She was driven not by the exposed side-paddle wheels, but by the new screw propeller of Ericsson's invention—the first commercial ship to use this revolutionary design. Ericsson had developed it for warships to decrease their vulnerability. It proved so efficient that it was tried on other ships, where it was equally successful. The *Vandalia* was taken up the Welland and entered into the Lake Erie service. Other propellers soon followed the trail of the *Vandalia.* In 1843 the propeller *Hercules* steamed out to Chicago. The voyage demonstrated anew the economy of her design. The engines in the side-wheelers were forward of amidships. They took up valuable space, the smokestacks showered soot and sparks over the decks, and enormous quantities of wood were required to drive the vessel. The engines of the propellers, as these ships were called, were located aft out of the way. The fifty horsepower engine of the *Hercules* occupied only six square feet of space. It could run on ten cords of wood a day at a cost of $17, whereas the steamships were using two cords an hour at a cost of $80 or more a day. Fifteen years after the *Vandalia* was lifted around Niagara Falls there were, according to *Lloyd's Steamboat Directory* of 1856, 118 propellers in service on the Lakes, and 120 steamers, besides the 1,149 sailing ships of various types and rigs.

The railroads also came in with a rush at about the same time. The first road in Michigan was incorporated as early as 1832. It crossed the wrist of the state from Detroit to St. Joseph on Lake Michigan. The 32-mile strip between Toledo and Adrian, Michigan, was opened in 1836. A 211-mile line was laid from Cincinnati to

Sandusky in 1846, connecting the river with the lake and competing with the Miami-Erie Canal. Buffalo became a rail center as well as the bridgehead to the Lakes from the East. By the end of the 1850's there were eleven main lines converging into five passenger terminals in that booming city. Fourteen freight and 300 passenger trains entered and left this lake port every 24 hours, and in the five years between 1850 and 1855 the Buffalo population jumped from 42,261 to 74,214. Simultaneously, rails extended out in all directions from the central depot on the water's edge at Cleveland: 100 miles to Pittsburgh; 67 miles to the Mahoning; across Ohio to Cincinnati; and along the lake shore to Toledo. Canada's Great Western ran across Old Ontario from the Suspension Bridge and Fort Erie to Windsor, with branch lines from London to Port Stanley and connecting with lines joining Toronto and Hamilton with Georgian Bay and Lake Huron ports.

These lines did not at first damage the steamship trade; rather they supplemented and stimulated traffic on the Lakes in the years when the immigrant flood was at its height, flowing westward. Some of the railroads went into the steamship business themselves. The Michigan Central Railroad operated daily passenger service across Lake Erie from Buffalo to Detroit, where the ships made connection with their trains for Chicago. The 1,830-ton *Mississippi,* launched in 1853, and the famed 2,000-tonners *Plymouth* and *Western World* of 1854 plied this route, one of them leaving the Erie Street docks at Buffalo each evening at 9 p.m. except Sunday, for the overnight run.

The Michigan Southern Railroad rivaled this service with its three 'new and popular ships,' the *Southern Michigan* (1853), the *Western Metropolis* (1860), and the big 2,200-ton *City of Buffalo* (1857). Not to be outdone, the C. C. & C. Railroad put into service, with calls at Cleveland, the *Crescent City* and the big *Queen of the West,* built at the Buffalo yards in 1853. And when the Sault was opened, the Cleveland, Detroit & Lake Superior line placed three new first-class propellers in service between Lake Erie ports and Superior City. The flagship was the *Iron City,* advertised as one of 'the fastest on the Lakes.'

Even before the Civil War temporarily closed the flourishing Mississippi River traffic and diverted it to the Great Lakes, more and more people were coming in to Chicago to make this portion of their journey to the East an excursion cruise on one of these palatial new steamers or propellers. But the panic that swept the country at the end of the 1850's, the rapid extension of improved railroads, and the devastation of the war itself seriously hurt the over-expanded luxury liners on the Lakes. Several of them had to be withdrawn from service, and some were broken up or decommissioned.

When the country and the Great Lakes passenger trade recovered in the 1870's and 1880's, still another era had already dawned in the structure of the ships. The sails rapidly disappeared, and the old wooden-hulled and wood-burning side-wheelers were outmoded. Steel hulls and coal-burning engines had made their appearance to haul the ever-increasing bulk freight of ore and grain down the Lakes. And the new passenger ships from the yards at Buffalo and Cleveland, Detroit and Manitowoc reflected the revolution. The passenger ships never recovered the dominance they enjoyed in the 1840's and 1850's, but they remained, and still are, significant. The new pace was first set in the 1870's by the *India,* the *China,* and the *Japan,* all of Buffalo, built by Edwin Townsend Evans for the Anchor Line. But these graceful vessels were surpassed two decades later by the Northern Shipping Company's *Northland* and the *North West,* both Jim Hill ships that were for many years the finest on the waters between Chicago, Detroit, and Buffalo.

The lead in passenger ships on long-run voyages across the Lakes, however, passed over to the Canadian companies, particularly the Canada Steamship Lines and the Canadian Pacific Railway. The Canadian Pacific decided in the early 1880's that the time had come for genuine ocean-going type ships to sail the Great Lakes, especially to bridge the water gap from their Port McNicoll on Georgian Bay to the Lakehead cities. That decision required imagination and some boldness. The ships were built and launched on the other side of the ocean in the Clyde and sailed to Montreal in 1884. They were 363 feet 5 inches long, and too big therefore to get through the locks on the St. Lawrence canals. They were placed in dry dock, cut in two, and towed by tugs up the river, across Lake Ontario, and through the Welland Canal to Buffalo. There they were put together again, and began their long and lucrative career in the Upper Lakes—except the *Algoma,* which joined many other fine ships when she went down in a blizzard on Lake Superior in 1887. Two more larger ships were brought up in the same way in 1907. One of them, the *Assiniboia,* 336-feet long, has been for over three decades one of the popular ships on the run from lower Georgian Bay ports up to the Lakehead.

The Canada Steamship Lines' Northern Navigation Division ships, *Hamonic, Huronic,* and *Noronic* (unpleasant names for very pleasant ships), compete with the Canadian Pacific fleet. They leave Windsor, cross the river to Detroit to pick up passengers, then steam up to Sarnia. There they take on a cargo of package freight and the automobiles of passengers who wish to motor west from Port Arthur. They stop again at the dingy wharf at Canada's Sault Ste. Marie for coal, package freight, and more automobiles and passengers. They go through the small Canadian lock at the Sault, and head across Lake Superior for Thunder Bay. They make an overnight side trip down to Duluth, and return, completing the round trip in seven pleasant days with long stopovers at each port.

The *Hamonic* is 341 feet long and over 5,000 tons, and the larger *Noronic* is 362 feet long and almost 7,000 tons. They are operated much like Mediterranean cruise steamers, with excellent cuisine, music, and dancing, and generous promenade decks and salons. As these ships steam up Lake Huron or across the center of Lake Superior, surrounded on all sides by blue water and swelling seas, with a long gray wake fanning out to the stern, with gulls trailing and flashing white wings in the sun, with the master on the bridge and lookouts posted, it is hard to believe that this is a fresh-water ship on an inland ocean 2,000 miles from the Atlantic. Many lesser ships ply the seven salt-water seas.

Many other passenger ships on shorter runs brighten the shipping lanes on the Great Lakes. Several lines operate out of Chicago to

the Michigan ports of St. Joseph, Benton Harbor, Ludington, up
the shore to Milwaukee, and through the Sault to Duluth. The
Canada Steamship Lines have some good vessels on Lake Ontario, crossing from Toronto to Niagara, and serving the route to
Kingston and Prescott. And the overnight service on Lake Erie is
still somewhat reminiscent of the great days of the 1850's. The big
side-wheelers of the Detroit & Cleveland Navigation Company,
the *Greater Detroit* and the *Greater Buffalo*, are familiar sights on
Lake Erie. They are 550 feet long, they accommodate 1,200 passengers, they are splendidly equipped, and they race through the
night past Long Point and Pelee Island at a speed of 21 knots.
They are fitted with rudders both fore and aft to enable them to
make quick turns and maneuvers in the narrow channels in spite
of their great length. The gigantic 6,300-ton excursion steamer
Seeandbee, of the Cleveland & Buffalo Line, was converted into
an aircraft carrier for naval training on Lake Michigan in World
War II. With her superstructure cleared and a flight deck built
over her mammoth width and length, this speedy ship made an
ideal practice landing field on the tossing waters of the Great Lakes.

Hundreds of handsome steamships have come and gone on the
Great Lakes. Most of them lived out a useful life and were honorably broken up, decommissioned, or converted into tows or floating
docks. Others went down in screaming tragedy, and their wreckage through the decades strews the floor of the Great Lakes. Some
of them are almost legends. The steamer *Clarion* lies on the bottom
of Lake Erie near the old British naval base at Amherstburg. She
is weighted down with a cargo of locomotives. The steamer *Temple-
ton* is anchored to the floor of Lake Michigan off South Manitou
Island by an even more valuable cargo of 350 barrels of fine whiskey. In August 1865 the steamers *Meteor* and *Pewabic* mysteriously
collided while passing shortly after sunset off Thunder Bay on
Lake Huron. The *Pewabic* had made a sudden turn in the rolling
sea, and the *Meteor* crashed against her, ripping a huge gash in her
side. Water poured into the *Pewabic* and she quickly plunged
down 20 fathoms to the lake floor with a rich cargo of copper. Of
her 180 passengers, 125 were lost. She lay there until 1917, with

legend accumulating around her. By that time diving apparatus had improved sufficiently to withstand the pressure of that depth. The diver who went down found a macabre scene of skeletons in the cabins, period costumes of Civil War days strewn about the ship, beer and beef in the galley, and playing cards on the table in the salon. The treasure, however, amounted to only $7,000.

Boiler explosions and fires took a heavy toll from the steamers of the 1840's and 1850's. The ships were built of wood, and many of them were decorated with heavy coatings of inflammable varnish. For many years they also burned wood in their boilers. They were firetraps on the windy lakes. The records are full of annual disasters, which combine all the horrors of burning and drowning. From a long list we choose one example which, if the details are slightly varied, tells the story of them all.

In the summer of 1841 the *Erie* steamed out of Buffalo. Of her list of about 200 passengers, 140 were Swiss and German immigrants packed in the steerage for the last lap of their journey to the land of prosperity and peace. It was a mild and pleasant day on Lake Erie, though a late afternoon wind was rising. The voyage was proceeding well. Then at 8:00 o'clock in the evening the *Erie* burst into flames. Almost before anybody knew what was happening, the flames swept through the ship, lapping up the painted and varnished timbers, devouring the furnishings, and driving the passengers into uncontrollable panic. The evening winds fanned the flames. Men and women screamed and leaped into the water, many of them trailing flames from their burning clothing. Some burned to death in the ship, others drowned in the lake. The lifeboats capsized. The life preservers were caught by the flames and burned in storage. Only twenty-eight men and one lone woman were saved. Some painters on their way to Erie to finish a new steamship had placed their cans of turpentine and varnish directly over the boilers of the *Erie*. No one suspected them or discovered them. They got too hot and exploded, scattering flaming liquid all over the tinder-dry ship.

Scores of passenger and immigrant ships perished in wrecks and collisions. The destruction of the famous side-wheeler *Atlantic* is typical. In August 1852 she put in at Erie, Pennsylvania, where 200 Norwegians were crowded on the wharf awaiting passage for Quebec. The *Atlantic* already had a near capacity load of passengers from Detroit. She could take only 125 of the immigrants. The disappointed 75 were forced to wait at the dock as their companions boarded and sailed off into the night. The *Atlantic* held her course past Long Point. She was nearing her destination with her passengers asleep and comfortable in their cabins and in the steerage dormitories. Out of the fog that was forming over the lake after midnight came the propeller *Ogdenburg*. She hit the *Atlantic* port side, but without apparent damage. Both ships continued on their course.

Two miles to the east the *Atlantic* began to flood and go down. The alarm was sounded and the passengers rushed topside to prepare to abandon ship. They threw overboard for life preservers everything that would float. The procedure was orderly and under control. But the Norwegians understood no English. They did not comprehend the captain's orders. They became panic-stricken and leaped overboard, wild and screaming. The *Ogdenburg* heard them two miles away and hurried back to the rescue. The ship sank in the darkness. Three hundred people, including almost all the immigrants, were drowned. The *Atlantic* still lies 25 fathoms deep on the Lake Erie floor, with $60,000 of Adams Express money and much treasure of the passengers and immigrants aboard.

The greatest tragedy of all did not occur in a storm or in a wreck on the open Great Lakes waters, but in the narrow channel of the Chicago River at the Clark Street Bridge dock. And it was not in the careless 1840's and 1850's, but on July 24, 1915. The steamer *Eastland* had worked up the river and was tied to the dock to receive 2,500 Western Electric Company passengers for a holiday excursion across Lake Michigan to the dune country. She was a fine, 1,900-ton three-decked ship with a record of ten years of service on the Lakes. As the gay crowd of passengers swarmed aboard at 7:00 a.m., the *Eastland* began to list. First she swayed toward the dock. Captain Pederson ordered the sea cocks opened to trim the ship. She came back to even keel, and then listed at a reckless angle away from the dock. Passengers below were thrown against the bulkheads, and bottles in the bar crashed. The captain attempted to work the ship out to the channel, but she continued to list. Frightened passengers began to jump overboard. At about 7:30 the strangely behaving ship turned over in the river with her starboard side turned topside above the water. Scores of people caught in the panic and confusion drowned in the river a few feet from the dock. Hundreds were trapped in the cabins and below decks. Only a few could crawl through portholes or stay alive inside until the rescuers with acetylene torches cut their way in. Eight hundred and fifteen people died, including 22 entire families.

No satisfactory reason for the capsizing could be given. The passengers had not crowded to either side, and the ship itself is still sailing the Lakes. She was converted to a naval training ship, and renamed *Wilmette*. Her berth is the pier by the Naval Reserve Armory on the inner harbor, in plain sight from the bridge on Wacker Drive.

((((XXVI))))

Great Lakes Melting Pot

ONE day in 1840 a trim clipper ship hoisted sail in the harbor of the Swedish port town of Gävle. She had a cargo of Swedish iron for New York. She could also carry a few passengers at $26 each, provided they would bring their own bedding and rations.

Young Gustav Unonius held a small government post at Uppsala. The outlook for the future was unpromising in the stratified society of his homeland. But across the sea in fabulous America all was bright and shining. 'I have heard about America,' he said. 'Every workman has there the same right of citizenship as the nobles. Conventional judgments, class interests, and narrow-mindedness do not hang to your coat tail nor trample on your heels.' Unonius took his bride and her maid down to Gävle and boarded the clipper. Three young men—two university students and a relative of Unonius—joined them, and the little party sailed to New York.

They were still uncertain where to settle in the promised land. They talked with New Yorkers about the Great Westlands, only to find that New Yorkers, as one might expect, knew less about the country than the Swedes of Uppsala. They met a fellow countryman who had made good money in Illinois and was now returning to the homeland. He described that country to Unonius as 'one of the most wonderful regions in the world, with extensive, fruitful, easily cultivated plains. If one desired to engage in agriculture, the emigrant could choose from a great surplus of vacant lands. There are many opportunities to earn an income.'

Those words decided Unonius. The party set out for Illinois.

They sailed to Albany and crossed to Buffalo on a canal boat. On that leisurely leg of the journey they fell in with a rival booster from Wisconsin. Go to Wisconsin, he urged them; it is 'the most beautiful and most fruitful region in the great west, and under present conditions the best for emigrants.' They boarded the lake ship torn between the two prospects. Crossing Lake Erie, a Milwaukee enthusiast added his word that all the best land in Illinois was cornered by speculators. The ship sailed through the Straits of Mackinac and across northern Lake Michigan to booming Milwaukee. When most of the immigrants went down the gangplank, Unonius, his bride, her maid, and their young friends were among them. They had chosen Wisconsin.

They looked at the land and selected a spot at Pine Lake about 30 miles west of Milwaukee. Others soon came to join them: middle-class men and women, army officers, decadent nobles, young, un-placed university graduates. They built log cabins and in 1841 founded the first Swedish colony in that state.

It was a pity, however, that with all the good land lying around they took the Pine Lake tract. The soil was poor, and these particular men were unschooled in pioneer farming. Few prospered. Most of them remained at the log-cabin level. Fredrika Bremer, a novelist on tour, called at the colony in 1850. A half-dozen families were still there struggling along, and one, a member of the gentry in Sweden, but a 'practical peasant' in Wisconsin, was well, happy, and optimistic. Others had scattered to better fortune elsewhere; Unonius had become a successful minister of the gospel and Episcopal missionary to his countrymen in the New World. But all rejoiced that they were in a land where at their own desire they could shift and change their fortune on their own volition.

Unonius's party was an insignificant atom unit in one of the greatest epics in all the history of mankind. That was the mass migration of men and women from Europe to the Lake states in the nineteenth century. They did not know it at the time, but never to any people anywhere in any age had such an opportunity come on such a scale and so swiftly. The mind dwells upon it. It was like a microcosmic drama of man's adventure upon the earth. The Mediterranean basin was scarred with age and battle; its towns were crowded, its soil thin and long ago pre-empted. Europe was so old, so cramped, so weary, so hopeless, its forests gone, its land partitioned, its society rigorously classified. But around the Lakes were not just crofters' plots, not mere acres, but whole square miles of lands and forests. It was not buried under the mists of Jutland. The soil was not rocks or sand or swamps, but thick with fertility; not tilted up on end but flat or gently rolling. The summers were long. This Eden was open to all who cared to come, and titles to it were theirs almost for the asking. The United States even urged land upon the immigrants and helped them to get to it.

So the young men and women of all Europe enthusiastically streamed into the new land. They came by the thousands, their number reached millions. They came as conquerors, but in peace, armed not with guns but with plows for their field pieces. Men from all nations converged on the Lake country. Their governments had made wars on their neighbors for ages past, their fathers and grandfathers had fought across their borders. Here they were meeting as friendly and helpful neighbors. They were meeting not in different uniforms to blow each other to bits, but as human beings on a common quest. They were uniting on the basis of their mutual need for co-operative development of a virgin territory. They were crowding centuries into a few hours; they were enacting a telescopic drama of the experience of the race. Not generations but a decade or two separated a wilderness from prosperous towns, villages, and farms. There was nothing but land and forest and waterways when they came. Whatever rose here would be their handiwork. They could build to the limit of their strength and wisdom.

A few men from New England and the Atlantic states, not many, had gone to the Lakes and laid out towns with the American stamp upon them. But no force was applied to the masses of immigrants who came from other cultures. One of the reassuring proofs of the virility of the principles upon which the Nation was founded was the ease and naturalness with which men from all countries embraced them and flourished under them. Jefferson would have rejoiced to see these Swedes and Danes and Norwegians, these Germans and Poles and Irish, these Cornishmen and Frenchmen and Englishmen, these Dutchmen and Rumanians and

Italians, helping to form new states, working together under the basic appeal of the growing American tradition. No gendarmes spied upon their homes, no gauleiters inspected their schools and churches. They could retain any of their homeland traditions they might choose: the *weinstube,* the *turnverein* of their German towns, the *klopfen* of Holland streets, the *sauna* of their Finnish villages. Their own emotional needs were their sole guide and authority. They could wear their hats or toss them in the air before the President himself at their own pleasure. Yet they became Americans and made the Lake region one of the marvels of the globe.

Hardships? Plenty of them, severe and devastating.

Cheats, swindlers? As everywhere.

Failures, frauds? Naturally.

Loneliness, misery, homesickness? Yes, and on the deepest plane that cut and seared the heart, as in Rölvaag's *Giants in the Earth*— but still persevering giants.

Sickness, hunger, despair? Yes, but no more than flesh is heir to.

But always they were sustained by their sense of political, financial, and personal dignity, and by their hope for the future. So they sacrificed to build schools they could never attend, but where their children would be educated as free, participating citizens of the towns and commonwealths they were building on the Great Lakes shores and on the timber and prairie land adjoining. It was a thrilling epic of America and mankind. It was the formative period of the Great Lakes.

The Scandinavians were among the first to come. Their experience and adventures were representative. The wonders of the new world around the Great Lakes were the talk of young men in every crofters' cottage, in university halls, in the lumber and mining villages, and in the seaport towns of Norway and Sweden. Men who had already been to America and prospered there returned with heavy gold watch chains across their waistcoats and with money in their pockets. Sometimes their passage was paid by lumber companies in the Wisconsin pineries, or by the mining firms of Michigan, Wisconsin, and Minnesota, if they would induce men to come

to America to work in these new industries. They were even given
bonus commissions for recruiting labor. These personal emissaries
dropped their words into ears already made eager to hear. Sons
and neighbors who had gone ahead wrote back home of the opportunities to build railroads, mine copper, or sail ships for good
wages, and of the ease with which this cash could be used to buy
farms.

Pamphlets describing the country and giving full directions for
reaching it were published in the native tongue and circulated
as early as 1837 and 1841. They stressed the point that in this
Lake territory there were few taxes, there was no privileged class,
and no militaristic government quartered troops in your home.
There was room for all who would come—smiths and tailors and
shoemakers and carpenters as well as miners, lumberjacks, and
farmers. Servant girls should come, too; they would be treated
with respect and they could marry at their pleasure. Drunkards
and lazy people should stay away; they would find only misery and
short welcome. But for solid folk there was no limit to the opportunities. They could buy land for $1.50 an acre, a good horse or a
yoke of oxen for $40 to $50, a cow for $10, a fat hog for $4, or a
large sheep for $1.25. Wheat was 50 cents a bushel, flour $3.50 a
barrel, and butter 8 cents a pound. A man could go from Sweden
to the Lake region for about $50. If the wives were too reluctant
to leave their neighbors and the impoverished but familiar life for
the new and untried land, husbands were advised to use the technique of planning to leave them behind. If that failed, they should
command under authority of the marriage vow. So the women
came.

Before the vision of even the most reluctant floated the enticing
pictures drawn by those who had already spied out the land. As
immigrant ships tossed through the weeks of passage on the rolling Atlantic, as the Lake boats wrestled with Huron storms, the
weary, seasick travelers recalled the glowing promise of Fredrika
Bremer, their own novelist, who toured the Lake country and
found it good. 'What a glorious new Scandinavia might not Minnesota become!' she had written. 'Here would the Swede find again

his clear, romantic lakes, the plains of Scania rich in corn, and the valleys of Norrland . . . The Danes might here pasture their flocks and herds and lay out their farms on less misty coasts than those of Denmark . . . The climate, the situation, the character of the scenery agree with our people better than that of any other of the American states.'

John Ericsson, who grew up on a small foundry estate in the Province of Värmland, came in 1839 to put screw propellers on steamboats and to build the turret battleship *Monitor*. News of how the *Princeton*, equipped with the Swedish inventor's submerged propeller, won handily a race with the side-wheeler *Great Western*, the finest steamship then afloat, caused rejoicing among his people. He became an American citizen and stayed on in New York.

Jenny Lind came, and with her nightingale voice and P. T. Barnum's showmanship captured the hearts of everybody. She returned to Sweden leaving her countrymen in America heartened and inspired and calling themselves Jenny Lind men. Ole Bull came and also conquered.

On and on came the nameless little people, shipload after shipload of them, to go to work around the Lakes. They landed at Quebec, at Boston, New York, and Baltimore, and streamed west.

The *Superior* sailed across the Atlantic in 1844 with 50 passengers. Three ships sailed from Gävle with 250 passengers in 1849. The *Charles Tottie*, with a cargo of 300 tons of ore, advertised for 250 to 310 passengers at about $15 each. The tide rolled higher and higher. The American Emigrant Aid and Homestead Company, with a capital of five million dollars, soon established direct and scheduled steamship service between Scandinavia and New York, with five big ships like the new *Ottawa* sailing from Gothenburg to New York with 635 passengers in only 15 days. The Company operated a land office through which the immigrants could purchase and sell farms, an insurance and employment office, and a banking and exchange department for converting riksdalers into American money. It was only one of several such companies. The Lake Superior Copper Mining Companies sent the Reverend B. F.

Tefft, formerly a consul at Stockholm, to Sweden in 1864 to get
10,000 miners and artisans to come to the Lakes. They paid him
$6,000 a year and commissions for his services. The company of-
fered to advance all expenses, including passage, to be repaid by
the immigrant in labor at the mines. Tefft chartered the steamer
Ernest Merk in July 1864 to send over a group of 500.

The Lake states themselves sent out their own agents. Wisconsin
men offered free transportation and two weeks' free bed and board
to men who would come to rising industrial towns like Green Bay.
Minnesota established its own Board of Immigration in 1866, and
had her agents at the ports of entry to interpret for the new arrivals, to look after their baggage, and give them literature about
the Minnesota region. The chamber of commerce of St. Paul, the
city authorities, and the transportation companies clubbed together
to maintain a 'Home' to give shelter, aid, and comfort to the needy
immigrants. Abe Lincoln encouraged them, and the Homestead Act
of 1862 lured them.

All this publicity about the free, peaceful New World came at
the very moment when Sweden, worried by German military might,
passed a military conscription act (1860) for all men between the
ages of 20 and 25. This fanned the enthusiasm of Scandinavia for
the Great Lakes region. Fifteen thousand of their citizens passed
through the single port of Milwaukee in 1866, ten thousand went
through Chicago, and fanned out into the virgin lands. A fifth of
the entire population of Norway and Sweden moved to the New
World, over a million of them in the two decades from 1877-98.
By 1900, just to pay passing notice to formal statistics, there were
225,900 people in Minnesota either born in Sweden or having a
parent born there. And, in the same category, there were 200,032
in Illinois, 49,790 in Michigan, and 48,382 in Wisconsin. It was,
indeed, Fredrika Bremer's 'glorious new Scandinavia.'

New Scandinavia was not ready-made and waiting. The journey
itself was enough to daunt all but the stout hearted. Take the case
of the party with which Eric Norelius, later a great leader in the
Swedish Lutheran Church, came to the Great Lakes. The year was

Ore freighter of the Bethlehem Transportation Co., upbound toward Lake Superior, on Soo Canal.

Cleveland grain elevators on the waterfront. *Photograph by A. F. Sozio. Courtesy of Philip Gendreau, N. Y.*

1850, and Norelius was seventeen. One hundred Swedes left Gävle aboard a clipper loaded with iron for New York. They paid only $8 each for passage, but they furnished their own food and bedding. Clippers were romantically beautiful to look at, making full sail through the Skagerrak, but they were cramped, smelly, and uncomfortable to live in. Some of the party slept on deck. They were almost three months on the sea because the wind was sore against them. Some died of cholera and smallpox.

It was late autumn when they finally docked in New York. They took the steamer to Albany and crossed to Buffalo by train. It was a crude, slow, cattle train, but it was the first the party had ever seen and they made no complaint. They were dumped out and stranded at Buffalo. They knew no English, and their interpreter had left them at Albany. The Norwegian hotel keeper who found them and took them in sharply overcharged them. They got aboard the lake steamer *Sultana* only to discover that there were no staterooms left. It was cold November on the Lakes, and the oncoming winter wind was biting at night, but they had to sleep on deck. For $40 they did get two cabins for the sick and the weak who could not endure the exposure. On Lake St. Clair the steamer ran aground and the passengers had to be unloaded. They got under way again the following day, and steamed on up Lake Huron and down Lake Michigan to Chicago. The voyage had taken ten punishing days and nights.

There were no trains out of Chicago in 1850. The party took passage out over the new Illinois and Michigan canal at $1.50 per person. It was very cold, the snow was falling, and there was no heat inside the canal boat. Per Anderson set up in the baggage room the cookstove he had bought in Chicago. The immigrants huddled about it to keep warm. It took three days to negotiate the canal from Chicago to Andover. They were still sixty miles from their chosen destination at Peru when Per Anderson cooled his stove and carried it from the baggage room to the wharf. They had their choice of walking those miles or waiting for teams and wagons, at $10 a load. Fifteen of them walked, the others waited.

When they got to Peru, they found only a few crowded frontier

houses—not enough to put roofs over the immigrants' heads. Many
of them were now penniless, even after borrowing from those
who could lend, but they were undaunted. They did what other
thousands of their countrymen did: they hired themselves out
hither and yon at whatever they could find to do. And after a few
months or a few years of labor, they got land of their own and
started the hard upward climb to independence.

Wherever work was going on in the Great Lakes country, the
Scandinavians were there. Swedes went under contract to the iron
and copper ranges of Michigan for a guarantee of $260 a year.
They moved over into northwestern Wisconsin and hewed out
farms along Lake Superior, around Iron River and Poplar, and
around Brule, where their sons and grandsons saw Calvin Coolidge
fish in the summer of 1928. They worked as lumberjacks in the
Wisconsin pineries and drove rafts down the Illinois River. They
made sail on Great Lakes ships and pushed grain and copper and
iron in wheelbarrows from the wharves to the hatches. They cleared
right-of-way and laid railroad ties and rails in construction gangs.
They laid out Swedish villages, built churches, and cultivated their
farms in the Chicago Lake district on the St. Croix River on the
borders of Minnesota and Wisconsin. Their artisans and professional men went into the cities to make furniture and shoes and
clothes, to become musicians, doctors, lawyers, and civic leaders.
Eric Norelius, whose journey to this land we have just followed,
founded Gustavus Adolphus College. His countrymen in the new
world, including Norwegians, endowed the celebrated St. Olaf
College at Northfield. They have supported the great state universities and educted their children there. They have retained enough
of their native culture to lend color and dignity to their heritage;
they have made New Scandinavia a treasured portion of new
America.

Such records as their governments kept merged Norwegians with
the Swedes until about 1850, but the Norwegians did not merge.
Even to this day, though friendly in spirit, they seldom mingle with
the Swedes; they keep their settlements distinct. They were among

the first Scandinavians to come to the Great Lakes. Back in 1825, the year the Erie Canal was opened, Cleng Peerson, a vigorous and restless personality, met the little sloop *Restaurationen* with 53 Quaker Norwegians from Stavanger, and took them to Kendall, New York, to plant a colony. A decade later, with the new West and the Great Lakes casting their spell over the East, Peerson and his colonists moved on to the Fox River in Illinois and founded in 1834 the first permanent Norwegian Colony in this country. They called it Norway. A century later in that village the great commonwealth of Illinois erected a monument to Peerson in recognition of his leadership in planting Norwegian colonies, and of the work of his people in the growth of the state.

That ceremony was symbolic of the pride and achievement of the Norwegian Americans. Their hardships were exactly parallel to those of their more numerous neighbors, the Swedes. For over a hundred years they have been helping to build up the country around the Great Lakes. They followed closely behind the American citizens of the eastern states who came in the 1820's and 1830's to found the villages and set the pattern of industry. They toiled in the mines of the Vulcan vein in Upper Michigan, and called their little village Norway. They populated the lumber camps of the entire Northwest, and then took the cutover lands of Michigan and Wisconsin to transform them by back-breaking labor into prosperous gardens and farms. They acquired most of the Red River section of Minnesota, and made it into a transplanted homeland. They developed towns like Manister on the east shore of Lake Michigan.

They had an especial fondness for Wisconsin, with its lakes and rivers and rolling countryside. Back in Norway, as in Sweden, they read glowing accounts of its wonders. They read Ole Rynning's *True Account of America* (1837), and Reiersen's *Pathfinder for Norwegian Emigrants to the North American States and Texas* (1844). From the 1840's through the 1880's they came in everswelling numbers. They also sailed on iron-carrying sailing ships with all their attendant miseries. They slept in rows of bunks hurriedly erected of rough boards. The only light came through

the hatches that had to be battened down in rough weather. Two
or three lamps burned day and night down there, and the stale air
made the passengers ill. There were no separate rooms for men
and women. Children were born and mothers died there. They
fed themselves on salt or smoked meat, flat bread, and cakes of sour
milk. They cooked where they could. Water was doled out to
them. Dysentery struck and killed them in large numbers. But
the survivors came bravely on.

They settled in the port and shipbuilding town of Manitowoc on
Lake Michigan, and grouped themselves in a near-by farming village which they named Valders for the mist-filled valley from
which they came. They followed the Yankees into the farm and
garden country around Madison, around Waukeska, West Salem,
and Richland Center. They helped drain the swamps at Black
Earth in the 1850's and planted gardens there in the deep dark
soil they had reclaimed. Some of them went to the iron ranges
back of Duluth. Some settled on the Wisconsin shore of Lake
Superior. In a dozen communities they have placed a Norwegian
stamp on the villages. The Norwegian script name is still visible
on the old mill in their hog and horse-trading town among the
springs of Lodi. At Stoughton and Albion, where they make up
three-fourths of the population, Norwegian is still much spoken
and native festivals are celebrated. At Westby, named for Norwegian Ole Westby, in the tobacco district of Wisconsin, the the-
atres use the native tongue. These Norwegians raise peas and
tobacco; they make cheese, and tend their herds. In Milwaukee
and Chicago they publish their own newspapers. At Little Norway,
near Madison, they display their native arts in a replica of a Norwegian village, complete with blue casement windows and sod roofs.
Their Lutheran church spires rise above the trees in scores of
towns and villages. Their lives in America are brilliantly inter-
preted by their greatest literary master, the late O. E. Rölvaag of
their own St. Olaf College. Their achievements are recorded and
their culture is encouraged by the active Norwegian-American Historical Association and their publications.

Danes left their fog-covered fjord pasturelands of Jutland to carry on their expert dairy technique in the Great Lakes states. All through the 1850's and 1860's, and again through the 1870's and 1880's to the turn of the century, they arrived in numbers only a little fewer than the Norwegians. They stopped in Michigan, they crossed into Illinois, they settled in Minnesota, but like the Norwegians they found Wisconsin especially to their liking. Their gift for dairying and cheese making far surpassed anything in America in the middle of the nineteenth century, and their solid, quiet industry is largely responsible for Wisconsin's position of leadership in this field.

The hardy, oppressed sons of Finland also came to the Lake region in large numbers. The Russians had taken over the Finns from the Swedes in 1809. They treated their new subjects with consideration for several years, but toward the end of the century the Czar began to exploit them without mercy. The only defense of so small a subject nation with pride and independence of spirit was migration. The bright beacon of American freedom guided them to the Great Lakes shore, where there were ships to be sailed, ore to be mined, timber to be cut, and farms to be cleared and developed.

The first groups came at the close of the Civil War and went into the copper mines of the Upper Peninsula of Michigan. They moved on along the Lake Superior shore to Wisconsin, to work the Gogebic range, or to transform the rocky cutover land into small gardens and potato farms. They dumped ore into the first steamers at Superior in the days before the great loading chutes were devised. They helped build those grain elevators and ore docks which now tower over the harbors. They flocked to the Vermilion and Mesabi ranges back of Duluth, when they were opened in the 1880's and 1890's. Thousands upon thousands of them people the mining villages throughout the range and keep the river of ore flowing into the freighters at Duluth Harbor.

Other thousands, unhappy in the ore pits or smitten with the respiratory diseases that go with mining, moved to farms beyond

the iron hills and built villages at Eski, at Embarass, and at New
York Mills. They have engaged in dairying in Minnesota and Wisconsin. They live in communities in Ashtabula, Conneaut, and
Cleveland, where the ore is unloaded on Lake Erie. They have
gathered in Detroit and Milwaukee and Chicago. They publish
their own newspapers. They have led in the organization and
spread of the co-operative movement in the Lake states. Near
Lake Superior, on the Bois Brule River, they have their own co-
operative summer camp. And in most of their settlements they have
preserved their old-world custom of the *sauna,* the steam bath,
which the Finns brought to America with them. In almost any
Finnish community you will see these log bathhouses, either private or co-operative, which the Finns find so necessary to their
happiness. In the center of these air-tight bathhouses they heat
stones and then pour water on the stones to create steam. Whole
families gather into them, lounge on planks, beat themselves with
twigs while they steam their bodies, and then finish their bath with
a douse of cold water.

The Finns have made themselves a significant element among the
people of the Great Lakes. They have toiled against great odds,
and wrestled with some of the least profitable land. But in general
they have prospered in their new Finlandia, and the names of their
sons appear on the Phi Beta Kappa lists of the Universities of
Minnesota and Wisconsin.

Of all the people from northern Europe who streamed into the
Great Lakes region, the Germans were the most numerous and
influential. They began coming in mass to the Great Lakes region
in the 1830's. They settled in Sandusky on Lake Erie and spread
down the Miami-Erie Canal toward Cincinnati, which they made
into a German city. They selected Milwaukee and for many
decades, right down to World War I in fact, gave it all the color
of a city of the Rhineland, complete with great breweries, singing
and debating societies, German newspapers, and *weinstubes.* Milwaukee became as much the symbol of German-America as Keokuk
and Kalamazoo were in later years of the mid-western American

town. The Germans especially favored the Great Lakes. They liked the shoreline, the waterways, the smaller lakes, and the rivers. They were pleased with the woods and forests, with the untouched soil, with the opportunity to build a new society where none had ever been before.

America was fortunate in the quality of the Germans who came to her shores. All of them, even the poorest peasants, were industrious and glowing with ambition, and the percentage of well-educated men, gifted with leadership and endowed with good will and family background, was exceptionally high. Among them were the liberals in thought, men like Carl Schurz, who militantly opposed the despotism of the German states after the Napoleonic wars. They came from Brandenburg and Pomeria, from Swabia, Hesse, and the Palatinate, from Westphalia, Thuringia, and the Rhineland. They refused conformity to the state church. They coveted the kind of religious and political freedom guaranteed by the American Constitution and fought for by American patriots. Many of them had been educated at the German universities which were then reaching the height of their prestige as centers for liberal thought. They rebelled against the expanding militarism of nineteenth-century Germany with its years of compulsory army service. They tried to place their fatherland on the democratic road of development in their revolution of 1848. But they lost that revolution and Germany plunged forward into its militaristic, intensely national monarchy that led straight into the two world wars.

It was America's good fortune that the Nazi refinements in torture had not been perfected in 1848. The great band of liberal men were not herded into prison camps. No cordon of armed guards surrounded the Reich. No stormtroopers, no Gestapo hunted them down to prevent their escape from the regime which they had opposed and tried to overthrow. They departed for a land where freedom was already a tradition jealously guarded. Agents went to Germany to encourage immigration. The state of Michigan published a guidebook for them and sent its commissioner of immigration, E. H. Thompson, into Germany in the year of the Revolution to urge Germans to buy Michigan land. They came to

America in a steady stream and in the two great waves of the early
1850's and the 1870's and 1880's. Schurz, to take one outstanding
example, fled from Germany in 1849. He went to Watertown, Wisconsin, about fifty miles northwest of Milwaukee, in 1855, where
a colony of Germans had received the title of Latin Farmers because they spoke in Latin. Schurz was a major general in the
Civil War, became Secretary of the Interior, and was Lincoln's
minister to Spain. The monument to him on Lake Shore Drive in
Oshkosh calls him 'Our Greatest German American.' But we should
not overlook the important contribution to American living made
by such great artists as Pabst and Schlitz.

Much of the hard work requiring patience and physical endurance was performed by the Germans. They toiled alongside the
Irish through the years from 1836-48 in the big ditch of the Illinois-
Michigan Canal. They helped build the Illinois Central Railroad in
the 1850's. They helped dig the Soo Canal. They liked the forests
around the Great Lakes, and felt pride in owning them because
in the Fatherland the forest preserves were the symbol of privi-
lege and power. They operated bakeries and creameries, wineries
and breweries. They owned stores, manufacturing plants, and busi-
nesses of all kinds. Their trained physicians doctored the people
and made Minneapolis, St. Paul, and Milwaukee into clinical centers of world importance. Each town had its music clubs where
Bach and Beethoven took the place of banjo-plucked frontier ballads, and where symphony orchestras displaced the church organ.
They founded schools from kindergartens to universities. They
came in such overwhelming numbers, so rapidly, that their communities were, until World War I, like transplanted German towns.
They spoke German, conducted church services in German, erected
signs in German, and published newspapers in German. They
stamped large areas with their culture as effectively as the English did the villages of New England. Instead of New Bedford,
New London, New Haven, or Plymouth and Southampton, a
journey around the Great Lakes leads you through New Ulm, New
Berlin, Germantown, and Dheinsburg. Their neat farms are distinctive, and the big houses of the prosperous merchant and manu-

facturing class overlook the Lakes from Buffalo all the way to
Duluth.

Twenty-one different nationalities have joined together around
the Lakes. Their reasons for coming, the hardships endured in
breaking ties in the homeland, crossing the Atlantic, and making
the long journey to their new homes ran along the pattern which
we have just been tracing. Each racial group, while taking on
American characteristics, retained some elements of its national
life and contributed some of them to the Great Lakes region. The
Irish moved on from the Lake Ontario section and the Erie Canal
to the Ohio, Indiana, Illinois, and Wisconsin canals. Many came
as contract laborers and were herded about under the most rigorous conditions. Many were wretchedly poor, many came to escape
extreme poverty or outright starvation in Ireland. The great harbors into which the ships now steam so smoothly were improved
and deepened by the Irish. The deep pits in the mine regions were
dug largely by Irish muscle. The railroad tracks over which a
thousand trains rush day and night without jostling the coffee cups
in the diners were laid by the Murphys and Sweeneys from Ireland. They have been a part of the bone and sinew of the Lake
states. They represent the largest single immigrant group in
Canada.

The Poles are in all the cities and towns on the Lakes. Many
came as recruits for the timber cutting on the invitation of the
lumber companies. Others came to the Superior mines. Thousands
of them gathered into their own distinctive community at Buffalo,
where they comprise a fifth of the population. Others jammed into
Cleveland, Flint, and Saginaw. Often they have kept apart from
other groups, as in their Hamtramck section in Detroit. They are
in the little port towns on Lake Huron. At Rogers City, when the
depression lay heavy over the Lakes and men were discouraged,
the community band gathered in their band stand and kept up
morale with their music. They work in hundreds of factories, in the
lumber camps, and at the mines.

Expert Cornish miners and mine foremen came to the copper

hills and the iron mines of Michigan, Wisconsin, and Minnesota.
Italian laborers by the thousands swarmed to the mining towns
and the port cities. Eighty thousand of them stayed in Buffalo.
Educated Bohemians and well-to-do peasants migrated to the Lakes
after their efforts toward independence were suppressed by Germany in 1848. The lumber companies employed them all through
the timber lands. Artisans, professional people, students, and
workers gathered into communities at Milwaukee and Chicago,
Detroit and Cleveland. Slovaks came to occupy cutover lands along
the lake shore between Ashland and Superior and to labor in the
mills at Gary and Lorain. Rumanians, Russians, Czechs, Greeks,
and a few Turks, Persians, and Spaniards found their place in this
vast melting pot.

Canadians and French-Canadians crossed over by the thousands;
Englishmen, Welshmen, and Scotchmen gathered in Old Ontario
and on the American side of the waters. The Dutch came bringing
their tulips and wooden shoes, their sturdy independence and strict
religious zeal, their Dutch dishes and their tight Sabbaths. They
bought government lands along the Lakes. They founded Hollan-
dale in Minnesota, Holland and Leeland in Michigan, Oostburg in
Wisconsin. They are fine gardeners and dairy farmers. They raise
baby chicks at Leeland and celery in the temperate climate of the
east shore of Lake Michigan around Kalamazoo. They crowd Grand
Rapids, where they were imported to work in the furniture factories. They poured in from the mid-1840's on toward the end of
the human mass movement of the nineteenth century.

Ten miles down the Lake Michigan coast from Sheboygan near
their village of Oostburg they have erected a sign as a monument
to these pioneers, especially to those who, like the children of
Israel, had crossed the Red Sea and braved the wilderness of Peran
only to perish in sight of Canaan itself. The sign reads: 'Holland
Settlement—Settlers came to this vicinity in 1846 under the leadership of G. H. Te Kolste. Just north of here in 1847 the steamboat
Phoenix with many new recruits to this colony was burned. 127
Hollanders were lost in this disaster.' It might have added that of
the 209 immigrants who were within sight of the shore at the end

of their pilgrimage, ready to begin a new life, all but 46 were burned to death or drowned on that disastrous night.

Men, women, and children from almost all the nations of the earth were drowned, burned, killed by boiler explosions, or destroyed by cholera, dysentery, and 'ship fever' on their way to the Lake settlements. But the ranks were closed, the good men kept coming on, and the Great Lakes were transformed from the lonely wilderness of the fur trappers to the vast garden and manufacturing region it has become in the space of a few short decades. Their children are at work as never before, sending back and forth across those miles of blue waterways such rivers of ore and grain and coal as the world has never before seen in all its history. In this spot men of all races toil jointly side by side in a common cause with a common and universal motive.

In June in Duluth a flower show is held in the lobby of a public building. Men and women of all the nations who have built that prosperous city bring their prize iris and peonies to the display benches and tables. The peonies especially are magnificent. Their color is rich and lustrous, their size prodigious. They rival those of the peony capital of the world at Van Wert, Ohio. Rival them? Perhaps no better example of the spirit of this new America could be found than in the accented words of the Polish woman who was caring for the huge vases of scarlet-colored peonies. 'We grow the finest peonies in the world here at Duluth.' And when the first passenger and package freight steamer of the season left Duluth, the dining room was gay with prize-winning peonies.

((((XXVII))))

Timber

In the mid-century years, when this river of humanity was flowing into the region of the Great Lakes, there was one sight that filled with wonder the eyes of families from timberless Europe. That was the endless expanse of forests which they sailed past, and the prodigious piles of sawdust, log jams, and rafts towering over the flat port towns and villages. One traveler, viewing Michigan from the deck of a steamer for the first time, remarked, 'If I were going to build a house in Michigan, I would first build a hill.' The only hills were artificial mounds of sawdust and stacks of timber. They sent the sharp damp odor of freshly cut timber over the towns, and the northwest winds blew it over the harbors and out into the Lakes. You could tell when you were passing Manistique, even at night; the deck of the ship was enveloped by the sweet resinous smell of the millions of feet of pine boards sawed, stacked, and ready to go to Chicago to build houses for the people who were sailing by.

Ships sailing up the St. Clair River had to keep well over to the edge of the channel to let the lumber boats go by. Passengers on their way to the West crowded the rail to see them pass down the river in tow. These once stately ships had grown old in service, and their timbers had been strained fighting ice and wind and high seas on the roadsteads of the Lakes. They were no longer tight enough to carry cargoes of grain and flour, but they could haul lumber to build the spreading acres of new houses in Detroit, Toledo, Cleveland and Buffalo. So their rigging had come down, most, if not all, of their sails had been removed, and they were now to be seen in tandem tow of four or more ships ('hookers,' the Lake men called them). They were pulled to market by a steam

256

tug or by a steam barge which also carried immense quantities of lumber in its hold and acres of shingles and lath topside.

If the immigrants were bound for Bay City or up the river to Saginaw, they might have to stand by for hours while huge rafts that filled the river were broken up and coralled into the booms at the sawmills that lined both shores. Or, as their ship sailed in close to dock at Milwaukee, they might see steamboats towing rafts of logs or sawed timber on the short haul down from Manistique to build the big sprawling, turreted wooden castles which the lumber barons were already affecting along the coast as their wealth accumulated. In a few weeks many of the men who now leaned on the ship's railing and marveled at these sights would be swinging axes and shouting 'Timber!' in a dozen accents in the pine forests. In a few days, perhaps, scores of them would be rafting this sawed lumber into cribs and towing it out to the ships anchored in deep water off the shallow sawmill town harbors.

The Lakes themselves are so vast that they seem to stimulate in men only the most gigantic enterprises. When they built grain elevators at Port Arthur, at Milwaukee, at Chicago, Buffalo, and Toronto they had to build the biggest ones in the world. When they shipped grain and flour, it was in the mightiest stream ever witnessed by man. Astor's fur trade around the Lakes was on a scale never before imagined. When the ore docks were erected at Duluth, they were the most stupendous on the planet. When the freighters were launched to carry ore to the iron and steel mills of Gary and Pittsburgh, they were the longest and most cavernous cargo ships on the waters of the globe. When the Yankees from Maine and Vermont and immigrants from beyond the seas streamed into the new land, it was in a mass migration undreamed of in previous history. The lumbering era was on the same colossal scale. No wonder the lumberjacks themselves created a Paul Bunyan to represent their feeling for size and superhuman exploits. A less Gargantuan figure would have been inadequate and woefully out of scale, a pigmy lost in the immensity of the pineries. Bigness and speed was the slogan of exploitation.

It is idle to talk about acres and board feet. The acres ran into millions and the board feet into trillions, and the mind simply does not manipulate statistics in such astronomical rows of digits. But we can sweep our mind's eye along the Mohawk Valley, through northern Pennsylvania, the Western Reserve and the Firelands of Ohio, around the 2,400 miles of Michigan shoreline, over Green Bay and the entire state of Wisconsin, down through Illinois, up through Minnesota, on to Fort William, and all the way back through sprawling Ontario to Niagara Falls, to Toronto and Kingston. We can see that entire region standing thick with virgin timber, 200,000 square miles of great trees whose rings recorded their hundreds of years of patient growth. The solid stand is unbroken except for a few savannahs, a few oases cleared out for a farmhouse and corn patch, or a crescent-shaped port town, and the scores of streams and rivers that cut a pathway through the timber to the Lakes and provide the only highways into the wilderness.

Up these rivers the lumbermen first went with their axes and saws and peavies. They did their first cutting along the lake shore and on the banks of the rivers where the logs or the lumber could be skidded into the water and floated off to the markets. There was no other way to get to the markets with a heavy and bulky cargo like lumber in large quantity. There is hardly a town or village in all Michigan, Wisconsin, or northern Illinois, and few in the Erie basin of Ohio, that did not begin humbly as a crude sawmill with a gristmill attached. It was usually set up and operated by some enterprising Yankee, who had come West to make his fortune —and he usually made it.

Daniel Whitney was a worthy representative of this early tribe of lumbermen who set the pattern for the hordes who came hot on the heels of his pioneering. He had gone out to Green Bay in the 1820's in the days when that ancient trading post was primarily a fur center and Astor had cast his rapacious net around it. Whitney, in fact, bought land and platted the first lots in present Green Bay in the year 1829. That winter he went from Green Bay up the Fox River and crossed over into the pineries on the upper Wisconsin to cut shingles. The military at Fort Winnebago seized his output, carried away all they could and destroyed what they left.

Whitney then got an official permit from the War Department and proceeded to erect a sawmill at Whitney Rapids (Nekoosa), the first, and for four years the only one, in that unbelievably rich stand of timber. Then the Black Hawk War carried the motley frontier militia (including young Abe Lincoln, Zachary Taylor, and Jefferson Davis) well back into the Wisconsin forests in 1832. The campaign revealed and popularized for the first time the riches of that region. Other lumbermen moved in, hauling their machinery on rafts or on canoes lashed together. They claimed and took the timberlands along the waterway, and within a few short years there were more than a hundred sawmills buzzing furiously through the pines. The same scene was enacted along every stream in Michigan. The big boom was on.

The demand for timber seemed to be as great and inexhaustible as the forests. The population in all the Great Lakes towns was climbing by the thousands with each passing year. 'Watch us grow!' was the slogan. Chicago quickly overran its one muddy street. Houses crowded round the fort, sprang up on the opposite side of the river, and began spreading up and down the lake, lining the river, and racing out into the prairie. The story was repeated at Buffalo, Detroit, Milwaukee, Bay City, and a score of thriving towns. It took a lot of timber to supply joists and weatherboarding, floors, laths, and shingles for those endless rows of stores and dwellings. There were also ships and wharves to be built, wagons, buggies, and canal barges to be fashioned, factories and elevators to erect, railroads and buckboard sidewalks to be laid. Everybody seemed to be calling for lumber. And as more people came in the second half of the century, the call grew louder. More and more timber crashed faster and faster, the sawmills screamed in shriller tempo, and more thousands of men went into the forests as lumberjacks.

The Lake towns swarmed with 'lookers,' ambitious Yankees for the most part, who went into the woods to look over the timber and select a 'big forty' for themselves. They picked out a good stand as near to a market as possible, close to a waterway, and surrounded by Government land. They bought their chosen site for $1.50 per acre and proceeded to cut right and left 'around their forty' all over the place until somebody got round to stopping them—if they ever did. The public forest domain was not very sacred to many of our ancestors. The boom reached such proportions right after the Civil War that it quickly outran the supply of lumberjacks, raftsmen, and river rats, who had come on from the New England and New York lands. The companies had to rush agents over to Norway and Bohemia, Germany and Hungary, to fetch in more labor. The whole industry spread in geometrical progression and spiralled dizzily upward.

Prodigal America was never more wasteful or rapacious than during the four or five decades of the lumbering era around the Lakes. It was a rape of the forests. They were not lumbered—they were mined. The waste was simply staggering. No one took any thought of the morrow. The timber lands were treated as if they were inexhaustible. As a matter of fact, thousands of acres were never even lumbered. They were merely cleared and burned. A Yankee from Maine or Connecticut, tired of piling up rocks and scratching on unyielding soil, would move out to Michigan or Wisconsin or northern Ohio and take up land. He would wade into a magnificent forest of walnut, oak, chestnut, pine, spruce, and start swinging. He would band the boles, or cut partway through them in a long row, leaving them standing but ready to fall. Then he would cut through a tall, heavy pine tree so that it would crash into the line of prepared trees. They toppled over like a row of dominoes and piled up into twisted heaps. Millions of dollars' worth of choice wood was only a brush pile or a windrow to men who wanted to farm the land. They set fire to it and rejoiced to see it go up in flame and smoke. Where the forest had stood, they planted a few bushels of wheat.

The work of farmers, however, made only a minor dent compared to the big-scale cuttings of the lumber barons. The port towns like Bay City and Saginaw, Grand Haven, Menominee, and Muskegon rose like mushrooms both as sawmill towns and as supply and shipping centers for the logging camps back up the rivers in the pineries. Ships brought in supplies, and steamboats

The skyline of Detroit.

The City of Buffalo. *Photographs by Hirz. Courtesy of Frederic Lewis.*

carried uncounted tons of pork and beans up the rivers to feed
the camps. An outline history of almost every small town in the
Lake region can be written in the same three short sentences: 'The
town began when Silver John Smith of Maine set up a sawmill
here in the 1830's. It boomed for about a quarter of a century
when the timber was piled high around it. But the timber was soon
cutover and exhausted, the population was left stranded or moved
away, and the once thriving settlement decayed into a ghost town.'
In the port of Au Sable on Lake Huron there were nearly 5,000
people at the height of the lumbering era. Now there are 61.
Oscoda had nearly as many people in 1890 when the logs were
flowing down the Au Sable River. Now it is a pleasant, stagnant
little fishing town: population 600. The list would be endless. Some
of them, however, have been able to add a bright postscript in the
present century: 'A paper mill, a furniture factory, a creamery, or a
cannery was established near the site of the first sawmill and the
town has enjoyed a mild prosperity.' That would be Piscomming
with its chicory and cheese; Alpena with its limestone; Manistee
with its fruitlands; Traverse City with its cherry canning; and
Muskegon with its motors.

While the fever lasted it was epochal in intensity. Lumber camps
were everywhere along the lakes and rivers. Thousands of lumberjacks went into the forests. Green Bay boasted proudly in 1854
that her mills alone would saw 80 million feet of pine that year,
and that the activity along the Saginaw would employ 100 span
of horses, 300 yoke of oxen, and 1,500 men. They were hardy,
tough, roistering men, these lumberjacks, about whom legend inevitably accumulated. They were more colorful in character as well
as in their bright-shirted garb than the fur traders whom they
drove from the woods. It doesn't matter what pinery you go to,
the pattern of life was as uniform as were the rows of houses built
with this lumber on the new side streets of American cities. The
lumber camps on the Saginaw, the Green, the Menominee, or the
Fox were crude and grim affairs—cheap shacks thrown up to eat
and sleep the lumberjacks during the night hours when they weren't
actually cutting timber.

Dr. Frank P. Bohn, who spent his professional life sewing up cuts and setting broken bones in the pineries of the Upper Peninsula, has left a graphic account of the life in these camps. It differs little from what I myself have seen in the camps of this more modern age. The sleeping bunks were shelves secured to the walls one above the other and softened slightly with a layer of straw or pine needles held in by a railing nailed to the bunk. Generally there were no windows, but there was a door at each end. In the center of the room was the barrel stove set in a bin of sawdust where the men could bake their shins, dry their feet, and spit. They hung their two or three pairs of socks, wet with snow and sweat, on strings stretched above the stove. All night long socks and shirts and Mackinaws gave off the odorous steam of drying. All night long the fire burned and the lamps smoked. The doors were closed tight. Fifty to a hundred tired lumberjacks snored away in this hot, fetid confinement, while the winds were howling in sub-zero winter outside the board walls.

All season long these huskies fed on pork, beans, onions, biscuits, pies, and coffee. They sat on rough benches at a long table in the cookhouse and reached for what they wanted. No word was spoken. Then, as now, when the cook announced a meal, the men sat down and gorged. They looked neither to the right nor to the left. It would have been bad manners to hold a conversation at meal time. When you ate, you ate. Yet, as Dr. Bohn points out, there was never a healthier lot of men.

The secret, of course, was long hours in the crisp, pine-scented air of the forest. For twelve hours each day, later cut to only ten, the lumberjacks swung axes, pulled cross-cut saws, and wrestled logs with their long-handled peavies. They worked up the rivers of Michigan, Illinois, and Wisconsin with slaughtering speed. There was no more science to these lumbering operations than in the depredation of a weasel striking a fang tooth into the breast of a mallard duck to suck a few drops of blood from its heart and leave the carcass otherwise untouched on the lake shore. The lumbermen were after pine, and only the big boles at that. Perfectly good but slightly smaller trees were bruised, battered, or cut out of the way. Even the chosen big ones were cut several feet above the ground, and hacked off at the top where the trunk began to taper. Only a fraction of the useable wood was saved. The wasted tops, 'slashings' they were called, were scattered in huge piles all through the cutover wreckage ready to become a tinder box for forest fires. Out of the pineries in the daylight hours came a continuous crackle and roar as the lumberjacks struck the finishing blow with an ax and yelled 'Timber' while the giant trees tumbled, toppled, and crashed down into the smaller growth about them.

So the choice logs piled up through the autumn and winter around a thousand camps in the Great Lakes region. The piles grew bigger and bigger in the 1870's and 1880's, reaching an all-time gigantic peak in the 1890's, and falling back to a mere trickle in the days before World War I. They were rolled, dragged by oxen, carted by team, hauled over wooden tramroads, and piled mountain high on the banks of the rivers and in the channels ready for the spring drive. When the winter was over and the spring thaws and rains came to swell the rivers to turbulent rapids, the most exciting drama of all the year began—driving the logs, or cribs of sawed timber, to the markets.

The spring drive was a general stampede. Down every river and every stream that could float them they were rushed on the spring floods. The rivers were narrow, winding, interrupted by falls. The logs jammed, saturated the streams, piled up in confusion. They dammed up the rivers, caused overflows, and even flooded towns on the banks. One jam on the Wisconsin was eight miles long. Daring lumberjacks and river rats climbed into the congestion to hunt the key logs. Many of the tragedies of which the old lumbering era ballads sang were enacted when the obstructing log broke loose. The logs often lunged suddenly forward with a terrific rush and force. The men on the banks watched the checkered shirt and hobnailed boots with the red-sock band at their tops disappear under the madly heaving and rolling logs as the bold victim plunged to death trying to leap across them to safety. Next season, as these same men sat around the stove in the evening, some passing ballad singer would teach them a song about the lonely maiden

of Menominee waiting for some word of her red-headed sweetheart
who was coming back to marry her when the spring drive was over
and he had money in his pocket.

Each log was stamped with the branding hammer of its owner.
There were log harbors at certain wide, quiet pools where the logs
were sorted and made into rafts or towed in booms down the larger
rivers or on the Lakes. They were guided and tended by a pilot
and crew who worked the huge sweep oars at each end and steered
the raft around the bends as it floated slowly on the last lap of its
journey to the river and lake towns.

By 1889 there were about 112,000 men working the Great Lakes
pineries. The lumberjacks got their pay—perhaps $20 or $30 a
month—and rushed into the grim little lumber supply towns for
their big spree. Throughout the slow days of the logging season
they had slept like sardines in the bunkhouses, eaten hurriedly in
the cookhouse, seen no one but themselves, heard nothing but their ·
own voices, the timber wolves, and the crash of falling trees. Their
only relaxation was sitting around the box stove chewing and smoking, singing a ballad or two, or matching tall stories about the size
of Paul Bunyan's shoes, his blue ox, or the length of his ax helve.
Then somebody yawned, stretched, and said, 'Danged if I ain't
bushed tonight,' and they pulled off their boots and crawled into
the hard bunks.

A season of that dull, masculine life stirred the lumberjacks'
desire to 'blow their stakes.' The only things a man wanted, they
said, came in bottles and corsets. The sorry little one-street saloon
towns, gleaming like the bright center of civilization, had an abundance of both. The lumberjacks swarmed in and all hell broke loose.
They rolled into Saginaw by the train load from miles around. As
many as twelve packed and jammed coaches would pull into the
Père Marquette station (blessed name) with every pane of glass on
the train shattered by the roistering, lusting lumberjacks.

Little Jake (4 feet 4) Seligman furnished the first round of amusement. He paraded a band and then tossed a vest out of his store
window to the milling, shouting lumberjacks in the street below.
Whoever brought the vest into the store got a suit of clothes free

to go with it. The vest was usually in rags when it got back to Little Jake's counter, and he was salesman enough to offer a new one at a good price. But Little Jake's was only an introductory side-show. The lumberjacks invaded the dozens of saloons for the bottles and then took their choice of the many well-advertised houses for the climax of their entertainment. These scaled downward from Belle Stevens' five-dollar house to the dives on the sawdust. It was Belle Stevens who distributed the elegant little cards, later much publicized by Hollywood, inviting her friends to 'Come down and see Belle when in Town.'

Every town around the Lakes has its own vivid legends and memories of those days and nights. Eccentrics abounded. People still remember the short thick man who used to weave down the streets of East Saginaw and other towns, tearing with his teeth at a hunk of raw liver dripping blood on his shirt front and barking loudly, 'I am T. C. Cunnion, the man-eater from Peterborough, Ontario.' 'Lumber Beasts' and 'Rum Hogs,' the woodsmen were called by the townsmen. All restraints were off. Lumberjacks in calked boots paraded up and down the duckboard side walk, going from saloon to saloon. Fights were inevitable through sheer brute energy unchanneled by idleness and inflamed with booze. Black Jack Smith, the giant six-foot-four champion of this camp, was maneuvered into a battle with Iron Mike Murphey of a rival camp, who had licked every challenger along the Fox or the Grand or the Chippewa. So these two giants met in the streets outside Little Gus's saloon and battled it out in the mud. They say that at Pres-cott, Wisconsin, a hundred men fought in the mire in a single pitched battle. Each town had its own name for its street of saloons. Bay City called its Water Street 'Hell's Half Mile.' Oshkosh, La-Crosse, Marinette—they were all alike. They said that a stranger could ask for a ticket to hell and the agent would hand him a ticket for Seney, Michigan.

All this hell-raising, however, makes it easy to misrepresent the true human heart of the lumberjacks. Their one weekend in town has obscured the rest of the year of patient toil just as one night of college-boy roistering after a big game may overshadow a semes-

ter of unassailable conduct. With rare exceptions, the heart of gold
beat in the tough giant's breast. Let a buddy get his hand ripped
by a saw or a leg broken in a fall, and one of them would go fifty
miles through a blizzard at night to fetch the doctor, and they
would tend the patient like a baby when the doctor was gone. They
were as sentimental and docile as wondering children when a 'good'
woman did by some chance come among them. Anyone who has
ever spent any time at a lumber camp must have remarked this
incongruity. I have heard from a woman who lived for a season
with her husband in a Canadian camp the story of how these rough
woodsmen with brawling reputations would come humbly and re-
spectfully to her cabin door, cap in hand, just to look worshipfully
at her and her baby. They were childishly happy to have the privi-
lege of carrying a pail of water, of fetching in logs, above all to
rock the baby's crib. And if any villain had dared touch one strand
of her hair, or made a disrespectful remark about her, they would
have bashed in his face.

We have already observed that the saga of Paul Bunyan has now
collected around that one picturesque figure most of the lore of
all the Great Lakes lumber camps. Like the legend of King David
or the jokes of Abe Lincoln, the isolated exploits of the mighty
men of the pineries were combined and attached to Bunyan. The
piled-up snows of northern winters became Paul Bunyan's blue
snow. The enormous boots of a six-foot-six Norwegian lumberjack
became the seven league boots of Bunyan. Such a pair of enormous
shoes is actually on exhibit at the Rhinelander Logging Museum
on the Wisconsin River, itself a reproduction of a logging camp.
The prize oxen of a Green Bay pinery became Bunyan's acre-
covering Blue Ox of the ballads. The immense labor of loosing a
log jam, or floating them when the spring floods did not come,
became the story of how Paul freed the billions of feet of logs
that were landlocked at the banking grounds of northern Minnesota. Paul's blacksmith made an enormous shovel. Paul commenced
to shovel before breakfast one morning, and by sunset he had
scooped out a channel all the way to the Gulf of Mexico. He was
back at the camp by nightfall. The dirt thrown out to the left and
right became the Appalachians and the Rockies, and the channel

between them became the Mississippi River. The sand drifting over
his shovel is now Florida, and the Lower Peninsula of Michigan
is his sand-filled mitten.

Scores of turbulent characters were thrown up by the hard life
in the timber. Take 'Silver Jack' John Driscoll and multiply him
by, let us say, 500, and the Great Lakes lumberjack stands before
us. This giant came over to the Saginaw pineries when he was
eighteen. He learned all there was to know about lumbering. He
worked the Saginaw, the Muskegon, the Tittabawassee in Michigan,
took a 'ticket to hell' and worked at Seney, and moved on through
Wisconsin to Duluth. His reputation grew as he went from one
camp to the next, and other men called themselves 'Silver Jack'
in covetousness of his legend and his prowess. He was an expert
in the 'Hell's Half Mile' school of fighting—biting off ears, gouging
out eyes, head butting, kicking, fist punching, wrestling and, in the
mud or sawdust, 'putting the boots' to a man—i.e., driving the sharp
calks into his face and giving him scars for life, if he survived.

Yet his friends who knew him best swore that he was a lovable,
generous, kindly man whose battles were on behalf of a weaker
man being bullied around, or in defense of his staunch Catholic
faith. One of the hundreds of lumberjack ballads records his fight
with Bobby Waite, who said the Bible was fable and Hell a hum-
bug.

> 'You're a liar!' someone shouted,
> 'And you've got to take it back!'
> And everybody started,
> 'Twas the voice of Silver Jack.
>
> 'Maybe I've not used the Lord
> Always exactly white;
> But when a chump abuses Him
> He must eat his words or fight.
>
> 'It was in that old religion
> That my mother lived and died;
> Her memory's ever dear to me,
> And I say Bob has lied.'

So Silver Jack fought Bobby Waite for forty minutes, chewed off Bobby's ear, and slugged him with his iron fists and vindicated the ways of God to the lumberjacks.

Silver Jack was employed by lumber companies which could not get their logs down past rival companies. Jack McGovern was one of these bullies of the log drives. He intimidated rival crews. So Silver Jack took the job for an abused company and agreed to go past Jack McGovern. The big men promptly met and fought. An eyewitness said the two men battled for an hour, punching, clinching, 'weaving around on the ground, clutching and clawing at each other.' Silver Jack finally caught Jack McGovern with a paralyzing uppercut on the point of his jaw and stretched him out. Then, being a fair sportsman at heart, he did not stomp his face with his calks, but stepped back from his prostrate rival. Jack McGovern finally came to and managed to get up on his feet. Then he shook hands with Silver Jack. 'I believe we can work together,' he said. And they did. Both companies ran their timber for years in peaceful co-operation. Such are the stories that still fall from the lips of the old men of the ghost towns who remember the good old days of the lumber camps.

The lumber barons also have their saga. They were the shrewd, driving, ambitious men of rugged and ruthless individualism. They were the new species of the post-Astor era, the rags-to-riches legend of the Great Lakes pineries. Their rise from ax-swinging poverty to millionaire splendor was meteoric. Their number was legion. Forty of them were created in a few seasons in Muskegon alone. The philanthropic C. H. Hackley, whose benefactions and foresight brighten the modern civic scene in Muskegon, was one of their best representatives. He arrived back in the spring of 1856 ready to ride the crest of the timber wave. He was 19 when the steamship put in alongside the sawdust heaps of Muskegon harbor, and he had just seven dollars. On the afternoon of the same day he began work in the mills. At 22 he and his father bought into a sawmill. The call for lumber sounded from all the crowded, growing cities;

Hackley hired it cut and sawed, and made his pile in the good old nineteenth-century American way. Some of the Victorian, gingerbread palaces of the forty barons, museum-like, still overlook Muskegon Lake and the sand dunes along Lake Michigan.

Over at Saginaw and Bay City, where 112 saw mills lined the river, there were 98 millionaire lumber barons. Their wealth came rolling down a dozen rivers, the mere repetition of whose names resounds with a Miltonic or Sandburgian rhythm: Shiawassee, Flint, Cass, Tittabawassee, Au Sable, Bad, Rifle, Au Gus, Kawhawlin. Fleets of Lake freighters steamed and sailed in and out of the bay and river carrying the white-pine lumber off to the Lake-port cities and down to the Erie Canal and Albany. Fifty times a day the bridges over the Saginaw lifted and lowered to let them through. With such lucrative activity going on, it was only a few years for the shrewd ones from woods boss to lumber baron. Then they put off their calked boots, their checkered shirts, and their red sashes for white beaver hats, heavy linked watch chains, and gold-headed canes. They sported a span of horses and a coachman.

Some of the most diverting characters did not take on the new ways when they became barons. One of the most amusing was Curt Emerson. He was big, rough, vulgar, and prosperous. He was celebrated for his crude diction, which we shall forego reprinting. His big moment upon which his present fame rests occurred on the night of September 7, 1859, at the formal gala opening of the Bancroft House in Saginaw. The Bancroft was the kind of marvel Hollywood loves to reproduce as its masterpiece of decor. It covered an acre of the sawdust which by that time lay packed 40 feet deep along the river. Its four magnificent stories were crowned with a cupola. As proudly as its successors advertise 5,000 rooms, 5,000 baths, the Bancroft announced a box stove, a brass cuspidor, and a plush bellcord in every room. Curt Emerson, then in his sixties, received no invitation to the banquet, so he crashed the party. He jumped up on the table under the big, gas-lit chandeliers, and ran all the way down its elegant length kicking bouquets, champagne glasses, china, and silver to right and left into the faces and laps of the millionaires and their ladies. Curt regretted if anybody was hurt, and he took keen pleasure in paying for all the damage. It was worth much more than it cost.

Philetus Sawyer, one of the best-known lumber kings of Wisconsin, made his fortune by speculating in the timber lands. He began the hard way. At the age of 17 he left his Vermont home to work in a New England sawmill. Like Hackley and so many others, he was shrewd and enterprising and he looked ahead. Also like Hackley, he leased a poorly managed mill and resold it at a handsome profit. He came west in 1847 in time to get in on the ground floor of the lumber boom. It was just at the beginning of the great migration of Yankee lumbermen to the Lake states when they had nearly exhausted the white pine of Maine and were moving on to bigger fields with their 'Bangor Tiger' lumberjacks. Sawyer was just 31. Again he bought out a failing mill and made it prosperous. He read the future accurately. At the fast rate the Lake region was receiving a new population, it was clear to Sawyer that it would not be long before the rich pineries of Wisconsin would be invaded. He became the best 'looker' of them all. He spied out the land to select the best timber regions; then, when the Government sold them off at auction, Sawyer was there to purchase. He bought for a song and resold almost immediately for millions. He later entered politics and became a United States Senator.

Robert M. La Follette spent a large portion of his career in exposing the methods of Sawyer and the barons and in breaking their tight hold which was anchored in the state of Wisconsin and reached into the Senate at Washington. La Follette's own sketch of Sawyer in his *Autobiography* is worth repeating. 'I can remember how he looked climbing into his carriage—a short, thick-set, squatty figure of a man with a big head set on square shoulders and a short neck—stubby everywhere . . . He had no humor, but much of what has been called "horse sense." His talk was jerky and illiterate; he never made a speech in his life . . .'

This great lumber baron attempted to bribe La Follette, and tried to get a bill through the Congress to sell off the pine timber from the Menominee Indian Reservation. This procedure seemed perfectly normal to the great baron. No better summary of the man and his era could be phrased than this passage from the man who helped bring the era to an end and a new beginning. 'Sawyer,' La Follette wrote in the *Autobiography,* 'was a man of striking individuality and of much native force. He was a typical lumberman, equipped with great physical strength and a shrewd, active mind. He had tramped the forests, cruised timber, slept in the snow, built saw mills—and by his own efforts had made several million dollars. So unlearned was he that it was jokingly said that he signed his name "P. Sawyer" because he could not spell Philetus. He was nevertheless a man of ability, and a shrewd counselor in the prevailing political methods. He believed in getting all he could for himself and his associates whenever and wherever possible. I always thought that Sawyer's methods did not violate his conscience; he regarded money as properly the chief influence in politics. Whenever it was necessary, I believe that he bought men as he bought sawlogs . . . He believed quite simply . . . that anything that interfered with the profits of business was akin to treason.'

These lumber barons sent their lumberjacks tearing through the pineries. It took only a few seasons to destroy a forest. LaCrosse was a typical sample of the era. It rushed up the climbing wave in the 1890's for seven fat years. It had nearly 2,000 mill hands in 1899. Five years later there were 34. The timber that supported it was gone. Or, more accurately, perhaps half of it had gone off to market, the rest lay in pitiful wreckage and huge piles of slashings drying ominously on the forest floor. Much of that floor was Government land and Indian reservation. In 1864 the Wisconsin state forest rangers found nearly 12,000 acres of Government pine lands trespassed on. The following year they found 19,000 acres encroached upon, and the trespassing increased. In 1873 one lone forester employed by the St. Croix & Lake Superior Railroad to protect their land grant found eleven million feet of logs stolen from their property by the lumber barons. That lucrative steal was practiced on a gigantic scale all over the lakelands forests.

The forest fires completed the havoc and destruction. The slashings, the wastage, the six-foot stumps accumulated in all the pineries during the autumn and winter—square miles of them. The droughts of summer came and baked them powder dry. Then a hunter's match, a spark from a farmer's fire, or a crackle of lightning touched the tinderbox and another and more literal hell broke loose. It happened again and again. Following the drought of 1863, fire raged over the southwest shore region of Lake Superior and devoured a million dollars' worth of forest. It was like a saturation bombing raid over the Rhineland. Vast towers of flame shot up and cast a glow over the dark surface of Lake Superior at night. Smoke billowed several thousands of feet into the sky and spread out over an area of a hundred miles. The atmosphere was dense with smoke all the way to Milwaukee, and even over western Lake Michigan it was like a haze from the dust bowl of the 1930's.

The following year, in mid-May, the Wisconsin forests again burst suddenly into flame after an unprecedentedly dry spring. The pineries along the Chippewa, the Black, the Wisconsin, and the Wolf Rivers blazed in 1868, and along the entire line of the Chicago & Northwestern Railroad from Escanaba to Marquette five great fires burned. The year 1871 is fixed in everybody's memory because of Mrs. O'Leary's cow and the fire that wiped out Chicago. That was disaster enough, God knows, but few people know that in the same year one of the worst conflagrations of its kind in all history exploded in the slashings of the Wisconsin pineries only a few miles to the north around Green Bay.

With Chicago competing, this disaster in the forests barely made back-page copy. It is known as the Peshtigo fire because that town with most of its population was burned to a crisp. For three months the summer drought continued without relief. Pine needles and withered leaves, dry as excelsior, dropped on the forest floor. The bark on the slashings curled up and the sap evaporated. Then the whole cutover seemed to explode into flame. It broke along both shores of Green Bay and swept northeastward. A west-southwest wind drove it on in early October, ravaging a thirty-mile-wide strip from Appleton, Wisconsin, to Menominee, Michigan. On the eighth, a hurricane roared up from the Mississippi Valley and fanned the

cauldron to a roaring, crackling inferno. In one night of the wildest
orgy it seared and blackened eight whole counties.

For six weeks the fire raged. It devoured villages and lumber
camps, isolated shacks and farmhouses. Livestock from the farms,
living things from the woods, fled before the smoke and flames
through the shower of sparks that sprayed out in front of them
with the wind. People fought it, lost the battle, and tried to flee
to safety on foot, in buggies and wagons, and in boats. Some hid
in dry cisterns. Over a thousand never reached safety. The fire
rushed round them and hemmed them in. They collapsed in the
suffocating smoke and heat and were horribly burned to death.
John Leach, survivor, buried eleven of his family. A thousand or so
people who did outrun the fire were badly burned. Boats blazed
in the harbors. Ships stood by for rescue in the port towns along
Lake Michigan, and raced to safety at the last minute when the
heat got too intense to bear. Men stamped out falling embers on
deck as the ships steamed through the flames.

All around the Lake region in towns and forest this story of
irresponsibility was repeated. Marquette was burned in 1868; Holland was burned in that disastrous year of 1871; Oshkosh, with all
its lumber waste, was such a match box that it was swept by fire
four times in 15 years: 1859, 1866, 1874, and 1875. As you drive
from Saginaw to Muskegon on the edge of the Bad River pinery,
you pass through the little settlement of Merrill. Grateful citizens
gave their village its name to honor the locomotive engineer who
braved the great fire of 1881 to haul the endangered people to
safety.

The Hinckley fire swept disaster over eastern Minnesota in September 1894. For days the sky over Hinckley had been ominously
pallid with smoke that darkened the sun at noon. Ashes sifted
lightly over the little sawmill town of 1,200 souls. Word came in
of villages and many of their citizens burning to the southwest.
Then a south-southwest wind struck and sent glowing sparks into
the Hinckley woods and the dry sawdust piles. Almost instantane-
ously the town roared into uncontrollable flames. Houses went up
in a blaze. Men, women, children, horses fell in the street and were

cremated. Nearly a hundred were burned to death in the clearing along the railroad as they tried to escape. Others plunged into the water in a gravel pit and survived. Refugees were hurriedly loaded onto a train and rushed through the flames, while the paint burned off the cars and men fought the blazes that broke out in the train as it raced toward safety. The bridge over the Kettle River just north of Hinckley collapsed and burned just as the train cleared it. Jim Root stopped his southbound train, took on refugees and backed north to Skunk Lake, where they rushed into the water. His train was aflame when he stopped, but the lake saved some 300 men, women, and children. Four hundred and thirteen had been cremated.

The forests are now gone. In their stead are the monotonous miles of cutover land. Where lumber barons once snatched fortunes from the virgin timber, Hungarian immigrants and second-generation Italians gather huckleberries. The boom towns are ghost villages. Shelldrake, Michigan, is a kind of museum piece. This once model lumber town of Whitefish Bay, equipped with cold storage, bathrooms, hospital and school, a long board walk and running hot water, now has a population of 25. They live among the ruins and look out over the bay in the sluggish river. Once it was jammed with logs and lumber; now it is clogged with dirt and sand. It is one of the many grim monuments to exploitation.
There are a few other monuments that are more inspiring. As time passes, the lumbering era gathers a halo of antiquity. Rhinelander, Wisconsin, has a Logging Museum with a bunkhouse and cookhouse and a display of tools and relics. Michigan has erected a Lumbermen's Memorial on the Au Sable River overlooking the remains of one of the great pineries of the Lake region. A Lumberjack Festival is held at Edenville on the Tittabawassee to keep green in the memory the skills of aging lumberjacks. Michigan and Wisconsin are returning to the commonwealth vast acreages of cutover lands and reforesting them. Their universities are educating the people and training experts in the science of conservation and sustained lumbering. William Dempster Hoard has taught lumberjacks

how to run dairies. Paper mills, furniture factories, and plywood plants have replaced the old sawmills. The big spring log drives that once monopolized the rivers and lake harbors are over. In their stead you will now see a Coast Guard boat dart out into the St. Mary's River to warn your ship's captain through a megaphone that a boom of pulp wood is coming round the bend. And you will stand in the wheelhouse watching a half-dozen ships idle along with just enough speed to make way, or actually drop anchor, while a couple of tugs maneuver a huge boom of loose, bobbing little pulp logs through the narrow channel and into the basin above the Sault.

River of Gold

ACROSS the full length of the Great Lakes flows the river of gold which is grain. It rises in thousands of fields in Illinois, Wisconsin, Iowa, Minnesota, Nebraska, and the Dakotas and on the immense plains of Saskatchewan and Manitoba. It streams across the prairie lands to the giant elevators at Fort William and Port Arthur, at Duluth-Superior and Ashland, at Milwaukee and Chicago. There it pours with a dry, quick roar down the hoppers into the holds of the grain fleet to be sailed down through the Sault, up through the Straits of Mackinac, down Huron and over the length of Erie to Buffalo, or around Niagara through the Welland Canal to Toronto, Montreal, and Quebec. This golden stream is about one third of the volume of the red stream of ore and the black stream of coal that make up most of the tonnage on the Lakes.

The coal and the ore are a domestic commerce. Ships pick up ore at one end of the Lakes, bear it cheaply to the foot of Lake Michigan or the south shore of Lake Erie to meet the coal and limestone, and the transaction is just about complete. But the grain flows far and links the Lakes and their vast farming hinterland most intimately and delicately with the markets and the peoples of the world. The saga of grain is an American-Canadian and also a world phenomenon, but one part of its dramatic cycle is set on the Great Lakes.

We have seen the hordes of settlers sailing westward over the Great Lakes. We have glimpsed the little clusters of houses at the ports, spreading along the shore and back into the disappearing forests, growing into settlements, then into villages, then into towns and cities swarming with men and women on the move, bursting with the activity of land sales and the commerce of receiving and sending in and out the people and the goods and the produce. And through the decades the people kept coming on and fanning out over the virgin land, breaking the sod, planting grain, harvesting grain, hauling it back to the port cities and shipping it to the four corners of the world.

As the canals opened, Ohio, Indiana, Illinois, and Wisconsin filled up. Travelers were arriving and leaving Buffalo at the rate of a thousand a day in July 1831. Six hundred people came to Cleveland alone in a single fortnight after the opening of the Ohio-Erie canal. Twenty thousand arrived in Chicago in 1833, and most of them went on onto the plains. Wagons of grain soon crowded the crude wharves at every port, and the canal boats piled up grain produce in the basins at Cleveland and Toledo and Chicago to be carried away by the schooners and steamships that were soon thick on the Lakes.

There was great rejoicing at Chicago in the year 1831. The harvest was good on the flat lands back of the city. Farmers hauled their grain to the new western port, where it was weighed and sacked in the Newberry and Dole warehouse. The brig *John Kinzie* was worked in over the sandbar and up to the dock. The bags of grain were then carried aboard by Irish roustabouts, and the brig with the first cargo of western grain put out again into Lake Michigan bound for the mills at Buffalo. Eight years later, in October 1839, the brig *Osceola* put in at this dock to take on a cargo of grain in bulk. It was not bagged, but lay loose in the watertight hold of the ship. For the enterprising Newberry and Dole firm had just built a crude grain elevator with a chute to channel the grain from the unloading platform of their commission house out to the ship dock. Instead of emptying directly into the brig, however, the grain fell into a bin on the wharf. Two men then carried this bin aboard ship and dumped it into the hold. It was all very primitive, but it was the beginning of the stupendous commerce of grain from the new West. There were cheers at Chicago when the brig set sail.

The celebration at Buffalo was no less spontaneous when the ship arrived to link the two terminal cities with a new bond. That Lake Erie port had already jumped from a population of 8,668 in 1830

to 18,000 when the *Oceola* lay to in the improved harbor below
Main Street. She was tied up there for a week while hustlers unloaded her mere 1,678 bushels by hand. Clearly that would never
do. Among the men who watched this slow process of unloading
was Joseph Dart. He went to work on machinery to speed it up,
and invented the steam-propelled grain elevator for handling this
kind of cargo. That was the beginning of those tremendous for-
tresses that now cut the skyline at Buffalo and Toronto, and at the
upper lake ports where a 12,500-ton cargo is poured in or sucked
out of the hold in a few hours.

Milwaukee was soon a third city in the grain trade. She spent
over $100,000 to remove the bar upon which so many ships visiting
her harbor had run aground, and to improve her anchorage. New
settlers came in by the thousands, as we have seen, and grain
poured back to the port for shipment. Milwaukee's proudest year
was 1856 when the schooner *Dean Richmond* loaded 14,000 bushels
of grain at the Milwaukee elevator in mid-July and sailed, not to
Buffalo, but direct for Liverpool. She reached the English port
safely in mid-September. The news of this epic-making voyage
spread across the grain-growing plains. It was of front-page interest
to the Twin Cities of Minnesota. Nothing could take us back more
freshly into the spirit of the day than this exuberant piece that
appeared in the St. Paul *Advertiser* following the announcement in
the *European Times* of the schooner's arrival in Liverpool.

In this simple announcement is contained the initial fact of a new
era in commercial history [the philosophical editor wrote]. It virtu-
ally makes our inland lakes the Mediterranean Sea of North America, and Chicago becomes the Alexandria of modern times. It peels
off the littoral rind of the New World at a stroke—and splits the
ripe apple of the continent to its core. Ocean commerce will follow
that entering wedge. Direct transportation will inevitably supersede
the expensive and complicated machinery employed in conveying
Western grain through its present channels—which, besides involving several expensive trans-shipments, is attended with an important
diminution of bulk. The Atlantic, the far Bosphorus, the Baltic, and
the seas of the old hemisphere, will flow in through the rent torn
by the keel of the *Dean Richmond,* and the majestic commerce of

the ocean overleaping the huge complications of human ingenuity—
passing in triumph past the monuments of Clinton's genius, past
canals and railroads, railroads and canals—through rivers and lakes,
2,000 miles into the interior—will plant its sea-worn flags upon the
shores of Lake Michigan, and sit in royal state like another queen
of Sheba, on the throne that Western industry shall build for her
in the chief city of the interior plain of North America . . . The
application of steam will overcome the delays of navigation, and
the path of the *Dean Richmond* will be thronged with the flags of
every nation.

That was the rhetoric-studded vision of western men on the eve
of the Civil War. It was not too far in advance of supporting fact.
All through the 1840's and 1850's the epic of western grain swept
on toward its climax in a feverish tempo. The grain marked at
Chicago was in the international spotlight. Fortunes were made
and lost in speculative trading. The pit was on its way to the stage
of Frank Norris's novels. When famine struck in Europe in the
'forties and 'fifties, wheat soared upward: $1.25, $1.50, $2.00 a
bushel. Long wagon trains toiled through the mired autumn roads,
sleighs slid over winter snows, and lined North and South Water
Streets, where the commission houses were centered. Runners from
rival firms even hustled out onto the prairie to meet the wagon
and sled trains, to bargain for a price, and to buy up the grain.
The increasing quantity of grain could not be shipped at once,
though the sails of the grain fleet dotted the Lakes all the way from
Chicago to Buffalo. The first storage warehouses were built in 1841
to hold the grain over in Chicago through the winter. One hundred
thousand bushels were stored that first winter; 700,000 bushels were
held in 1845-6; and the volume climbed—and the warehouses became elevators.

Thrilling progress in methods of farming the wheat lands was
building up a terrific pressure behind the flow of grain. The wheat
center moved west and northwest in the middle and late years of
the century. When the *Dean Richmond* made her epochal voyage,
Ohio, Indiana, Illinois, and Wisconsin were the western leaders in
wheat. One by one these states dropped from the front ranks as
the Missouri Valley took the lead. By 1900, only Ohio was left

among the first six, and she withdrew by the time of World War I. The vast prairies, geared to Chicago, and later to Duluth and the Lakehead, poured out their rising harvests, and industries to support the farms rose in the Lake cities. The prairie sod was tough and heavy, and the ancient wooden plows could not cope with it. John Deere on an Illinois farm in 1837 faced his plow with cutting steel and started a revolution. Henry W. Oliver (whom we shall meet again) developed his chilled steel plow in the 1860's, and a hundred improvements were added to break the sod deeper and faster: sulky plows, gang plows, steam-gang plows with seeder and harrow. With this machinery the man-hour time required to produce a bushel of wheat was reduced, according to Department of Agriculture estimates, from 32.8 minutes in 1830 to 2.2 minutes in the 1930's.

Reaping in the first wheatfields was also a back-breaking and time-consuming process. The methods in 1830 were not greatly different from those used by homesick Ruth when she stood in tears amid the alien corn. Cyrus McCormick remedied that shortly after the Black Hawk War. In 1840 his machine reaped six acres of wheat in a single day. With accurate foresight he set up shop in Chicago and spread his reapers to almost every farm in the West—a quarter of a million of them were on the farms ready to meet the acute man-power shortage when the boys departed in droves for the Civil War. Threshing machines soon followed the plows and the reapers, to add the exciting tradition of threshing week, which relieved the monotony of life on the bleak farms on the western plains. The wire binder came along in 1872, the Appleby twine binder shortly thereafter, and the reaper-thresher, drawn by 20 to 40 horses, in the 1880's. This machine even bagged the grain ready to be hauled away to the elevators. Then came steam and finally tractors to replace the horses, and the wheat fields were harvested at the rate of 75 or 80 acres a day.

War in the far-off Crimea raised the price of wheat in the crucial years of the 1850's to $2.00 a bushel, and the World War of 1914-18 pushed it up again to that high price. A thousand scientists in the state universities and colleges and in the experiment stations worked to increase the yield. Mark Alfred Carleton got interested. Among the millions of immigrants who were raising wheat in the West were a group of Russian Mennonites. They settled on the Santa Fe Railroad lands and planted seed which they had brought all the way from Russia and husbanded in America. It resisted the black rust and the drought that destroyed the Fife and Blue Stem varieties on our southern plains. That gave Carleton an idea. He journeyed to the far steppes of Russia beyond the Urals in 1898 and brought back Kubanka wheat. It proved to be perfectly adapted to Minnesota, the Dakotas, and Saskatchewan, and became the staple winter wheat of that region. Carleton later brought in the hardy Kharkov wheat which flourished in our southern wheat plains. The yield jumped year by year, subject of course to the periods of depression, which sent prices down and threatened ruin to the over-expanded industry.

Down on the lake shore the farm machinery manufacturing plants, the elevators, and the ships charted the upward curve by their ever-increasing height and length and breadth. Small elevators rose at intervals along the western railroads to receive the grain, and the trains rolled it across the prairies to the docks on the Lakes. Brigs and schooners crowded with canvas, and the growing steamship fleets sailed it over the Lakes at a good profit. Steady improvements went on in the complicated mechanism for receiving, storing, loading, and unloading. The giant elevator tubes shot up into the skies, and clustered together in such huge batteries that they dominated the harbors and even overshadowed the ore-docks. From far out on Thunder Bay the great elevators at Port Arthur and Fort William reflect the morning sun and are the first objects on the shore to be lifted against the gigantic background of up-flung rocks. The vast gray batteries first catch the eye as you approach the Duluth-Superior Harbor. They dominate the harbor and skyline of Buffalo, they overshadow the yachting basin at Toronto, they fill up the triangle of the lower city of Quebec.

Between these ports ply the grain fleet. Like the ore vessels, they have steadily lengthened in the past few decades, culminating for the time being in the Canadian Steamship Line's giant *Lemoyne*,

633 feet long and 75 feet at the beam, which carried a cargo of 571,960 bushels of wheat down from the Lakehead in her enormous hold. Yet even this long ship looks small when tied up under the elevators on the shore of Thunder Bay, and her tonnage leaves no hole in the bins. The grain has overflowed the regular elevators, spilled out into massive frame sheds for 'distress storage,' and in the early 1940's lay piled up under the snow on the Canadian wheatfields.

((((XXIX))))

Fish and the Fishing Fleets

WINTER fishing at the Sault a century ago was an exciting festival. The water at the entrance to Lake Superior, eighteen miles above the falls, freezes over to a thickness of two or three feet. The big salmon trout lie quietly beneath at depths of from thirty to fifty fathoms. The Indians had discovered long ago just where the schools collected, and the white men at the Sault had learned the lore of the Indians. They went up over the smooth ice of the river to Whitefish Bay. They cut round holes in the clear ice. They baited large hooks with small herring, or gobbets of beef or pork, dropped them through the holes, lowered them on a long, stout line to the level of the school, and waited. A big fish would swallow the bait and the hook, and with a powerful lash of his tail give a sharp tug on the line. When the fisherman felt that signal challenge from far down under the ice, he threw the line over his shoulder and hurried away with it at top speed. At the end of the pull he gave the line a quick, careful jerk, and a salmon trout, four to five feet long and weighing half as much as a man, shot up through the hole and floundered on the ice. The trout were so abundant in those days that a single fisherman would haul out fifty in a single day, and the colony at the Sault feasted through the long, cold winter on baked salmon trout.

Once in summer the winds blew strong from east-southeast and drove the waters of Lake Superior back toward Minnesota and Thunder Bay. The St. Mary's River abruptly ceased to flow over the Sault; it lay calmly in shallow pools in its bed above the falls. Whitefish, mullets, trout, and fat siskowits tossed about in the pools. Word spread through Sault Ste. Marie and everybody rushed to the river with pails and baskets, with nets, spears, gaffs, and bare

283

hands, to capture them. The phenomenon lasted for several hours and the catch was tremendous. Then the St. Mary's resumed its flow. It came back with such a rush that some of the fishermen did not have time to reach the bank, and had to struggle for their lives.

Down on Lake St. Clair, on Sandusky Bay, and around the Bass Islands in western Lake Erie, the fishermen's shanties appear each winter as soon as the ice is strong enough to support them. Acres of these shacks dot the region like miniature derricks in a crowded oil field. They are hauled out on sled runners by automobiles, or dragged along by the fishermen themselves. Inside is a stove and a stool or bench for the fisherman. He builds a warm fire. He chops a hole in the ice and drops a hand line through the opening in the floor. He will sit there all day long pulling up saugers, pike, perch, and pickerel as fast as he can lower and raise his line. It is an industry as well as a favorite form of winter sport.

From a hundred wharves around the Lakes the little fishing fleets put out each morning in the season—and the season is almost the full year round on the southern edges of Michigan, Erie, and Ontario. The nets lie on the wharves in the sun, smelling of fish and evaporating lake water. They are wound on huge ten-foot reels, inspected, and mended. They line the wharf at the Fishing Village a few yards from Navy Pier at the mouth of the Chicago River. Each morning at daybreak the motor-driven fishing boats put out past the control locks at the river's mouth, and run several miles out into the lake to the fishing grounds. They drop acres of nets overboard to the lake bottom and haul in those they had set the day before. They toss the flapping perch and lake herring into the boats and motor back to the odd little village where the fishermen live and market their catch.

Crossing Lake Superior on a summer's day on a Canada Steamship Line ocean-going style ship, you sit in the dining room with a steaming platter of whitefish before you, delicately browned with butter and garnished with lemon. It is a gourmet's dinner on the

Lakes. Words of praise for this dish have been spoken since white men first visited these waters. Henry R. Schoolcraft was moved to write a long poem about it.

All friends of good living by tureen and dish,
Concur in exalting this prince of a fish;
So fine in a platter, so tempting a fry,
So rich on a gridiron, so sweet in a pie;
That even before it the salmon must fail,
And that mighty bonne-bouche, *of the land-beaver's tail.*

You look out across the promenade deck to the deep blue of the lake. You see a cloud of gulls circling and sweeping. A flag buoy comes into view. The number of gulls increases. They swoop down to the lake against the wind, strike, and soar upward. And in a few minutes the big ship is steaming past a unit of the Lake Superior fishing fleet, anchored within its signal buoys, calmly hauling in fish from the cold waters. The fishermen wave, their boats rock on the swells, the gulls scream, and you go on with your dinner of whitefish as the ship glides along and the boats drop from sight in its lengthening wake.

The islands in western Lake Erie take their name from the bass that were once so prolific in those waters where they found ideal spawning grounds. The fishing fleet that daily puts out from Sandusky is as old in tradition as the town itself, which was and is the market center and outlet port for the millions of pounds of whitefish and bass, of pickerel, perch, sturgeon, herring, and catfish that have been taken from these grounds. The launches run out through the bay and up to the waters off North Bass Island just south of the shipway from Detroit to Buffalo around Pelee Point. The fishing district is blocked off by buoys topped with brightly colored flags. It is several miles long and may be seen from the texas house of the freighters or the promenade decks of the big excursion steamers going east from Detroit. The fishermen lower miles of trap nets equipped with sinkers to hold them ten fathoms under. Each day they haul them up, dump their catch into their specially constructed boats, and speed back to the slip alongside the fish houses. Here the catch is scaled by machine, packed in Lake Erie ice, and shipped out by fast express to Chicago, St. Louis, and the markets of the East.

The smelts run by the millions in silver schools in the rivers and creeks around the rim of Lake Michigan. They are imported fish, first brought to Crystal Lake in 1912 to feed the Mackinac trout. They spawned much faster than the trout could eat them. In a few years they were running in and out of the lake in vast schools and increasing in numbers annually. Regularly they leave the lake in crowded runs upstream to their spawning grounds. They overflow little Cold Creek at Beulah on Crystal Lake. Along this creek at night, by lamp and torch light, the people gather by the thousands to scoop up these fish in nets and buckets while the run is on. They take them by the ton. The smelts are also hooked as a part of the winter sports. Fishermen drag out cabins like those on Lake St. Clair and Lake Erie and fish through holes in the ice. The catch is run ashore by automobiles. You can even rent a shanty and hire a taxi to carry you out across the ice to the fishing village on the frozen lake.

This same scene is enacted on the Upper Peninsula when the smelts run up the Ford, the Escanaba, and the Menominee, usually in early April. The smelts run at night, and the fishermen gather along the river banks or wade out in hip boots with dip nets to scoop up the 8- to 10-inch silver fish. It has become an annual festival in some of the Michigan cities. At Escanaba they call it the Smelt Fishing Jamboree, and they parade the streets in carnival spirit. Menominee calls its season the Smelt Carnival. They crown a king and queen, sing and dance under the light of bonfires in the spirit of a New Orleans mardi gras. They fish from the inter-state bridge that leads to Marinette, from boats in the river, from crude barges with open centers into which they dip their hand nets. They haul them out in big nets operated with ropes and pullies— hundreds of tons of them. The fish houses freeze them, hundreds of them caked together in big flat slabs like giant bars of peanut brittle, and rack them up in the refrigerator rooms for storage and the markets.[1]

Fishing on and around the Lakes is big business as well as sport and recreation. Indians depended on lake fish for much of their food supply. The French acquired their hunting and fishing techniques along with a love for this diet. Alexander Henry at the Sault and Mackinac strained his simple vocabulary to praise the fat whitefish upon which he fed through a bitter winter in the North. The War of 1812 cut the tenuous food-supply lanes between Detroit and the East. The soldiers, both British and American, in that wearisome campaign survived on whitefish, sturgeon, bass, and perch from the Detroit River, western Lake Erie, Lake St. Clair, and southern Lake Huron. From that day on, Detroit was a fish market for both consumption and distribution. Commercial fishing by professionals with seines began in the St. Clair River around 1812, and in Maumee Bay about 1815. Whitefish were especially bountiful in the Detroit River in those early years. Immigrants went west by the thousands before the lands were open and before the local food supply was adequate. Food ships sailed west instead of east. Great Lakes fish became a staple in western diet. The early mining communities in northern Michigan depended upon fish. Fisheries at Detroit built their own ships and sent them out to the near-by fishing grounds. Schooners were hauled on rollers over the falls in the St. Mary's River in 1841 to sail to the fishing banks of Lake Superior. Salt was sailed up from Lake Erie, or brought up the Erie Canal, to Detroit and Mackinac for packing the fish in barrels for shipment. Thirty-five thousand barrels were packed and shipped in 1840; over 100,000 barrels went out in 1857. A hundred years ago fishermen took out of the Lakes sturgeon up to 100 pounds, trout up to 60 pounds, muskellunge up to 40 pounds, and mullet and pickerel from 10 to 15 pounds—and took them in quantity.

[1] Catastrophe struck the smelts in Lake Michigan and Lake Huron in the winter of 1943-4. They died by the millions. Instead of the expected ten million pounds, the catch was only *two pounds*. The smaller schools in Lakes Superior, Erie, and Ontario were not affected. Pathologists were completely mystified because the dead smelts showed no signs of disease.

The luscious whitefish and trout were the basic catch. Splendid small speckled or brook trout were thick at the Sault and in the rivers flowing into Lake Superior. They are still abundant in the protected streams.

Georgian Bay in those days teemed with whitefish, salmon trout, and muskellunge. The growing city of Toronto was supplied in the mid-nineteenth century and afterward from the fishing grounds of Nottawassaga Bay. Trout and other fish sought the mouth of the Nottawassaga River for their spawning grounds. The calcareous rock formation on the lake bed was warm and drifted over with fine sand. The fish swarmed in and lay vapid on the sun-heated banks. Fishermen gathered them in by the ton and shipped them across the arrowhead neck to the Toronto market.

The take of the commercial fishing fleets increased through the decades following the Civil War. By 1873 the Michigan fishing grounds in the four Upper Lakes were yielding 28,000,000 pounds of fish each year—a quantity equal to the present-day catch by improved and more expensive methods. The equipment of the fleets represents a capital of about $4,000,000; and about 5,000 men are employed in the industry. Toward the end of the century little Sandusky, Ohio, was sending out over 10,000,000 pounds of lake fish each year. The annual catch of the thousands of private fishermen and sportsmen added many tons not entered in the records.

As the supply diminished, the scale of the operations increased until the danger of over-fishing became acute. The fishing methods are pretty deadly. The whitefish, trout, and yellow perch pike are taken in large mesh gill-nets webbed from 4½ to 5 inches. The mesh is now increased to from 7 to 8 inches on the spawning grounds. For herring, chubs, and other rough fish the mesh is reduced to 2¼ to 2¾ inches. Netting of from 4½ to 9 feet wide is secured to two heavy lines, on one of which is tied 6-ounce leads, on the other small wooden or aluminum floats, at intervals of from 6 to 12 feet. The leads hold one edge of the net down, the floats raise the other, and the net stands upright like a chicken fence. It may be set at any depth, sometimes as far down as 600 feet. The fish swim head-on into this fence, ram their noses through the opening, and get caught behind the gills. They are often dead when the net is raised.

The nets are set from the little fleets of fishing boats that may be seen putting out from the harbors at daybreak or moving slowly along over the fishing grounds. Some of the boats are 65-foot steam tugs, others are 40- to 50-foot gasoline- or oil-burning launches, with a cruising radius of 100 miles or so. The vessels tending the gill-nets are generally enclosed, and they carry crews of from 5 to 7 men to work the nets. When the boats put out, the nets are stowed neatly in boxes, each of which holds about a half mile of net. The fishermen bend a line to a buoy, secure an anchor to the other end of the line, and cast it overboard. To this anchor and marker the fishermen fasten both the heavy float and lead lines of the first net. As the boat moves slowly along, one man pays out the lead line, and a second man the float. When they reach the end of one net, they tie a second buoy and anchor, and attach another net. They string them out in a gang that reaches from 4 to 8 miles, with each buoy flying its signal flag. Special revolving drums on the stern of the boat lift the nets and roll them in. It is an interesting sight to see the miles of net hoisted in vertical position, with one man tending it as it is hauled up, one man clearing it, separating the fish, and throwing them into 'lake boxes,' and a third man folding it into the containers.

Pound nets, trap nets, and fyke nets, all impounding types, are also extensively used on the Lakes. The fish are shunted into a net trap through a tunnel and are taken alive. They are fished to depths of about 90 feet, where they are anchored by long stakes driven into the soft bottom of the lake bed. They are tended by small crews in open, shallow draft (2½-foot) motor boats 30 to 40 feet long. You see them on western Lake Erie, in Saginaw Bay and other relatively shallow fishing grounds.

Trout are taken on hooks attached to short, four-foot lines. These lines are secured to a long trot line at intervals of about 16 feet with 350 to 400 hooks to a single box of line. A half dozen or more boxes make up a 'gang.' The fishermen bait these hooks with bloaters—small fish that swell up with the change of water pressure on

them—and pay out the lines from the stern of the fishing boat. The
gangs lie on the bottom of the lake and may stretch over the fishing grounds for a distance of ten miles. They are raised periodically,
by hand, the trout are thrown into the boxes, the hooks rebaited,
and the launch races back to the fish market with the catch.

The annual herring run on the Upper Lakes generally begins in
November. It is one of the big events in the year of Great Lakes
fishing. The herring swarm in to the shallow waters along the lake
shore from Munising to Duluth to spawn. These 9- to 15-inch fish
are trapped in the gill nets and hauled in to the hundreds of motor
and steam fishing boats by the wind-bitten fishermen who know
no rest during the three or four cold and stormy weeks of the run.
Each year they take from 17 to 23 million pounds of herring during
the season.

The supply of good fish in the Great Lakes has been diminishing
through the years. It has fallen off markedly in our time, while
rough fish, like the sheepshead, have been increasing. Old Michigan
fishermen around Ludington and Benton Harbor will tell you that
the big commercial fisheries have destroyed the young by lifting
them up in their nets; the sudden release of pressure on the fish
as they come to the surface causes them to explode and die. This
is probably a fisherman's tale. There are other more significant
causes. The grounds have been over-fished as the prairie lands were
once over-grazed. Small fish have been slaughtered by close-mesh
net fishing. The attempts to exterminate sturgeon and sheepshead,
which fill the nets, tear holes in them, and drive fishermen mad,
have also sacrificed other fish. Fishing in the spawning grounds has
been very wasteful and damaging. And pollution from hundreds of
towns, mills, and factories has been disastrous.

Many agencies have made studies of the problem and recommended interstate and international plans of action. The Ohio State
University maintains a laboratory on little Gibraltar Island in Lake
Erie, where Jay Cooke used to live during the summers. The scien-
tists there are also studying the causes and possible remedy for
the sharp decline in commercial fishing on the Lakes. They have
found that chief among the causes, aside from the heavy catches

of earlier years, is the rapid silting over of the lake floor by the rivers that carry down pollution and the eroding soil from the lake bowl and destroy the plant life in the lake. More care in cropping the take, closer regulations of the spawning season, stringent protection for the young, restocking from the hatcheries, and the united conservation movement that is underway may in time restore the Lakes to their former place as one of the greatest and handiest fish-producing areas in the world.

Part IV   DEVELOPMENT

We went through fire and through water: but thou
broughtest us out into a wealthy place.

PSALM 66:12

XXX

Keweenaw, Marquette, and the Sault

THE Great Lakes in our time are rimmed and girt with steel. The very mention of them calls up before the mind's eye the vision of giant black and red and green hulls with nearly 500 feet of steel hatches separating the gleaming white superstructures of the wheel-house and texas house forward from the after deck house.

These strange, whale-like monsters are distinctive on the Lake waterways. They are found nowhere else in the world. But on the Lakes they are everywhere. You see them squeezed into such tight slips in little harbors, like the one at Huron, Ohio, that they seem to be sitting on the stockpile grounds and overshadowing them. You see them putting their awkward length gracefully into the har-bors at Gary, at Detroit, at Lorain, Cleveland, and Buffalo. You see them gliding down the Maumee channel under the high-flung bridges of Toledo, and between the buoys of Sandusky Bay. They march along in a continuous column down the St. Mary's River and through the Sault, down the dredged channel of Lake St. Clair and through the Detroit River. In a busy season they are never more than a few minutes apart all the way from Duluth to the Sault, from the Sault to Chicago and Indiana Harbor, or to Con-neaut and Buffalo. In winter, when the ice closes over and naviga-tion ceases, you may see them by the score huddled side by side in protected anchorages along the entire 2,000 miles of the route. They account for the enormous shipping which the statisticians love to feature when they say that more tonnage passes through the Sault in one brief seven months' season than through Panama and Suez combined in a full year.

The figures are true enough. What the statistics omit is the fact that the tonnage is mostly a few items of bulk freight mechanically

tumbled through hoppers and chutes into these vast bottoms. I remember a pleasant afternoon in company with an old citizen of
Chicago on a clubroom terrace high above Michigan Avenue with
a magnificent view of Lake Michigan. Ships were moving about in
the harbor, and passing up and down the lake. The Chicago citizen,
himself something of a sailor, remained quite indifferent to the
spectacle. 'Monotonous,' he said. 'No color, no surprise. Just ore
and coal and grain, and a cargo of peaches from across the lake.'
That also was true. This traffic does not include the endless variety
and design of the ships that ease through Suez with cargoes of
spices and tea, ivory and jade, silks and sandalwood. These lake
ships are cumbersome, many of them are labeled 'red-bellies,' but
in their own way they have a saga of romance and a mission that
will stand up with the best of them.

The great cities that rim these shores draw their daily sustenance
from these ships. They link Cleveland, Youngstown, and Pittsburgh
furnaces with the greatest ore pits on earth. They join the coal fields
of Kentucky, West Virginia, and Pennsylvania with the cities and
towns of the Northwest. Through their endless bottoms flows the
wheat from the prairies of Minnesota and Manitoba to the granaries
of Buffalo, Toronto, Montreal, and Quebec. The cities are dependent upon the Lakes. And the saga of both in the modern era is the
saga of metal for a new America that began to roll on steel, to
build bridges and skyscrapers of steel, to sail ships of steel.

The lust for metal was never long absent from the minds of the
explorers who laid the Lakes open to the white men. Champlain
always pricked up his ears when his Indian friends from the Lake
region told him about the chunks of copper lying in the hills along
the Lake Superior shore. He always hoped to find this treasure
chest; he charged his personal scouts to hunt for these legended
deposits. Fur and not minerals, however, was for another 200 years
the chief product of the Lake region. Fish, lumber, and grain also
preceded the flow of copper and iron ore on the Lakes. But the
hunt for metal went on through the two centuries. Indians picked
it up along the trail east of Duluth, now the Douglas Copper
Range. They had found it on the Apostle Islands, and had created

a legend that one of these islands (now Madeline Island) was pure copper, guarded by spirits. Louis Denis, Sieur de la Ronde, commandant of the French fort in those parts in the early 1700's, actually mined some of the copper there.

The great Copper Country around Michigan's Keweenaw Peninsula was equally fabled. Explorers in this desolate region came upon holes and pits where Indians of a long-forgotten race and era had extracted the precious metal and left only the scars of their activity to suggest what manner of men they really were. We still do not know. But even in Champlain's old age, Frenchmen were publishing pamphlets in Paris about the Copper Country, and a hundred years later our friend Alexander Henry was out there exploring and digging tentatively into this hidden wealth.

In this desultory manner interest in the copper mines and knowledge of their whereabouts were kept alive, waiting the coming days of big-scale exploitation. They began modestly in the 1840's—along with the discovery of iron ore. On this lonely but spectacular Keweenaw Peninsula, a few miles from Copper Harbor, is a dirt trail leading back to the abandoned village of Cliff. By the roadside is an almost forgotten and seldom visited copper plaque, set into a boulder, bearing this inscription: 'On November 18, 1844, on the bluff west of this point, named Cliff Mine, Pure Metallic Copper was first discovered in the world by John Hays of Pittsburgh, Pa.' This and other mines in the vicinity were immediately put into operation and a trickle of copper began to move down the Lakes. The flow was seriously handicapped by the rapids and falls at Sault Ste. Marie. Everything that was shipped down from Lake Superior had to be unloaded in the St. Mary's River, portaged around the Sault, and reloaded below the falls. In the 1840's and early 1850's, Mr. Sheldon McKnight, a member of the Michigan House of Representatives, transported all the merchandise around the falls with one or two horses hauling a string of wagons or cars on a tramway.

Something, of course, would have to be done about the Sault. In the meantime there was some copper below the falls on the Ontario shore of Lake Huron. A lode had been discovered at Bruce on the North Channel, fifty miles from the Sault. The Montreal

Copper Mining Company started workings there within easy reach of the Lake ships. It was a port of call for the excursion steamers that came up from Collingwood, 290 miles away. In the 1850's the summer tourists stopped here to visit the copper mines. Twelve shafts went down about 300 feet to the lode. Three hundred miners, all Europeans who had come to the New World to find work, toiled in the crude, dark underground shafts. They were lowered in buckets. The ore, which looked like gold when the sun struck it, was hauled up by teams of mules hitched to the end of a cable. The ore was crushed and puddled at the mine, and then shipped off on the long voyage to Swansea, Wales, for smelting. Later on, as the Lake cities grew, some of it went to Buffalo, and some on to Baltimore to be turned into cables for the new telegraph lines that were beginning to bind the big country together.

These copper deposits first stirred up the speculators and sent hundreds of prospectors into the Lake Superior region to stake out claims. Most of them returned from devastating winters broken and impoverished. But millions of dollars' worth of copper were, and still are, taken out of these ranges. It was iron ore, however, and not copper that converted Lake Superior into the wonderland of natural resources.

The young state of Michigan did not want to be saddled with the wasteland of what we now call the Upper Peninsula. She was much more interested in northern Ohio and the mouth of the Maumee, and she even fought a small war with her sister for the prize of Toledo. She did not get Toledo or Maumee Bay, and the Federal Government made her take the wilderness between Lake Michigan and Lake Superior, like it or not. Since she was burdened with it, she might as well have it surveyed to learn its extent and find out just how worthless it really was.

Two great explorers and surveyors went in. One was the Michigan geologist, Douglas Houghton. He was young, strenuous, and frail. He had been with another great scientist and explorer, Henry Schoolcraft, on the upper Mississippi in 1832. He had persuaded the new Michigan legislature to appoint him to survey this reluctantly acquired peninsula in 1837. When the limited funds provided by Michigan were exhausted, he turned to the Congress and got authorization for a geological survey of federal lands up there. He went diligently to work, traveling along the Superior coast and around the Keweenaw Peninsula by canoe, tramping over the iron and copper ranges, and quietly filling his notebooks with the data which, as he well knew, would bring men in a rush to these fabulous mineral deposits, once the news leaked out.

Houghton was not eager to have the news spread prematurely. On February 1, 1841, when he made his report on the Copper Country, he also mentioned, very cautiously, the 'possibility' of iron ore on the Marquette Range. He went on with his work until 1845. He was closing the season's survey for the year, and was making his way along the south Superior shore back toward the Sault on October 13, when a sudden fierce storm struck. Houghton and the four men who were with him in the Mackinaw boat fought vainly against the storm. About a mile and a half from Eagle River the boat was lashed by the wind, the seas rose and hurled it up ten feet above the normal level of the lake, and smashed it against a rock. The boat was broken to pieces. Houghton and two of his men were injured and drowned. Two of the men escaped. Houghton's body was not found until months afterwards, but by a miracle his notes were saved. The disaster helped to spread the news of the wealth of this Upper Peninsula. A monument and a mining town in the Copper Country honor the memory of this scientist and martyr to the age of iron.

The other surveyor was William A. Burt, and a mountain of iron still perpetuates his name. He was one of the many capable, inventive, resourceful men produced in the mid-nineteenth century. He was an able surveyor and woodsman. He invented the solar compass and the equatorial sextant. He tinkered with the idea of a typewriter, and patented a crude but workable machine which he called a 'typographer.' He was also a legislator and a judge in Michigan's territorial days. He was not a geologist or mine prospector; he was a surveyor running accurate section and township lines for his state.

Burt took a party of eight men and two Indians into the district

around Marquette in 1844. On September 19 of that year he set
up his magnetic compass on the hill where the town of Negaunee
now stands. When he leveled it up to set his course and take a
sight, the needle began to flutter and whirl crazily around in the
box. He must have looked around impatiently to see which of his
axmen had got too close to his compass, for the needle always
jumped when one of them came up and craned his neck to watch
the instrument operate. But this time it was no ax that disturbed
the needle. It had gone completely wild and was twirling irregu-
larly through an arc of 87° variation. You would have to hold an
ax directly over the needle and move it back and forth to cause
that much deflection. Burt told his men to look for iron. They
kicked up leaves and dirt, poked under trees and bushes, and
hunted around among the loose earth and rock. They found chunks
of almost pure iron ore along an outcropping where the earth had
eroded. They were, in fact, standing on a mountain of iron, but
they did not know it.

Burt's new solar compass was independent of the magnetic
deflection. Quite understandably, he took more joy in his great
invention than in the discovery of an iron mountain. The season
was growing short. Already the cold winds were blowing over the
range, winter was approaching, and they were far from home. Burt
was not looking for iron in this faraway place; he was running
section lines. He went on with his work, but when the party got
back to the Sault, they told of what they had found, and the word
was picked up by interested ears.

Ambitious men, eager to make a quick fortune, pressed into the
peninsula on the heels of the surveyors. There were many of them.
One was Philo M. Everett of Jackson, Michigan. He was prowling
around up there hunting for copper when he picked up the spreading rumor of iron ore back of Marquette. In the spring following
Burt's difficulty with his compass, Everett persuaded a superstitious
Chippewa Indian to guide him through the wilderness hills to a
spot near Negaunee, where lay, according to Indian legend, such
quantities of ore that it was guarded by Spirits. The guide led
Everett to the edge of the sacred mount, but no further. Then, like

Moses advancing alone up Sinai, Everett went forward to the pits
and outcroppings of the eerie, polychrome hill that became Jackson Mountain, one of the richest of the reservoirs of ore on the
Marquette Range.

So, acre by acre, the land was explored and mines were opened
and workmen were brought in. A few ships were hauled up over
the barrier of the Sault Ste. Marie. They were inched along on
rollers and dragged over the ice and snow on sledges, a few feet
each day, until they could be launched again on the river above
the falls. Six schooners of from 20 to 110 tons, and two larger
steam-driven ships were hauled into Lake Superior in the seasons of
1845 and 1847. Five other steamers were taken up between 1850-53
as the new mines increased their operation and the demand for
transport grew.

It was perfectly obvious that this crude and expensive hauling
of ships around a mere nineteen-foot falls between Lake Superior
and the lower Lakes was an intolerable makeshift. With eight
canals already in operation across the rim of the Lake bowl, all
involving more labor and engineering genius than the Sault would
require, it was inevitable that this barrier should be overcome.
That was to be the work of another young pioneering genius,
Charles T. Harvey.

Harvey, at the age of twenty-five, had come out to this new
country to sell scales for Fairbanks. He picked up some typhoid
germs at the Sault, and his weeks of illness and convalescence gave
him plenty of time to weigh and consider the spectacle before
him. He walked along the St. Mary's River, and stood on the bank
watching the water foaming and tumbling over the rocks into the
channel and placid pool below the falls. On the Canadian side still
lay the wreckage of the old Northwest Company's canal and locks,
which they had built in 1798 for the canoe fleets. Major Holmes
had led a force up there in 1814 and destroyed the canal, along
with three ships at the Sault. Harvey saw the little steamships of
Captain Ward's fleet from Detroit come up as far as the barrier
of the Sault, unload, reload, and return without entering Lake
Superior. He saw the steamers, sloops, and schooners come down

to the foot of the lake above the falls, cast anchor and unload. Only a few feet of rapids prevented through navigation. As his strength returned, he went on a tour of the mines of the Upper Peninsula. Ore in what seemed inexhaustible quantities lay on and under the ground, and was already piling up around the mine shafts and at the developing ports on the south shore of Lake Superior. Again he thought of that nineteen-foot falls at the Sault. It was the only obstacle to a free-sailing route over a thousand miles and more of water to the cities that were already calling for ore. He would clear away that obstruction.

Michigan was easily persuaded. In fact she had already taken some hesitant steps toward a canal at the Sault, but the route was through federal land around Fort Brady and the War Department had stopped the project. Now, in 1851-2, new plans and surveys were made, the Congress gave its consent and set aside 750,000 acres of land to help pay for the construction. This was the occasion for Henry Clay's classic remark during the congressional debate, 'It is a work beyond the remotest settlement of the United States, if not the moon.' Mr. Clay had not been in the Copper Country or on the spirit-haunted summit of Jackson Mountain; he had not seen the ships being rolled round the falls at the Sault, or the ore piling up on the Superior shore.

Harvey had seen all this. He persuaded Fairbanks and others to back him with equipment and operating funds. The Saint Mary's Falls Ship Canal Company was formed under contract with the commissioners appointed by the state of Michigan. Harvey assumed the gigantic task of field manager of the operation, and the work commenced in the spring of 1853. It was to be completed within two years. Harvey worked like a man possessed. This was not so much a digging as a blasting job. It was a mile long. Holes had to be drilled by hand, one man holding the drill and two men swinging sledge hammers to make a cavity for the blasting powder. The powder had to come all the way from Delaware. The nearest machine shop was far down the Huron coast on Saginaw Bay. The stone for the canal and the locks was quarried and shaped at Aberdeen, near Malden, Canada, where Barclay's fleet had lain before it sailed out against Perry; and at Marblehead, across the bay from Sandusky, where the acres of deep-sunken pits still scar the region, and from which the Perry monument may be seen gleaming in the sun at Put-in-Bay. A fleet of 25 sailing vessels carried these stones across Lake Erie, up the Detroit, across the St. Clair Flats, up the St. Clair River, up stormy Lake Huron, and through the island-studded lower St. Mary's River to the workings at the Sault. Wrought iron—103,437 pounds of it—had to be fashioned and transported to the Sault; 38,000 pounds of it went into the gates of the locks. Eight thousand feet of oak timber had to be cut and shaped in the forests and brought to the falls.

And while all these supplies were coming in, Harvey was driving his men on the job to the limit. The summers were short and pestilential. Cholera broke out among the laborers, but the 200 victims were borne silently away at night and laid in shallow graves out of sight of the operations. The digging and the blasting went right on. The winter winds blew sub-zero cold down over frozen Lake Superior, over Whitefish Bay and the St. Mary's River, and the camp cook hacked meat from frozen carcasses of beef with a sharp ax. Sleet and hail battered the camps; snow piled up in the canal; men's ears and hands and feet were nipped by the frost; but the work went on. When labor grew desperately short, Harvey sent agents to the seaport cities to board the immigrant ships and sign on more men to swing the hammers, to drive the oxen, and push the wheelbarrows. He had from 1,200 to 1,600 men on the job. When they struck in protest against the harsh working conditions, Harvey closed the cookhouse and starved them back to the ditch. It was a heroic but agonizing epoch in the building of America. Through two short summers, followed by two long, grueling winters, Harvey drove on, and in June 18, 1855, he was able to hand over to the commissioners the completed canal.

The Governor of the State, his official family, and the Commissioners came up formally to inspect the work. They saw a ship canal one mile and 304 feet long around the turbulent falls. It was 115 feet wide at the top, 100 feet at the water line, 64 feet at the bottom, and 12 feet deep. The stone walls were 25 feet high and 10 feet thick at the bottom. They saw two fine locks, each 350 feet long, each 70 feet wide at the top and 61½ feet at the bottom. The upper lock lifted and lowered ships 8 feet, the lower 10 feet. They watched the three pairs of folding gates, each 40 feet wide, open and close. They inspected the upper and lower caisson gates that shut off the water of the river from the canal. They walked along the 180-foot lower wharf and the 830-foot upper wharf, from 16 to 30 feet wide. Then they watched the S.S. *Illinois* lock through the canal with ease and dispatch, and steam out a few minutes later into Lake Superior. It was, indeed, a stupendous achievement, entirely acceptable to the authorities. As a reward for building the canal in the record-setting time of two years, the company received the 750,000 promised acres of land. They selected 39,000 acres in the iron ranges, 147,000 acres in the copper region, and 564,000 acres in the timbered Lower Peninsula. All in all, not a bankruptcy return for the construction company.

On August 14 of this remarkable year, the trim, two-masted brigantine *Columbia*, with the American flag gracing the yardarm of her mainmast, dropped her white sails, eased her white-banded sides into the new locks at the Sault, and was lowered gently into the St. Mary's River below the falls. She was carrying the first cargo of iron ore for the Cleveland-Cliffs Iron Company, headed by Samuel L. Mather, direct from the wharf at Marquette on Lake Superior to the harbor at Cleveland. The river of red had begun to flow.

XXXI

Duluth and the Vermilion Range

Two seasons after the canal was opened, Harvey was invited to address the House of Representatives at Lansing on 'The present state and future prospects of the commerce of Lake Superior.' He proudly cited statistics to his gratified listeners. He told them that the first steamer had floated on Lake Superior in 1851, just six years ago; that in 1855, the first year of the canal, 1,400 tons of iron ore passed through the Sault. But in 1856, 11,000 tons had locked down from Lake Superior to Detroit and eastward, an increase of 800 per cent; and in addition, $2,250,000 worth of copper had gone down, and $2,500,000 worth of merchandise had gone *up* the canal. Over $6,000,000 worth of cargo had passed through his canal in seven months, whereas only fifteen years ago, he said, the traffic out of Lake Superior was zero. In Harvey's opinion the future prospect of the commerce of Lake Superior was impressive, and the Representatives at Lansing cheered the canal builder and his vision.

Not even a Charles T. Harvey, who had toured the iron ranges and built a canal to reach them with cheap transportation, could foresee the momentous stirrings and the national tragedy of Civil War that were rushing into action in 1857. Neither could the tourists who now began to book passage on excursion steamers to view the wonders of the canal and of Lake Superior. In the summer following the opening of the Sault, a Cleveland newspaper carried an exuberant advertisement of 'Two Grand Pleasure Excursions around Lake Superior.' For a fare of $40 'the new, staunch, upper-cabin and low-pressure steamer *Planet*, Captain Joseph Nicholson,' of 1,200 tons' burden, would take excursionists through the canal at the Sault, past the Pictured Rocks in daylight, and visit the iron

305

and copper country of Lake Superior. Though the *Planet* boasted
of splendid accommodations for 300 people, the passenger list
would be limited to 175, and there would be a band in attendance
'to enliven the scene.'

Passengers who made the trip on this luxurious ship found
plenty to see around Marquette. The town had been founded on
the fine harbor at the mouth of the Carp River by Robert Graveraet
of Mackinac in 1849, and given the name of Worcester in honor
of the New England town. But it seemed more appropriate to give
such an honor to the great Jesuit missionary and explorer who had
labored for souls and not for iron or gain in this region, and the
name was changed to Marquette the following year. When the
Planet called in 1856, there were ships in the harbor, the wharf
was buzzing with men and wheelbarrows and ore, and the little
town was expanding from the lake shore back toward the hills
and rocky bluffs that lent grace to the rough newness of Marquette.

The mines were from 12 to 30 miles back on the range from the
lakeport dock. The Jackson Iron Mountain had driven away the
Indian gods and was sending ore down for the Sharon Company.
Two miles away was Cleveland Mountain, operated by William
H. Gordon and others of Cleveland. It employed 30 men who
could ship down from 30 to 40 tons of ore daily (about three
dipperfuls and a few minutes' time on the Mesabi range today).
Sleighs had already been superseded by tramways for hauling the
ore. The tourists saw the plank road, laid with flat iron rails, that
led from the docks to these mines, and the little five-ton ore cars
pulled by a span of horses or mules and driven by swearing Canuck
teamsters recklessly along the irregular route.

A few miles further on the range were the New England Iron
Mountain and the Burt Mountain. They were already enjoying the
swift improvements of an expanding industry, for a railroad with
heavy T rails and a real locomotive was reaching back to these
mines. Fourteen miles of it were in operation, and ore was being
laid on the Marquette dock at $3.50 per ton instead of $5.00, with
no sacrifice in profit. Teams cost as much as $1,400, hay for them
was around $100 a ton, and every so often one of these expensive

animals was crushed under the wheels of the on-rushing ore car on the grades. The new iron horse ran no such risks and consumed no hay several hundred miles from the nearest meadow.

If the excursionists had gone back on the range, they would have seen desolate little clusters of shacks around the towering shaft houses and stockpiles. Some of the ore lay near the surface, where the earth could be stripped away and the ore blasted into chunks. Most of them were shaft mines. Cornishmen, chiefly from the Ohio and Pennsylvania bog mines and charcoal furnaces, climbed into buckets and were lowered from a hundred to three hundred feet to the workings. They were big-muscled men, grim and earnest about their job, and they took pride in their work. They fastened a long candle to their caps (four candles lighted them through a ten-hour shift down in the hole) and began drilling, digging, blasting, and loading the buckets. One man held and turned the drill, two men swung sledge hammers to drive it down ready for a charge of powder. They ate pasty (Welsh variety of meat pie) and drank tea warmed over a candle in the pit. When their long day was over, they were hauled up in the buckets, they changed their ore-red clothes in the dry-house, and went home with ore-stained hands and face to sleep in the shacks with their wives and children. During many months of the year they seldom saw daylight or the sun. They kept the ore rolling down to the lake.

On around the lake, at Superior City, as it was then called, the same hum of activity was transforming the port. The year before the Sault was opened, two steamers and five sails called at this wharf. During the first season of the operation of the Sault, 23 steamers and 10 sails came into the harbor. In 1856, 40 steamers and 16 sails arrived. And that was only a beginning and a suggestion of the traffic that was about to stream over the lake and down through the canal.

The big cities called for more and more ore. The shipyards all around the Lakes sent new and bigger bottoms sliding down the ways and into carrier service. Captain Alvah Bradley hoisted sail on a brand new fleet of schooners and brigs in 1858 to carry ore:

the *London*, the *Exchange*, the *Wagstaff*. For nearly two decades, much of the ore was sailed down the Lakes in brigs and schooners. Their masts and rigging hampered loading and unloading, and their tonnage was small, but they kept the ore flowing. They made an unforgettable spectacle in the lake harbors, particularly at the ore ports where a score or more of them fought and jockeyed in the wind for first place at the loading docks. Many of them were owned and operated by the captain who leased his ship for the specific haul. (Individually owned ships are still an important item in the total Great Lakes-St. Lawrence traffic.)

There was always drama at the docks. In these first years, the small ships were loaded by wheelbarrow pushed by Irish hands and shoulders from the wharf to the deck. This slow process was soon superseded by hoppers with chutes to the hatches. A tight little professional group controlled the loading of the hold—ore trimmers they were called. It was a science in those early days to keep the ore evenly distributed throughout the ship. Too much on the port side would cause the ship to list and make her hard to steer. Too much at the bow or stern would make her ship high seas, throw her off course, or cripple her speed. The boss trimmer stooped over topside with measuring line and plummet to direct each shovelful to its appointed place in the hold. The men below, stripped to the waist and hustling out of pride in their work as well as because they were paid by the job, handled pick and shovel to move the ore as it poured down in a cloud of red dust into the hold. They kept a lookout for heavy chunks, especially when the chutes were first opened into the empty cargo space: a particularly huge lump shot down like a thunderbolt into the hold of the *Inter-Ocean* and went right on down through the hull into the lake, taking with it soon afterward the ship itself. Sometimes they worked day and night without ceasing from the time the ore ship secured to the dock until it was loaded and ready to put out on an even keel for one of the big and growing mill towns down the Lakes.

A few other improvements along the water route between this rising new industry and the Lake Michigan and Lake Erie industrial cities were now necessary. The harbors were all shallow. Most of the port cities had been founded at the mouth of the short rivers draining down into the Lakes. The years of erosion had brought sand, soil, and gravel down and deposited them in sandbars in front of the cities. These obstructions had now to be cleared away, better breakwaters and anchorages constructed, and lights and buoys installed or improved. The first Rivers and Harbors Congress had been held at Chicago in 1847 to consider the problem, lay plans for improvement, and solicit congressional aid. Harbors and channels were rapidly improved. The treacherous sandbars at Milwaukee, upon which so many sailing ships and steamers had run aground, was cleared away. The harbors at Chicago, Cleveland, Buffalo, and Toronto were dredged, deepened, and enlarged. The difficult and shallow channel across the St. Clair Flats was first dredged in 1855 by Mr. Barton of Buffalo. With the aid of Mr. Osgood he also deepened the channel of the St. Mary's River.

The waterways were cleared, the harbors in good shape, and the mines opened with their basic operating pattern already formed when the Civil War hit the nation. It was an amazing coincidence of the greatest significance to the North. Guns and wagons and railroads and ships were all needed in quantity. The hundreds of small furnaces scattered through southern Ohio and western Pennsylvania, dependent upon the limited output of ore in those regions, could not meet the demand. The Marquette Range had opened just in time.

Peter White was already a legended figure of nearly Paul Bunyan proportions in the iron country of Michigan before the war broke out. As a lad he had worked his way on a schooner up to the Sault from Detroit. He was with Robert Graveraet when that far-sighted pioneer selected the harbor at the mouth of the Carp River as the best outlet for the Marquette ore, and he had helped build the dock with logs and rock from which the first load of ore was shipped down the Lakes. He had tramped over all the region in snowshoes, he had guided prospective iron barons to the ranges, he had carried the mail to the mining towns, and he had helped to persuade the Government to grant its lands to aid the railroads to tap the workings. He had no doubt of the future of this iron country or of the coming greatness of Marquette.

As the war came on, this strangely gifted backwoodsman bought up all the ore he could find in the stockpiles at the mines, on the wharves of Lake Superior, at the harbors on the other Lakes. Then he went down to Cleveland and on to Pittsburgh, where he promptly sold every ton of it at a fat profit. He laid the foundation for his family fortune and gave another boost to the ore production on the Lake Superior ranges. In 1904, the city that he helped to build erected to him the kind of monument he would have approved—the beautiful Peter White Public Library, which also houses the local historical society's museum of maps, pictures, manuscripts, and specimens of the minerals of the region.

The war gave a tremendous impetus to the Great Lakes. Back in April of 1848, when the Michigan-Illinois canal was opened to join the Lakes with the Mississippi at Chicago, the *General Thornton* came up from New Orleans with a cargo of sugar. She crossed the low lake ridge on the canal, and sailed proudly out on Lake Michigan from Chicago, her course set for Point Betsie and the Straits of Mackinac, her destination Buffalo. The crescent empire, so long dreamed of by the French, was now a reality for the Americans. But the sectional war between the states cut the long water route in two, and the South closed the Mississippi River. Traffic from the American West was immediately diverted northward over the canals and railroads to the Great Lakes, and still more volume was added to the Lake fleet of passenger and freight ships. The towns from Chicago to Buffalo, and on to Toronto and Kingston felt the impetus. Canada opened more mines, built more ships, and laid more rails over the Ontario arrowhead. At the close of the war, Canada confederated her provinces (1867) and pushed her Canadian Pacific Railway on to her own great West. Immigrants poured in on both sides of the international border—and the search for ore went on.

The scene now shifts farther west.

Geologists and surveyors were busy running lines and testing minerals all through the Upper Peninsula and around the northwest coast of Lake Superior in Minnesota. Both the Federal Government and the states concerned were eager to learn just what value might be placed on this wilderness area about which the owners knew nothing. This ignorance has its amusing and ironic sides. We see the high commissioners from America and Britain sitting in knee breeches under powdered wigs around the conference table at Paris at the close of the Revolutionary War, debating the boundary between the United States and Canada. Not one of them had ever seen, or even been anywhere near, this Michigan-Minnesota wilderness. It was just a few lines on the maps before them. Ralph D. Williams, writing about Marquette's notable Peter White, said that his saga 'might have been a Canadian tale had it not been for the foresight of the great Benjamin Franklin, who deflected his pencil a bit on a certain memorable occasion and caused the Upper Peninsula of Michigan to be included within the American boundary.'

That pleasant story may well be apocryphal, but the error that gave Minnesota the Vermilion and Mesabi iron ranges is a matter of record. The commissioners had before them John Mitchell's map of the Lake Superior country. (See page 312.)

It is a curious piece of cartography, a combination of imagination and near accuracy. Where did the surveyor dream into existence the Isle Philippeaux? And who counted out all the other islands in the Apostle group to leave the Biblical number twelve? There is no Long Lake on the Superior coast, and the Lake of the Woods does not drain down through the Pigeon River into Lake Superior. Pigeon River is only 30 miles long. But on John Mitchell's map it made a logical boundary line, and the commissioners agreed to adopt it instead of the St. Louis. England unwittingly gave up Fond du Lac, the undiscovered iron ranges, the Minnesota arrowhead, and the site of Duluth.

If Britain did not know what wealth she had ceded, neither did America suspect what resources she had acquired. Both preserved their ignorance for almost a century. That great traveler in the West, James Flint, crossing Lake Erie on the *Walk-in-the-Water* in 1820, met on deck a captain in the United States Army who was

returning from Green Bay. Flint expressed the geographical sense
of his generation when he wrote in his journal that the captain had
taken some soldiers into banishment at that Wisconsin fort, Green
Bay being 'a place of exile, so far removed from the other settlements of the United States, that culprits have it not in their power

Redrawn from John Mitchell's Map of the British Colonies in North
America, February 13th, 1755

to escape from thence.' That great United States Senator and frequent candidate for President, Henry Clay, thought, on the eve
of the Civil War, that the Sault was a remote spot on or beyond
the moon. One of the most hilariously funny speeches ever made
in the Congress, where the competition has been keen, was delivered in January 1871 by J. Proctor Knott, Representative from
Kentucky, when he spoke with an ignorance of epic proportions on
'The Glories of Duluth,' and the projected St. Croix and Bayfield
Railroad. The error that gave the iron ranges to the United States
was scientifically precise by comparison.

After pouring out a stream of irony on the urgent need for a railroad built at government expense in 'those vast and fertile pine barrens, drained in the rainy season by the surging waters of the turbid St. Croix,' Mr. Knott unloosed the full flood of his oratory on the wonders of Duluth. Just where, he asked, would this mighty railroad have its terminal? 'I knew that neither Bayfield nor Superior City would have it,' he said. But in his moment of darkest despair, he continued,

I accidentally overheard some gentleman the other day mention the name of 'Duluth.' DULUTH! The word fell upon my ear with peculiar and indescribable charm, like the gentle murmur of a low fountain stealing forth in the midst of roses . . . DULUTH! 'Twas the name for which my soul had panted for years . . . But where was Duluth? Never, in all my limited reading, had my vision been gladdened by seeing the celestial word in print . . . Its dulcet syllables had never before ravished my delighted ear . . . I asked my friends about it, but they knew nothing of it. I rushed to the library and examined all the maps I could find . . . but I could nowhere find Duluth.

At that point in his desperation, when he was convinced that he would go down to his grave whispering with his fleeting breath, 'Where is Duluth?', the legislature of Minnesota furnished him with a magnificent map. 'As I unfolded it a resplendent scene of ineffable glory opened before me . . . There, there for the first time, my enchanted eye rested upon the ravishing word, "DULUTH."' And he kept the House in an uproar while he elaborated on the wonders of Duluth. The speech focused national attention upon the beautiful town at the head of Lake Superior, which soon made real the glories of which J. Proctor Knott had spoken in ironical jest.

In 1865, shortly after General Grant had sent the soldiers of the conquered South home with their horses to start the spring plowing, a geologist (of sorts) came down from Lake Vermilion with the report that gold lay in that region. The rumor spread like a Wisconsin forest fire, and almost over night adventurers and prospectors were swarming inland over the tough muskeg with all kinds of mining paraphernalia to pick up their fortune.

In the vanguard was a very wise man, tough of body and philosophical of mind. He was George R. Stuntz, one of the truly admirable characters of the Northwest. He was primarily a surveyor.
He ran township lines for the Government in the wilds of Wisconsin, then moved on in 1852 to the Duluth section to survey
northeastern Minnesota. He was a gifted amateur archaeologist and
mineralogist as well as woodsman and pioneer. He studied the
mounds and Indian artifacts of that country and speculated upon
these early men and their habits of life. He was captivated by
the prospect of Duluth. He must often have climbed up the hills
behind the future city, where his bones now lie in the Oneota
Cemetery on the Parkway Skyline, and from the outjutting rocky
headlands viewed the wide expanse of Lake Superior and the
natural harbors at the mouth of the St. Louis River and Bay below
him. Someday, and soon, he knew a city would grow there on the
terrace and the lake would be a crowded shipway. He was not
personally ambitious, but he had confidence in the future of this
region which he preferred to more civilized areas.

Stuntz was too wise to believe the reports of gold in those hills,
but he was also too curious not to explore the locale. He hurried
on across the hundred miles of rough terrain to Lake Vermilion.
He picked up some nuggets of the bright metal and weighed them
in his hands. He nodded his head in confirmation—just what he
expected, sulphur and iron, fool's gold. The prospectors returned,
all of them disillusioned and many impoverished. Stuntz, however,
had found something that men would gladly pay gold to obtain.
He saw iron ore all over the place, and he lugged back to Duluth
a heavy sample. He had it analyzed; it was phenomenally pure.

The woodsman, after thinking it over in his cabin during the
bleak winters, finally decided to take his samples to the East.

For nearly two decades, Stuntz pressed this treasure chest upon
eastern millionaires and labored in season and out to get a railroad
to the range and the mines in operation. Most eastern men had
about as much understanding of this part of their country as Flint,
Clay, and J. Proctor Knott. They were not helpful. But his old
friend, the Surveyor-General George B. Sargeant, sent him to Jay

Cooke, then at the height of his enterprise, with his samples and the specific proposal to build a 70-mile railroad to let the ore flow down to the ships on Lake Superior. The imaginative Philadelphia millionaire and railroad magnate was intrigued by the idea, and promised to build the road. The great man himself actually came out to Duluth to see what all the excitement was about. Surviving accounts of that visit indicate that the millionaire in the flamboyant baron's costume of the 1870's—top hat, cloth shoes, long coat, colored waistcoat, gold watch chain and stick—cut a figure in the shabby boomtown at the head of the lake. Duluth spread with excitement under his all-powerful interest; the road was as good as built. But, alas, there were forces in America bigger even than her formidable barons. The panic of 1873 hit the nation and carried down in the crash the empire of Jay Cooke and the proposed road to Vermilion. The town of Duluth almost perished in the debris, but after losing three-fourths of its population, it rallied and hung on. A handsome statue, however, on London Road at 8th Avenue East, pays Duluth's tribute to Cooke's interest in the city.

While all this Jay Cooke furor was raging, a significant little drama, typical of expanding America, was enacted at the entrance to the harbor. The natural location of Duluth is beautiful from the land or from the lake. A low sandbar, only a few score feet wide and now covered with houses whose backyards touch the bay, lies across the harbor for over six miles, pointing toward the Wisconsin shore at Superior. It is still known as Minnesota Point. A similar bar juts out about half as far from Wisconsin, leaving a 500-foot space of water between them as the natural entrance to the land-locked harbor. This is now the Federal-controlled Superior Ship Canal, through which most of the 10,000 seasonal ship arrivals pass into the Duluth-Superior Harbor. Duluth wanted a canal across this bar near her own shore in order to save her fishing boats the six-mile voyage down to the channel. Ambitious Superior objected to her rival's plan, and when Duluth began digging in 1871, Superior protested to Washington, where her promoters had powerful backing. Washington entertained Superior's demand for an injunction to halt the work and dispatched an army engineer to serve it on Duluth. The news reached Duluth three days before the engineer and the injunction. The aroused citizens pitched in to help with the digging and the shoveling. They worked day and night from Friday to Monday morning, and when the order to cease and desist arrived, the tug *Fero* was already steaming through the completed ditch with her whistle blowing and the crowds on both sides cheering in triumph. It was characteristic of the spirit of Duluth. Today ships pass through this improved canal under the high arch of the Aerial Lift Bridge. Three blasts of the ship's horn send the traffic platform up the steel towers of the bridge, and the cars going back and forth from the Point to the City pause while the ship glides through and eases into its wharf or slip.

Stuntz saw and relished this American episode, which proved his confidence in Duluth. The collapse of the city two years later pained him but did not defeat him. Another enterprising man with risk capital always rose when one fell. Charlemagne Tower, a Pottsville, Pennsylvania, millionaire, agreed to back the road whose profit was now a mathematical certainty. He sent out his son, Charlemagne Tower, Jr., to oversee the work. He depended heavily upon George Stuntz, who knew every mile of the terrain. Stuntz's surveyor's eye located the route and directed the driving of the stakes and the clearing of the right of way. It was one of the toughest construction jobs of its kind so far undertaken in the United States. The terrain was rough and hostile, the living conditions for the gangs were harsh, the problem of supply was formidable. The 70-odd miles of track cost the huge sum of $4,000,000. It was called the Duluth and Iron Range Railroad, but its Lake Superior port was not Duluth but Two Harbors, a few miles up the lake shore.

The road was finally ready to haul ore in the spring of 1884. The usual big celebration was held on June 30 to see the first train of cars, loaded with Vermilion ore, roll down to the dock at Two Harbors. The steamer *Hecla* and a barge were at the dock to receive the cargo and carry it down to Cleveland. It was the beginning of the stupendous mining on the ranges back of Duluth that would pile up vast fortunes for the operators. As for George Stuntz, that philosophical gentleman remained indifferent to these fortunes. He bought up for his employers 17,000 acres of Vermilion ore land for a mere $40,000, and he lived a happy life on his princely salary of $8.00 a day.

((((XXXII))))

Mesabi

THE hunt for ore around Lake Superior was now on in epic proportions. It extended westward and southward from the Marquette Range and southwestward from Lake Vermilion. While George Stuntz was exploring the Vermilion Range and hunting capital for his railroad, John Longyear, another great woodsman, was tramping about over the hills just north of Green Bay. He carried a compass, and kept close watch on the needle. It jumped around nervously in its box on the Menominee hills, and disclosed the rich Menominee iron range with its center at Iron Mountain on the Wisconsin border, and its outlet port at Escanaba, 40 to 80 miles away on Lake Michigan. It was in full operation by the late 1870's.

Longyear then went on westward to open up the Gogebic Range, about 50 miles back of Ashland, Wisconsin, its big Lake Superior port city. Charles Whittlesey had gone out there in 1849 to survey the region for the Government. He had found a long, irregular ridge extending about 80 miles across Michigan and Wisconsin, and rising nearly a thousand feet above Lake Superior. Everywhere along its blue summit were evidences of ore. Operators moved in, railroads were built connecting the Gogebic with outlets at Ashland and Escanaba, and the first ore went out to the Lower Lakes in 1885. Most of the ore on the Gogebic Range lay deep underground. The Newport mine, opened in 1886, kept going down and down to 2,300 feet, sending up millions of tons of ore. The Geneva Mine in the same district at Ironwood, Michigan, has gone deeper and deeper, straight down to 3,150 feet.

That is a long way down. When you have dropped from the observation floor of the Empire State Building to the street level, you have traveled considerably less than half the distance these miners descend each day to the lowest platform in the mine. They are lowered, 75 at a time, in double-deck cages in a little more than three minutes from top to bottom. Enormous fans pump in fresh air for the workers through huge canvas air ducts, and other pumps and pipes force the water out of the shaft and crosscuts. Powerful hoisting machinery whisks the ore out of the shaft and dumps it on the stockpile.

The same big hunt was on in the Minnesota hills. Prospectors and speculators poured in. They recklessly bought and sold shares and stakes they had never seen, bidding up prices, bringing on panics, and creating the typical scene and cycle of an American boom—whether it be a California gold rush, a Michigan copper craze, or a Florida land swindle. In the rush there were always a few wise, persistent, or lucky ones who held on and made good. Among this group back of Duluth were the Merritt Brothers and Nephews, the 'Seven Iron Men' of De Kruif's book of that title, and they are, indeed, exciting subjects for a full volume. They, like Stuntz, and perhaps even more perfectly than he, epitomize the entire epic of the iron-hunting era.

Their father, Lewis Merritt, was an expert woodsman. He was in the Lake Vermilion gold rush, and, like Stuntz, he too picked up some nuggets of ore. He kept his discovery in his cabin, he looked at it often, and he talked to his stalwart sons about it, but he never went East with it. These sons, with fine period names like Leonidus, Cassius, and Napoleon, rather slowly absorbed the wisdom of the old gentleman while they carried on their trade and profession of cruising the Minnesota forests, and estimating the stands of timber. This work, of course, led them to the still-undiscovered ore ranges to the south and southwest of Lake Vermilion. Here they came upon the northeast end of the range known today throughout the world, under a half-dozen variant spellings, as the Mesabi. The odd phenomenon of this range was that the ore, instead of being flint-hard and far underground, as at Vermilion and Gogebic, was loose and lay near the surface under a relatively thin layer of earth. It hardly seemed believable that it was really iron ore, or that it could be good ore. It was too much for the human imagination that God should have, in a sense, already mined this ore and left it here in a stockpile ready to be shoveled up and carted away to the Ohio and Pennsylvania furnaces!

The Merritts hewed a road through the timber from Tower (on the south of Lake Vermilion) to their discovery. They took out samples of the soft, hematite ore, and engaged the mining expert, Captain J. A. Shields, to aid and advise them. They got an analysis of their ore. It tested 64 per cent pure—the finest yet discovered in the treasure chest of Lake Superior. With some repetition and lack of imagination, they named the place Mountain Iron.

The Merritts, now sure of their find, began to buy up rights and plan operations. They acquired 141 leases in 1890. They extended their search on down the ridge, finding ore on every hand.

All they needed was financial backing to build a railroad back to the mines. Leonidus was chosen as the salesman, promoter, and special ambassador to the money bags of the eastern capitalists. It was a heartbreaking task for the timber cruiser and looker. Duluth meant about as much to the barons as it did to J. Proctor Knott. Among others, Leonidus called on Henry C. Frick, the great Pennsylvania iron magnate of Carnegie Steel. Frick was irritable and short-tempered with his visitor. That meeting is a dramatic and unforgettable scene: the powerful, well-dressed baron scowling and growling at the rough Minnesota giant who stands before him ill at ease in his new clothes among the unfamiliar appointments of a steel magnate's office. Leonidus felt that he was being bullied and browbeaten by an arrogant man who would not even listen patiently to a few important facts about Minnesota ore. He returned empty handed.

The Merritts finally got local backing for their projected railroad, and by some miracle, plus the capital liquidated from their own small lumber business, they built the Duluth, Missabi & Northern R.R. to link their mines with Lake Superior. Duluth, however, refused them entrance to that port. Brother Cassius had to locate the tracks from Mountain Iron around Duluth to its rival, Superior, across the St. Louis River. The first train load of ore was rolled down in October 1892.

Henry W. Oliver, the big Pittsburgh plow-and-shovel man, was in Minneapolis that year as a delegate to the Republican Convention. Naturally he heard the excited talk that ran through the hotels about the Merritt Brothers' mines and their new railroad. Oliver was a man of action. He hastened up to Duluth, slept, or at least lay, the night on a pool table, because booming Duluth was overflowing, bought himself an expensive horse, and trekked over the muskeg to the Merritts' camp. With his own eyes he saw the fabulous wealth of loose ore. He tested it, promptly leased a mine, and rushed back to Pittsburgh to complete the complicated series of organizations which led, step by step, stage by stage, to the gigantic Oliver Iron Mining Company. When the United States Steel Corporation was organized in the spring of 1901, the Oliver Iron Mining Company became its subsidiary as owner and manager of its iron-mining division, which embraces every district of the Lake Superior Ranges.

The Merritt Brothers, we are sorry to record, were crowded and squeezed out by the big concerns. They ran into tight financial crises, and had to turn again and again to the East for help. They turned once too often, this time to John D. Rockefeller, in the most ruthless days of a ruthless and uncontrolled era. The details of the deal have never been made clear, but the results were spread before everyone who knew or had any knowledge of the Merritts. They lost their mines, they lost their railroad, and they died as poor men, while the ore flowed down in an ever-increasing red flood into the expanding furnaces of millionaires. Their bones lie in the same Duluth cemetery on the Parkway Skyline that gives peace to George Stuntz. But the scene that pleased contented and philosophical Stuntz could give no solace to the restless and defrauded Merritts, to whom the cars of ore rolling down from the range, the red dust at the docks, and the coming and going of the big ships in the harbor must signify industrial war, failure, and personal defeat.

There was one other boom in the crescendo of discovery, and it involved the greatest of all the mines. It is dramatically fitting that the exploration should have moved mile by mile down from

Vermilion, growing richer at each stage, to reach its climax in the area of Hibbing. The stand of jackpine in this region had brought the lumber camps on westward in the late 1880's and early 1890's, and the usual rowdy villages with a saloon-lined Main Street had sprung up to service them. But lumbering in the early 'nineties was less exciting than ore hunting. The story is that Jim Kennedy, the foreman of a camp near present Hibbing, was talking one night with a well digger who was sinking a shaft not far from the bunkhouse. The well digger said he had struck some loose red dirt that was easy digging but very heavy shoveling. Kennedy thought about that remark during a restless night, and finally got up in the dark to investigate. He found the pit, lowered himself, struck matches to examine the sides and bottom, and was convinced that under this cheap jackpine he was cutting lay a fortune in ore. He sent for Captain Frank Hibbing, who was operating eight miles away, to come and look at it. Hibbing was at the pit by noon. He knew iron ore when he saw it, and this was it. By mid-afternoon four different gangs were sinking test pits around the well, and the most productive of all the mines on the ranges was on its way to exploitation.

This Frank Hibbing, for whom the famous mining city was named, was another of those remarkable German immigrant boys who had come over with nothing but his talents and his capacity for work. He arrived at the right time, and he made his fortune on the range which he helped uncover. He thought the Vermilion and the Mountain Iron section were not the center of the ore deposit but rather its northeastern edge. He wandered back into the western end of the Mesabi, where he stumbled upon the incredible storehouse of ore that lies between Virginia (once upon a time Virginia City), Chisholm, Marble and Coleraine, with Hibbing in the center. Railroads were promptly built to the new mines, and by 1895 the ore was rolling down to the freighters in Duluth harbor to swell the red tide that flowed a thousand miles to Lorain, Cleveland, Ashtabula, and Conneaut on Lake Erie.

This ore deposit around Hibbing is one of the wonders of the world. It was formed there in the astronomical past during the

slow but cataclysmic earth changes that formed the rocks behind
Fort William and created the Lake Superior bowl, as we saw in
Part I. The glaciers covered it over with drift when they were
processing the present form of the Great Lakes. On this part of the
range, the drift is a thin blanket that can be peeled off with steam
shovels, leaving the naked ore exposed in the open pit. The greatest exposure is at the Hull-Rust mine, a pit so vast and overpower-
ing to the eye that superlatives fail to cope with it.

It must be seen to be believed or understood. It is almost four
miles long. It is irregular in width, varying from a half mile at
the Susquehanna and Webb Mines on the east to a full mile at the
Mahoning, Hull-Rust Mines on the west. It is approximately 350
feet deep. The stripping and mining has lifted and moved as much
material out of this tremendous hole as was handled in digging
the great Panama Canal itself. It has gone down and down on a
series of vast terraces. In some places you can count thirteen of
these giant steps leading down from the surface to the bottom
floor where the cranes and shovels are scooping up ore and the
locomotives are shuffling the cars around over 75 miles of track-
age. The mid-morning sun hits these scarred sides and the terraces
and they glow in a variegated mass of red and brown and bluish
green. Then they look more like the threshold steps to Lucifer's
Palace of Pandemonium than anything in this world of ordinary
mortal men.

The sinking of this pit has involved the entire cycle of modern
industrial technique in the last half century. The first layer of
earth was dug with picks and shoveled by hand into horse-drawn
dump wagons. This method was slow, crude, and costly. Steam
shovels, also crude affairs, took the place of hands and backs in
1898, and little 10-ton, dinkey locomotives displaced the horses.
From that day to this, each few seasons, this equipment has grown
in size, speed, and capacity for work. The dump cars got longer
and higher—from one cubic yard up to 3, then to 7, then to 20
with a special air-dumping device, and on to the present 50-ton
ore cars. The dinkeys grew up to be 100-ton locomotives, and then
to 127 tons with an auxiliary engine under the tender to boost the

power in getting a train of 17 cars under way. The shovels have kept pace. They jumped from 50 tons to 90, from 90 to 250, from 250 to 350 tons lifting 16 tons of ore at a single scoop and operating on caterpillars.

The movement of the ore became so rapid during World War I that the town of Hibbing, which had seemed to be a safe distance away from the mine, found itself sitting almost within the pit. The operations surrounded it on three sides, and a wealth of ore, immensely more valuable than the town, lay beneath it. The Oliver Iron Mining Company then bought the whole foundation of the town and moved the houses off to a new site about a mile and a half away. It wasn't much of a town to move, mostly a slovenly hodgepodge of frame houses and shacks, some of which were too flimsy to survive transplanting. A good picture survives of the collapse of the tired old Sellers Hotel that gave a sigh and fell to pieces on the road from Old to New Hibbing in 1921. Cass Gilbert's stone Christ Memorial Church was razed and rebuilt on the new site. Even the graves in the cemetery were lifted out gently with steam shovels and transplanted.

This new Hibbing is a smart and swanky town with a municipal income from the mines that enables it to live as a city in incomparable luxury. It has a War Memorial Building, covering a city block, fitted up with club rooms, bowling alleys, dancing floor, and 'the finest indoor skating rink in the Northwest,' complete with a plant for quick-freezing a sheet of ice over the big dance floor in a mere twelve hours. Its High School and Junior College covers four city blocks, and it takes a lengthy chapter to chronicle its marvels from its imported china in the home-economics departments, to its kindergarten, its 2,000-seating-capacity auditorium, its swimming pools, its machine shops, and its fully equipped stage.

It is a far cry from modern Hibbing back to the early mining towns around Lake Superior and northern Lake Michigan. Some of them were as wild as they get, and some took pride in their ill repute. On the Gogebic there was a saying in the 1880's that 'the four toughest places in the world are Cumberland, Hayward, Hurley, and Hell.' And many who saw Hurley in those days agreed that of the four, Hurley was worst of all. Not even Seney, the lumberjack hell-hole on Lake Michigan, could equal it with its saloons, whorehouses, bloody fights, and bartender murders. A few places gave it more interesting competition. Ely, on the east end of the Vermilion Range, had its celebrated Daisy Redfield and her roughly elegant house of white slaves. Daisy's reputation spread down the Lakes to Chicago, where young Billy Sunday heard of her. He went to Ely and preached earnestly and forcefully, from a distance, to, or at, Daisy and her girls, but they were not among the throngs who rushed to kneel before the altar of the Lord. When the evangelist departed, the irredeemable Daisy is said to have said that he had done her more good 'than a whole free barrel of sloe gin woulda.'

Down on the Menominee Range the notorious Old Man Mudge created unprecedented excitement and near war before he was run out of town. He still trails his legend of sin, which probably has grown a little more scarlet with time and the repetition of his chief exploit. This Satan of vice followed the miners and lumberjacks back to the range from Escanaba. He built a big drinking, gambling, whoring den, stocked it with liquor, adorned it with his daughter Mina and a staff of girls, and surrounded it with a stockade. Near the gates he kept fierce gray wolves chained to posts, but left a safe passageway for the customers, and the customers were many and varied. This outrageous place flourished for a time, but the good citizens rebelled when its notoriety became too much for the Great Lakes area. They organized a posse, raided the house, and dispersed its denizens.

Such episodes were the inevitable by-products of the rip-roaring wild era of a pioneer industry in an unsettled region suddenly flooded with lumberjacks and miners from nearly every country in the world. The crude towns soon grew up to be reasonably staid and progressive communities, as they are today, lavish in their expenditures for schools, churches, and clubs, and industriously mining and processing and shipping more ore than mankind ever dreamed would be possible or necessary.

XXXIII

The Ore Fleets

THE trim little brigantine *Columbia,* which spread her white sails
on Lake Superior and stood out from Marquette's log-and-boulder
wharf with that first cargo of ore in August 1855 while the loaders
cheered, was a pioneer indeed. She was not designed for the ore
trade. If she lay under one of the enormous ore docks at Duluth-
Superior at the present time, she would look like a toy vessel in
hiding. And one single chute from those acres of hoppers would
spill out enough ore in less than a minute to overflow her hold
and anchor her to the bottom of the harbor. A whole fleet of such
ships could not hope to move the ore which the Cornwall men
were digging and scooping.

Around all the shafts and pits of all the mines towered the stockpiles of red ore.

Down from all the ranges to the port cities rolled the mountains
of ore.

A thousand miles away, in the steel valleys of Pittsburgh and
Youngstown and Cleveland, the great furnaces roared on. Thousands upon thousands of tons of ore were dumped into their white-
hot mouths to feed them, but the more they engulfed, the louder
they sputtered for more. They made guns, cannon, and cannon
balls for Grant and Sherman, and rails for the railroads. Carnegie's
empire spread and grew fat. William Kelley of Kentucky and Henry
Bessemer of Britain (later Sir Henry) attacked the problem of
converting the hard red ore into tough white steel. The technique
proved to be simplicity itself: just force air through the liquid-hot
ore and burn away the impure substances. The big pear-shaped
Bessemer cup was perfected, the molten ore was poured in, the
flames and sparks shot out while the mixture roared through most

of the colors of the rainbow as the oxygen met the carbon and silicon of the iron, and in a few minutes only good steel was left ready to be poured out of the converter into molds. Carnegie converted his mills along the Monongahela to the new process. Greater quantities of better steel for railroads and engines, ships, farm machinery, saw mills, and skyscrapers rolled from the plants; the Slavs and Magyars toiled in his mills twelve hours a day, seven days a week; the Carnegie profits jumped up and up until they reached $40,000,000 a year in 1900, and still the furnaces called for more ore.

The supply route from the ore beds to the furnaces was the Great Lakes and the bridge was ships. No means of transportation has ever been devised that is at once so cheap and so efficient, and nowhere on the globe has God himself set up so stupendous and accessible a combination of ore at one end, coal and limestone at the other, with a free waterway between them. The average carrying distance is about 800 miles, and the Great Lakes ships can sail the ore over that waterway at a cost of only about 70 cents a ton. To haul it by rail would cost $5 a ton. The average sailing distance for coal is about 500 miles; the cost by ship is 40 cents a ton, by rail $3. So sharp is the difference that dealers make money by transferring cargo from cars to ships at Toledo for the market at Detroit, only about 70 miles away.

The great forward strides in the industry had their immediate counterpart at the ports and harbors and in the ships that served them. Little brigantines like the *Columbia*, captain owned and company leased, were inadequate. In the rapid growth of the Lake ships, the *Columbia* is like the chrysalis out of which the giant emerged. He elongated and changed his shape gradually. The Cleveland-Cliffs Iron Company of Cleveland, which had chartered the *Columbia*, got into the shipping business for themselves in 1867 by acquiring a half interest in the barquentine *General Sherman*. They have been continuously in the trade ever since, and now own and control a large fleet of ore freighters.

All around the Lakes the shipyards on both sides of the border expanded. As fast as one set of plans left the drawing boards for the construction yards, a new set, calling for greater capacity, more speed, and increased efficiency in loading and unloading, was already under way. The clean white sails grew fewer and fewer. Their masts and sailing gear, under the best designs, were always in the way and usurped carrying space. After their wooden structure had improved in strength and size to the limit of their material, they were still too small and too slow to cope with the accelerating pace and volume of the age of steel.

Two small iron steamers had been launched on the Lakes in 1844. The *Surveyor,* of 133 tons, was built at Buffalo; the *Michigan,* of 583 tons, at Erie. Both were for years employed in the United States Government's coastal survey of the Great Lakes. They pointed the way toward future construction. A few years after the opening of the iron ranges, ships of steel put in to the same Lake Superior harbors from which the ore out of which they were fashioned had been shipped. Four famous ones of the 1880's comprised the iron fleet which bore the proud names of the *Iron Duke, Iron King, Iron Age,* and *Iron Cliff.* These big steamers could each carry the immense load of 2,000 tons of ore.

In 1889 and on through the 1890's the radical McDougall whalebacks, or 'pigs,' made their appearance on the Lakes. They were purely functional, and so ungainly that they were interesting in their very ugliness. They looked like Moby Dick himself, all blackened with coal dirt and carrying Captain Ahab's quarter-deck on his stern, a wheelhouse and navigating bridge on his shoulders, and railings along the dorsal side to keep the hands from washing overboard when they crawled from bow to stern. This self-propelled cargo hull was dreamed up by Alexander McDougall, a Scotch immigrant who had settled in the Lake Huron port and shipbuilding center at Collingwood, Ontario. After more than ten years of sailing the Lakes as deck hand, mate, and master, he turned designer. His idea was to construct a stout ship that could carry the greatest possible cargo at the lowest cost through the storms and choppy waves of the Lakes. His general model was the blunt nose and round back and belly of the whale. His ships were successful. They thrust their stubby prows into the high seas on Lake Superior, nosed their way through, shook the waves off their moulded deck, and wallowed placidly on to their destination with heavy cargoes of ore.

Dozens of these marine monsters were launched from the big yards at Superior between 1890 and 1900. Some of them may still be seen operating over the route between Duluth and Conneaut, under the flag of the steel trust fleet of the Pittsburgh Steamship Company of Cleveland. The *J. B. Neilson*, 308 feet long and of 2,234 tonnage, began service back in 1892. The *Frank Rockefeller*, 366 feet long and 2,759 tons, and the *Sir William Fairbairn*, 414 feet long and 3,807 tons, were both launched in 1896. The *Frank Rockefeller* was later rechristened *South Park;* wrecked at Manistique in 1942, she was salvaged and converted into a tanker in 1943, and again renamed the *Meteor*. The *John Ericsson* of the Peterson Line used to be a familiar sight on Lake Erie, shoving along like a deep-water animal at play in the sun. Until World War II stopped production, Detroit citizens used to watch the Erie Steamship Company's one 'pig' go up the river with a load of automobiles glistening on her remodeled deck. And Chicagoans are familiar with the old *Christopher Columbus*, a passenger-style whaleback, the only one of its kind, built for the World Exposition in 1893 for the Goodrich line. A 362-footer with five decks, she carried nearly two million sight-seers during the Exposition, and she is still in service on Lake Michigan as a curiosity and museum piece.

Whalebacks were fascinating oddities, distinctive on the Lakes, but they were not the answer to the insistent transportation problem between mines and mills. The answer lay with the long steel freighters so characteristic of the Great Lakes of today as to be synonymous with them. The first important step toward them was Ericsson's screw propeller. The sloop *Vandalia*, of 138 tons, Oswego built in 1841, was the first commercial ship to use it. Her engine was aft near the screw, and the cumbersome side-paddle boxes were discarded. These, of course, would have to disappear in any event, because they filled up the narrow sides of the canal locks, and seriously cut down the pay load aboard the ship. With engine

and propeller compactly housed aft, the space between them and
the wheelhouse forward was left free and unobstructed for the
hatches. These kept lengthening as designers learned how to build
them of steel, and the wheelhouse withdrew farther and farther
from the engine room.

The iron-hulled, government-owned *Michigan* demonstrated the
ease with which iron could be substituted for cedar and oak
beams in shipbuilding. An enterprising yard at Buffalo built the
first commercial iron ship in 1861 and placed her in service on the
Lakes. Under the name of the *Merchant* she carried quantities of
rich cargo during the hectic days of the Civil War and for a decade
afterwards. The Cleveland yards followed with their *R. J. Hackett*
in 1869, whose lines and general arrangement forecast the present
freighter design. The giant 300-footer *Onoko* went into the ore
trade in 1882, and stayed there until she was lost in the first year
of World War I. She fixed the model for the hundreds of ships
that have followed her into this service, with her vast, unobstructed cargo space for 3,000 tons of ore, her funnel aft, and her
navigating bridge forward—a tough, navigable shell equipped with
an engine, a single screw propeller, and a rudder. Ships of this
vintage and model began to move in quantity the ore that Stuntz,
Houghton, the Merritts, and Hibbing had found on the ranges.

The early freighters had their troubles. They foundered in
storms, and were weighed down with ice as they rushed to get in
just one more run before the season closed. They dragged keel on
the shallow channels which were not steadily deepened to corre-
spond to the deeper drafts of the ships. Many a ship scraped bottom on the St. Clair Flats and loosened its plates. But the channels
got dredged, and the technique of steel making, welding, and shipbuilding steadily improved to make the ships tight and secure at
any length.

And they went right on lengthening and widening. The story
of the ore fleet in the last half century might, indeed, be written
in a table of lengths and tonnage. The advanced ships of 1892
were from 308 to 330 feet long: the *J. B. Neilson* was 2,234 tons,
the 320-foot *Maritana* was 2,914 tons, and her 330-foot sister *Mari-*

posa was 2,898 tons. When the old Bessemer Steamship Company was formed in 1896, it had in its fleet of 21 ships some new and still longer models launched in that year. The *Queen City* was 400 feet long and 3,785 tons; and the *W. E. Corey* took a tremendous stride to a length of 549 feet and a tonnage of 6,363. The *Sir Henry Bessemer*, of that same year 1896, was 412 feet long, with a tonnage of 3,850, and a carrying capacity of 6,700 tons of ore.

The 454-foot *Malietoa* of 1899 astonished the trade by loading 7,500 tons of ore in her hold, and also by the lavish appointments of her captain's quarters and the red plush of the owners' rooms and lounge. She served decade after decade and carried ore to the mills in World War II. The 540-foot *Augustus B. Wolvin* of the year 1904 surpassed this record by taking on 10,500 tons. This ship also set a record by loading that tonnage in just 90 minutes. The 590-foot *William P. Snyder, Jr.* of 1912 took on a load of 12,200 tons. But the 580-foot *D. G. Kerr* of 1916 broke both records at Duluth on July 15, 1919, and then, just to show that this was no record at all, the same ship actually cleared the ore docks at Two Harbors in sixteen and a half minutes with a cargo of 12,506 tons. The 607-foot *Henry Coulby* of 1925, named for the general manager of the company who began as an immigrant boy, carried 14,000 tons.

The Canada Steamship Line fleet kept pace with these ships under the United States flag. It launched its 604-foot *Donnacona* in 1914, its 529-foot *Westmount* in 1917, its 582-foot *Gleneagles* in 1925, and its sensational 633-foot *Lemoyne* in 1926—a ship so vast in length that it achieves grace and pleasing lines. She was built to carry a load of 14,500 tons. On May 28 she took on 16,577 tons of coal, and two months later steamed down from Lake Superior with 571,960 bushels of wheat in her hold.

No record, however, holds for long on these Lakes. The *Leon Fraser* of 1942 was 639.5 feet long, and she carried to Conneaut 16,863 tons of ore, the greatest amount ever carried up to that time by a single ship. The big *Lemoyne* then surpassed this record by hauling 17,080 tons of ore from Superior to Hamilton. But the next year, when every man on every one of the 300 ore ships was

straining to deliver over 90,000,000 tons of ore to the mills of war
in a 250-day season, the new *Irving S. Olds* set still another record
by carrying 18,161 tons. It would take a fleet of 60 sailing ships of
300 tons' capacity to hold that much ore, and the *Irving S. Olds*
would be down to Conneaut and back to Duluth before the sailing
fleet got through the Sault. As men learned long ago to say on
these Lakes, 'The wildest expectations of one year seem absolutely
tame the next!'

As the carrying capacity of the ships increased, the loading and
unloading techniques improved. The machinery at the two ends
of the haul are among the marvels of the age, both to the eye as
a part of the Great Lakes scenery and to the imagination as a
tribute to man's ingenuity. The 600-foot freighters can run from
Duluth-Superior to Calumet or Cleveland and return in seven
days because the *average* loading time has been cut to about three
and a half hours, and the unloading time for a cargo of 15,000
tons to a mere eight or ten hours. The highly co-ordinated process
begins as the freighter fastens down its hatches and steams out
from Cleveland. If it is a U. S. Steel ship, the Cleveland office will
know what mixture the blast furnaces will require, and it will instruct each ship where it is to go and what kind of ore it will
load. These orders are sent on to the mines on Lake Superior, and
the grader there has three days to get the specified cargo ready
and on the docks while the ship steams up Lake Huron and
through the Sault. At the mines on the range the ores are carefully graded into groups, chiefly on the basis of their phosphorus
content. If it is to be processed in a Bessemer converter, there
must not be more than 0.045 per cent of phosphorus. If it is open-
hearth, there may be a little more. Samples of the ore are taken
from the cars in the shipping yards and sent to the laboratory for
immediate analysis. While the cars are moved down to the sorting
yards near the docks, the chemists make their reports on the com-
position of the ore in each car. With this report in hand, the grader
then breaks up the shipment into lots or blocks, exactly filling the
order for so many tons of such and such a grade. And when the
freighter eases in alongside the docks with its hatches clanking

open, the load is all ready and waiting to be spilled into the cavernous hold.

The Great Northern Docks at Superior have 1,352 pockets, and 16 ships can load simultaneously at this one battery of docks. Despite their 600-foot length, the ships are dwarfed by these docks with their miles of hoppers. There are no Escanaba ore trimmers here with picks, shovels, and measuring lines. The bumper beam spreads the ore evenly as it flows in, the water ballast is pumped out, the big ship settles lower into the water, and within two or three hours or so is again under way on even keel back down the Lakes.

Even greater marvels are performed at the Lake Erie and Calumet ports. Unloading was once a slow and tedious process. But now, as soon as the freighter comes alongside, the nimble giants known as Hulett unloaders, begin to work. The huge machines, a complicated maze of steel arms, bars, scoops, cables, and tracks, operate in a series and travel on rails. They are designed to fit the big steel hatches of the freighter. The operator has a control cockpit just above the jaws on the end of the giant's arm. He rides it right down into the hold where it closes its jaws on 15 to 18 tons of ore, rises out of the hatch, swings daintily back to the wharf, and drops its mouthful into a waiting car. The car moves off automatically, runs out to the stockpile, dumps itself, and returns for more. In a few hours the ship has disgorged her 15,000 tons and is on her way back to Lake Superior for more.

The appointments on these ungainly, businesslike vessels are always a surprise to visitors going aboard for the first time. Almost any luxury liner in the trans-Atlantic trade would be proud to display them. The *Leon Fraser*, 639.5 feet long, built in 1942, has a lavish captain's office and stateroom, two owners' staterooms, and an observation room forward in the texas house, all insulated and sealed with fireproof material. The red plush of the 1890's is gone, and in its stead is smart stainless steel and moving-picture style interior decorating, including palatial private baths. The officers and crew are only a little less pampered. The staterooms for the First, Second, and Third Mate are in the forecastle; they are spacious, each has a private bath, and there is a recreation room for their relaxation and pleasure. There are also attractive quarters for the watchmen and wheelsmen, though they do share a common bathroom, near the neat deck crew laundry. Quarters for the deck hands and deck watchmen are on the main deck forward. The Chief Engineer and assistants have fine staterooms, each with private bath also, and an office in the aft deck house. The firemen and coal passers, however, like the deck crew forward, share a common bathroom. Also in the aft deck house are the commissary, the officers' dining room, the galley, pantry, and mess room, a spare room, and a recreation room. All the hardware and cooking utensils, the lining of the huge refrigerators, the galley sinks, the shelves, tables, and such items are of stainless steel.

The two deck houses, separated as they are by the long rows of 18 hatches, are connected by an enclosed passageway, entirely unobstructed. These hatches are spaced at 24-feet centers, and the 12,500-pound steel hatch covers are lifted and stowed away by electrically operated traveling cranes.

The propulsion and navigating equipment also rival the best on the ocean liners. Engineers have preferred a single rather than a double screw propeller because of the narrow channels through which they operate. The *Leon Fraser* has a single solid-bronze wheel propeller that is 17½ feet in diameter. Like the other newer ships in Great Lakes service, the *Leon Fraser* has a ship-to-shore radio, a radio direction finder, an Auto Pilot, and a Sperry gyro compass. The ship is intricately connected from the bridge to the farthest recesses of the engine room, the spar deck aft, and the pilot house roof by a talk-back loud-speaking system. There is nothing slovenly or inland about these Great Lakes ships.

Life aboard them is informal. There are no smart uniforms with caps and gold braid. The master may be in a straw or felt hat and slacks. Except in emergencies his duties do not seem to be urgent. He is generally in his middle or late years, he has sailed the Lakes so long that he knows by instinct just what his ship's position is day or night, and his salary is $5,000 or more a season. The big companies have their own special boot-camp training schools for the ships' crews, and the wages of the lowliest deck hand in the forecastle is now about $109 a month with quarters and food. The food is the best the country affords; the big stainless steel refrigerators bulge with prime porter-house steaks, roasts, ham, poultry, fresh fruits, and vegetables. The Lake Carriers' Association operates a marine bank for their officers and men. The crews of 284 of these ships deposited a grand total of $2,681,717 in the season of 1941. They also have their own library service. It is located at the Sault, and packets of books are hoisted and lowered over the side as the ship locks through. The variety and quality might surprise those who do not know the type of young men attracted to the service on the Lakes. They read Shakespeare and Shaw as well as Zane Grey, and they call for technical books as well as mystery stories.

All in all, sailing the Lakes is about as pleasant and well-paid marine duty as may be found anywhere. In the active seasons, an ore freighter sails the equivalent of twice around the world. There is a lay-up of three or four months between seasons. The rapid loading and unloading leaves but little time in port, and the wild days and wilder nights of drunken sailors on the loose in Ashtabula Harbor, on Canal Street at Buffalo, and along the Superior water front are gone, except as they live in the memory of a few veterans of nearly a half century's experience. The present generation of sailors has time for only a few hours of relaxation on shore at the Saratoga Bar in Duluth, at the Round Bar in Indiana Harbor, or at Wilson's Tower in Conneaut. And one of the most human scenes along the waterway is that of the officers and crew waving to their wives and sweethearts along the Detroit and the St. Clair Rivers, and along the St. Mary's and at the Sault, or calling a greeting to them through a megaphone.

XXXIV

Parade of Ships

THERE are more than 2,000 vessels on the Lakes, about 800 of them being cargo carriers, and about 300 of them belonging to the Canadian companies. The elongated freighters of course dominate the scene on the Lakes by their spectacular size and the clocklike regularity of their procession, like an endless column of great whales following a leader through a thousand miles of ocean way. But there are other ships on these Lakes, too, and they provide much of the color at the Sault, at the Straits, and across the crowded channels of the St. Clair Flats. The big American and Canadian grain fleets are quite similar to the ore freighters. They carry the enormous crops of the Northwest United States and of the upper plains of Canada from Duluth-Superior, Milwaukee, and Chicago, and from Fort William and Port Arthur. They speed down the Lakes in an early spring and last-minute autumn rush to the gigantic elevators at Buffalo, and through the Welland Canal to those at Toronto, Montreal, and Quebec. They look tiny as they huddle under the great circular walls of these elevators, slowly sinking to the water line as the stream of grain flows into the hold, slowly rising as it flows out again at the lower end of the Lakes.

Another familiar sight in the parade is the coal fleet, carrying on deck their own elaborate steel-armed self-unloaders. This complicated device is folded in upon itself as the ship sails down the Lakes; when the ship docks, it unfolds like a living worker and is ready with buckets and conveyors to empty the hold in a few hours in a steady black stream from ship to dock or stockpile. They move millions of tons of coal from the Illinois fields up Lake Michigan, and from the Pennsylvania, West Virginia, and Kentucky mines up from the Lake Erie cities.

On Lake Huron and Lake Erie particularly the ships of the limestone fleet are constantly easing in and out through the narrow breakwaters and channels of the little limestone ports at the quarry cities of Michigan and Ohio. These ships are built on the same model as the ore fleet. Sometimes the captain puts his ship in under its own power as though he were bringing in a motor launch. More often the big vessel is seized in the harbor by two or three tugs and towed slowly and gently into a slip only a few feet larger than the freighter, while the tugs blast signals back and forth on their throaty whistles. They ease the ship under the battery of hoppers projecting out of the docks where the crushed limestone is stored ready for quick loading. They carry millions of tons of limestone to the mill cities to meet the flow of coal and ore.

The oil tankers are relatively new on the Lakes. They are specialized vessels designed to utilize the cheap and safer haul over the American waterways for the ever-increasing volume of oil that now flows toward the Great Lakes. Acres of refineries have been concentrated on both the Canadian and the American sides of the waters. Their clusters of silver domes reflect the sun at Toronto, at Buffalo and Cleveland, at Toledo and Detroit, along the Chicago and Calumet strip of Lake Michigan, and crennelate the skyline of scores of smaller cities. Tankers built to the dimensions of the locks on the St. Lawrence come from the Caribbean and the Gulf of Mexico, up the Atlantic Coast, and then all the way up the St. Lawrence into the Lakes, with crude oil, gasoline, petroleum, and benzine. Others go up the Ottawa canal system to the interior. These tankers comprise the Canadian fleet of the Imperial Oil Company, Ltd. They are at present limited to a length of 250 feet and a beam of 43 feet, 8 inches. The larger tankers, owned by Standard Oil and other American companies, are longer—some nearly 400 feet—and operate only on the Upper Lakes. There are few accidents. Their hulls, like those of the ore fleet, are tightly and firmly constructed; they receive the liquid in bulk form directly from the pipe lines. They are elaborately equipped with pipes and pumps, and are quickly emptied with maximum safety. They put in gingerly at the crowded ports and harbors, with lookouts posted on the alert, horn sounding, and other ships giving them a wide berth. The boiler and engine are located far aft, and the most careful watch is kept for leakage or pools of oil on deck, and for stray sparks from the ship or from passing vessels.

Two of these tankers, the *Panoil* and the *Mexoil,* had an experience typical of Great Lakes ships a few years ago. They had been caught and icebound at Saginaw. They lay there for the winter, impatient for the season of 1922 to open on Lake Huron. The ice seemed to be weakening in Saginaw Bay in April. The *Panoil* and *Mexoil* attempted to break through the 24-mile-long ice field in the bay. They hit the ice at full speed, but the ice gave way slowly. After 24 hours of capacity propulsion, the tankers had made only three miles, and were ice bound. It just happened that the *Naugatuck,* a new Coast Guard icebreaker, was out on a trial run. It decided to turn its theoretical practice into a genuine test. The *Naugatuck* ran in to the bay. The thickest and toughest parts of the ice field slowed down this little, up-to-the-minute vessel only to half speed. It plowed through to the stranded vessels at the phenomenal pace of 7½ knots, and set them free.

Another interesting sight on Lake Erie is the sand and gravel fleet. You may see these vessels, like the 186-foot *Kelley Island,* operating out in the lake as you sail round Pelee Island. Strangers on the passenger ships wonder what these vessels are doing at anchor off the Erie islands. They are sucking up clean sand from the inexhaustible supply on the lake bed. They have powerful suction pumps aboard which can haul up 9,000 gallons of watery sand in one minute. As the era of steel and concrete spread eight-lane trunk-line highways and 80,000- to 120,000-capacity stadiums across the country, this sand and gravel commerce grew, and it has continued to be an important item in the complex Great Lakes shipping.

Still others of this same general Great Lakes type of vessel, with the long, free deck space between the forward and aft deck houses, are constantly encountered on the sealanes loaded with lumber or automobiles or farm machinery.

The total Great Lakes fleet also includes a large squadron of package freighters. On any voyage down the Lakes you will encounter perhaps a dozen of these busy vessels plowing patiently along the main route, or turning off to one of the smaller Canadian or American ports along the way. They carry an immense quantity of merchandise between the inter-lake cities and to and from the seaboard ports. The Canada Steamship Line alone has a score of these vessels in service along their 2,000-mile thread of waterway. Their ships range in size from 1,600 tons up to 2,400 tons. The *Fernie*, of 2,418 tons, built in 1929, is the largest, with a length of 250 feet, a beam of 42⅔ feet, and a draft of 26½ feet. Those that can get through the St. Lawrence canals run from Quebec and Montreal, past the St. Lawrence River towns, up to Kingston, Toronto, and Queenston; they pass through the Welland Canal to Port Colborne and Windsor; and they traverse the lanes through the Sault to the Lakehead cities. Some of them, like the *City of Montreal*, the *City of Toronto*, and the *City of Windsor*, afford fast express service up the river and across the Lower Lakes.

These vessels do a spritely trade from Sarnia and the Georgian Bay ports of Midland and Collingwood, which are outlets for the rich region of Old Ontario, and are connected by rail and canal across the narrow arrowhead neck with Hamilton and Toronto. It is a long, expensive haul overland around Georgian Bay and the north Lake Superior shore from these southern ports to the Lakehead. The region is generally desolate, isolated, and thinly settled. The package freighters bridge this gap over the natural waterway with a cheap and reasonably fast form of transportation. They pick up almost every imaginable item of merchandise at the big warehouses on the docks at these ports—drugs, processed foods, drums of oil, stoves, refrigerators, lard, bacon, bags of onions, canoes, radios—the list is endless. Hour after hour the fast little electric trucks scurry through the warehouses, rattle across the wharf and down the gangplank to the hold. Husky French Canadians push two-wheeled hand trucks rapidly in and out among the piles of goods on the wharf and in the ship's cargo space. Some of the vessels are equipped with elevators to lift and lower them up from and down into the hold, and most of them carry cargo booms and steam deck winches.

The car ferries are another type of vessel distinctive on the Great Lakes. All the year round, summer and winter, through the ice fields and through open channels, these serviceable craft go right on methodically with their work. They cross every few minutes at the Straits of Mackinac, pitching up and down in their slips until cars have trouble going aboard, and riding out high seas that sicken some of their passengers before they catch a clear sight of the hotels on Mackinac Island. They operate on the Detroit River. They cross Lake Erie from Ashtabula, Ohio, to Port Burwell, Ontario; and across Lake Ontario from Charlotte, N. Y., to Cobourg, Ontario. And on almost any trip on Lake Michigan you will see them crossing from the Lower Peninsula towns of Frankfort, Ludington, and Muskegon to the Wisconsin ports of Milwaukee, Manitowoc, Kewaunee, and Menominee.

Since the early days of the immigrants and the railroads, considerable traffic has always gone east and west over the land-water route. It crosses at Niagara or Buffalo-Fort Erie, shoots across Old Ontario to Windsor-Detroit, crosses Michigan to, say, Ludington. There it boards a big car ferry for Manitowoc, Wisconsin, saving a couple of hundred miles or more on a journey into the Northwest. Loaded railroad cars cross in this fashion, and, since the fine highways have netted both Old Ontario and the American states, it has become a route of ever-increasing interest to motorists.

The vessels in this service are not mere ferries; they are big and interesting and costly ships. The Père Marquette Railroad operates a fleet of ten of these vessels, two on the Detroit River and eight on Lake Michigan. The *City of Flint* and the *City of Saginaw* are 381 feet long. A still bigger one, *City of Midland* 41, the largest ever built, was launched at the Manitowoc Ship Building Company's yards in September 1940, and went into Père Marquette's service in 1941. It cost two million dollars. It is 406 feet long, 58 feet in the beam, and displaces 8,200 tons. It makes two round trips

Cleveland's Civic Center. *Courtesy of Philip Gendreau, N. Y.*

Business section of Milwaukee. *Photograph by R. Gates. Courtesy of Frederic Lewis.*

daily between Manitowoc and Ludington. It is a big ship on any waterway. It has four standard railroad tracks running the full length of its deck, and it can carry 34 loaded freight cars at one time. It also has a special upper deck that accommodates 50 automobiles. It can carry 376 passengers. There are 72 staterooms for their comfort, with controlled air circulation, and Pullman type upper and lower berths. There are also included about a dozen master staterooms or parlor suites. The satin-finished dining room with its stainless steel furniture seats 60 guests. There are two smoking rooms with glass partitions, a semi-enclosed promenade that circles the main deck, and a radio room. Well-appointed quarters for the officers and crew are forward, the neat and spacious captain's room is aft of the wheelhouse. These sturdy vessels provide a thrilling sight on Lake Michigan when other shipping is tied up for the season in safe harbors. They plow their way through the ice and emerge in the winter mists at their appointed slip to the sound of breaking and crackling ice sheets and the relief of the little cluster of people always gathered at the wharf to see them come in.

In addition to these ships there are also hundreds of other vessels on the Lakes: the sea-going type passenger ships, the few big side-wheeler passenger-excursion ships on Lake Erie, the flat-topped barge canal freighters, the little Coast Guard boats that rush out to give messages to the captains of the passing ships, the few ancient training ships, the lake- and ocean-going tugs, the huge barges with their mast for sails in case they break loose from the mother ship or tug, the light and busy tenders, the icebreakers, the motorized fishing fleet, and the wreckers. And almost every Lake town has its basin crowded with yachts of every size and description. They range from the little 12-footers up to big palatial vessels that rival the swanky ocean-going yachts. Toronto boasts the largest fresh-water yacht club in the world. The yachts and clubs of Buffalo, Cleveland, Belle Isle, and Milwaukee are famous. Much of Detroit's summer social life is made pleasant and sometimes exciting by its yachting and yacht racing. From Chicago's clubs, yachts of every length and design put out into Lake Michigan and on fair weekends the larger ones race toward Point Betsie.

Scatter all these thousands of vessels over the length and breadth of the Great Lakes, and they present a cheering and neighborly spectacle of industry and pleasure not to be duplicated anywhere on the waters of this crowded and troubled globe.

((((XXXV))))

White Hell

WINTER comes sharply and suddenly to the Great Lakes. Sometimes at the end of November, usually in early December, a gale rolls a frigid mass of continental polar air down over Canada and Minnesota into the Lake Superior bowl. It slides over Chicago, whips the scurrying pedestrians on Michigan Avenue, hits Lake Michigan, rages across Lake Huron and Georgian Bay, and blankets Lake Erie and Lake Ontario with freezing air. A few hours later the harbor at Duluth-Superior is a sheet of ice, Thunder Bay at the Lakehead is locked in, Whitefish Bay begins to pile up ice floes, the St. Mary's River and the Sault Canal congeal into tough clear blue ice, and another navigating season has come to an end. It is a melancholy and somewhat desolate period over the Lakes. It means the end of the activity that makes these Lakes of such spectacular importance to the world; it brings to a close the last-minute rush of the ships to complete just one more voyage before they tie up.

Sometimes the first freeze strikes without warning. When this happens the ships are trapped. A few seasons ago, in early December, 98 ships loaded with ore and grain reached the Sault on their last voyage down, and 149 arrived on their way up to the Lake Superior ports. They were caught in a sudden quick freeze that iced over the river to such a depth that automobiles could drive on it. There were 5,000 sailors on these 247 ships. Ford cars cruised out to carry food to them. Captain Charles Autterson was particularly proud of the fact that he had hailed a passing taxi cab and was driven from his ship into port in an automobile. The ships were imprisoned for days. They made an unforgettable picture massed around the Sault and embedded in glittering ice. Their release was equally memorable. When the frigid cold finally warmed and lifted, and the Coast Guard icebreakers could set them free, they departed one behind the other in both directions from the St. Mary's River in the most concentrated movement of ships ever seen on the Lakes. They still talk about it at the Sault.

The ships generally find safe harbor before the routes are sealed with ice for the duration. They tie up one against another in tight anchorage, as many as 25 to 50 staggered in a close huddle like cattle in a byre on a snowy evening, or rows of parked cars on a crowded lot. All winter long they lie dormant in the frozen bays with fires pulled and hatches battened down. You will see them massed at Duluth-Superior, in Maumee Bay below Toledo, in the slips at Chicago, Indiana Harbor, Detroit, Cleveland, Conneaut, and Buffalo; at the Sault, at Collingwood, at Port Colborne, and at Toronto.

The people of the Lake cities feel the melancholy and the isolation. They wait anxiously for the last voyagers to reach safe port, for the toll in men and ships has always been heaviest on the Lakes during this last run. The citizens of Duluth look out across the frozen bay at the mouth of the St. Louis River to view the 'Necklace,' as they call the harbor with its string of elevators and docks, and to see the lift bridge settle into its place at street level. Then they settle in for the sixteen weeks of waiting until the harbor is cleared, the channels opened, and the new eight months' rush season comes again in April.

Down at the Sault the commander of the Coast Guard chops holes and measures the deepening ice. Down it goes, inch by inch— one foot, two feet, three feet of clear hard solid ice over the channel, sealing it firmly for 63 miles. Above this tough sheet in Whitefish Bay the ice floe moves into the narrow river channel. It piles up in layers and windrows as the current moves down, and the winds, gathering force along the unobstructed sweep of Lake Superior, drive it toward the lower edge of Whitefish Bay. It banks up for 40 miles, one layer pressing down upon another until the iceberg-like mass is from 15 to 20 feet deep, or even pressed down on the bottom of the channel. At Spectacle Reef Lighthouse, on a limestone reef ten miles out in Lake Huron near the entrance to the

Straits of Mackinac, the ice piled up around the tower in 1874-5 to a height of 30 feet. When the keepers returned in the spring, they had to cut through the ice, which was seven feet above the doorway, before they could enter and put the light in operation.

Green Bay, Georgian Bay, Saginaw Bay—all are sealed up. Lake Michigan and Lake Huron are frozen over, or full of ice sheets lying so close together that Eliza could cross from Milwaukee to Collingwood. Lake Erie is the last to yield, but the ice spreads over from Ontario and out from the Lorain-to-Buffalo coast, and Erie too is often a sheet of ice. The last spot of all to close is usually between Toledo and Detroit, and in milder seasons it may remain open most, if not all, of the year.

As the ice grips the Lakes, the little shacks of the fishermen appear off the Lake Erie islands, around Mackinac, at the Sault and on Whitefish Bay. They cut holes through the ice and take their catch from the cold water beneath. A few Indians still fish with lines through holes in the ice. Automobiles cross from Sandusky to the Bass Islands, and people walk, drive, or cross the channels and rivers by sled. The summer resorts around Lake Michigan on both sides crouch on the edge of the icebound waters, and the few permanent residents hibernate like the Lake ships to wait out the winter and welcome the spring and the new season of tourists. Their lives, like the activity of the ships, revolve around the seasons, and they are marked by the two rhythmic heartbeats of Winter and Spring—the coming and going of the blanket of ice.

It comes in stillness following the slap of the blizzard. It goes with a mighty crackling and a roar. It always opens first at the southwestern tip of Lake Erie between Toledo and Detroit, and between Detroit, Lorain, and Cleveland. Some days later it begins to loosen on Lake Superior. Up at Duluth and at the Lakehead cities the news spreads up and down the miles of waterfront that the ice is going out. People gather along the shore to witness the phenomenon. The great sheets crack and split. They break loose from the shore and are driven out into Lake Superior by the warming winds. The frozen spray that has decorated the rocky headlands into a winter faeryland melts and drips back into the Lake, sparkling in the sun.

The excitement is general, and it has been repeated so often that it has become a tradition. Everybody knows that in a few more days the ships will be released and will begin to steam in and out of the harbors. At Fort William the good citizens present a silk hat to the captain who brings his ship into the harbor first in spring. At Duluth the excitement used to be so great that the people deserted their church on a Sunday morning right in the middle of service when they heard the long, rich sound of the horn on the first ship to break through the ice and open a new season. They operate a pool for guessing the day and hour of the arrival of the first ship through the canal. In the unusually early season of 1942, a coal dock worker named Carl Erickson laid his number at 19 minutes and 37 seconds past 11:00 a.m. on March 26 as his prediction for the opening. The *W. G. Mather,* Captain A. J. Rathburn, steamed through the canal and the photo-electric signal registered the hour. It was 11:19:37 on the 26th. Erickson received $1,000, and Duluth-Superior began to hum with the most furious activity ever undertaken on the Great Lakes.

This seasonal drama, however, centers at the Sault. Until that narrow, vital channel is open, traffic cannot flow between the Lakes. And the ice is always clear, thick, tough and persistent in the St. Mary's. The icebreakers go to work on it the minute there is any chance of opening it and keeping it open. Sometimes they go out too soon. In the 1942 season the sturdy *Tahoma* ventured out in mid-March. She hit the blue ice field again and again, but could not break through. When she gave up, she had battered her propeller to pieces; one blade was broken off, the others were twisted like the blades on a crash-landed airplane.

The icebreakers seldom fail, however. They are remarkable ships, powerful, sturdy, and ingeniously constructed for their difficult work. They were born out of the Scandinavian ice cutters, and developed for the particular job in the Great Lakes channels. Their prows are heavily reinforced, and the ballast system is arranged so that the draft at the bow may be quickly lifted or lowered according to the specific task. We have already noted how the *Nauga-tuck* ran through the 24-mile ice field in Saginaw Bay at a speed of 7½ knots to clear a channel for two tankers that had failed to make way and had been frozen in.

It is little short of amazing to see these vessels at work at the Sault in late March or early April. They look so tiny beside the huge freighters, and it seems incredible that the little ice cutters can break through where the big ore fleets cannot move. They take a run at a strip of solid ice and hit it like a fullback plunging into a tight line. Sometimes nothing happens, and they must fall back and take another lunge. A few such battering-ram attacks usually force the ice to give. It splinters for yards around with a sharp crackling sound like a battalion of exploding rifles. The cutter then races on easily for a hundred feet or more until it reaches another tough obstacle. There it repeats its performance. If it fails to break through after repeated assaults, or gets stuck in the ice, the ballast is shifted to raise the prow, the vessel runs up on the ice layer and breaks it down with its weight of steel. Hour after hour the determined little ship beats away at the formidable barrier.

A shout of triumph goes up when the first icebreaker gets through the Sault and out into Whitefish Bay. In the early season of 1942, when every town on the Lakes was tense with eagerness to get to work, the honor went to Captain Paddy Brown of the icebreaker *Ste. Marie*, when he forced his vessel through on March 23. But the weather over the Lakes is capricious, and one never knows when it will play one of its tricks on the ships that try to rush spring into the far north. The cutters do not melt or destroy the great ice fields; they merely batter through a narrow channel for the ships. There is still danger lurking for the ships that follow the icebreakers. If a strong wind blows down over Lake Superior toward the Sault, as it frequently does, it will drive the heavy broken ice cakes into Whitefish Bay and force them down the channel with a powerful drive behind them. This happened on Easter Sunday of 1942 and held up nearly a half-million tons of precious shipping. The big 600-footer *Dunn, Jr.* was going up the channel at reduced speed, in the vanguard of a long line of freighters. The wind was straight ahead, coming right down the channel and driving the ice floe before it. The wheelsman of the *Dunn, Jr.* saw the ice coming at his ship head on, but there was nothing he could do about it. The channel was too narrow for the ship to turn or even to veer. The *Dunn, Jr.* steamed into the ice which struck it with force and plowed right on down toward the other vessels. The ice floe was too overwhelmingly powerful for the ships to handle. The big *Dunn, Jr.* was pushed back, then shoved aside and run aground. The *William A. McGonagle* and the *William B. Schiller* were also forced aside like a couple of canoes. In a short time 80 ships were jammed and entrapped in the region of the Sault, and they were held there for almost a week before they could be set free.

From the disappearance of the *Griffon* right down to the present season, the shipping losses on the Great Lakes have always been stupendous. The weather is full of vagaries, the storms are fierce and tremendous, and there is no room on the narrow Lakes for a ship in distress to run before them as they can upon the ocean. A bare outline record of these disasters would fill a folio. Of the 199 steamships on the Lakes between 1818 and 1853 as listed by Disturnell, 14 were burnt, 4 blew up, and 36 were wrecked. The losses among the sailing ships were probably even greater. There were 118 lives lost in 1855, and 407 lost in 1856. Cargo losses mounted in the middle years of last century by approximately a million dollars a year. Ninety-seven ships were lost or broken up by a four-day hurricane that swept the Lakes clean in 1869. In the two decades between 1878 and 1898, 5,999 vessels were wrecked on these Lakes; 1,093 of them were total losses of both ships and cargo and an appalling number of men. And, with all the improvements in navigation aids that have come on ships and shore in recent years, 116 ships and 326 sailors have gone down in two decades.

In one single disastrous night in early November 1913, 13 ships and 235 men went down. A storm of hurricane proportions circled in cyclonic path out of the Canadian Northwest and lashed the Lakes from every direction from Sunday November 8 to Monday the 9th. It was one of the worst and longest storms ever experienced on the Lakes. The *L. C. Waldo* was crossing Lake Superior with a cargo of ore. She plunged through 35-foot seas. Ice coated her over. One particularly heavy sea ripped the pilot house from the ship and washed it away. She was driven before the wind through the dark night toward the south Superior Shore and was cast on a reef near Keweenaw. For 48 hours the captain and crew clung to safety in the deck house forward, waiting for the ship to break up. It survived the ordeal of the battering waves, and the men were rescued by the Coast Guard as the storm abated. The *Turret Chief* was driven across the Lake and smashed against the rocks on the south shore, not far from the *L. C. Waldo*. The *William Nottingham,* loaded with grain from the Lakehead, was caught in the middle of Lake Superior. She fought the storm for two days and nights, used all her fuel, and then burned her cargo of wheat to keep her engines running. She reached Whitefish Bay before she too was cast on a shoal. The Coast Guard rescued all but three of her crew.

All round the Lakes these experiences were repeated. The people on the Lakes and in the Lake cities know these tragic facts, but inland citizens and those who take a summer cruise or a vacation on the Lakes are seldom aware of the hazards of what appears to be a safe, colorless, routine movement of Lake ships.

Disturnell, a great traveler and writer of guide books to the Lakes in the middle years of the century, blamed the early captains for these losses. He said, 'Were it not for the almost criminal carelessness or recklessness of many of the owners and masters of steamers navigating these lakes, whereby hundreds of valuable lives have been lost and millions of property destroyed, no more safe, instructive, or grand excursion could be found on the face of the globe.'

Actually the greatest number of tragedies have occurred in the late autumn when, in their eagerness to get in one more voyage, the owners have exposed their ships to devastating storms and the white hell of ice. Some of these ships, like the *Griffon*, simply disappeared, leaving not a trace behind to solve the mystery of their passing. The *Bannockburn* left Duluth late one season with a full cargo for the Lower Lakes. She carried a crew of twenty-two men.

She was sighted once the following day about halfway across Lake Superior. She was never seen again and never heard of. A freighter was pulling two tows down Lake Huron when a storm kicked up high seas and the tow ropes broke. The freighter lost sight of them. Neither tow was ever seen again and the six sailors aboard them were never found.

The *Chicora* attempted a crossing from Milwaukee to St. Joseph in mid-January 1895. She carried one passenger and a crew of 23. A sudden storm struck and lashed Lake Michigan with wintry gales so fierce that the ship could not ride them out. She went down with all hands. Weeks went by with no trace whatever of the lost ship. Later in the season some fragments of wreckage were washed up on the shore at South Haven. The steamer *Telegraph* disappeared on northern Lake Michigan leaving no clue behind her except a persistent legend that she was taken by the Mormons, who operated a colony on one of the islands off the Lower Peninsula. The big grain freighter *James Carruthers* left the St. Mary's River just before the terrific snow storm and gales struck in November 1913, and disappeared under the wild waters of Lake Huron without being sighted again.

One of the most poignant of all the disappearances was that of the schooner *Rouse Simmons* in the pre-Christmas season of 1912. Her captain was Herman Schuenemann, the genial and well-beloved dealer in Yule-tide evergreens who each year brought in his shipload of trees from the Manistique forests to the dock at the Clark Street Bridge in Chicago. He had begun the business with his brother August, but August was lost with his ship in 1898, and Herman carried on alone. He had been coming regularly for fifteen years, and many Chicagoans made a point of going to the bridge to buy a tree from him.

That Christmas season Captain Schuenemann cut and loaded as usual, but as he made sail down the Wisconsin coast, the winds hit him head on, the storm raced in, a blizzard struck, and heavy seas began to batter the schooner and coat her with ice. She was sighted once, with distress flags out, but the Coast Guard could not ride out the heavy storm to reach her. Somewhere off Two

Rivers Point the ship with her Christmas trees and all hands went down with no survivor to tell her story. Three messages, however, were brought back by the Lake from the dead. One was a note on the ship's log written by the captain, and corked in a bottle which was found on the beach. It read, 'Friday: Everybody goodbye. I guess we are all through. Sea washed over our deckload Thursday. During the night the small boat was washed over. Ingvald and Steve fell overboard Thursday. God help us. Herman Schuenemann.'

Twelve years later a man was idling on the beach near Two Rivers Point. He found a water-soaked wallet cast up on the sands. He picked it up and examined it. It belonged to Herman Schuenemann. The rubber band was still tight around it and the papers still legible. In 1927 another bottle was cast up on the shore. The note within read, 'These lines are written at 10:30 p.m. Schooner R. S. ready to go down about 20 miles southeast Two Rivers Point between fifteen or twenty miles off shore. All hands lashed to one line. Goodbye. Charles Nelson.'

The next season after the *Rouse Simmons* was lost fishermen found evergreens afoul of their nets in that region. Next season also a Schuenemann schooner worked in with a load of trees to the old wharf at the Clark Street Bridge. Aboard were the widow and two daughters of Herman. For twenty-two years they carried on the business and were a brave part of the Christmas spectacle in the city under the shadow of the towering skyscrapers.

The fates of other ships caught in high seas or lashed by late season storms were all too tragically known. Heavy winds, bred over the northwestern plains and driven over the Lakes, lash the waves to heights of 25 to 35 feet, and dash them against the windows of the pilot houses. They wash all the way across the long rows of hatches between the forward and aft superstructures. At times the wheelsmen cannot see the after deck house for the seas or the spray. The *John P. Geistman* put out from Detroit with 50 automobiles lashed to her deck. One of these storms hit the ship, waves washed her spar deck, and when she came through her four-hour battle, only 6 cars remained; the other 44 had been swept overboard.

When the season is late, the cold rains may turn to sleet, or the dashing spray may freeze as it hits the ship. In a few minutes or a few hours the ship will be coated with the 'white hell' of ice. Each wave that breaks against the prow flings up another coating of spray. The wheelhouse cakes over, the railings are like fence-posts, and great heavy stalactites hang from the prow and drop from the deck over the side. Even the Gloucester fishing fleet coming in on a Nor'easter carries no more ice. Ships have foundered and gone down under its massive weight under the battering of a Great Lakes ice storm.

The *W. F. Sauber*, heavy with ore, reached Whitefish Point in a sleet storm driven by a gale. She was weighted with tons of ice that gradually slowed her down and began to founder her. She was sighted by the steamer *Yale*, which stood by to aid. For eighteen hours the storm continued to rage and the ice to accumulate while the steamer waited for a chance to rescue the crew. Finally Captain James Jackson with volunteers from the *Yale* put a boat alongside in the high seas; and while the boat pitched and tossed, and the cold wind lashed the bay, he succeeded in taking off the crew. Captain W. E. Morris of the *W. F. Sauber* stayed with his doomed ship, and when the ore, the ice, and the battering seas pulled her under a few minutes later, the Captain also went down.

At the end of November 1905 four big freighters stood out of the harbor at Duluth loaded for their last voyage of the season. They were only an hour or so out on Lake Superior when an early winter storm hit them with tremendous force, dashing them about like chips and washing them with heavy seas. All the ships turned and ran for safety toward the Duluth-Superior anchorage. The first two ships made the entrance and secured. The third was hit at the entrance, and plunged against the pier, but she cleared and made the harbor before she sank. The fourth and last ship, the *Mataafa* and her tow *Nasmuth* are still talked about in the bars and on the wharves at Duluth.

By the time the *Mataafa* reached the harbor entrance, the storm was pounding Duluth with full fury and the seas were running fierce and high in and then out of the channel. The outrushing water caught the *Mataafa* head on in the narrow canal just as a battering sea struck her from the stern and flung the big ship against the pier. Then the storm, in no hurry for the kill, began to play with its doomed victim. It tore off her rudder, tossed her onto the rocks near the shore, and broke her long frame in two. People gathered on shore by the thousands in the storm to watch the struggle. The rescue squads exhausted every means for saving the crew. They shot a line to the stricken ship, but it broke under the weight of the cable as the rescue workers tried to pull it ashore. All efforts failed. The night was freezing cold. The men aft had no fuel to keep warm. They froze to death, nine of them, in sight of the bonfires on the shore. Those forward survived and were taken off when the storm passed next day leaving the terraced city buried under six feet of snow. The tow had cast free of the *Mataafa*. It dropped anchors, the hooks held, and it lived through the terrible night.

No; sailing the ships on the inland Lakes is not always a pleasant summer cruise. These Lakes are mean and tough, and the soft air, the calm, glossy-blue surface under a full moon or a summer sun, as seen by the casual traveler, give no hint of their latent ferocity and the tragedies they can pile up in a few hours of swift and terrible anger.

World War II and the Deep Waterway

WINSTON CHURCHILL proudly announced in September 1943 that in the preceding three months there had been no losses in the convoys on the Atlantic. The news was heartening. Not so many months earlier the sinkings were alarming. German submarines in wolf-packs had been slaughtering Allied shipping; prowling submarines were torpedoing American ships and tankers in plain sight of the eastern coast cities, and were even operating in the mouth of the St. Lawrence River. The Prime Minister's report was, among other things, a glowing tribute to the wartime activity on the Great Lakes in the heart of the North American continent.

Long before the United States entered the conflict, the Canadians were building ships along the 2,000-mile shoreline. All round the Lakes the shipyards, old and new, were humming with unprecedented energy. At Port Arthur on Thunder Bay, as far up Lake Superior as ships can go, the shipyards were building corvettes to protect the convoy lanes on the Atlantic. I watched the ceremonial launching of one of these bluff little fighting ships in June 1941 on the day Germany invaded Russia. A gnarled old lake-man took me in a motorboat from the city pier down the bay to the shipyards. We passed a jam of pulp logs bobbing in the choppy waters. We beat past the overwhelming towers of the grain elevators and the acres of yellow boards that were becoming sheds for distress grain storage. Cool spindrift flew in our faces as we curved round a grain freighter heading toward the breakwater with a heavy load. We ran right up to the slip where the latest of the corvettes was dressed with flags, and ready to slide down the ways. High officials, companies of soldiers, guests and workmen were massed about the ship. When the proper words were said, the

354

anthem was played, the bottle of champagne was broken, the blocks were removed, and the vessel sped sideways into the slip with a splash as the multitude cheered.

A half-dozen corvettes at anchor near by were getting their guns and deck fittings, and the last touches to their superstructures. One of them was making a trial run across the bay; it grew smaller and smaller as it neared the Sleeping Giantess and turned in a graceful, sweeping arc toward Fort William. It would soon be on its way down through the Sault, down the Welland, down the Williamsburg, Cornwall, Soulanges, and Lachine Canals through the thirty-one locks into the free waters of the St. Lawrence and out into the Atlantic. It was an amazing sight to see in the heart of the continent at the very head of Lake Superior.

These corvettes, built in Canadian Great Lakes ports, are interesting ships. In the days of the old sailing navies, a corvette was a small, fast ship, next below the frigate, carrying a single tier of guns. It corresponded to a large United States sloop. The modern steel corvette merely perpetuates a legended name, for, as the Canadians say, the present design is 'out of the sturdy North Sea fishing trawler by the whaler's killer-boat.' It is under 200 feet in length, about 500 tons or less, and is comparatively cheap and quickly built. It is armed with a four-inch gun, light deck guns, heavy machine guns, Oerlikan dual-purpose guns, high explosives, and depth charges. It carries a complement of about fifty-eight men. Its draft is so shallow that it rides above the accurate depth line of a torpedo and is hard to hit. Its skipper says it can turn on a dime, but it sails like a saucer. It is a rough-riding ship and it is wet. It rides out heavy seas, pitching, tossing, yawing like a wild broncho. When it is acting up in the storm-tossed waters, no man can stay on his feet on the wet deck. Waves break over the corvette, and it rolls over as though it would capsize. The casualty list is large with broken skulls, arms, and legs, and there is no medical officer, usually not even a pharmacist's mate, aboard. Yet these bluff, broad-beamed little ships with their cramped living quarters patrolled the convoy routes, ferreted out submarines, depth-charged them, rammed them, or hovered over them until they surfaced and then went to work on them with their deck guns.

Canada had no navy in 1910; by the end of 1943 she had over 300 fighting ships with a personnel of over 50,000 men, most of them direct from the plains of western Canada, men who had never so much as sailed on the Great Lakes. The shipyards were, however, manned by experienced shipbuilders. In the long years of the post World War I depression, when English mills were idle and the British Navy and Merchant Marine were static, the shipyards closed down. Hundreds of men left the idle shipways on the Clydeside and emigrated to a brighter future in Canada. They went out to the wheatfields of Manitoba and Saskatchewan to raise the grain that piled up and overflowed at the Lakehead elevators. Then the desperate days of World War II came, with their urgent call for ships and more ships. The old Clydeside builders left their fields and came down to the shipyards at Port Arthur, Collingwood, Owen Sound, Midland, Maitland, and other ports, to start the flow of ships that turned the tide of the war in the critical years between 1941 and 1943—corvettes, frigates, submarines, and cargo vessels.

The Canadian activity was soon supplemented by the yards on the United States side of the waters. During the depressed decade of the 1930's no new ships were built. The yards at Cleveland, Detroit, Manitowoc, Calumet, all lay idle, and fine vessels rusted at anchor in a score of Great Lakes harbors. The war exploded them all into feverish labor. The yards at Ecorse, Michigan, and Lorain, Ohio, as we have seen, turned out giant super-freighters of 639-feet length to help bring down the ore from Lake Superior. Other yards began to build warships. In August 1943, newspapers carried on their front pages the story of Commander George H. Wales and his 'fresh water submarine.' It was launched in Lake Michigan at the Manitowoc yards, and was taken to sea under the Outer Drive Bridge at Chicago, and down the Mississippi past New Orleans. On its first cruise it reached the coast of Japan and sank a Japanese ship with its first torpedo. An undisclosed number of submarines left the yards on the Great Lakes to make this same phenomenal journey over the ancient discovery route of Marquette and La Salle to the war zone in the Empire.

The American Ship Building Company from its yards in Lorain slid 180-foot mine sweepers down its ways in the Black River. The yards of the Leathem D. Smith Shipbuilding Company of Wisconsin, with fewer than 50 men on the pay roll, were almost idle in September 1940. Then the company began to build ships for Great Britain under Lend Lease. The yards expanded back over an old swamp, some of it under 7 feet of water, and the number of workers jumped to 4,300. They built 8 frigates, 317 feet long and 37½ feet at the beam, for the Maritime Commission. They launched 175-foot subchasers for the United States Navy. They delivered the first ocean-going cargo vessel, the *Alden Gifford*, to come out of the Great Lakes in World War II, and they became the first Great Lakes shipyard to win the Maritime M 'for record production of coastal cargo vessels.'

The yards at Marinette, Wisconsin, at the mouth of the Menominee River, had been idle for years. They had, in fact, practically ceased to exist. There was scarcely even a memory left of the great days of lumbering, mining, and the sailing ships. World War II reopened them. Norse workers again went into the forests behind Marinette and Menominee, where recent scientific care had made lumber a crop industry, and sent timber down to the yards. Lumber and woodworking revived and reached full swing in these towns. And down the shipways in the spring of 1943 slid wooden barges to help carry the burden of war shipping. They were 750-ton vessels, 194 feet long, 33 feet wide, 18 feet draft, and bore the names of *White Pine No. 1*, *White Pine No. 2*, etc.

The auxiliary aircraft carriers from the Kaiser yards at Vancouver are propelled by engines built in the big Norberg Manufacturing Company's plants at Milwaukee. Above the factory flies the Navy E and the Maritime M burgee and victory flags as awards for making and delivering to the shipyards 'steam engines and Diesels speedily and efficiently.' And so it goes in all the yards—Calumet, Detroit, Ecorse, Cleveland. The natural protection of the Great Lakes, the concentration of industry around their shores, and the easy outlets to the Mississippi, the Hudson, and through the St. Lawrence to the Atlantic, have joined them more closely than ever before to the Seven Seas.

The war activity, however, was not all favorable to Great Lakes commerce. When the Great Lakes Harbors Association met in convention in Chicago in 1943, its members were disturbed. The war had cut sharply into lake transportation by assigning vessels exclusively to ore and limestone cargoes. Smaller ships, from 75 to 100 of them, had been taken out of the Lakes since 1940 for ocean service. Package freight shipments, one of the important items in lake commerce, were at a standstill. Building materials had dropped out of the shipments because of the curtailment of new construction. Automobiles and farm machinery had disappeared from the spar decks. The grain trade was down because of the operation of the permit system favoring ore shipments. The pig iron and scrap-metal trade had been diverted to the railroads for faster movement. And with the exception of ore shipping and shipbuilding, the lake ports were not sharing in the war boom. The convention expressed its concern for the restoration of Great Lakes shipping after the war, though there could certainly be no doubt about its resumption. The millions of people and the great cities around the shores of these Lakes, the concentration of natural resources and industry, and the existence of the unobstructed natural shipping lanes across the length and breadth of the Lakes made inevitable the continued flow of lake ships.

More important in the long run than the temporary diminution of the package freight trade was the reopening in World War II of the old controversy over the deep waterway from the Great Lakes to the Atlantic. President Franklin D. Roosevelt spearheaded the discussion by urging the project upon the Congress from time to time. The vision of this waterway is as ancient as the discovery of the peculiar profile of the Lakes. It has challenged men of every generation to overcome the few rapids and falls that impede free navigation over the long inland waterway. In the 1850's, when the

Dean Richmond sailed direct to Liverpool, men thought they had a deep waterway—and they did. But the term is purely relative, and what was deep to the mariners of 1850 was shallow to the heavy-draft ships of the twentieth century. The Welland locks are now 860 feet long, 80 feet wide, and 30 feet deep, making that canal a seaway. The opening in 1943 of the giant new MacArthur lock at the Sault made that canal an open gate to almost any vessel except the heaviest of modern battleships. But the six Williamsburg, Cornwall, Soulanges, and Lachine locks are, however, still only 270 to 280 feet long, only 43.67 to 46 feet wide, and 14 to 15 feet deep. They are the obstacle to the large and profitable ocean-going ships. Montreal sees that barrier in terms of wheat shipments. It gets less than one-third of the wheat, some of it by rail from the Georgian Bay ports; while Buffalo receives over two-thirds of the total shipments and sends it on by rail or the barge canal, much to her profit. If the canals were deepened, Montreal reasons, a large proportion of this shipping would pass her way instead of being diverted to New York.

On the other hand, the owners of the smaller ships that operate from Montreal along the upper St. Lawrence River and into the Lakes are vigorously against the seaway project. They do a thriving trans-shipping business. They are afraid they would perish if the big ships could sail direct to Kingston, Toronto, and Hamilton and the ports on the Upper Lakes. These captain-owners and their small vessels are so interesting, and they lend to the Lakes so much of their flavor of individual enterprise, that it would indeed be a pity to lose them from the waterways.

The discussions one hears around Toronto and Montreal, and at the Château Laurier and the Château Frontenac, reflect a somewhat different view. The big businessmen of the Dominion and the government officials speak rather frankly of the growing interdependence between Canada and the United States. They think that it will increase rather than diminish. The United States is the master partner. If the United States really wants a deep waterway, and the Congress puts up the money to finance it, the deep waterway will be constructed with Canada going along, reasonably, if not enthusiastically, co-operating. In the meantime, the project is so intriguing from a physiographic point of view that the engineers will never rest in peace until they have leveled these slight barriers between the Great Lakes and the Atlantic Ocean.

((((XXXVII))))

Cities on the Shoreline

THE sacrifice of the discoverers, the new beginnings on the ruins of war, the sweat and heartbreak and hope of the immigrants, the raucous and spendthrift waste of the exploiters, the flow of ships with their cargoes of grain and lumber, coal and ore, cattle and hogs, men and machines: from these things have emerged a fabulous region with a chain of cities that has become, almost within the memory of men still living, one of the richest and happiest on the surface of the earth.

Blot out of the North American continent the cities that rim the shores of the Great Lakes and it is astonishing to consider how much would be lost. The heart of Canada would cease to beat. Quebec and Montreal on the St. Lawrence River; Kingston, Belleville, Toronto, Hamilton, St. Catharines on Lake Ontario; Port Colborne, Port Dover, Port Stanley, Leamington on Lake Erie; Amherstburg and Windsor on the Detroit River, Chatham on the Thames; Sarnia, Southampton, Collingwood, Midland on Lake Huron and Georgian Bay; Sault Ste. Marie; Port Arthur and Fort William on Thunder Bay—all ports to the supporting hinterland.

The concentration on the American shoreline belt is equally imposing: Two Harbors, Duluth, Superior, Ashland, Marquette on Lake Superior; Sault Ste. Marie; Mackinaw, St. Ignace, Manistique, Escanaba, Menominee, Marinette, Green Bay, Kewaunee, Two Rivers, Manitowoc, Sheboygan, Milwaukee, Racine, Kenosha, the Waukegan-to-Wilmette towns, Evanston, Chicago, Calumet, Hammond and Gary, all on the outer Lake Michigan shore; St. Joseph-Benton Harbor, South Haven, Grand Haven, Muskegon, Ludington, Manistee, Traverse City, on the eastern shore; Rogers City, Alpena, Bay City, Saginaw, Port Huron on the western rim of Lake

Huron; Detroit, River Rouge, Ecorse on the Detroit River; Toledo,
Sandusky, Hudson, Lorain, Lakewood, Cleveland, Ashtabula, Con-
neaut, Erie, Dunkirk, Buffalo on Lake Ontario; Lewiston on the
Niagara; Rochester, Oswego, Sackets Harbor on Lake Ontario:
merely to catalogue their names is to sing a Homeric epic of
America.

These cities have risen where the ships put in with the wealth
of a continent and cargoes for the world. They spread along the
water's edge, and they reach back deep into the land. They are
the visible symbol of the energy of the men and women who have
chosen to live and work here. Their mill stacks and elevators, their
skyscrapers, their church spires and university towers that pierce
the skyline are an index to their proud triumphs.

The cities on the Lakes are alike in only one respect: each has
its vital water front with its docks and its ships. In all other
respects they are distinctive and individual.

A few impressions haunt the mind as it sweeps over the twenty-
mile belt around the thousands of miles of the Great Lakes shores.

Quebec on her rocks, with the St. Lawrence at her feet and the
ships sailing past Cap Diamond and around the Isle d'Orleans, is
still a lake port. The Citadel faces the Atlantic, but the statue of
Champlain significantly looks off toward the western waterways
down which comes the commerce that gives life to the walled
museum city.

Sprawling, busy Montreal is likewise a lake port. Ships from
the ocean come in and put out from her acres of wharves, her bins
and her elevators. From Mount Royal the smaller ships can still
be seen edging through the locks on the canal around the gleaming
rapids of Lachine. Their cargoes are bound for the Ottawa towns
and for the cities of the Great Lakes.

The Province of Ontario borders four of the five Great Lakes
and over a hundred miles of the St. Lawrence River. A third of
Canada's population, a third of her agriculture, over half of her
minerals are concentrated in Ontario facing the Lakes. The Old
Ontario arrowhead is washed all around by the Lakes and their

connecting rivers. Half of Canada's manufactures and industries are assembled here, drawing sustenance from the Lakes and the Lake region:

Kingston, boasting less of its lake trade than of Queens University, one of the ranking institutions of the Dominion, and wearing a martial cloak as the home of the Royal Military College. It got its start as the Buffalo of Lake Ontario, where the lake water flows past the Thousand Islands to become the St. Lawrence River. A hundred years and more ago it was one of the chief grain ports on the lake, but Buffalo and Montreal pulled this traffic to their wharves.

Pleasant old houses in wooded grounds overlook the expanse of Lake Ontario from the high bluff along the shore between Kingston and Toronto.

Toronto, city of 850,000, the financial heart of the Dominion. It rose out of the 1812 ruins of Muddy York. It is a cosmopolitan city, somewhat Americanized, very British, but aggressively Canadian. With Yonge Street as its arterial highway, it spreads over a pleasing, irregular terrain facing the freight yards, the wharves, the elevators, the yacht club, the basins, and the spacious harbor. The famous street leads back to Queen's Park, the University of Toronto and the Parliament Buildings. The Royal York, largest hotel in the Empire, symbolizes Toronto's importance in the business of the world. Americans and visitors from all parts of the Empire, in Toronto to buy and sell and trade, throng its lobbies. Four hundred United States and British companies have offices in Toronto.

Hamilton, below the Niagara escarpment, growing and versatile, maker of a hundred products: jewelry and road-building machines, electric bulbs and elevators, vinegar and fertilizer.

The fruit belt along the lake to Port Weller and St. Catharines.

The ships coming down the Welland Canal.

The dozen little Erie ports, outlet towns for Old Ontario with its tobacco farms, its dairies, its woolen mills, its orchards.

Windsor, the Johnny Walker signboard and the Ambassador Bridge.

Sarnia, the Blue Water Bridge linking it to Port Huron and the United States shore, the towering sign of the Imperial Oil Company.

Collingwood and Midland, great shipping ports across the jagged neck of the arrowhead.

Quiet little Sault Ste. Marie, with its dingy wharves, its trim ships, and its small canal, looking across at the procession of freighters through the four giant locks on the Michigan side of the St. Mary's River.

Port Arthur and Fort William on Thunder Bay between the elevators, the piles of pulp-wood, and the massive mountains of upheaved rock, magnificent link between the Canadian Northwest and the Great Lakes.

The great American cities flash their personalities indelibly upon the most casual spectator. Their tempo is faster than their Canadian neighbors', their noise is shriller.

Oswego, the canal port on Lake Ontario, with gasoline barges coming up from New York.

Rochester back on its height of land, reaching for pleasure rather than for business down toward the lake and the yacht basin; not a port but a canal and railroad city on the route of trans-shipped commerce out of Buffalo.

Buffalo, city of railroads and elevators, storage city for forty million bushels of grain. It faces its harbor filled with vessels of all kinds. It spreads north to the Niagara River, engulfing its ancient rival Black Rock. It expands eastward along the old canal. It reaches southward along the rim of the Lake toward the open country, the Lake Erie villages, and the vineyards on the protected shore. City of all races: the East Side Germans, the 80,000 Italians on the waterfront, the 15,000 Hungarians at Black Rock, teeming Little Poland. Eastern gateway to the Upper Lakes, trans-shipping point to the Hudson and New York.

Erie on her tree-covered slope, the Pennsylvania port, clustered around her quiet bay, facing the curling sandbar of Presque Isle.

Conneaut and Ashtabula, ore ports for Pittsburgh and the Mahoning Valley, colonies of Finns.

Spacious Cleveland, sixth largest city in the United States. While Cincinnati on the Ohio became the Queen City of the West, Cleveland lay dormant on Lake Erie. The cabins on the high ground overlooking the mouth of the Cuyahoga River huddled in isolation. There were only a thousand people there in 1830. The canal came down from Akron, the steamboats and schooners sailed in from Buffalo and Detroit, and in the single decade of the 1830's Cleveland increased 464 per cent. Canal basins, railroads, lake piers, harbor improvements, the opening of the Sault releasing the rivers of ore and coal and grain; the Civil War; oil; Euclid Avenue and millionaires' row: Rockefeller, Wade, Huntington, Gordon, Mather, Bradley, Hanna, the Van Sweringens.

Tom Johnson, Newton D. Baker.

The Cleveland *Plain Dealer*, Western Reserve University, the Play House, Severance Hall, and the Cleveland Symphony.

The 708-foot Terminal Tower, monument to the Van Sweringen Brothers, is a landmark visible for miles to the ships passing across Lake Erie. Below it the bronze figure of Moses Cleaveland surveys the Public Square and the Mall, and looks off toward the lake. Great bridges span the Cuyahoga gorge where the industries of Cleveland spread over the Flats, and the freighters ease round the bends in the river.

Businesslike Cleveland turned her back on the splendor of her lake. She made the shoreline repulsive to the eye. The hotels are several blocks from the lake; they give no view of its sunlit blue water. Thousands of Clevelanders, other thousands of visitors to the city, hardly knew Lake Erie was near by. Slums cluttered the lake front from the Mall to East Cleveland and Shaker Heights. The 1930's gave the city a brighter vision of itself. The New Lakeshore Boulevard, like the Leif Eriksen Drive along Lake Michigan in South Chicago, turned the city around and faced it again toward Lake Erie, as in the old days when watchmen on the rooftops signalled the arrival of a ship in the harbor.

Lorain, active under the pall of smoke from the industries along the Black River, bright in the sun on the lake front when the wind is northwest. American Shipbuilding, National Tube, the U.S. Coast Guard Station.

Sandusky on its bay, with its fisheries, its acres of Pennsylvania railroad track and coal yards and docks on the west, vacation land and the green islands and vineyards in Lake Erie to the north. City of famous wines, of E & K, of Dorn, and of M. Hommel.

Toledo on the Maumee, coal trans-shipping port to the Lakes. The estuary widens toward Lake Erie, lined with docks, railroad tracks, and oil refineries, bulging with great freighters going and coming to and from the lake port cities. The firm girdle of bridges, the 30-story Ohio Bank Building, the Toledo *Blade,* the Museum of Art, Libbey's Glass, the Gothic tower of the University of Toledo.

Detroit, Workshop to the World, resourceful, energetic, blatant.

Cadillac's city covers many of the 28 miles of the Detroit River shore, reaches along Lake St. Clair. The Ecorse shipyards and the acres of factories on the River Rouge. Grosse Isle and Fighting Island, Belle Isle and Windmill Point.

The skyline from the river, from the Ambassador Bridge, is a long inverted parenthesis piled up to a point in the mid-city area: the jutting assertiveness of the Detroit News Building, the 47-storied Penobscot, the tower of the Wayne County Building, the Statler and the Book-Cadillac, the Fisher and the Federal buildings, the General Motors and the New Center buildings, the City Hall Tower.

City of Ford and Chrysler, David Buick and William Durant, General Motors and United States Rubber, Hudson and Dodge, Packard and LaSalle, DeSoto and Plymouth, Cadillac and Lincoln, Burroughs Adding Machines and Parke-Davis Laboratories, the Detroit *News* and Wayne University.

Trim yachts, speed boats, excursion steamers, and heavy freighters.

The melting-pot city of Hamtramck within the city of Detroit.

Men from the mountains of Tennessee and the mountains of the Tyrol.

City of 1,600,000 gathered from all over the globe, set down on one of the busiest and most crowded waterways in the world.

Sault Ste. Marie, Michigan, climbing up the gentle slope from the giant new MacArthur lock to the heights overlooking the St. Mary's River and the Falls, and the church spires in Sault Ste. Marie, Ontario. The house of the great Schoolcraft; the lake freighters waiting their turn to be lifted or lowered in the four locks; the river ferries; hay-fever victims fleeing the pollen, spending the late summer at the Kachoo Club in the Ojibway on the park opposite the Sault.

Duluth on its terrace, climbing up the steep rocks, looking down on its ample harbor, its elevators and docks, the flats of the St. Louis River, the Necklace, and the haze over the low expanse of its neighbor Superior.

Ashland on the plain around Chequamegon Bay: sawmills and paper mills; coal and iron and black granite.

Marquette between its docks and its hills, the blue mist over the Gogebic Range.

The white ferries plying between St. Ignace and Mackinaw.

Pleasant Milwaukee, industrial and social, fronting the lake from the gray precipice of its shoreline.

Gracious Evanston, with the campus of Northwestern University extending along the lake shore, its spires rising above the trees.

And Chicago, a magic city on an early morning, with the sun on her towers, springing up out of the lake waters. From Lake Michigan you do not see the squalor of the slums behind the Gold Coast. You do not see the miles and miles of ugly, naked apartment houses set in harsh rows, set in dingy, soggy lots, caves of the Lonigans and the Druets. It is a city of monumental buildings lifting their heads and shoulders into the sky, a city of parkways generously spread over wide areas as befits the metropolis gateway to the endless West.

Chicago's most understanding poet, Carl Sandburg, who has his home and prize goat pens among the dunes on the opposite shore, has fixed the city in the minds of millions with a few stabbing phrases. This is the city of the broad shoulders, city of cunning, a laughing city—stacker of wheat, hog-butcher to the world, freight-handler to the nation. And the fog comes in from the harbor on little cat feet. Carl Sandburg knows the feel of modern Chicago.

Carl Schurz saw and felt a different Chicago. The year was 1854, and he was traveling to Milwaukee. The hotels were jammed with the hordes of immigrants and businessmen. There was no room at the inns, not even for one more cot in the corridors. Schurz was turned away into the night from house after house. He sat down on a plank sidewalk under a dingy street lamp. Rats swarmed out of the damp holes under the boards, scurried over his feet, and looked at him with their beady eyes. He had to fight them off. He crowded into a lobby and sat all night in a chair. After that night in Chicago, Milwaukee seemed to him a heavenly city, happy and well-planned.

Mrs. O'Leary's lantern, grim and harsh though the treatment was, did the city a service.

Between the era of slimy rodents under board sidewalks and the dreaming towers of the famous Boulevard throbbed eight strenuous decades.

Chicago is a city of names, city of contrasts, city of the Titans and city of the squids. Theodore Dreiser and the Cooperwoods have been here, Frank Norris and the speculators in the Pit. Al Capone and the Little Caesars of Cicero blackened her name in headlines round the world. William Rainey Harper more quietly built one of the world's great universities on the Midway among the marshes west of Jackson Park.

Swift and Armour of the Gold Coast, Swift and Armour in the stench of Halstead.

Marshall Field, the Store, and the Museum on the reclaimed esplanade where the sailing ships once dropped anchor.

Grant Park and Soldier Field; Jane Addams and Hull House thriving in the region of decay on South Halstead Street. Little Italy, Little Greece, Little Mexico.

The flamboyant clowning of political boss Mayor William Hale

Thompson, 'Big Bill the Builder,' and the lucrative vice of the 1920's. Anton J. Cermak, from Bohemian boy mineworker to mayor of the city, taking the bullet meant for Franklin D. Roosevelt.

Samuel Insull.

Joseph Medill McCormick, his grandson Col. Robert R. McCormick, the Chicago *Tribune*, the flying buttresses of the Tribune Tower, 'the most beautiful and distinctive office building in the world.'

Col. Frank Knox; the Chicago Daily News Building decorating the river front.

Sears, Roebuck and Montgomery Ward. Navy Pier and the Water Tower. Merchandise Mart and the Palmolive Building.

Park Commissioner Charles H. Wacker, clearing the debris along the south bank of the Chicago River, opening it to the sun with the spacious parkway; Wacker Drive and the Outer Drive Bridge, dedicating the achievement with President Roosevelt's 'Quarantine the Aggressor' speech on October 5, 1937.

The traffic roars and hums on the boulevards, the cars pause under the shadow of the Wrigley Building at the Michigan Avenue Bridge when the giant double-decked bascule rises to let the vessels pass up and down the river past the site of old Fort Dearborn. Lorado Taft's Fountain of the Great Lakes sparkles in its spray on the south terrace of the Art Institute, Lake Superior spilling from her shell the waters for her four sisters.

The railroad tracks on the lake shore are hidden in their trough like the ha-ha fence in an English park or a Virginia estate. The railroad stations: the old Dearborn, Central, Grand Central, La-Salle, North Western, the vast new Roman Doric Union Station on Canal Street: sending and receiving hundreds of trains day and night from all directions.

The crowded Loop and the new subway.

Airplanes landing and taking off from the great airport, flying the air lanes of the world.

The smoke-filled hotel rooms, the political conventions. Abraham Lincoln, Warren G. Harding, Franklin D. Roosevelt, the National Destiny.

BIBLIOGRAPHY

THERE is an immense quantity of material on specific matters related in one way or another to the Great Lakes. Francis Parkman's volumes on the early history of the French explorers, generals, governors, and missionaries are standard classics, and everybody who writes anything about that period is in his debt. The same may be said, with qualifications, of the work of Justin Winsor and of R. G. Thwaites. George A. Cuthbertson's beautiful marine paintings and his spadework study of the ships of the Great Lakes in *Freshwater* cause all students of the Lakes to honor him and his work. Stewart H. Holbrook has contributed two energetic and semi-popular books, *Holy Old Mackinaw,* on the lumber era, and *Iron Brew,* on the saga of the iron ranges around Lake Superior. And there are hundreds of volumes of somewhat similar character and purpose.

Few books, however, have attempted to view the region as a whole, or to deal with the Lakes as a unit. The sources for this particular volume are many and varied. They include such items as the Journals of Champlain, Brother Sagard, Father Hennepin, and other travellers to the region; detailed studies in the publications of the several active State Historical Societies; the annual reports of the Lake Carriers' Association; old newspapers; and hundreds of other sources which yield a few facts of significance to the unfolding story.

They also include pleasant conversations with friends and acquaintances from Quebec, Ottawa, and Montreal to the Lakehead cities and Duluth, men whose studies and experiences have made them authorities on various aspects of the lore of the Lakes: with W. D. Percival in the Parliament Building at Quebec and at the Château Frontenac; with the newspaper editor at Port Arthur; with the Ontario onion merchant on a package freighter going down from Fort William to Duluth; with Master Williams on the bridge and in the wheelhouse of his ship on a voyage from Port Arthur down to Detroit; with George W. Rightmire about J. Proctor Knott and the iron ranges of Lake Superior; with two retired Lake captains on a bench at Sarnia, watching the freighter go by on the St. Clair River; with the fishermen of Sandusky; with Lakemen at Milwaukee, Chicago, Toledo, Cleveland, and Buffalo; with the guardsmen at Lachine; with engineers, lumbermen, shipbuilders, and men who know and love the Lakes or some favored spot and activity connected with them. They contribute more than an author could ever specify or thank them for adequately.

It is a special pleasure also to thank the librarians of the United States and Canada—those indefatigable servants, consultants, friends, and confidants of writers and scholars—who have been so uniformly helpful to me.

The list which follows contains the more significant titles of the books, monographs, magazines, and articles relating to the Great Lakes and the contiguous regions.

I am in debt to Fola La Follette for her generous permission to quote from the *Autobiography* of her father, the late Robert M. La Follette.

Atwood, Wallace W.: *The Physiographic Provinces of North America,* New York, 1940.

Beasley, Norman: *Freighters of Fortune,* New York, 1930.

Butterfield, C. W.: *History of Brûlé's Discoveries and Explorations,* Cleveland, 1898.

Callahan, James Morton: *The Neutrality of the American Lakes and Anglo-American Relations,* Baltimore, 1898.

Catlin, George B.: *The Story of Detroit,* Detroit, 1923.

Champlain, de, Samuel: *Voyages,* 1604-1618, New York, 1907.

Channing, Edward, and Lansing, Marion F.: *The Story of the Great Lakes,* New York, 1912.

Chapelle, Howard Irving: *The History of American Sailing Ships,* New York, 1935.

Clowes, Ernest Seabury: *Shipways to the Sea,* Baltimore, 1929.

Colton, Calvin: *Tour of the American Lakes, etc., in 1830,* London, 1833.

Curran, James W.: *Here Was Vinland; the Great Lakes Region of America,* Sault Ste. Marie, 1939.

Curwood, James Oliver: *The Great Lakes,* New York, 1909.

Cuthbertson, George A.: *Freshwater,* Toronto and New York, 1931.

Dawson, S. E.: *The St. Lawrence, Its Basin and Border-Lands,* New York, 1905.

DeKruif, Paul: *Seven Iron Men,* New York, 1929.

Disturnell, John: *The Great Lakes, or Inland Seas of America,* New York, 1863.

—— *Sailing on the Great Lakes,* Philadelphia, 1874.

—— *Upper Lakes of North America,* New York, 1857.

Downing, Elliot R.: *A Naturalist in the Great Lakes Region,* Chicago, 1922.

Duncan, Dorothy: *Here's to Canada*, New York, 1941.

Foster, J. W.: *Limitation of Armament on the Great Lakes*, Washington, D. C., 1914.

Freeman, L. R.: *By Waterways to Gotham*, New York, 1925.

Garriott, Edward B.: *Storms of the Great Lakes*, Washington, D. C., 1903.

Grant, W. L. (ed.): *The Voyages of Samuel de Champlain*, New York, 1907.

Hall, J. W.: *Marine Disasters on the Great Lakes*, Detroit, 1872.

Hansen, Harry: *The Chicago*, New York, 1942.

Havighurst, Walter: *The Long Ships Passing*, New York, 1942.

Hennepin, Father Louis: *A New Discovery of a Vast Country in America*, Chicago, 1903.

Henry, Alexander: *Travels and Adventures*, New York, 1809.

Holbrook, Stewart H.: *Iron Brew*, New York, 1940.

—— *Holy Old Mackinaw*, New York, 1938.

Illinois, A Descriptive and Historical Guide, Chicago, 1939.

Janson, Florence Edith: *The Background of Swedish Immigration*, 1840-1930, Philadelphia, 1931.

Jansson, J. H. (compiler): *Great Lakes Red Book*, Cleveland, 1934-1936.

La Follette, Robert M.: *Autobiography*, Madison, c.1913.

Lake Carriers Association: *Annual Reports*.

Lazell, Warren (publisher): *Steamboat Disasters and Railroad Accidents*, 1843.

Leverett, Frank, and Taylor, Frank B.: 'The Pleistocene of Indiana and Michigan and the History of the Great Lakes,' *U. S. Geological Survey*, Vol. LIII, 1915.

Levermore, Charles H.: *The Anglo-American Agreement of 1817 for Disarmament on the Great Lakes*, Boston, 1914.

Lloyd's Steamboat Directory, 1856.

Mansfield, E. D.: *The Life and Military Services of Lieut.-Gen. Winfield Scott*, New York, 1862.

Marquis, Thomas G.: *The Jesuit Missions*, Toronto, 1921.

Martineau, Harriet: *Society in America*, London, 1837.

Michigan, A Guide to the Wolverine State, New York, 1941.

Mills, James Cooke: *Our Inland Seas, Their Shipping and Commerce for Three Centuries*, Chicago, 1910.

Minnesota, A State Guide, New York, 1938.

Nautical Gazette, New York.

New York, A Guide to the Empire State, New York, 1940.

Nute, Grace Lee: *The Voyageur*, New York, 1931.

The Ohio Guide, New York, 1940.

Parkman, Francis: *The Pioneers of France in the New World*, Boston, 1903.
—— *The Jesuits in North America*, Boston, 1903.
—— *La Salle and the Discovery of the Great West*, Boston, 1903.
—— *The Old Regime in Canada*, Boston, 1903.
—— *A Half Century of Conflict*, Boston, 1903.
—— *Montcalm and Wolfe*, Boston, 1903.
—— *The Conspiracy of Pontiac and the Indian War after the Conquest of Canada*, Boston, 1903.
Porter, K. W.: *John Jacob Astor, Business Man*, New York, 1931.
Putnam, George R.: *Lighthouses and Lightships of the United States*, Boston and New York, 1933.
Rogers, Robert: *A Concise Account of North America*, London, 1765.
Rynning, Ole: *True Account of America*, Minneapolis, 1926.
Sagard-Théodat, Gabriel: *The Long Journey to the Country of the Hurons*, Toronto, 1939.
Samuel, Sigmund: *The Seven Years War in Canada*, Toronto, c.1934.
Schultz, Christian: *Travels on an Inland Voyage, 1807-8*, New York, 1810.
Shepard, Francis P.: *Origin of the Great Lakes Basins*, Washington, 1938.
Spencer, Joseph W.: *The Duration of Niagara Falls and the History of the Great Lakes*, New York, 1895.
—— 'Origin of the Basins of the Great Lakes of America,' *American Geologist*, Vol. 7, 1891.
Stone, William L.: *Narrative of the Festivities Observed in Honor of the Completion of the Grand Erie Canal*, New York, 1825.
Strickland, William Porter: *Old Mackinaw*, New York, 1860.
Thwaites, R. G.: *France in America, 1497-1763*, New York, 1905.
—— *The Jesuit Relations, 1610-1791*, Cleveland, 1896-1901.
Trimble, George: *The Lake Pilots' Handbook*, Pt. Huron, 1907.
U. S. Steel News, June 1937.
Van Oosten, John: 'Michigan's Commercial Fisheries of the Great Lakes,' *Michigan Historical Magazine*, 1938.
Waldron, W.: *We Explore the Great Lakes*, New York, 1923.
Winsor, Justin: *Narrative and Critical History of America*, New York, 1889.
—— *Cartier to Frontenac*, New York, 1894.
Wisconsin, A Guide to the Badger State, New York, 1941.
Wittke, Carl F.: *We Who Built America: the Saga of the Immigrant*, New York, 1940.
Wood, William: *All Afloat*, Toronto, 1920.

INDEX

Index